LEISURE AND TOURISM
Advanced GNVQ

GW00320239

LEISURE AND TOURISM
Advanced GNVQ

Ray Youell MSc MTS

PITMAN PUBLISHING published in association with

PITMAN PUBLISHING
128 Long Acre, London WC2E 9AN

A Division of Longman Group Limited

First published in 1994

A CIP catalogue record for this book can be obtained from the British Library.

ISBN 0 273 60517 8

Typeset by M Rules.
Printed and bound in Great Britain by Clays Ltd, St Ives plc.

The Publishers' policy is to use paper manufactured from sustainable forests.

Please note the assignments included in this book are not part of the BTEC
designed assignments published by BTEC which meet the full requirements of
the BTEC specifications. They will however, provide opportunities for students
to produce useful evidence towards the full requirement.

Contents

Introduction

This book has been written specifically for individuals studying for the Advanced GNVQ in Leisure and Tourism. The material will also prove useful for students on BTEC National courses in Leisure Studies and Travel and Tourism, which are due to be replaced by GNVQs from 1995. The book is designed to be used by students following GNVQs offered by all three awarding bodies – BTEC, RSA and City & Guilds – which follow the same pattern of mandatory units developed by NCVQ (National Council for Vocational Qualifications) and offer broadly similar optional unit specifications.

The Advanced GNVQ in Leisure and Tourism is a new work-related qualification designed to offer a choice of opportunities in employment or higher education. Originally called Level 3 qualifications, GNVQs were recently retitled 'Advanced' in order to emphasise their equivalence to 'A' levels. GNVQs are part of the NVQ (National Vocational Qualification) framework, which provides a national system for work-related qualifications, endorsed by the TUC and CBI. GNVQs offer students a flexible qualification based around mandatory, optional and additional units. The mandatory units form the vocational core of the GNVQ while the optional units offer students the choice of extending their achievement. Additional units give the opportunity for further specialism and provide a focus for progression to higher education.

This book is structured around the eight mandatory units of the Advanced GNVQ in Leisure and Tourism (Units 1–8) and the seven optional units currently offered by BTEC (Units 9–15). Although BTEC has been chosen as the basis for the units dealing with the optional units, the reader will find sufficient material in the units to fulfil the requirements of the options offered by both RSA and City & Guilds. Revision test questions are included at the end of the seven mandatory units, which currently have an external test. Although not written in the same style as questions that appear on test papers produced by the awarding bodies, the revision questions cover the focus areas included in the test specifications and will prove useful for individual and group work. The sample assignments, which are included after each mandatory and optional unit, can be included in a student's portfolio.

Finally, I must thank all the people who helped in the compilation of this book. The individuals and organisations who kindly provided photographs, case study material and statistics are acknowledged in the appropriate sections of the book. Many former colleagues in FE provided helpful suggestions and advice; in particular, Sally Ross from Shrewsbury College was a constant source of help and encouragement. Particular thanks go to Jeff Hart and staff at Wealden District

Council who provided valuable material for many sections of the book. Thanks are due also to David Jux, UK Personnel Director of the Rank Organisation, who gave permission for the use of much useful material. Valuable source material was provided by many private, public and voluntary sector organisations, including Stena Sealink, National Trust, ETB, WTB, BTA, STB, Arts Council, CCPR, Sports Council, Forestry Commission, BWB, Britannia Airways, Thomson Holidays, HSE, Department of National Heritage, Baron Systems, YHA, Rural Development Commission, ABTA, Sally Line, British Midland Airways, P&O Ferries, London Tourist Board, Chessington World of Adventures, Dartmoor Area Tourism Initiative, Castlefield Management Company, Mid Wales Festival of the Countryside, Centre for Alternative Technology, NutraSweet London Marathon, Maesmawr Hall Hotel, and many more.

Last, but by no means least, a big thank you to Sue, Megan and Owen, who provided great support during a hectic six-month period.

Ray Youell
Sheffield, February 1994

Unit 1
INVESTIGATING THE LEISURE AND TOURISM INDUSTRY

Section 1 Overview of the industry

Just what is leisure and tourism?

Deciding on a comprehensive definition of the terms 'leisure' and 'tourism' is no easy matter. Most people associate leisure with either leisure time or leisure activities; they choose to use their spare time in ways which give them the most satisfaction. To many people, tourism is their annual holiday – perhaps two weeks on the Costa del Sol, a family holiday on a Welsh farm, a week at Butlin's or a trip to EuroDisney.

To the leisure and tourism professional, these simple ideas mask a highly complex industry, arguably the fastest-growing in the world, which spans many different activities:

- Sport and physical recreation.
- International tourism.
- Arts and entertainment.
- Heritage and other attractions.
- Community leisure provision.
- Hotels and the accommodation sector.
- Hospitality.
- Transport.
- Travel agents and tour operators.
- Home-based leisure.
- Countryside recreation.

As an industry, leisure and tourism is developing rapidly at local level, with new facilities being opened to meet the needs of the local community (leisure centres, arts centres and museums, for example), at national level, where prestige projects can attract a larger audience (Wembley Arena, Alton Towers and the National Museum of Photography at Bradford are good examples) and internationally, with steady growth in the number of tourist arrivals around the globe, particularly within Europe.

Above all, *leisure and tourism is a business*. This has long been the case with private sector operators in the UK, whose main aim is profit maximisation, but even within the public and voluntary sectors, with the introduction of such measures as compulsory competitive tendering (CCT) for local authorities, all organisations within leisure and tourism are becoming more business orientated in the way they plan and manage their operations. Managers with good communication skills, the ability to motivate others and the realisation that quality is paramount in meeting customer needs and expectations are being sought increasingly by leisure and tourism organisations.

Notwithstanding the business focus of much leisure and tourism activity, there are significant social, cultural, environmental and economic benefits which the industry can bring to regions. This topic will be explored in Section 3 of this unit along with leisure and tourism's negative aspects, which have recently become the subject of much debate.

Leisure explained

A random group of people asked to explain their understanding of the term 'leisure' would give very different answers. Some would regard leisure as time spent when they are not at work, while others would think of specific activities which they do in their leisure time, such as gardening, listening to the radio, playing tennis or going to the cinema. A few might mention that Britain is considered to be moving towards a 'leisure society' with the decline in many aspects of our industrial base and a move towards service industries, of which leisure is one of the most important. You could not say that any of these responses is wrong; they simply highlight the difficult task faced by anybody trying to define exactly what is meant by leisure.

A dictionary definition of the term 'leisure' says that it is, 'time free from employment'. This, too, does not give a complete answer to the question; it fails to take into account the many necessary duties and functions that we all have to perform in our daily lives, such as eating, sleeping and carrying out domestic chores. Unemployed people do not fit very easily into such a definition either with most agreeing that they have more leisure time than they want.

A comprehensive definition of the term 'leisure' would necessarily include all of the following elements:

- Time outside of a formal employment situation.
- Time over and above that devoted to necessary household chores.
- Time outside sleeping, eating and personal hygiene functions.

- Time at the disposal of the individual.
- Time when an individual has the freedom to choose what to do.

The last two elements concerning an individual's freedom of choice are perhaps getting us closer to the true meaning of leisure. Rather than a mechanistic calculation of the time left over when all necessary tasks have been completed, leisure is much more about time when an individual can strive to reach his or her potential as a human being and become a productive member of society.

What activities are included in leisure?

Official statistics collected and published by government departments include the following activities within their 'leisure' category:

- Watching TV.
- Listening to radio, records and tapes.
- Reading books.
- Gardening.
- DIY.
- Dressmaking, needlework and knitting.
- Visiting or entertaining friends or relatives.

Sources such as the General Household Survey (GHS) and Social Trends refer to the above as home-based leisure activities. The following are some of the activities categorised as leisure away from home:

- Going to the cinema, theatre and ballet.
- Visiting tourist attractions.
- Taking part in indoor sports, games and physical activities (e.g. snooker, swimming, badminton, ice skating, darts, etc.).
- Taking part in outdoor sports, games and physical activities (e.g. walking, cycling, fishing, sailing, jogging, etc.).
- Going to watch football matches.
- Taking holidays and day trips.

It is clear that leisure activities differ greatly in the degree of physical effort required from the individual; passive activities, such as watching television or listening to the radio, involve little in the way of exertion, whereas active leisure pursuits, for example gardening, sports and DIY, demand much greater effort (see Figure 1.1).

Factors affecting leisure activity

It is important for the leisure manager to be aware of the various factors that influence participation in leisure and the activities that are preferred by different groups in society. These are many and varied, and, as we shall see in the part of this book looking at the history of leisure and tourism, they change over time.

Some of the more important factors are:

1 *Availability of leisure time* – one of the most basic factors since no leisure time equals no leisure activity! Statistics published in Social Trends show, not surprisingly, that retired people have the most leisure time; in a typical week in 1991–92, retired men enjoyed nearly 90 hours leisure time and retired women 74 hours. Women in full-time employment also have less leisure time when compared with their male counterparts, the result of spending more time on household chores and looking after children.

2 *Income* – a low disposable income (that which is left over after all necessary household and personal expenditure has been met) leaves an individual with little, if any, money to use on leisure activities for which there are charges. Many facilities offer concessions for those on low income to help alleviate the problem.

3 *Personal mobility* – car ownership has risen dramatically in Britain in the last 50 years (see page 1.12). There is still, however, a sizeable proportion of the population which neither owns nor has access to a motor car (33 per cent in 1991 – GHS). This can influence greatly the ability to get involved in local leisure activities; the problem is particularly acute in rural districts and other areas where public transport provision is poor.

4 *Culture and demography* – factors such as age, marital status, gender, education, skills, cultural background, social class and personality, will all influence leisure participation and choice.

Fig 1.1 Active Leisure! *(courtesy of Utopia Leisure Centre, East Sussex)*

5 *Provision of facilities* – if you live in an area that offers high quality facilities at reasonable prices, the chances are you are more likely to seize the opportunities made available to you.

6 *Long-term changes in society* – the rise in the proportion of the population over 80 years of age, the increasing divorce rate, higher numbers of one-parent families, technological advances in communications, environmental awareness and the changing patterns of employment will need to be taken into account by leisure professionals to be able to plan effectively for the future.

Tourism explained

Tourism is the temporary, short-term movement of people to destinations outside the places where they normally live and work, and activities during their stay at these destinations; it includes movement for all purposes, as well as day visits or excursions (Tourism Society 1976)

The above is perhaps the most widely accepted definition of tourism in use in the UK today. It clearly demonstrates that people we would categorise as tourists are:

1 Away from their normal place of residence (although they will be returning home).

2 On a visit that is temporary and short term (but the definition gives no indication of whether there is a maximum or minimum time for a visit to be classed as 'tourism').

3 Engaged in activities that would normally be associated with leisure and tourism.

4 Not necessarily staying away from home overnight; they may be on a day-trip or excursion.

5 Not always away from home for holiday purposes; they could be on business but would still qualify as tourists.

Tourism is not just holidays!

Contrary to popular belief, tourism is concerned with much more than simply an annual two-week holiday in the sun. Tourist activity is often divided into leisure tourism and business tourism; Figure 1.2 indicates the main purposes under each of these two categories. As you can see, leisure tourism includes many of the types of activities that most people think of as 'tourism'. However, business tourism is an increasingly important sector since it is often of high value and earns hoteliers, caterers and transport operators significant income. Indeed, many city-based travel agents operate a separate department geared exclusively to the needs of the business client.

Some examples from each of the categories shown in Figure 1.2 will help to give a clearer understanding of the meaning of tourism.

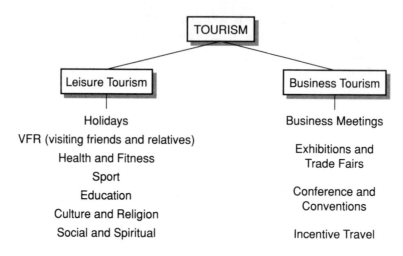

Fig 1.2 Different forms of tourism

Leisure tourism

Holidays
- A weekend break in a guesthouse in York.
- A two-week family holiday to the Algarve staying in a self-catering villa.
- A murder/mystery weekend at a hotel in Torquay.

VFR
- A fortnight staying with a friend who lives in France.
- Staying for three months with your sister-in-law in New Zealand.
- A family party in your sister's house 100 miles away.

Health and fitness
- A cycling tour in France.
- A weekend in a hotel with a fitness room and health suite.
- A walking holiday in Scotland.

Sport
- The British team's visit to the Olympic Games in Barcelona.
- Visiting Old Trafford to watch a one-day cricket international match.
- A weekend break to watch the Monaco Grand Prix.

Education
- A week at an Open University summer school in Durham.
- A weekend sailing course in Plymouth.
- A French student attending a College in Brighton to learn English.

Culture and religion
- A week studying Celtic folklore in the West of Ireland.
- A Roman Catholic visiting the Vatican to see the Pope.
- A weekend studying the churches of East Anglian villages.

Social and spiritual
- A weekend reflexology workshop.
- A one-parent family holiday to Suffolk.
- A week-long meditation course in the Lake District.

Business tourism

Business meetings – A British sportswear manufacturer on a two-week fact-finding tour of the west coast of the USA.
– An advertising executive taking a train journey from her home base for a meeting with a client in Leeds.
– A Member of the European Parliament flying to Brussels for the day for meetings with EC officials.

Exhibitions and trade fairs – A representative of the English Tourist Board visiting the Scottish Travel Trade Fair in Glasgow.
– The Gardeners' World exhibition at the NEC Birmingham.
– Attending the World Travel Market in London.

Conferences and conventions – Lawyers from EC countries attending a two-day conference on EC Directives in Copenhagen.
– Attending the TUC Conference in Blackpool.
– The ABTA domestic conference in Llandudno.

Incentive travel – A weekend golfing break at Gleneagles for achieving top monthly sales for your company.
– Free car hire for one week on your holiday for completing an important project on time.
– Two weeks in Florida for you and your family for clinching a new multi-million pound contract.

Tourism isn't just about going abroad!

There is a common misconception in Britain that tourism is only concerned with taking holidays abroad; this couldn't be further from the reality of the situation. Later in this unit (see Table 1.5), we shall see that Britons take nearly five times as many tourist trips within the UK compared with visits abroad. Also, overseas visitors to Britain contribute nearly £8 billion per year to the UK economy according to BTA statistics.

There are three principal strands within the tourism industry:

Domestic tourism – When people take holidays, short breaks and day trips in their own country.

Incoming/inbound tourism – That form of international tourism which deals with people entering another country from their own country of origin or another country which is not their home.

Outbound tourism – A form of international tourism that concerns people travelling away from their main country of residence.

A few simple examples will help to clarify what can sometimes be a confusing concept.

Domestic tourism – The Smith family from Birmingham enjoying a two-week holiday in a caravan in Scarborough.

Incoming/inbound – tourism	M et Mde Du Pont from Limoges sampling the delights of Cardiff as part of a driving tour of England and Wales.
Outbound tourism –	The Smith family from Birmingham deciding to give Scarborough a miss this year and taking a week's holiday at EuroDisney.

The history of leisure and tourism

Ancient times

It is clear that in ancient times there was little opportunity for true leisure pursuits and the distinction between work and leisure was often blurred. The leisure opportunities that did present themselves were usually associated with festivals and celebrations of a religious or spiritual nature. The early Egyptian civilisation displayed a primitive social structure that rewarded the 'upper classes' with time to enjoy such activities as archery, dance, music and drama. Travel in early times tended to be confined to one of two forms, either for the purpose of trade or associated with religious activities. There is, however, evidence of some travel for purely recreational purposes with the first Olympic Games taking place in 776 BC.

The Greek civilisation

The Greeks, and particularly the Ancient Greek philosophers, were the first to begin to distinguish clearly between work and leisure. They commended the sensible use of free time and promoted a balance between work and play as the route to a healthy individual and a healthy society. Sport was encouraged and many of the words we associate with sport and recreation derive from Ancient Greek, e.g. stadium, decathlon and gymnasium.

The Romans

Leisure activity in Roman times (27 BC until the fourth century AD) can be characterised as 'leisure with a purpose'; gone were the aesthetic pleasures the Greeks so enjoyed. The great Roman engineers built public facilities for the masses of the urban populations who practised recreation for physical fitness and in readiness for war. The extensive road network developed by the Romans meant that travel was faster and more convenient. Travel within the Empire for trade and to visit friends and relatives expanded and excursions further afield were not uncommon. The healing powers of spa waters were first recognised in Roman times.

The Middle Ages

The time between the fall of the Roman Empire (AD 400) until AD 1000 was known as the Dark Ages. As their name implies, these were austere times with few opportunities for the mass of the population to take part in leisure activities. The rise of Christianity during this period relegated leisure activities to those associated with worship and religious festivities. During the later Middle Ages (up to approximately 1500) leisure continued to be the privilege of those in power who enjoyed hunting, jousting, music and dance. The 'holy days' designated by the church were the main source of leisure for the bulk of the population; the familiar term 'holiday' is derived from 'holy day'. Travel for religious purposes was evident with pilgrimages to holy shrines increasing in popularity. Leisure in general towards the end of the Middle Ages was beginning to take on an unpleasant character with activities such as gambling, drinking and blood sports becoming the pastimes of the increasingly corrupt nobility.

Renaissance and Reformation

Renaissance literally means 'rebirth'; it signals that time in the history of civilisation (the fifteenth century) when we changed from a medieval system to a modern Western culture. In terms of leisure, the Renaissance heralded a time when leisure was no longer available only to the privileged classes; the loosening from the religious ties of Medieval times meant that such leisure activities as music, drama and dance were opened up to the masses. However, during this time the Reformation movement was also developing in Europe leading to the 'Protestant work ethic', which attacked the excesses and corruption of the pleasure-seeking nobility and led to a sharp decrease in the availability and respectability of leisure.

Post-Reformation leisure and tourism

During the seventeenth century, attitudes towards leisure and tourism were changing once again. From 1670 onwards, young gentlemen were sent on the 'Grand Tour' of the cultural centres of Europe to widen their education prior to seeking positions at court on their return. Centres such as Paris, Venice and Florence gave such gentlemen the opportunity to sample different cultures, societies and experiences. In the early seventeenth century, the healing powers of spa waters became widely accepted amongst the aristocracy, leading to the development of spa resorts both in Britain and on the Continent. Spa towns such as Buxton, Leamington Spa, Llandrindod Wells and Bath prospered until well into the eighteenth century, recognising the wider opportunities that tourism can create. Baden-Baden in Germany was one of the most frequented spa resorts in Europe.

The Industrial Revolution

The Industrial Revolution of the eighteenth and nineteenth centuries brought about profound changes to the way of life in Britain, not least in relation to leisure and tourism. There was rapid urbanisation in response to greater mechanisation and mass production techniques and a flow of population from the countryside to the towns. The often overcrowded housing conditions, with long working hours and low wages, gave few opportunities for leisure activities to the mass of the population. In the late nineteenth century it was not uncommon for men, women and even children to work in excess of 60 hours per week. Once again, however, there was a privileged minority (the emerging 'middle classes') who were fortunate enough to be able to indulge in all manner of leisure pursuits ranging from horse racing to prize fighting; leisure was available to those who could afford it.

As the Industrial Revolution progressed, the 'working class' element of society began to demand greater freedom from work. The physical nature of their employment, coupled with dirty and often dangerous working environments, made people want to get away from the urban sprawl and experience the relative calm and tranquility of the countryside and coast. The Bank Holiday Act of 1871 created four public holidays per year which, with the increased spending power of the more prosperous working people, led to the development of a variety of leisure and tourism facilities to meet their needs.

The development of seaside resorts

In the early eighteenth century, doctors began to realise that the healing and relaxing minerals present in spa waters were also to be found in the sea; Scarborough, with the twin benefits of spa and sea water, was quick to exploit its benefits. It was not, however, until 1752 with the publication of Dr Richard Russell's noted medical work *Concerning the Use of Seawater* that seaside resorts such as Southend, Brighton and Blackpool began increasing in popularity. Accommodation, catering and entertainment facilities were developed in the resorts, some of which benefited from the introduction of steamboat services in the early nineteenth century, a factor that led to the construction of many of the piers still seen at seaside resorts today.

Railways and steamships

The development of steam power was to have a very important effect on leisure and tourism patterns with the introduction of the railways from 1830 onwards and passenger steamships from 1840.

The first passenger train service between Manchester and Liverpool was opened in 1830. There followed a massive expansion of the network, principally to service industrial centres, but with the capacity to bring many of the seaside resorts within easy reach of the centres of population; Brighton was a notable success with some 132,000 visitors recorded on Easter Monday in 1862. The expansion of the railway network led a number of entrepreneurs to consider how they could capitalise on this new form of travel. One of the most successful was Thomas Cook who was destined to have a far-reaching impact on the early development of travel. In 1841 he organised an excursion from Leicester to Loughborough for his local Temperance Association. Within 15 years, spurred on by the success of his first trip, he was running a fully commercial travel company arranging tours and excursions both at home and overseas, including the Great Exhibition in London in 1851 and 'inclusive tours' to the Paris Exhibition in 1855.

Just as steam power on land in the early nineteenth century was radically altering travel and leisure patterns, the same was true at sea with the introduction of a new generation of ships serving North America, the near Continent and the Far East. The Peninsular and Oriental Steam Navigation Company (P&O) began the first regular long-distance services to India and the Far East in 1838. The Cunard Steamship Company started services to North America in 1840. Following on from successes in Britain and on the Continent, Thomas Cook organised the first excursion to America in 1866.

Sport and recreation in the Industrial Revolution

The Victorian era saw the public taking part in organised sport and recreation in ever increasing numbers; mass participation in leisure was becoming a reality. Sports such as football, rugby, cricket, tennis and hockey became regulated with modern rules being drawn up by governing bodies; the Football Association was founded in 1863. More informal recreational pursuits such as cycling, roller skating and swimming also increased in popularity; the Cyclists' Touring Club was founded in 1878. Leisure was at last available to all but the most deprived in society.

Twentieth-century developments

Leisure and recreation

The First World War (1914–18) brought a temporary halt to the more active forms of leisure with much time being spent on activities such as needlework, knitting, board games and reading. The inter-war years (1918–39) saw a return to many of the leisure pursuits that had become popular in Victorian times. 'Taking fresh air and exercise' was regarded as a very healthy activity either in the countryside around towns and cities or at seaside resorts. New forms of communication, such as posters, guide books and radio, stimulated the public to travel further afield in search of different leisure experiences.

The 1950's boom after the ending of the Second World War (1939–45) created more employment and meant that people had greater disposable income with which to purchase the many new consumer and leisure products coming on to the market. New labour-saving devices, many originating from the USA, meant that more time was available for leisure pursuits both inside and away from the home.

Fashion, music and youth culture were to have important influences on the pattern of leisure during the 1960s, 1970s and 1980s. The television became a powerful source of home entertainment to the detriment of, for example, cinema attendances. 'Fads' such as ten-pin bowling and skateboarding were to come and go. Sport at the highest level was becoming dominated by money, with the amateur/professional divide becoming blurred. The decade of the 1980s is sometimes referred to as 'the Thatcher years' after the Prime Minister of that time. During these years, the gap between the rich and poor widened; the terms 'yuppie' (young urban professional) and 'dinky' (double income/no kids) were coined; such people spent extravagantly on leisure and consumer products generally. High-risk activities such as hang-gliding, power boat racing and ballooning became commonplace for these privileged individuals.

Travel and tourism

Four elements can be singled out as major twentieth-century developments in travel and tourism:

1 The rise of holiday camps.
2 Increasing car ownership.
3 The development of jet aircraft.
4 The introduction of the 'package tour'.

Holiday camps

The first purpose-built holiday camp (what the industry now refers to as a holiday centre) was opened by Billy Butlin in 1936 at Skegness. Holiday camps worked on the simple principle that if the children were happy on holiday then the parents would be happy as well. To this end, they provided entertainment and activities both for parents and children at a low, all-inclusive rate with the added bonus of a child-minding service to allow the parents to enjoy themselves. Butlins and Warners became market leaders in this type of holiday, which still survives to this day, albeit in a different form.

Increasing car ownership

The increase in car ownership after the Second World War began to have serious effects on other public forms of travel, particularly rail and coach journeys. In 1970 there were approximately 11 million private cars on the roads of Britain compared with 2.3 million in 1950 and approximately 20 million in 1993. The dramatic rise in the use of the private car for tourism purposes has led to new types of accommodation being developed, e.g. motels, and growth in activities such as caravanning and day visits to tourist attractions.

The development of jet aircraft

The technological advances in aircraft design which resulted from developments during the Second World War, led to air travel becoming a reality for the masses of the population from the 1950s onwards. The Boeing 707 jet was introduced in 1958 and led to a surge in scheduled and charter flights, the latter being combined with accommodation, transfers and courier services to form the 'package holiday' that is so familiar to us all today. (See Figure 1.3.)

Fig 1.3 Boeing 767 *(courtesy of Britannia Airways)*

Package tours

The 1960s saw the beginning of the rapid increase in the number of package holidays sold. Destinations such as the coastal areas of southern Spain, the Balearic Islands and Greece were favourite locations for British and other European travellers. The convenience of an all-inclusive arrangement, coupled with the increased speed which the new aircraft brought, caught the imagination of the British travelling public. The age of mass tourism had truly arrived.

Leisure and tourism today

This section will look at the following aspects of today's leisure and tourism industry:

1 The scale of the industry – just how big and important is it?
2 The structure of the industry – private, public and voluntary sectors.
3 Employment and careers in leisure and tourism.

The scale of the industry

Leisure

Leisure in Britain is a multi-billion pound industry. According to figures collected by Leisure Consultants (see Table 1.1 on page 1.15), consumer spending on leisure in 1993 was valued at £102.9 billion, representing almost a quarter of all consumer spending by the British. The largest element of leisure spending was eating and drinking out (42.5 per cent of total leisure spending), followed by home-based leisure (28.2 per cent), holidays and tourism (19.3 per cent) and neighbourhood leisure (9.9 per cent).

Consumer spending on leisure

Data supplied by the Central Statistical Office shows that average weekly expenditure by British people on leisure items in 1981, 1986 and 1991 were as in Table 1.2.

Table 1.2 Average British weekly expenditure on leisure items

Year	Total weekly expenditure	% of total household expenditure
1981	£16.82	13.4
1986	£28.76	16.1
1991	£41.14	15.9

Source: Social Trends 23

What these figures don't show is that certain leisure activities and items showed increases of over 250 per cent over the same ten-year period, including purchases of home computers, DIY, holidays, trips to the theatre and admissions at sports events (other than football matches).

At the international level, spending on leisure is an important element of total

Table 1.1 Leisure time and money 1988–98

	1988	1989	1990	1991	1992	1993	1994	1995	1996	1997	1998
Time – hours of leisure											
Full-time worker:											
Annual hours	2513	2509	2519	2542	2546	2552	2567	2579	2594	2621	2648
% change	−0.3	−0.1	0.4	0.9	0.2	0.2	0.6	0.5	0.6	1.0	1.0
All people 16+:											
Total hours: bn	125.5	124.9	125.5	128.2	130.0	131.1	131.9	132.4	133.1	134.3	135.5
% change	−0.8	−0.5	0.5	2.1	1.4	0.8	0.6	0.4	0.5	0.9	1.0
All ages:											
Total hours: bn	151.0	150.4	151.3	154.3	156.4	158.0	159.2	160.0	160.8	162.0	163.4
% change	−0.8	−0.4	0.6	2.0	1.4	1.0	0.8	0.5	0.5	0.8	0.9
Money – Consumer spending on leisure											
Value: £ billion	76.33	83.78	89.94	94.52	99.82	102.90	107.54	113.55	120.16	126.23	130.84
Leisure as % of all consumer spending	25.0	25.0	24.7	24.9	25.1	24.5	24.2	24.2	24.2	24.1	23.7
% change on year ago:											
in value	9.2	9.8	7.4	5.1	5.6	3.1	4.5	5.6	5.8	5.1	3.6
in prices	4.8	6.9	7.5	8.0	5.6	3.5	2.5	3.3	3.2	3.1	3.0
in volume	4.3	3.3	−0.4	−3.1	0.2	0.1	1.3	2.4	2.8	1.9	0.3
The leisure pound – each market as % of leisure total											
Reading	5.1	5.0	5.2	5.1	5.2	5.3	5.3	5.3	5.2	5.2	5.2
Home entertainment	9.8	9.6	9.2	9.0	9.1	9.4	9.5	9.4	9.2	8.9	8.8
House & garden	8.1	7.8	7.5	7.5	7.5	7.7	7.8	7.8	7.8	7.9	8.0
Hobbies & pastimes	5.4	5.7	5.6	5.7	5.8	5.8	5.8	5.8	5.7	5.6	5.6
In the home	28.4	28.1	27.6	27.3	27.6	28.2	28.4	28.3	27.9	27.7	27.6
Eating out	19.4	19.7	19.6	19.2	18.5	18.2	18.0	17.9	17.9	17.8	17.8
Alcoholic drink	24.6	23.6	24.1	25.0	24.7	24.3	24.0	23.7	23.4	23.2	23.0
Eating & drinking	44.0	43.3	43.7	44.2	43.1	42.5	42.1	41.6	41.3	41.0	40.8
Local entertainment	2.5	2.5	2.6	2.7	2.7	2.6	2.6	2.6	2.6	2.6	2.7
Gambling	3.4	3.4	3.4	3.3	3.2	3.2	3.1	3.2	3.1	3.0	3.0
Sport	4.2	4.5	4.8	4.6	4.1	4.1	4.2	4.3	4.4	4.5	4.6
Neighbourhood leisure	10.2	10.4	10.8	10.6	9.9	9.9	9.9	10.1	10.2	10.2	10.2
Sightseeing	0.5	0.5	0.6	0.6	0.6	0.7	0.7	0.7	0.7	0.7	0.7
UK holiday accom.	5.2	5.8	6.8	6.5	6.3	6.1	6.1	6.1	6.2	6.3	6.3
Holidays overseas	11.7	11.9	10.5	10.8	12.4	12.6	12.9	13.2	13.7	14.1	14.3
Holidays & tourism	17.4	18.2	17.9	17.9	19.4	19.3	19.6	20.0	20.6	21.1	21.4
Away from home	71.6	71.9	72.4	72.7	72.4	71.8	71.6	71.7	72.1	72.3	72.4
All leisure	100.0	100.0	100.0	100.0	100.0	100.0	100.0	100.0	100.0	100.0	100.0

Figures include spending by foreign tourists where relevant. Alcoholic drink includes off-licence sales in UK. Leisure time is time left after essential activities (sleeping etc.) and paid work.

Source: Leisure Forecasts 1944–98, Leisure Consultants (1994)

household spending in many industrialised nations. Data from the Statistical Office of the European Communities shows that, at one end of the spectrum, Irish people spend 10.5 per cent and the Japanese 10.2 per cent of total expenditure on leisure while the people of Luxembourg (4 per cent) and Greece (5.6 per cent) spend the lowest proportion on leisure.

Tourism

Tourism is commonly referred to today as 'the world's biggest industry'. According to the World Travel and Tourism Council (WTTC), in 1990 the industry:

- Generated an annual turnover equivalent to 5.9 per cent of World GNP.
- Employed 118 million people worldwide.
- Accounted for over 6.7 per cent of the world's capital investment.
- Contributed over 5.6 per cent to total tax payments worldwide.

Figure 1.4 shows the growth in travel and tourism gross output (sales generated) between 1987 and 1993. Over the 20 year period 1970–1990 world tourism grew by 260 per cent (WTTC).

The growth in total world tourist arrivals 1970–89 is shown in Table 1.3.

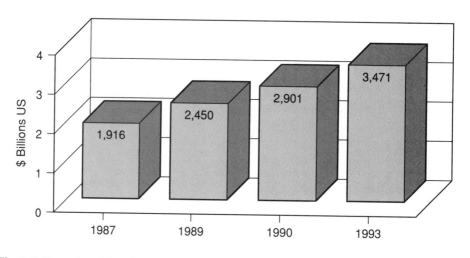

Fig 1.4 Travel and tourism gross output (source: WTTC)

Apart from the early 1980s when the world was experiencing a recession, Table 1.3 shows a steady growth pattern over two decades culminating in more than 400 million tourist arrivals in 1989.

Table 1.3 World international tourist arrivals 1970–89 (millions)

Year	Arrivals	Rate of growth (%)
1970	159.7	11.6
1971	172.2	7.9
1972	181.9	5.6
1973	190.6	4.8
1974	197.1	3.4
1975	214.4	8.8
1976	220.7	3.0
1977	239.1	8.3
1978	257.4	7.6
1979	274.0	6.5
1980	284.8	4.0
1981	288.8	1.4
1982	287.0	− 0.7
1983	284.4	− 0.8
1984	311.2	9.4
1985	325.9	4.7
1986	333.9	2.5
1987	358.9	7.5
1988	390.0	8.7
1989	405.3	3.9

Source: World Tourism Organisation (1990)

European tourism

The popularity of Europe as a tourist destination is shown in Table 1.4.

Table 1.4 International tourist arrivals by region 1988 (millions)

Region	Arrivals	% Share
Africa	12.0	3
Americas	72.5	19
East Asia and the Pacific	42.0	11
Europe	251.5	64
Middle East	9.0	2
South Asia	3.0	1
World Total	390.0	100

Source: World Tourism Organisation (1989)

Europe welcomed nearly two-thirds of all worldwide travellers in 1988 and is sure to dominate the international travel scene well into the next century. It can boast:

- Eight of the top ten world tourist destinations (in terms of receipts).
- Sixteen of the top 20 destinations visited.

However, Europe is coming under increasing pressure from other world destinations, such as America, the Far East, the Caribbean and Australasia, which are marketing themselves worldwide and increasing the products they offer tourists. During the 1980s, Europe's share of world tourist arrivals actually fell by 6 per cent, so the European tourism industry must work hard to regain its market share.

British tourism

During 1992, UK adults and children accompanying them took more than 118 million trips of one night or more away from home (see Table 1.5). These trips lasted for a total of nearly 653 million nights and resulted in a total expenditure of £25,070 million. Contrary to popular belief, trips and nights taken within the UK far outweighed those taken abroad; it is only when the figures for total spending are examined that figures for travel overseas exceed those within the UK.

Table 1.5 UK residents' tourism in 1992

	Trips		Nights		Spending	
	million	% of all destinations	million	% of all destinations	million	% of all destinations
All destinations	118.9	100	653.3	100	25,070	100
UK	95.6	80	399.7	61	10,665	43
England	77.2	65	306.4	47	8,080	32
Scotland	8.9	7	42.3	6	1,220	5
Wales	8.3	7	40.1	6	930	4
N. Ireland	1.1	1	5.3	1	135	1
Non-UK (rest of the world)	23.7	20	253.6	39	14,410	57

Source: Insights, September 1993

Notes:
A tourist trip is a stay of one or more nights away from home for holidays, visits to friends or relatives, business, conference or any other purpose except such things as boarding education or semi-permanent employment.
Tourist nights are those spent away from home using any type of accommodation, or in transit, on a tourist ship.
Tourist spending is expenditure while away from home and on advance payments for such things as fares and accommodation. Spending by the tourist on other people, e.g. children, is included. Spending on behalf of the tourist by other people, e.g. their spouse, is excluded.

Overseas visitors to the UK

In 1992, Britain earned a record £7.89 billion from the 18.53 million trips by overseas visitors to all parts of Britain (British Tourist Authority Annual Report 1993). This was in spite of the problems generally in the global tourist industry resulting from the world economic recession.

The structure of the industry

In broad terms, the British leisure and tourism industry is made up of three types of providers:

- The private sector.
- The public sector.
- The voluntary sector.

Each sector has its own distinct aims and objectives and different ways of managing its affairs.

Private sector leisure and tourism

This sector involves business units, both large and small, owned by individuals or groups of people whose principal aim is to maximise their profits. Revenue from the sales of their services or goods will hopefully be greater than the costs of operating the business so as to leave a surplus which can be either taken as profit or reinvested in the business in order to build a solid foundation for future success for owners, directors, employees and any shareholders who may have bought a stake in the business.

Leisure and tourism facilities provided by the private sector include:

- Theatres.
- Cinemas.
- Hotels and other forms of accommodation.
- Restaurants, cafes, pubs and bars.
- Discotheques and nightclubs.
- Travel agencies and tour operators.
- Airlines.
- Tourist attractions.
- Health and fitness clubs and studios.
- Mixed retail and leisure complexes.
- Transport operations.

Private sector leisure and tourism has a lively and dynamic image since the survival of many of its companies and individuals is dependent on adapting to new trends and fashions in society. For the same reason, customer service and customer care are vital components of any professional concern in the leisure and tourism field.

Structure in the private sector

As with many other sectors of the economy, businesses in leisure and tourism can be categorised into one of the following five classifications:

1 Sole trader.
2 Partnership.
3 Private limited company.
4 Public limited company (PLC).
5 Co-operative.

Sole trader

As the name implies, a business run by a sole trader is owned and controlled by that one person. Within leisure and tourism, such people often provide ancillary or support services for larger organisations, e.g. as couriers, guides, chauffeurs, caterers, fitness counsellors and instructors. Much maintenance work on property and equipment is also often entrusted to sole traders. It is not uncommon in the leisure and tourism business to find that an individual who used to work for a large organisation decides to leave and start a business as a sole trader free from the bureaucracy which sometimes frustrates talented employees.

This highlights one of the main advantages of being a sole trader, namely the ability to have personal control of the business and to be able to make decisions quickly. There are, however, disadvantages, which include the fact that the owner is personally liable for all the debts of the business and, often overlooked, the long hours the sole trader will have to work in order to be successful.

Partnership

There must be between two and 20 people in business together for a partnership to be legal. Not all of the partners are necessarily involved in the day-to-day running of the business, indeed some may choose only to put up capital in the hope of a return on their investment and show no interest in the management of the business at all; such individuals are referred to as 'sleeping partners'. An important point about partnerships is that the decision of any one partner is binding on all the other partners; this may cause problems if one partner proves to be unreliable or untrustworthy. In leisure and tourism, partnerships are often found in the hotel and catering field, with many pubs, cafes, restaurants, small hotels, guesthouses and inns being run as partnerships.

Advantages of partnerships are that extra capital is injected into the business when compared with the sole trader and that the responsibilities are shared by the partners. One disadvantage has already been highlighted, namely the decision of one partner being binding on the others; with the increased numbers involved in the partnership, decision making may be slower than is the case with the sole trader.

Private limited company

Any organisation within leisure and tourism which has the abbreviation 'Ltd' after its name is a private limited company. 'Limited' means that the company enjoys the benefit of 'limited liability', meaning that the investors in the business are only liable for the company's debts up to the amount they have actually invested; this is in stark contrast to both sole traders and partnerships who do not have limited liability. Those who invest in the business are known as shareholders although the shares of private limited companies are not offered for sale on the Stock Exchange as is the case with PLCs (public limited companies). Many leisure and tourism businesses are private limited companies with examples as diverse as tourist attractions, leisure centres and country house hotels.

Public limited company (PLC)

These are large organisations, often with hundreds and even thousands of people on their payroll. Some of the best known leisure and tourism companies in the UK are PLCs, e.g. Grand Metropolitan PLC, Ladbroke Group PLC, Airtours PLC, Forte PLC, Rank Organisation PLC and British Airways PLC, to name but a few. Investors in PLCs have the benefit of limited liability in the same way as those investing in private limited companies. The difference between the two lies in the word 'public', which indicates that the shares of a PLC are listed on the Stock Exchange and are therefore available to the public at large. Public limited companies often have a parent company acting as the head of a group with a number of subsidiary companies working beneath it, e.g. Forte Travelodge is a subsidiary of Forte PLC, the parent company.

As well as the advantage of limited liability, private limited companies and PLCs also have greater opportunities for expansion when compared with sole traders and partnerships. There may also be significant tax advantages of operating as a limited company. Disadvantages of private and public limited companies are that there is less confidentiality since they are both required to publish their accounts annually and they may be unable to react quickly to new market opportunities unless management and workforce are very flexible.

Table 1.6 on page 1.22 shows the turnover of some of the largest limited companies involved in leisure and tourism in 1989.

Co-operatives

The number of co-operatives within leisure and tourism is quite small, but they are to be found in community activities such as art galleries, music workshops, street theatre entertainment and countryside groups. Co-operatives work on very democratic principles with one vote per shareholder rather than one vote per share. They work within simple guidelines with elected managers organising the venture on behalf of the workers.

Table 1.6 Turnover of selected leisure and tourism companies 1989

Company name	Turnover (£000s)
Grand Metropolitan PLC	9298000
Ladbroke Group PLC	3659500
Whitbread PLC	2488300
Granada Group PLC	1636400
Rank Organisation PLC	1093000
Mecca Leisure Group PLC	588438
Stakis PLC	143223
Chrysalis Group PLC	95590
Wembley PLC	76275

Source: Jordans (1992)

CASE STUDY

The Rank Organisation PLC

The Rank Organisation was founded and created by J Arthur Rank more than 50 years ago. Rank became the dominant influence in the British film industry by the end of the Second World War and has subsequently developed and expanded into other leisure and entertainment businesses. Today it is one of the world's leading leisure and tourism organisations and one of the 100 largest companies in the UK. It currently employs some 40,000 people in four operating divisions:

- Film and television.
- Holidays and hotels.
- Recreation.
- Leisure.

Film and television operations include the famous Odeon Cinemas, which have been part of the Rank Organisation for over 50 years. Odeon operates over 300 screens at more than 70 locations in the UK and has an important presence in London's West End where the Odeon in Leicester Square often stages Royal Film Premieres. All Odeon cinemas are equipped with computerised box offices and offer advance booking facilities. Rank owns Pinewood Studios near London, the premier and best-known film studio in Europe, offering facilities to producers of feature films, TV commercials, training films and corporate videos. Other film and television work includes film distribution, video duplication and film processing services. In all, the film and television division employs approximately 7,000 staff.

Butlin's is the jewel in the crown of Rank's holidays and hotels division. Butlin's is a brand leader in the UK holiday market and sells in the region of 1.6 million holidays per year. It operates five Holiday Worlds and five Holiday Hotels at UK coastal resorts. The Holiday Worlds provide facilities for the family market, with a range of sports and leisure facilities, while the Holiday Hotels are aimed at older customers. Butlin's is the leading contractor of star entertainers in the UK. Rank also owns HavenWarner, offering self-catering and half-board holidays in 60 UK locations, and, through its Haven France and Spain brand, self-drive and caravan holidays at some 40 parks in Europe. HavenWarner sells over one million holidays each year. Shearings is part of the Rank Organisation and is the leading coach holiday operator in Europe with a fleet of some 350 coaches travelling to 300 UK and 250 continental European destinations.

Through its recreation division, Rank operates businesses that are regulated by the Gaming Board of Great Britain. These include around 150 amusement centres spread throughout the UK and 28 casinos trading under the Grosvenor Clubs banner. Rank is the leading bingo and social club operator in the UK with some 160 outlets known by the 'Top Rank' and 'Mecca' brand names, attracting about 700,000 customers each week.

Rank's leisure division operates around 50 nightclubs and theme bars, the best-known being Ritzy, Fifth Avenue and Central Park. The division also develops and manages multi-leisure centres that typically include a mix of multi-screen cinema, bingo, ten-pin bowling, nightclub, amusement centre, bars and restaurants. Resorts USA owns and operates 14 'Outdoor World' campground resorts on the Eastern seaboard of the USA and sells second homes in Pennsylvania. Rank Leisure USA owns and operates ten Hard Rock Cafes in Europe and America. There are also 12 franchised Hard Rock Cafes in other parts of the world.

Rank is also an equal partner in Universal Studios Florida, a film and TV studio complex and motion picture theme park which opened in Orlando in June 1990.

(Information courtesy of the Rank Organisation PLC)

Leisure and tourism in the public sector

Public sector leisure and tourism facilities in Britain exist side by side with those in the private sector. Indeed, with the trends towards privatisation (the transfer from public to private sector ownership and control) and compulsory competitive tendering (see page 1.32), the distinction between the two is becoming increasingly blurred. Unlike private sector provision, where profit maximisation is generally the main objective, the public sector is concerned with providing a service to the local community and the wider public. This does not mean that public sector providers are not concerned with giving value for money within the facilities they provide. Increasing competition from rival facilities has forced public sector managers to adopt many private sector practices in order to survive and expand their operations.

Facilities provided by the public sector include:

- Sports and leisure centres.
- Libraries and museums.
- Arts centres and galleries.
- Visitor attractions.
- Tourist information centres.
- Community centres.
- Parks, sports grounds and play areas.
- Swimming pools.
- Special events.

The structure of leisure and tourism in the public sector

Public sector provision can be at either one of two levels:

1 National government.
2 Local government.

National government involvement in leisure and tourism

The Department of National Heritage (DNH) was created after the general election of April 1992 as a totally new Ministry that would try to co-ordinate the many different activities that go to make up leisure and tourism within Britain. The Department, which is headed by a Cabinet Minister, the Secretary of State for National Heritage, has responsibility for:

- Broadcasting.
- The arts.
- Sport.
- Tourism.
- National Heritage.
- The film industry.
- The Millenium Fund (dedicated to projects to celebrate the start of the twenty-first century).

Before the DNH was formed these activities were the responsibility of many different government departments resulting in overlap and unnecessary duplication of effort. Staff have been transferred from these departments into the DNH, which has five directorates:

- Heritage and Tourism Group.
- Broadcasting, Films and Sport Group.
- Arts and Lottery Group.
- Libraries, Galleries and Museums Group.
- Resources and Services Group.

Figure 1.5 shows the structure of the Department of National Heritage.

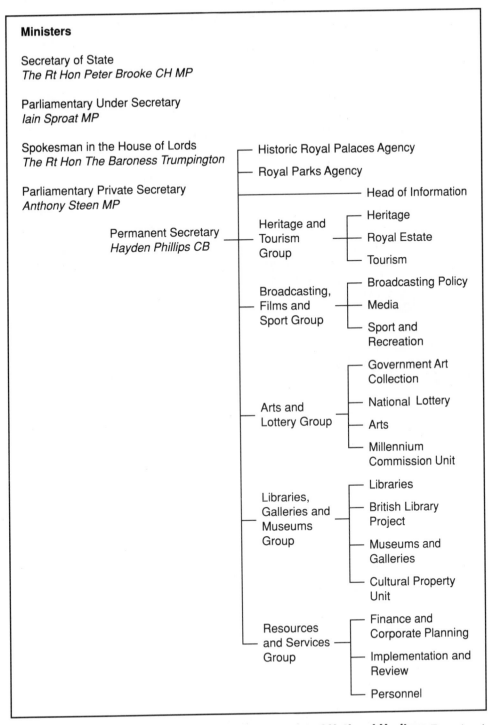

Ministers

Secretary of State
The Rt Hon Peter Brooke CH MP

Parliamentary Under Secretary
Iain Sproat MP

Spokesman in the House of Lords
The Rt Hon The Baroness Trumpington

Parliamentary Private Secretary
Anthony Steen MP

Permanent Secretary
Hayden Phillips CB

- Historic Royal Palaces Agency
- Royal Parks Agency
- Head of Information

Heritage and Tourism Group
- Heritage
- Royal Estate
- Tourism

Broadcasting, Films and Sport Group
- Broadcasting Policy
- Media
- Sport and Recreation

Arts and Lottery Group
- Government Art Collection
- National Lottery
- Arts
- Millennium Commission Unit

Libraries, Galleries and Museums Group
- Libraries
- British Library Project
- Museums and Galleries
- Cultural Property Unit

Resources and Services Group
- Finance and Corporate Planning
- Implementation and Review
- Personnel

Fig 1.5 Organisational structure of the Department of National Heritage *(Reproduced with the permission of the Controller of Her Majesty's Stationery Office) (source: DNH Annual Report 1993)*

The following public bodies are sponsored directly by the DNH:

- Arts Council of Great Britain.
- British Film Institute.
- British Tourist Authority.
- English Tourist Board.
- English Heritage.
- Sports Council.
- Football Licensing Authority.
- National Film and Television School.

They are sometimes referred to as quangos (quasi-autonomous non-governmental organisations) which, although linked to a government department, are left, to a greater or lesser extent, to manage their own affairs free from political bias.

Other government departments also have some influence in leisure and tourism policies, for example British Waterways, English Nature and the Forestry Commission are all supported by the Department of the Environment while the Ministry of Agriculture, Fisheries and Food promotes diversification into such activities as farm tourism and leisure pursuits. The Department for Education indirectly funds many leisure classes in local schools and colleges.

British Tourist Authority

The 1969 Development of Tourism Act established the British Tourist Authority (BTA) along with the Wales, English and Scottish Tourist Boards; the Northern Ireland Tourist Board was set up in 1948. Unlike the national tourist boards who try to encourage visitors to their own particular country, the BTA is responsible for promoting the whole of Britain to overseas visitors. BTA's objectives are:

- To maximise the benefit to the economy of tourism to Britain from abroad while working worldwide in partnership with the private and public sector organisations involved in the industry and the English Tourist Board, Scottish Tourist Board and Wales Tourist Board.
- To identify the requirements of visitors to Britain, whatever their origin, and to stimulate the improvement of the quality of the product and the use of technology to meet them.
- To spread the economic benefit of tourism to Britain more widely and particularly to areas with tourism potential and higher than average levels of unemployment.
- To encourage tourism to Britain in off-peak periods.
- To ensure that the Authority makes the most cost-effective use of resources in pursuing its objectives.

In order to meet these objectives, BTA works in close co-operation with the national and regional tourist boards, local authorities, media and trade interests, as shown in Figure 1.6.

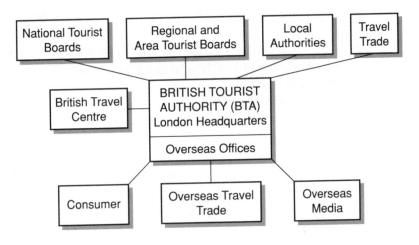

Fig 1.6 BTA's co-ordinating role

As well as running the British Travel Centre in London, BTA operates a network of 22 offices worldwide which act as information points for potential visitors to Britain and pass on information about the market from that particular country to the BTA's headquarters in London. This 'market intelligence' helps shape the various travel and tourism products that Britain has to offer to overseas visitors. In 1991/92 BTA received £29.2 million of grant from the government and generated a further £13.6 million from other commercial activities. The grant-in-aid figure for 1993/94 was £32 million.

Source: BTA

The Sports Council

The Sports Council is an independent body, established in 1972 by Royal Charter, and funded largely through funds from the Department of National Heritage. It has a remit covering British sport as a whole although there are separate Councils for Scotland, Wales and Northern Ireland. It consists of members appointed by the Secretary of State and around 550 permanent employees.

The Sports Council has four main aims:

- To increase participation in sport and physical recreation.
- To increase the quality and quantity of sports facilities.
- To raise standards of performance.
- To provide information for and about sport.

Increasing participation

The Council has an extensive programme to increase participation by:

- Providing regional participation grants to help a range of local organisations to get local people into sport.
- Running campaigns to persuade people to get involved in sport.
- Funding development staff to help governing bodies to increase participation in their particular sport.
- Organising programmes such as 'Action Sport' to promote sport through a wide range of formal and informal agencies.

Facilities

The Council works to improve facilities by:

- Encouraging the development of new or improved sports facilities through advice and financial assistance.
- Preparing standard design solutions for sports buildings and systems.
- Developing innovative facilities and systems such as artificial playing surfaces.
- Identifying examples of good practice in facilities and management.
- Funding research into local and national sport facility requirements.

Raising standards of performance

Action by the Sports Council in the area of standards of performance includes:

- Running five centres of excellence at:
  - Crystal Palace (National Sports Centre).
  - Bisham Abbey (National Sports Centre).
  - Lilleshall (National Sports Centre).
  - Holme Pierrepont (National Water Sports Centre).
  - Plas y Brenin (National Centre for Mountain Activities).
- Offering support to governing bodies of sport.
- Financing the National Coaching Foundation (NCF) to help meet the demand for trained coaches.
- Encouraging sponsorship of sport by the private sector.
- Running the campaign against drug abuse in sport.

The Council is the country's main central source of information and data about sport. It provides a national information centre and a network of nine regional centres based at its regional offices. The Sports Council researches and publishes a wide range of data on sport, briefs journalists, politicians and other interested parties and runs sport's largest annual conference 'Recreation Management'.

Source: Sports Council

The Arts Council of Great Britain

The Arts Council is the national body established to foster the arts throughout Britain. It was formed in 1946 to continue in peacetime the work begun by the Council for the Encouragement of Music and the Arts during the Second World War.

The Council operates under a Royal Charter, which defines its objectives as:

1 To develop and improve the knowledge, understanding and practice of the arts.

2 To increase the accessibility of the arts to the public throughout Britain.

3 To advise and co-operate with departments of government, local authorities and other bodies.

Structure

The Arts Council is the central part of a funding structure that includes the Crafts Council, British Film Institute, the Scottish and Welsh Arts Councils and the ten Regional Arts Boards (see Figure 1.7).

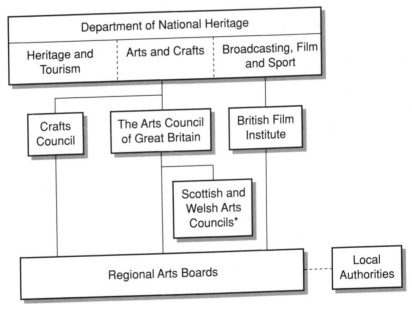

* Autonomous bodies from April 1994

Fig 1.7 The arts funding structure in Great Britain (source: Arts Council)

From April 1994, the Scottish and Welsh Arts Councils will become autonomous and directly accountable to their respective Secretary of State. A separate Arts Council will be set up with a new Charter to continue the work of the current Council in England.

Funding

The Arts Council received £225.63 million for 1993/94 from the Department of National Heritage. It allocated £44 million to the Regional Arts Boards and £23 million and £13 million to the Scottish and Welsh Arts Councils respectively. Four per cent of the Council's grant is spent on administration of the Arts Council itself.

Priorities

The Arts Council has identified the following priorities for its work:

- Quality in the arts generally.
- Access for all to the arts.
- Growth of the arts economy.
- Quality of service.

Source: Arts Council

Local government involvement in leisure and tourism

Local government in England and Wales consists broadly of three tiers. Working from the most local these are:

1 Parish or community councils.
2 District or borough councils.
3 County councils.

At each tier there are elected representatives (known as councillors) who implement central government decisions at local level. Local government officers, the equivalent of civil servants in central government, carry out the decisions of the councillors which, if the democratic system is functioning correctly, should reflect the views and wishes of the majority of the local people.

Local authorities exist to provide services to the local population; whether a service is provided by the county or district, for example, is not always clear-cut. In general, county councils are concerned with broader issues, such as education, social services, highways and strategic planning, while the district councils confine themselves to more local needs, such as refuse collection, environmental health, leisure and housing.

Provision of leisure and tourism facilities

There is no statutory (legal) duty on local authorities to provide the range of leisure and tourism facilities we see in most areas of the country today. They only have a legal duty to provide recreational opportunities through schools and libraries, but most go far beyond this and use their wide discretionary powers to provide the best possible leisure and tourism facilities within their local area. This discretionary provision does have its drawbacks, however, since in times of financial cut-backs it is often leisure and tourism that has its budget cut first.

Local authorities use their resources to provide a wide range of leisure and tourism facilities, which in a typical district might include:

- Playgrounds.
- Parks and gardens.
- Playing fields.
- Libraries.
- Art galleries and museums.
- Theatres.
- Sports/leisure centres and swimming pools.
- Outdoor activity centres.
- Tourist information.

Some of these facilities may be dual use or joint use when, for example, a college and the local community share the use of a sports centre in order to make better use of the facility.

How important is local government leisure and tourism provision?
The influence of local authorities on the provision of facilities and amenities for leisure and tourism is immense. In purely financial terms, local authorities were estimated to spend nearly £1.5 billion on such provision in the financial year 1992/93 (DNH figures). This compares with a spend of approximately £1 billion at national level by the Department of National Heritage itself.

Local councils in England and Wales are also significant employers within the leisure and tourism sector. According to the Employment Department's figures for 1993, employment in libraries, museums, art galleries, sports and other recreational services amounted to 380,000 out of a total leisure and tourism employment figure of around 1.4 million. Figure 1.8 shows the structure of a typical local authority leisure services department.

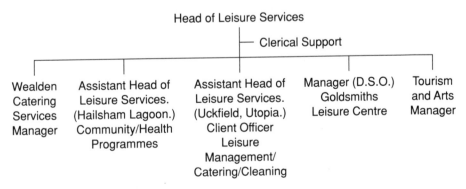

Leisure Services Department, Wealden District Council

Head of Leisure Services

— Clerical Support

| Wealden Catering Services Manager | Assistant Head of Leisure Services. (Hailsham Lagoon.) Community/Health Programmes | Assistant Head of Leisure Services. (Uckfield, Utopia.) Client Officer Leisure Management/ Catering/Cleaning | Manager (D.S.O.) Goldsmiths Leisure Centre | Tourism and Arts Manager |

Fig 1.8 The structure of a typical local authority leisure services department
(courtesy of Wealden District Council)

Compulsory competitive tendering (CCT)

CCT is the process by which many local services traditionally provided exclusively by the local authority are opened up to competition from the private sector. It is not privatisation in the strict sense of the word since the local authority retains ownership of the facilities involved. Within the leisure and recreation sector, all local authorities in England and Wales are required to have put the management of their sports and leisure facilities out to tender by the end of 1993. 'Management' in this case includes:

- Taking bookings.
- Providing catering services.
- Marketing and promoting the facility.
- Collecting and accounting for fees and charges.
- Making the facility secure.
- Cleaning and maintaining the facility.
- Hiring out equipment.
- Providing instruction.
- Supervising activities.

Current employees of the local authorities may submit a bid for the management of a facility and, if their tender is successful, they are known as the DSO (Direct service organisation).

Sport and leisure facilities that fall within the scope of CCT include:

- Sports centres.
- Leisure centres.
- Athletics grounds.
- Cycle tracks.
- Bowling greens.
- Artificial ski slopes.
- Golf courses.

The principle underlying CCT is that increased competition will provide an improved service and better value for money for the local population. Opponents of the legislation argue that CCT may lead to certain services and facilities being phased out since they are unprofitable but are, none the less, fulfilling an important local need, such as services for the disabled.

Leisure and tourism in the voluntary sector

Not all leisure and tourism facilities and services in Britain can be provided solely by public and private sector organisations. A third important source of provision, the voluntary sector, exists to supplement private and public facilities.

The voluntary sector includes charities and trusts involved in:

- Conservation/environment.
- Community activities.

- Play schemes.
- Heritage.
- Minority groups.
- Youth organisations.
- Cultural/entertainment organisations.
- Clubs and societies.

Voluntary organisations vary enormously in their size and aims. At one end of the scale, a small group of like-minded people may decide to form an aerobics club in their local village hall purely for the purpose of improving their level of fitness. At the other end are large organisations such as the National Trust and the Royal Society for the Protection of Birds falling within the voluntary sector of leisure and tourism, each having its own objectives in terms of environmental conservation. Voluntary organisations at both national and local level often receive advice and financial help from both the public and private sector, sometimes in the form of grants or sponsorship (see Section 4 of this unit).

Organisation within the voluntary sector

The grouping of individuals to achieve a common purpose may be either formal or informal. Generally, the more formal an organisation is, the more structured it becomes. Taking the earlier example of the group of people deciding to form an aerobics club, it is likely that they will form a committee to manage the affairs of the club. As a minimum, the committee will normally include:

- A chairperson.
- A secretary.
- A treasurer.

There may also be a social secretary or membership secretary and co-opted members (people who are appointed because of their particular skills or experience). The committee is elected by the members of the club and all who volunteer to serve on the committee are accountable to all club members for its smooth running.

Larger organisations within the voluntary sector are not able to meet all their needs through the recruitment of volunteers alone. Salaried professionals are employed, sometimes alongside volunteers, to manage the affairs of the organisation and help it meet its objectives. Certain individuals may be invited to become honorary members in recognition of loyal work or exceptional financial contributions to a particular organisation. Ordinary members are members of the general public who wish to further the cause of an organisation by paying a membership subscription. A particular society or trust may invite a celebrated individual to become its patron to add prestige to the organisation; the Queen, for example, is the patron of the Youth Hostel Association.

The National Trust

Introduction

The National Trust, or to give it its full title, The National Trust for Places of Historic Interest or Natural Beauty, was founded in 1895 as an independent charity in response to the spread of industrialisation, which was affecting both town and countryside at the end of the last century. Although its name might suggest that it is run by the government, the Trust is jealously independent of the State. It depends on the generosity of those who give it properties and the money to maintain them, on more than two million subscribing members and on its friends and supporters everywhere. Today, the National Trust protects more than 600,000 acres of land in England, Wales and Northern Ireland as well as over 200 houses and parks.

Structure

The day-to-day administration of the Trust is carried out by its executive staff at head office in London and in 16 regional offices covering England, Wales and Northern Ireland. The governing body is a council of 52 members, half of whom are elected by the members and half appointed by relevant bodies.

Activities

The Trust plays host to an immense number of people. Each year, some 11 million people visit its 400 buildings and gardens, open at a charge, and on a fine summer weekend untold millions freely enjoy the coastline, hills and woodlands which the Trust preserves for us all. The Trust must ensure the right balance between the often conflicting interests of preservation and presentation to the public. Too great a pressure of visitors could destroy the atmosphere they seek. The Trust is at present running several special appeals including Enterprise Neptune, launched by the Duke of Edinburgh in 1965, which aims to preserve unspoilt coastline and set itself an initial target of raising £2 million. By the end of 1992, the appeal had raised £17.5 million and over 530 miles of coastline were under the permanent protection of the National Trust.

Source: National Trust

Employment and careers in leisure and tourism

Employment

We have seen earlier how tourism alone is estimated to employ 118 million people worldwide and, closer to home, how leisure and tourism creates a significant number of jobs in the private, public and voluntary sectors. Leisure and tourism's ability to create jobs is one of its main economic benefits and often the principal reason why a country, region or local area considers tourism as an option for economic development.

The scale of employment in leisure and tourism

Figures from the Employment Department give the breakdown of employment in the different sectors of the leisure and tourism industry in Britain for June 1992 shown in Table 1.7.

Table 1.7 Leisure and tourism employment in Britain – June 1992

Category	%
Restaurants, cafés, etc.	20.5
Public houses and bars	22.3
Nightclubs and licensed clubs	9.4
Hotels and other tourist accommodation	20.6
Libraries, museums, art galleries, sports and other recreational services	27.2
	100.0

Source: Employment Gazette

As Table 1.7 shows, the bulk of jobs are to be found in the private sector. The total employment figure for the same month was approximately 1.5 million. In addition to this, the Labour Force Survey estimates that there are around 183,000 self-employed in the leisure and tourism sector.

Trends in employment

Being a service industry, which by its very nature is labour intensive, trends in employment in leisure and tourism tend to reflect the peaks and troughs in the industry. Much of the growth in jobs in tourism is very recent; it is only with the introduction of package tours and the advent of 'mass tourism' within the past 30 years or so that we have seen tourism develop as a provider of jobs. Sectors of leisure and tourism employment which have grown rapidly over this time period include:

● Airlines.
● Travel agency and tour operations.
● Restaurants and cafés.
● Licensed entertainment venues.

One or two areas, notably employment in hotels and public sector leisure and tourism, have remained fairly static over this time period while the number of jobs in cinemas has actually fallen. The recent upsurge in popularity of home-based leisure activities (watching TV and video, playing video games, etc.) is creating new jobs but sometimes at the expense of others, e.g. jobs in video rental go up while those in cinemas go down.

Along with other sectors of industry, leisure and tourism is likely to see more part-time and short-term employment particularly in times of world recession. The nature of tourism particularly, means that many jobs are seasonal, only employing people for part of the year. Many agencies, however, are working hard to encourage more use of facilities and attractions off-peak so as to increase further the economic benefits of tourism.

Careers in leisure and tourism

People who work in leisure and tourism, or who are considering a career in the industry, should:

- Be a 'people person'; in other words, like working with the general public and serving their needs.
- Be prepared to work unsocial hours.
- Be aware of the importance of high standards of customer care and customer service.
- Be patient and able to work under pressure at times.
- Be able to know where to find relevant information in answer to enquiries.
- Be accurate in their work, particularly when dealing with money matters.
- Be prepared to learn fast!
- Be able to accept responsibility and work with little supervision.
- Be able to demonstrate basic computer skills.

In return, the leisure and tourism industry offers:

- A satisfying job where employees get pleasure from helping others make best use of their leisure time.
- Opportunities for travel, both at home and abroad.
- Great variety in the work that is undertaken.
- Excellent prospects, often at a young age, for those with the talent and determination.

Jobs in leisure and recreation

The range of possible careers in leisure and recreation is very broad and includes:

- Hotel management.
- Conference planning.
- Leisure centre management.
- Sportsman/woman.
- Arts administration.
- Pub or restaurant management.
- Countryside management.

- Contract catering.
- Event management.
- Teaching/lecturing.
- Outdoor pursuits.
- Sports coaching.
- Casino/betting shop management.
- Sports administration.

Jobs in tourism and travel

The main employment opportunities within tourism and travel occur in:

- Airlines and airports.
- Tour operators.
- Tourist attractions.
- Coach operators.
- Tourist information centres.
- Ferry and cruise companies.
- Travel agencies.

- Local authority tourism departments.
- Hotels and other accommodation.
- Car hire companies.
- Guiding.
- Training.

Fig 1.9 Overseas representatives advising holidaymakers (courtesy of Airtours PLC)

The future of leisure and tourism

We have seen how leisure and tourism has developed very rapidly to become one of the world's biggest industries. But what of the future? Will this dramatic growth be sustained or will the bubble burst?

Influences on future developments

1 *Social factors* – Demographic trends (those concerned with the characteristics of the UK population) and social changes will have important impacts on the future development of the industry up to and beyond the year 2000. The fact that people are living longer, the fall in the number of young people, the increase in one-parent households, more couples choosing not to have children or to delay having children until later in life all point to the fact that the type of leisure and tourism products and services will change dramatically as we move into the next millenium.

2 *Political and economic factors* – On a global scale, the late 1980s has seen historic world developments with countries emerging from State control and embracing the Western 'market economy'. Events such as the demolition of the Berlin Wall will have profound effects on leisure and tourism developments; tourists from Western countries are now more able to visit the former Eastern bloc countries, while those from the former East will be curious to sample Western hospitality by travelling further afield. The completion of the Single European Market in 1993, with the easing of border controls, has the potential to increase travel within EC member countries. Closer to home, recession will continue to hold down expansion in certain sectors of leisure and tourism.

3 *Cultural/environmental factors* – The 1980s saw the emergence in Britain of a greater environmental awareness and a society that was beginning to take its health and fitness seriously. These factors are likely to remain important influences on leisure and tourism developments in the future with so-called 'green issues' high on the agenda.

4 *Technological factors* – Leisure and tourism has always been an industry that has made extensive use of new technology equipment. Central reservation systems (CRS), the use of computers in leisure centres and sophisticated databases for marketing purposes are now commonplace. Increasing competition within the industry will force organisations to use new technology to the full. New developments in transportation make extensive use of new technology; the Channel Tunnel is a good example of this as are the advances in aircraft design, opening up new 'long haul' destinations.

The future of tourism

When the present economic recession ends, most experts in tourism and travel predict there will be growth of between 2 per cent and 4.5 per cent per annum up to the end of this century. The higher figure would increase the volume of world tourism by over 50 per cent to 600 million international arrivals by the year 2000. Such growth could produce an extra 38–55 million jobs worldwide by the end of the nineties (World Travel and Tourism Council).

The trend towards British tourists choosing 'long haul' destinations is likely to continue, reflecting the desire to seek out new places, which has characterised much of the historical development of tourism. Visitors will continue to want challenge and some degree of education from their travel. Tourists will increasingly demand holidays and other travel products that conform with the principles of sustainable tourism; it is likely that environmental quality will be one of the major factors affecting consumer choice in tourism up to the year 2000.

The future of leisure

Figures produced by Leisure Consultants show that UK leisure spending between 1992 and 1998 will increase from around £100 billion to more than £130 billion. Specific leisure activities that are likely to increase in popularity over the same period include:

- New forms of home electronic entertainment and education.
- Creative and productive leisure.
- 'Green', healthy and active leisure.
- Purposeful travel.
- Social and community leisure.

Of declining interest up to 1998 will be:

- Established 'mass' leisure (e.g. cheap package holidays, network TV).
- Socially discouraged activities (e.g. heavy drinking).
- Activities with health or environmental hazards (e.g. some DIY goods).
- Young adult leisure (e.g. going to pubs, discos and pop concerts).

The priorities in the use of leisure time up to the year 2000 will be activities aimed at improving the home environment and leisure away from home, which will provide interest and stimulation to both mind and body. People will expect high quality in all aspects of leisure provision, and particularly in the levels of customer service they receive. Life-style concerns, such as environmental protection, importance of the family, health and security will greatly influence the choice of leisure activities and products. Changing patterns of working will necessitate a more flexible approach to the provision of leisure facilities.

We are all familiar with the term 'product' in our everyday lives. We all buy products such as food, clothing and newspapers. In leisure and tourism, the majority of 'products' that we buy or use are intangible, i.e. we can't see or touch them; examples are holidays, short breaks, aerobics sessions, swimming lessons and West End shows. Tangible leisure and tourism products include sports goods, restaurant meals and travel goods.

This section looks at the full range of leisure and tourism products available in the UK but concentrates first on Britain's natural resources, which influence many of the products on offer.

UK natural resources

Climate

As we all know, weather plays a crucial role in determining how we use our leisure time; British people will often travel thousands of miles to escape our cool temperate climate in the hope of 'guaranteed' sunshine. There are marked differences in climate even across Britain, with the south generally experiencing warmer summers and less severe winters than the north. This is due in part to the warming influence of the Gulf Stream, an air current that originates in the warm atmosphere of the Gulf of Mexico. The weather will also influence the location of many sports and leisure activities; surfers will usually prefer the warmer waters of Cornwall to the cooler climate of, say, Northumberland. Britain's wet climate will lead to more indoor activities and the use of all-weather surfaces for sports events. The west and south of Britain do best of all when it comes to sunshine hours, but the west has the areas of highest rainfall, a consequence of the prevailing westerly wind, which the British Isles experiences and the highest altitudes, e.g. Snowdonia, the Lake District and the West of Scotland.

Topography

The varied landscapes found in Britain today are the result of man's activities over thousands of years, the effects of climate and the underlying geological formations. The dramatic scenery of North Wales, the Pennines and the Scottish Highlands, for example, attract visitors in their millions. Some choose simply to sit and marvel at these works of nature while others follow active leisure pursuits such as rock climbing, walking, fell running or camping. The 'patchwork' of fields in the traditional British landscape, when coupled with the delights of clusters of small towns and villages, are a magnet for home and overseas visitors alike. As a result of the last Ice Age, the countryside abounds with natural lakes, some of which are extensively used for activities such as windsurfing, sailing, water-skiing and power boating.

The range of UK leisure and tourism products

We have already seen how leisure and tourism facilities are provided by organisations in either the private, public or voluntary sectors. Table 1.8 shows how these 'providers' are linked to the types of 'products' they supply.

Table 1.8 The relationship between providers and products in leisure and tourism

Sector	Providers	Types of products
Private	Hoteliers, leisure companies, tour operators, travel agents, transport operators, catering outlets	Holidays, short breaks, flights, attractions, health and fitness clubs, events, entertainments, hospitality
Public	National government (indirectly), local authorities, quangos	Leisure centres, tourist information centres, sports facilities, catering outlets
Voluntary	National Trust, YHA, Royal Society for the Protection of Birds	Historic houses, nature reserves, wildlife centres, accommodation

Table 1.8 demonstrates the very broad nature of the UK leisure and tourism industry, with just a small sample of the types of products on offer to the general public. We will now look in more detail at these and other products' highlighting the key features of each.

Holidays

Tour operators are in business to sell holidays. They negotiate with hoteliers and airlines to put together a package holiday that would normally include:

- Accommodation (full-board, half-board, bed and breakfast, or room only).
- Flight or ferry crossing.
- Transfer arrangements at the holiday destination.
- The services of a courier or representative.

The tour operators invite travel agents to sell the holidays on their behalf to the general public. For this service, the operator pays the agent a commission (an agreed percentage of the total holiday price, normally in the region of 10 per cent, although this fluctuates according to the level of sales). Travel agents also sell a host of other products, again earning commission on sales. These include:

- Travel insurance.
- Foreign exchange and travellers cheques.
- Car hire.
- Coach travel.
- Theatre tickets.
- Short breaks.
- Ferry tickets.
- Cruise bookings.
- Airline tickets.
- Train tickets.

By a process known as vertical integration (where companies at different levels of the distribution chain are linked), the major tour operators have gained control of the biggest travel agency chains. For example, the number one tour operator in terms of volume of sales, Thomsons, owns the Lunn Poly travel agency. Similarly, Going Places is owned by tour operator number two, Airtours. The third biggest tour operator, Owners Abroad, has an 'alliance' with Thomas Cook agencies. Some operators also have their own airlines, e.g. Thomson owns Britannia. Horizontal integration is when companies at the same level in the distribution chain merge, for example British Airways' recent takeover of Dan Air.

Short breaks

Although the traditional British two-week holiday is in something of a decline, short breaks have been a resounding success story since the early 1980s. Many innovative accommodation operators and destinations have responded to the need to fill their bedspaces at weekends and slack periods of the year by offering short holidays, often based on a theme or activity. According to independent research quoted by Cresta, one of the main operators, the total outbound short-break market is also developing, with a growth rate of 67 per cent since 1987, with city breaks alone accounting for 600,000 travellers per year. The top operator is the Bridge Group (including Paris Travel Service) with 136,000 clients in 1991, substantially ahead of Thomson Citybreaks at 80,000. Travelscene and Cresta each carry over 60,000, the next biggest being BA Holidays and Time Off each carrying well over 20,000. The popularity of short breaks lies in the changing leisure habits of much of the population, linked to changes in working practices, making the traditional 14-day break unpopular with a large section of the travelling public, many of whom have sufficient disposable income to be able to enjoy more than one holiday each year.

Sports facilities

The majority of sports facilities are provided by local authorities, sometimes with financial assistance from the Sports Council or other funding agencies. Sport is very popular in Britain, yet the level of participation remains low. According to Sports Council figures, 56.5 per cent of adults participate in sport of some kind – only 66.7 per cent of all men and 47.6 per cent of all women. One-third of the population play an indoor sport at least once a month and 40 per cent participate outdoors. Local councils, as well as the Sports Council itself, are doing a great deal to raise the overall level of participation by offering as wide a selection of products as their resources allow. A local authority is likely to offer:

- Sports facilities.
- Sports coaching.
- Health and fitness programmes.
- Events for young people.
- Events for 'minority' groups, e.g. disabled, ethnic minorities.

Some sports facilities will be provided by the private sector wherever they can ensure a reasonable return on their investment. Most of the large sports spectator facilities, such as football grounds, are provided by private sector companies, e.g. Tottenham Hotspur PLC.

Entertainment and catering facilities

While local authorities are generally only involved in a small way with providing facilities for entertainment, this activity is a major money-spinner for the private sector, with such names as the Rank Organisation and Granada being major players. Everything from bingo halls to casinos and nightclubs are the preserve of private companies, large and small. Catering services ranging from a simple meal, through bar services to large hospitality events are all within their scope.

Accommodation services

The British accommodation sector is essentially a private sector concern although the voluntary and public sectors are represented to a small degree, e.g. the Youth Hostels Association and outdoor activity centres operated by local authorities. Accommodation is generally classified as either serviced or self-catering. Serviced accommodation, as its name implies, refers to accommodation which involves guests coming into contact with staff or proprietors who provide the services they need during their stay. The types of accommodation that fall into the serviced category include:

- Hotels.
- Guesthouses.
- Inns.
- Farmhouses.
- Motels.

The services they provide range from the provision of meals to the cleaning of rooms. Self-catering accommodation, so popular with families who like the freedom and flexibility that this category of accommodation offers, includes:

- Static and touring caravans.
- Cottages.
- Villas and chalets.
- Camping.
- Apartments.
- Motorhomes.

Although there will nearly always be an element of service provided with self-catering accommodation, the guests are essentially catering for themselves by preparing their own meals and doing the housekeeping.

According to English Tourist Board figures, hotels, motels and guesthouses accounted for the largest proportion of all spending on accommodation in the UK in 1992 at 36 per cent with VFR (visiting friends and relatives) next at 22 per cent. Staying in a self-catering house was third at 8 per cent, closely followed by static caravans at 6 per cent of total spending.

One recent development in the accommodation sector is worthy of note. Timeshare is the name given to the purchase of the right to stay in a particular property at a specific time in the year, rather than buying the property outright. Timeshare is usually sold in blocks of weeks, with a week in the high season costing more than the same length of time out of season. The person who buys the week or weeks has the option of letting the property out for rent or swapping properties with another timeshare owner, perhaps in another country. The week or weeks can also be offered for sale. Timeshare is most common in the USA and Mediterranean countries, but there are properties in Britain including apartments in country house hotels, in major cities and in seaside resorts, such as

Torquay, as well as purpose-built timeshare villas in Wales, the Lake District, Scotland and other country areas.

Arts and entertainment facilities

While much sport, leisure activity and tourism takes place in the outdoor environment, many arts and entertainment activities take place indoors, including in the home. We have seen that home-based leisure is set to grow substantially up to the end of the century, based to a great extent around electronic media. While such products are provided by private sector companies, the public sector does have an important role in providing arts facilities in the local community, e.g. art galleries, museums and theatres.

Visitor attractions

When a visitor is safely installed in his or her accommodation, having travelled to the destination by any one of a variety of modes of transport, the third element of the tourist product, namely entertainment, comes into play. Visitor attractions are one of the entertainments that visitors look for to give them excitement, education, stimulation and interest. Visitor attractions may be either natural or man-made.

Natural attractions

Britain has an abundance of fine landscapes, from Land's End to John O'Groats. Visitors are attracted to the beautiful coastline, the rugged mountains and the picturesque dales. Many of these areas have been given special status to protect the environment and provide facilities for their enjoyment by the public. The job of overseeing these 'protected' areas in England lies with the Countryside Commission, whose aim is to conserve and enhance the natural beauty of England's countryside and help give people better opportunities to enjoy and appreciate it. The Countryside Council for Wales does a similar job in the Principality. The main areas for which they are responsible are as follows.

1 National Parks

The ten National Parks in England and Wales (see Figure 1.10) were established under the 1949 National Parks and Access to the Countryside Act (the Broads in Norfolk and Suffolk is not a National Park as such but has equal status). The word 'national' does not mean that the Parks are owned by the government; most of the land within National Park Boundaries is privately owned and often under severe pressure from visitors and their vehicles. The Peak District National Park is a good case in point being located between the huge conurbations of Sheffield and Manchester. The total number of visitors to the National Parks in England is more than 70 million in a typical year and, when combined with the three Welsh Parks, they cover approximately one-tenth of the land area of England and Wales.

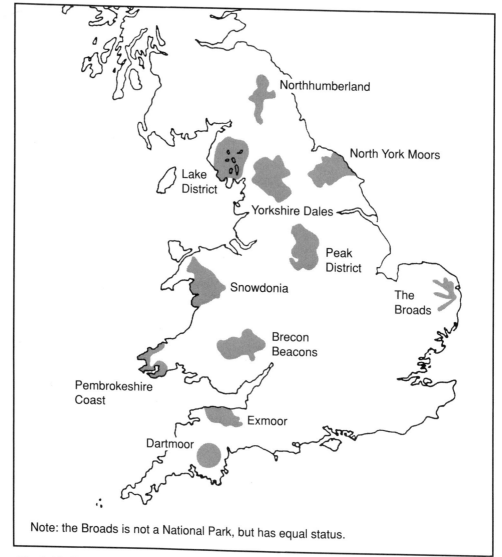

Note: the Broads is not a National Park, but has equal status.

Fig 1.10 The national parks in England and Wales

2 Areas of Outstanding Natural Beauty (AONBs)

Thirty-five of England's most cherished landscapes are protected as AONBs. They range from the wild open moorlands of the North Pennines to the green belt countryside of the Surrey Hills and the intimate valley of the Wye, which straddles the border with Wales (there are another four AONBs wholly within Wales itself). AONBs can be popular destinations for leisure and tourism, although, unlike National Parks, they are not designated for their recreational value. The Countryside Commission has proposed stronger measures for their management and more funding for their upkeep. In total, AONBs in England cover around 15 per cent of the landscape.

3 Heritage Coasts

There are 44 Heritage Coasts in England and Wales. They are among the most precious assets for wildlife and landscape, as well as for leisure and tourism. Concern over the harmful impact of increasing numbers of visitors led to their designation and a plan of action that includes creating and repairing footpaths, cleaning up bathing water and removing litter.

Man-made attractions

The range of man-made visitor attractions is vast. They can be grouped under the following headings:

Sports facilities	– e.g. swimming pools and dry-ski slopes.
Heritage attractions	– e.g. stately homes and castles.
Entertainments	– e.g. nightclubs and discos.
Theme parks	– e.g. Alton Towers and the American Adventure.
Leisure shopping	– e.g. regional shopping complex and car-boot sale.
Animals and plants	– e.g. zoos and botanical gardens.

Statistics from the BTA show that the most popular visitor attraction in Britain in 1992 was Blackpool Pleasure Beach with an estimated 6.5 million visitors. Table 1.9 gives the number of visits to the top ten historic properties in Britain in 1991 and 1992.

Table 1.9 shows that the number of visits to historic properties remained fairly constant between 1991 and 1992, except in those attractions with a strong appeal to overseas visitors, which enjoyed welcome increases in levels of business, notably Windsor Castle, Hampton Court Palace and the Tower of London.

In order to remain successful, attractions have to respond to changing public tastes and fashions, hence the introduction of such new developments as virtual reality. Other recent trends in the attractions sector include the introduction of holiday centres, theme parks, leisure pools and a revival in museums. We will consider each of these in detail.

Table 1.9 Visits to the top 10 historic properties in the UK 1991–92

		1991 visits	1992 visits
1	Tower of London	1,923,520	2,235,199
2	St Paul's Cathedral	1,500,000*	1,400,000*
3	Edinburgh Castle	973,620	986,305
4	Roman Baths and Pump Room, Bath	827,214	895,948
5	Windsor Castle, State Apartments	627,213	769,298
6	Warwick Castle	682,621	690,000
7	Stonehenge, Wiltshire	615,377	649,442
8	Shakespeare's Birthplace, Stratford	516,623	577,704
9	Hampton Court Palace	502,377	580,440
10	Blenheim Palace, Oxfordshire	503,328	486,100

Source: Insights, July 1993

* = An estimate

Holiday centres

The old concept of the holiday camp has been replaced by the new holiday centre. Butlins camps underwent a major refurbishment in the 1980s to create Butlins Holiday 'Worlds', e.g. Summer West World in Minehead. Center Parcs have introduced to Britain their well-tried and tested European formula of a complex centred on a covered leisure pool and offering up-market villas in a woodland setting for those seeking an active break or holiday. The first British Center Parc was built in Sherwood Forest, the second near Cambridge with a third opening at Longleat in Wiltshire in mid-1994.

Theme parks

The bigger British theme parks have been modelled on North American examples, principally the immensely popular Disneyworld in Florida and Disneyland in California. Theme parks often provide thrilling 'white knuckle' rides and a range of other attractions and catering facilities aimed at families and young adults who usually pay one all-inclusive entry fee which permits an unlimited number of rides. Some of the most successful UK theme parks are Alton Towers in Staffordshire (nearly two million visitors per year), Chessington World of Adventures (1.5 million) and the American Adventure in Derbyshire (one million visitors).

Leisure pools

Many local authorities and private operators have upgraded existing swimming pools or built new complexes to house leisure pools. In many cities, towns and rural areas, the stark, rectangular municipal baths have been replaced with pools boasting such facilities as wave machines, jacuzzis, saunas, flumes, waterslides and splash pools. These leisure pools often have themed events, e.g. a Caribbean evening or a birthday party, in order to maximise revenue and make full use of the facility.

Museums

In recent years, many museums have tried to change their image from one of dark, dreary and unwelcoming places to one where visitors can find fun, excitement and entertainment. Some have been changed into living museums, for example Beamish Open Air Museum, Ironbridge and Wigan Pier, where actors and actresses play the roles of those who lived in the past to entertain the visitors. Others have made imaginative use of new technology to bring history to life through animated displays; two good examples are the Jorvik Viking Centre in York and the Oxford Story. To appeal directly to children, some museums have introduced a 'hands-on' policy that allows people to touch exhibits, e.g. Eureka! in Halifax, which is set to achieve its target of 500,000 visitors per year within three years of opening (Unit 13 has a case study on Eureka!).

Leisure and tourism infrastructure

In leisure and tourism, the term infrastructure is used to denote all the services that an area needs in order to develop its full potential and provide the level of facilities that both local people and visitors demand. The main categories are:

1 *Transportation* – including roads, railways, airports, seaports.
2 *Utilities* – for example electricity and telecommunications.
3 *Other services* – including health care and security.

The infrastructure of a region can be thought of as the skeleton around which the superstructure components (hotels, attractions, etc.) are built. In most cases, the public sector will take on the responsibility for developing the infrastructure and the private sector the superstructure, although partnerships between the private and public sectors are increasingly common.

Transportation

A good transport network is vital for a country, region or local area to develop its full economic potential for leisure and tourism. We have seen in Section 1 of this unit that the number of cars on our roads is set to increase dramatically up to and beyond the year 2000, with the government pledging even more money to expand

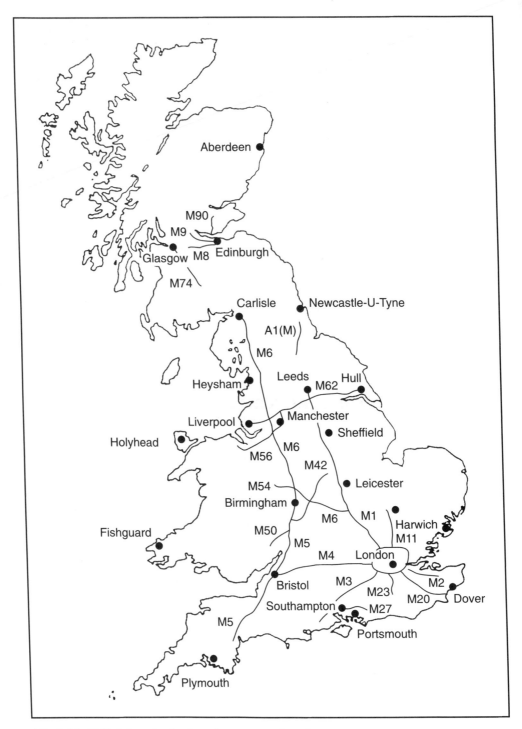

Fig 1.11 Britain's principal motorways and ports

the motorway network and by-pass towns and villages. Figure 1.11 shows Britain's network of principal motorways and main ports of entry and exit.

The private car is the predominant mode of travel for tourists in Britain, whether UK residents or overseas visitors. The car accounted for 78 per cent of holiday tourism trips in 1990 and, if hire cars, bus and coach travel are included in the statistics, the figure rises to 87 per cent (*Insights*, January 1993). The number of people using rail services for tourism has fallen significantly over the last 40 years. Britain's airports are important 'gateways' for overseas visitors, with Heathrow and Gatwick between them handling over 70 per cent of all UK air passenger traffic (Unit 13 on the UK holiday industry looks in more detail at transportation in the UK).

Main tourist receiving areas

The section on the historical development of tourism showed that seaside resorts and spa towns were some of the first areas to be developed for tourism in Britain. Today, seaside towns are still popular with the British and many spa towns are enjoying something of a revival, e.g. Llandrindod Wells and Cheltenham. What we have seen in Britain in more recent times has been the rise of inland 'resorts', for example the historic towns of Chester and Shrewsbury, towns exploiting their industrial heritage (Bradford and Ironbridge are good examples) and towns and cities attracting visitors via imaginative events and excellent sporting facilities, for example Edinburgh and Sheffield respectively.

Section 3 Impacts of leisure and tourism

There are three main types of impacts that leisure and tourism can have at national, regional or local level:

1 Economic impacts.
2 Environmental impacts.
3 Social/cultural impacts.

It is important to remember that within each of these categories, the impact that leisure and tourism can have may be either positive or negative or, as is often the case, a mixture of the two.

Economic impacts

Income generation

The leisure and tourism industry generates income and wealth for private individuals, local authorities, companies, voluntary bodies and national governments. At the international level, tourism can make a considerable contribution to a country's balance of payments, which is a statement of the inflows and outflows of currency to and from a particular country. Tourism and leisure are services and are known as invisible items on the balance of payments, while visibles include goods such as food and manufactured items. Table 1.10 shows Britain's travel balance between 1976 and 1990. As you can see, the balance has gone into a negative (deficit) situation in recent years reflecting the growth in overseas holidays taken by British people and a slowdown in the growth of overseas visitors to Britain.

Table 1.10 Britain's travel balance 1976–90

Year	Earnings from inbound tourism (£m)	Spending on overseas tourism (£m)	Balance (£m)
1976	1768	1068	+700
1977	2352	1186	+1166
1978	2507	1549	+958
1979	2797	2109	+688
1980	2961	2738	+223
1981	2970	3272	−302
1982	3188	3640	−452
1983	4003	4090	−87
1984	4614	4663	−49
1985	5451	4877	+574
1986	5405	5927	−522
1987	6260	7280	−1020
1988	6184	8216	−2032
1989	6945	9357	−2412
1990	7475	9905	−2430

Source: BTA/ETB figures

At a local level, revenue generated by leisure and tourism facilities is often vital to the economic well-being of an area and is boosted by an important concept known as the multiplier effect. Research has shown that the amount spent by visitors to an area is recirculated in the local economy (by, for example, the wages of somebody working in a leisure centre being spent on goods and services in local shops) and is actually worth more to the area than its face value. For example, £200 spent by a couple on a short break in a hotel could be worth £200 × 1.4 (the hotel multiplier effect for that area), i.e. a total of £280.

The actual value of the multiplier (1.4 in the above example is merely an illustration) varies between regions and different sectors of the leisure and tourism industry. The multiplier for, say, a farm guesthouse is likely to be greater than for a city centre hotel which is part of a large multi-national chain. This is because the farm guesthouse is likely to buy its food and other services locally, while the goods and services for the large hotel may well be brought in from outside the area as part of a national distribution contract; i.e. income is lost to the area (in economic terms this is known as a leakage from the local economy).

Job creation

We have seen already that leisure and tourism is a significant employer in the private, public and voluntary sectors, providing around 1.5 million jobs nationally (see page 1.35). The creation of new jobs is one of leisure and tourism's major benefits.

Investment

Investment in large and small leisure and tourism projects not only provides short-term benefits for an area in terms of jobs in construction, for example, but also offers a base for the longer economic regeneration of regions by providing employment and revenue for many sectors not directly related to the industry, e.g. more business for petrol stations, printers, accountants, etc. Leisure and tourism is increasingly used as a 'springboard' for the regeneration of run-down areas of towns and cities; the Albert Dock in Liverpool and the Castlefields development in Manchester are excellent examples of this (see case study on Castlefields in Unit 13).

Environmental impacts

Although leisure and tourism can have positive environmental benefits to a local area, for example the Britain in Bloom scheme, restoration of redundant buildings and improvements to derelict areas, there is much evidence to suggest that the industry could do a lot to improve its negative environmental impacts. In Britain, the coast, countryside, towns and cities all suffer from the pressures of increasing numbers of visitors and their transportation. Some of the worst problems include:

- *Physical erosion* – the wearing away of soil and vegetation by walkers, horse-riders, cyclists, cars and motorcycles.
- *Litter*– both an eyesore and a threat to safety.
- *Congestion and overcrowding* – in popular holiday areas we all see the effects of too many people and too many cars.
- *Pollution* – of water and air, not forgetting noise pollution.
- *Loss of habitats* for flora and fauna.
- *Spoiling of the landscape* that people have come to see and enjoy.

Better education, improved visitor and traffic management techniques, use of the price mechanism and better signposting, are some of the possible solutions which are being tried in our towns and countryside to reduce the harmful environmental effects of leisure and tourism.

Social/cultural impacts

Some people believe that the negative social and cultural impacts of leisure, and particularly, tourism are far more harmful in the long run than the environmental problems we have just seen. This is based on the belief that many of the negative environmental impacts can be easily corrected with the right management and funding. The social and cultural problems, however, can be far more deep-rooted and may take generations to improve. Some of these problems are:

- Overcrowding, which may cause a reduction in the quality of life for the 'host community' (those living in the area visited by the tourists).
- Traditional activities (e.g. farming) may lose labour to the seemingly more attractive jobs in leisure and tourism.
- Tourists' behaviour can distort local customs.
- Religious codes may be altered to adapt to the needs of visitors, e.g. Sunday opening of facilities.
- Local languages may be lost through under-use.
- Traditional crafts may be lost in favour of mass-produced souvenirs.

Leisure and tourism can, however, have positive impacts, such as the revitalisation for visitors of neglected regions, the rebirth of local arts and crafts, refurbishment of local architecture and greater understanding of cultures.

The growth of sustainable tourism

Concern about the harmful environmental and social/cultural impacts of tourism has led to a lively debate about 'green' or sustainable issues in relation to the industry. The Tourist Boards and private sector companies are developing principles and practices which all sectors of the leisure and tourism industry will need to consider in order to ensure a healthy industry for the future.

Every organisation within leisure and tourism must have income in order to survive. Without sources of revenue, there will not be the finances needed to meet the day-to-day operating costs, such as wages, interest charges and advertising costs, nor the longer-term investment needs, such as new buildings and equipment (often referred to as capital items).

The sources of the necessary funds vary, depending on whether the leisure and tourism organisation is in the public, private or voluntary sector. We will look at each in a little more detail.

Funding in the public sector

The way in which funds are generated and distributed in the public sector is shown in Figure 1.12.

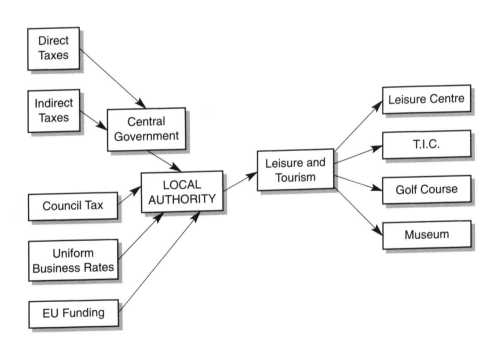

Fig 1.12 The funding of leisure and tourism in the public sector

The figure shows how a typical local authority receives funding from a number of sources and uses it to finance, amongst other things, its leisure and tourism provision. There are two principal stages involved:

Stage One: The local authority receives money from four main sources:

1 *Central government* – through its fiscal (tax) policy, the government levies taxes on private individuals and companies. These may be either direct taxes (e.g. income tax on individuals, corporation tax on companies) or indirect taxes (e.g. VAT, duty on petrol and alcohol). A proportion of these funds is given to each local authority to provide services in its local area.
2 *Council Tax* – this is a tax levied by the local authority on people living in their area in order to supplement national government funding for local services. Council Tax used to be known as the rates and, more recently the Community Charge (poll tax).
3 *European Union (EC) funds* – some local authorities will bid for funds from the EC for specific projects that often include leisure and tourism because of its economic and social benefits. The main EC sources for leisure and tourism projects tend to be the European Social Fund and the European Regional Development Fund, which provide finance for schemes such as infrastructure improvement and the development of new facilities.
4 *Uniform Business Rate (UBR)* – in the same way that local residents pay Council Tax, local businesses, such as shops and restaurants, have to pay Uniform Business Rates to the local authority for services provided.

Stage Two: Once it has received its funding, the local authority will decide on its own priorities and allocate budgets to each of its departments accordingly. Figure 1.12 shows how the leisure and tourism department will then allocate individual sums to its facilities, for example to a leisure centre, golf course or tourist information centre, so as to provide the best level of service to both the local community and visitors to their area.

One very important point about public sector funding of leisure and tourism is that it is purely discretionary; in other words, the local authority does not have a duty to provide leisure and tourism services and facilities in the same way that it is duty bound to provide social services and education, for example. This discretionary nature of leisure and tourism funding makes it rather vulnerable, particularly in times of recession and economic stringency when the government is looking for further cuts in local authority budgets. Leisure and tourism is likely to be one of the first budgets to be cut because of its non-statutory status.

Department of National Heritage (DNH)

The DNH was established in 1992 as the single Ministry that would co-ordinate government involvement in the field of leisure and tourism (see Figure 1.5 for details of the structure of the DNH). The expenditure plans of the DNH for 1993–4 are shown in Figure 1.13.

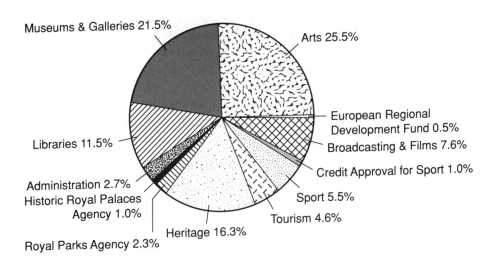

Museums & Galleries 21.5%
Arts 25.5%
European Regional Development Fund 0.5%
Broadcasting & Films 7.6%
Credit Approval for Sport 1.0%
Libraries 11.5%
Administration 2.7%
Historic Royal Palaces Agency 1.0%
Sport 5.5%
Tourism 4.6%
Royal Parks Agency 2.3%
Heritage 16.3%

Fig 1.13 Expenditure plans of the DNH 1993–94 *(Reproduced with the permission of the Controller of Her Majesty's Stationery Office) (source: DNH Annual report 1993)*

The pie-chart shows that out of a total allocation for the year of £990.5 million from the Treasury, more than a quarter was allocated to the arts, over 20 per cent to museums and galleries, and 16.3 per cent to heritage.

Funding in the private sector

The sources of funding for a private sector leisure and tourism organisation often depend on the size of the business and its legal identity. A sole trader, for example, may start his or her business purely from private savings or gifts from friends and relatives. A large public limited company (PLC), however, will raise funds by selling shares in its business on the Stock Exchange, in return for which its shareholders will expect a return on their investment, known as a dividend.

Most new or existing leisure and tourism businesses will generally approach the clearing banks (high street banks) first when they are looking for funding. The banks all offer a wide range of services to new or expanding businesses either through their branch network or specialised subsidiaries. The banks can offer overdrafts, usually the cheapest type of borrowing with the lowest rate of interest, for short-term needs, often important with the peaks and troughs of cash-flow experienced by some leisure and tourism operators. Loans are offered by the banks for periods ranging from up to three years (short term) to over ten years (long term). They are usually for the purchase of capital items such as replacement equipment or new land and buildings; commercial mortgages are also on offer for this type of purchase. In all cases of loans and mortgages, the bank will require security from the borrower in case repayments are not met; this can take the form of deeds on property or insurance policies.

Other types of funding in the private sector include leasing and hire purchase where equipment is not purchased outright.

Once a company is established, income from sales is vital for leisure and tourism companies in order to have a healthy cash-flow and to be able to trade profitably. In the case of companies that have shareholders, there will need to be sufficient profits generated to be able to pay a reasonable dividend. Some businesses within leisure and tourism, mainly those working as agents, will receive their income in the form of commission, which is an agreed percentage of the total price of a product or service, which is retained by the agent for services rendered. A travel agent, for example, earns commission on the sale of package holidays; if the agent sells a holiday valued at £1,000 and is given a 10 per cent commission by the tour operator, the agent will forward £900 to the operator and keep £100. In a similar way, many tourist information centres offer a bed-booking service for which they charge a small commission.

Private sector companies can apply to a whole host of public sector organisations and quangos within leisure and tourism for either a grant or a loan, to help with expansion or improvements to their facilities. These non-commercial sources of finance include:

- Sports Council.
- Department of the Environment.
- National Tourist Boards (except ETB).
- Countryside Commission.
- Rural Development Commission.
- English Heritage.
- Forestry Commission.
- English Nature.
- Arts Council.

Sponsorship is an important, if uncertain, source of income for some sectors of the leisure and tourism industry, particularly spectator sports and the arts. The extent of sponsorship varies enormously, from the local builder paying for the match ball for his local football team to Carling's multi-million pound deal to sponsor the Premier League in English soccer. The principle, however, is the same. Both the builder and the brewer expect a return on their investment in the form of wider publicity leading to increased sales; the builder is likely to get his picture in his local paper while Carling's name will be mentioned many dozens of times per week in the national media.

Voluntary sector funding

Many voluntary sector leisure and tourism organisations have charitable status since they aim to promote a cause or help individuals rather than make a profit. There are benefits to being a charity, such as exemption from certain forms of taxation and reductions in business rates. Whether a voluntary body is very large, as is the case with the National Trust, or very small, such as a local playgroup, the funding opportunities and sources open to them are very similar:

- *Sponsorship* – the sports goods company, Hi-Tec, contributes to the printing costs of the YHA, while a local countryside trust may be sponsored by a local company.
- *Subscriptions from members* – the RSPB, English Heritage and many local clubs receive funds from this source.
- *Grants from central and local government* – a local council may make a grant to its local choral society, while the Arts Council gives grants to individuals and organisations it considers are advancing the cause of the arts. The Countryside Commission gives grants towards training in countryside management and for environmental improvement projects.
- *Donations and gifts* – perhaps part of the estate of a deceased person, as is often the case with the National Trust.

Assignment 1A

Situation

You have recently taken up the post of Promotions Assistant reporting to the Head of Leisure and Tourism in a large District Council located in the west of England. The Council's Leisure and Tourism Department provides facilities and services for a local population of 180,000. It is a recent winner in the Sports Council Regional Management Awards.

Tasks

The Head of Leisure and Tourism, Ms Fairweather, has been asked to make a presentation to the Council's Leisure Services Committee entitled: 'The Council's leisure and tourism strategy – beyond 2000'.

She has asked you to write the draft of one section of the report, which will be an overview of the UK and European leisure and tourism industry. She will use your draft of the general industry trends as the basis for her own detailed analysis of the key features of the Council's policy in the medium term.

She has indicated that your draft should focus on:

- Recent historical developments in the leisure and tourism industry.

- Likely growth and decline in leisure and tourism sectors up to and beyond the year 2000.
- Factors which will affect leisure and tourism participation.
- The funding of leisure and tourism in the public sector.

Your draft should be no more than 1,500 words in length and should be supported by statistics on trends in leisure and tourism participation.

Assignment 1B

Situation

A property developer, Mr Owen, who has been active in your local area for more than ten years, has decided to diversify into leisure and tourism. Most of his business to date has been concerned with sheltered housing and work for housing associations and small housing developments for the local Council. He has little experience of the leisure and tourism industry, but has been told by your college Principal that you would be interested in helping him with some preliminary survey work to help him formulate some ideas as to the best way forward.

Tasks

Working through your leisure and tourism tutor, Mr Owen has indicated that he would like your group to prepare a report on the existing leisure and tourism facilities and services provided in your area. The report should include:

- An audit of the number and types of facilities which exist.
- Details of the local Council's plans for developments in leisure and tourism.
- An idea of whether existing facilities are in the private, public or voluntary sectors.
- A map of the area with the facilities highlighted.
- Any detailed information which you can find on current levels of use and financial performance of facilities.

Your submission should follow a normal report format and should include relevant local and national data.

Revision test questions

1 Give three examples of home-based leisure activities.
2 Using two examples of each category, explain the difference between active and passive leisure pursuits.
3 Name three factors that influence participation in leisure activities.

4 Statistics show that, in general, women have less leisure time than men. Why do you think this is the case?

5 Give four specific examples of leisure tourism and four of business tourism.

6 What is domestic tourism? Give two actual examples of domestic tourism.

7 What is the 'Grand Tour' that began in the late seventeenth century?

8 Give three examples of spa towns that prospered from the eighteenth century onwards in Britain.

9 What factors led to the increase in popularity of the countryside for leisure in the nineteenth and twentieth centuries?

10 In what year did Thomas Cook organise his first excursion in Britain?

11 Who was the pioneer of the holiday camp in Britain?

12 Which factors led to the beginnings of mass tourism in the 1960s?

13 Name three leisure products that grew rapidly in popularity during the 1980s.

14 What was the total number of world tourist arrivals in 1989?

15 Which continent attracts more visitors per year than all the others put together?

16 Where do the majority of British people go for their holidays – is it (a) abroad or (b) in Britain?

17 List five leisure and tourism facilities provided by the private sector.

18 What is a public limited company? Give three examples from within the leisure and tourism industry.

19 What do the initials CCT stand for?

20 What is the role of the Department of National Heritage?

21 What is a quango? Give three examples in the leisure and tourism industry.

22 What do the initials BTA stand for?

23 List five leisure and tourism facilities and services provided by local authorities.

24 In which sector of leisure and tourism is the National Trust?

25 Is the majority of employment in leisure and tourism in the private, public or voluntary sector?

26 List five skills and qualities needed by employees in the leisure and tourism industry.

27 Give three factors that will have a bearing on the future development of the leisure and tourism industry.

28 Tourism products are said to be 'intangible'. What do you understand by this term?

29 Give three examples of self-catering accommodation in the UK.

30 What is VFR?

31 Which was Britain's most popular tourist attraction in 1992?

32 What do you understand by the term 'infrastructure'?

33 Give two positive economic impacts of leisure and tourism.

34 Give two examples each of the negative environmental and social/cultural impacts of leisure and tourism.

35 What are the main sources of funding for a local authority leisure and tourism department?
36 Which sector of leisure and tourism is most heavily supported financially by the Department of National Heritage?
37 What is commission?
38 How many National Parks are there in England and Wales?
39 What is limited liability?
40 What are the main aims of the Sports Council?

Unit 2
HEALTH, SAFETY AND SECURITY IN LEISURE AND TOURISM

Section 1 Health and safety for all

Introduction

A basic function of all organisations involved with the leisure and tourism industry is to provide a safe and controlled environment for staff to work in, and for visitors to enjoy. The wide-ranging nature of leisure and tourism means that each sector of the industry has its own particular requirements in terms of health and safety. For example:

- Many indoor entertainment complexes are very large and often cater for the needs of hundreds, if not thousands, of people at any one time. Cinemas, theatres, sports stadia and indoor arenas must put health and safety very high on their list of priorities.
- The managers and staff of hotels and other types of accommodation have a number of health and safety concerns which they must address, e.g. the storage and handling of food, and ensuring safe means of escape in case of fire.
- Tourist attractions, especially theme parks with complex 'rides', have to be aware of dangers to both staff and visitors from machinery and electrical installations.
- Leisure centres will offer a range of sports activities which can, if not properly supervised, expose the participants and spectators to potential risks. Centres that offer swimming and other aquatic attractions need to be especially aware of health and safety requirements.
- Outdoor activity centres that cater for the needs of both young and old, must ensure that staff are fully trained in supervising potentially dangerous activities such as rock-climbing, watersports and fell-walking.

- Transport operators, including airlines, coach companies, ferry and cruise operators and car hire firms, have a duty to ensure that their vehicles are safely maintained and that all staff are capable of carrying passengers in a safe manner.

It is important to remember that health and safety can no longer be thought of as a 'bolt-on' to other management decisions. Health and safety should underpin all the decisions, operations and tasks that managers and staff in leisure and tourism facilities undertake. For example, decisions on staffing, budgeting, types of activities, events management, equipment, maintenance and so on, all have safety implications and ramifications.

Leisure and tourism facilities are used by all sorts of people, some of whom will have special needs, e.g. the very young, disabled people and the elderly. Health and safety policies and practices must take the needs of these special categories of visitors into account.

Health and safety is not only the concern of the private sector in leisure and tourism; it is just as applicable to both the public and voluntary sectors of the industry, as this extract from the 1993 National Trust Handbook indicates:

> *The Trust endeavours to provide a healthy and safe environment for visitors at its properties as far as is reasonably practicable, and to ensure that the activities of its staff and contractors working on Trust properties do not in any way jeopardise the health and safety of visitors. You can help the Trust by observing all notices and signs relating to this subject during your visit, by following any instructions given by Trust staff, by ensuring that children are properly supervised and by wearing appropriate clothing and footwear at outdoor properties (1993 National Trust Handbook)*

Health and safety legislation

There is a variety of legislation that imposes certain duties on the management and staff of leisure and tourism facilities in relation to health and safety issues. For anybody considering working in, or already involved with, the leisure and tourism industry at whatever level, it is important to be aware of the ever increasing impact of health and safety legislation.

To begin with, there is a common law duty of care, under which each citizen owes a duty to all others who may be affected by his or her activities. If a person takes insufficient care in relation to another citizen, and that person suffers damage as a result, the injured party may begin an action in the civil court to reclaim damages. However, this civil law only comes into action after damage has been suffered. Although the outcomes of civil cases have given the courts many opportunities to create precedents that guide the conduct of similar occurrences in the future, the civil law has always been considered an inappropriate instrument in the area of accident prevention. The advent of the Health and Safety at Work, etc. Act 1974 changed all this.

Health and Safety at Work, etc. Act 1974

The Health and Safety at Work, etc. Act (HSW Act) was introduced to provide the legislative framework to promote, stimulate and encourage high standards of health and safety at work.

Contents of the Act

The HSW Act is an enabling measure superimposed over existing health and safety legislation. In addition to placing duties of a general nature on employers, manufacturers, employees, the self-employed and others, the Act provides wide powers for the making of regulations. Part I of the Act, the part that concerns leisure and tourism organisations the most, aims to:

- Secure the health, safety and welfare of people at work.
- Protect other people against risks to health or safety arising from the activities of people at work.
- Control the storage and use of dangerous substances, e.g. chemicals, and preventing their unlawful use.
- Control the emission into the atmosphere of noxious or offensive substances from premises.

Scope of the Act

All 'persons at work', whether employees, employers or self-employed, are covered by the Act, with the exception of domestic servants in private households. About 8 million people who were not covered by previous health and safety legislation, such as the self-employed and those employed in education, health services, leisure and tourism industries and in some parts of the transport industry, are now protected.

The HSW Act aims to gradually replace existing health and safety requirements by revised and updated provisions, which take the form of regulations and approved codes of practice prepared in consultation with industry. Regulations relating to health and safety matters are usually made by the appropriate government minister on the advice of the Health and Safety Commission. In reality, most regulations are made by the Secretary of State for Employment. Codes of practice have a special legal status. Although they are not statutory requirements, they may be used in criminal proceedings on health and safety issues, as evidence that the statutory requirements have been contravened.

Duties of employers

It is the duty of every employer to safeguard, so far as is reasonably practicable, the health, safety and welfare of all those in his or her employment. This duty is extended to others who may be affected by the operation of the facility, e.g. contractors, visitors and members of the general public. In practice the employer must have specific regard for the following:

1 To provide plant and equipment that is not a risk to health.
2 To ensure that work systems and practices are safe.
3 To ensure that the work environment is regularly monitored in respect of health and safety requirements.
4 To provide safe storage for substances that could pose a threat to safety and ensure their safe use.
5 To provide a written statement of safety policy and bring it to the notice of employees (applies only to those employing five or more staff).
6 To provide adequate information and training for all staff in matters relating to health and safety.

Duties of employees

Employees have a duty under the HSW Act to:

- Take reasonable care to avoid injury to themselves or to others by their work activities.
- To co-operate with their employers and other agencies to ensure that the requirements of the Act are carried out.
- Not to interfere with or misuse anything provided to protect their health, safety and welfare under the Act.

Figure 2.1 is an example of advice to employees contained in Butlin's Staff Handbook.

Enforcement of the HSW Act

The Act established the Health and Safety Commission (HSC) and the Health and Safety Executive (HSE) both to publicise the need for safety at work and to begin prosecutions for breaches of the Act. The HSC is responsible to the Secretary of State for Employment for taking the necessary steps to secure the health, welfare and safety of people at work and also to protect the public against risks to health and safety arising out of a work situation. The HSE is the operating arm of the HSC and is responsible for enforcing the legislation under the HSW Act. HSE appoints and controls teams of inspectors who have wide powers to enter premises and examine records and staff to check that the Act is being complied with. Inspectors can also make enquiries into accidents that have occurred at places of employment. This covers accidents not only to employees themselves,

Butlins are very conscious of their responsibility to protect the Health & Safety of team members and the customers that visit the Centre. In the buildings you will find the Company Policy statement.

A Health & Safety committee meet regularly so that there is an opportunity for you to mention any problems you become aware of. The secret of safety is to **BE ALERT** because under the act **you too have a very important responsibility.**

> **HEALTH
> &
> SAFETY
> AT WORK**
>
> **COMPANY
> POLICY**

At Stars Introduction you will be told about some of the problems you may encounter at work. Here are some guidelines to help you.

1. **Good Housekeeping**

   Keep the work area tidy - if you don't want to be treated like a cabbage, don't keep your work area like a pig sty.

2. Please wear the protective clothes provided. It's in your own interest.

- Only use equipment that is in a good state of repair, e.g. steps/ladders.
  Remove any faulty equipment and report it.

- Don't overload sockets so that they overheat - one plug, one socket.

- Beware of wet slippery surfaces especially floors in kitchens and food halls when they've been washed.

- Do not leave things lying around for people to fall over.

- **Have respect for chemicals** read the instructions. If in doubt ask!!! Only use the correct chemical for the job. **NEVER** mix chemicals and make sure you have been told how to use them properly.

- Report any hazards or accidents to your Manager immediately.

Fig 2.1 Advice to employees at Butlins from the staff handbook *(courtesy of the Rank Organisation)*

but also to visitors and would include, for example, people using sports centres and other leisure and tourism facilities.

If an inspector discovers a contravention of one of the provisions of the HSW Act or any of the earlier legislation that is still in force, he or she can take one of several courses of action:

1 The inspector can issue a prohibition notice if there is a high risk of serious personal injury. This effectively stops the activity in question until the specified action to remedy the situation has been completed. The notice can be served either on the person undertaking the activity or the person in control of it.

2 An alternative course of action would be to issue an improvement notice if there is a contravention of any of the requirements of the Act. This notice gives a time limit for compliance with the relevant contravention.

3 Over and above the issuing of either a prohibition notice, an improvement notice or both, any person found contravening the Act or any of its regulations may be prosecuted. Contravention of some of the requirements can lead to prosecution in either the magistrates' court (Sheriffs' Court in Scotland) or the Crown Court in England and Wales (Sheriffs' Court in Scotland). The

maximum fine for most offences is £2,000 and imprisonment for up to two years can be imposed for certain offences.

4 The inspector has powers to seize, render harmless or destroy any substance or article considered to be the cause of imminent danger or serious personal injury.

Examples of prosecutions brought under the HSW Act include:

- In 1985 inspectors of the Health and Safety Commission brought an action against Mendip District Council because they did not have enough lifeguards on duty when an 11-year-old girl tragically drowned in a pool.
- A school was fined £2,000 in 1989 after admitting two breaches of the Act which led to the death of its groundsman when a new type of steel rugby post fell on him while it was being manoeuvred into position by staff and pupils.
- In 1983 Holiday Inns were prosecuted for contraventions in respect of the swimming pool at one of its hotels which had a number of alleged safety and supervision defects.
- In 1991 Alton Towers was fined £1,500 with £1,920 costs for inadequate operator training procedures. An incident occurred on the first day of the 1991 summer season when two cars on a rollercoaster collided leaving six people injured.

New EC directives on health and safety

Six new sets of health and safety at work regulations came into force at the beginning of 1993. They apply to almost all kinds of work activity, including leisure and tourism, and like the health and safety laws we already have, they place duties on employers to protect:

- Their employees.
- Other people, including members of the public, who may be affected by the work being carried out.

These new UK regulations are needed to implement six European Community (EC) directives on health and safety at work. They are also part of a continuing modernisation of existing UK law. The directives are part of the EC's programme of action on health and safety, which is an essential ingredient in the move towards a single European market. Most of the duties in the regulations are not completely new. They clarify what is already in current health and safety law. Any leisure and tourism organisation already complying with the HSW Act and the regulations linked with it should not find the new regulations at all daunting.

A lot of old and out-of-date laws have has been repealed by the new regulations. More modern laws, for example COSHH (see page 2.13) and the Noise at Work Regulations remain in place.

HSE inspectors' approach to the new regulations is initially to make employers aware of their existence and content. During this initial period, formal enforcement of the regulations will only take place if the risks to health and safety are immediate or what needs to be done is not new, i.e. it should have been put right under the existing legislation. Also, any employer who deliberately flouts the law will be liable to prosecution under the new regulations.

What do the regulations cover?

The new regulations cover:

- Health and safety management.
- Work equipment safety.
- Manual handling of loads.
- Workplace conditions.
- Personal protective equipment.
- Display screen equipment.

Health and safety management

The Management of Health and Safety at Work Regulations 1992 set out broad general duties that apply to almost all work activities in Great Britain and offshore. The regulations make more explicit what is already required of employers under the HSW Act and are principally aimed at encouraging them to take a more systematic approach to dealing with health and safety matters. In general terms, the regulations require employers to:

1 Systematically assess the risks to the health and safety of employees and anyone else affected by the work activity, e.g. visitors, spectators and contractors. Employers with five or more employees will need to record their findings by drawing up a risk assessment.
2 Put into practice the measures outlined in the risk assessment. This will involve planning, organisation, control, monitoring and review; in other words, the management of health and safety.
3 Appoint competent people to help devise and apply the measures.
4 Set up emergency procedures.
5 Provide employees with information about health and safety.
6 Co-operate with other employers who may share the same work site.
7 Provide adequate training for employees in health and safety.
8 Provide temporary workers with particular health and safety information to meet their needs.

Work equipment safety

The Provision and Use of Work Equipment Regulations are designed to pull together and tidy up the laws governing equipment used at work. Instead of piecemeal legislation covering particular kinds of equipment indifferent industries, they:

- Place general duties on employers.
- List minimum requirements for work equipment to deal with selected hazards whatever the industry.

'Work equipment' is broadly defined to include everything from a hand tool, through machines of all kinds, to a complete plant such as a leisure centre or indoor arena.

The regulations include both general duties placed on employers and specific requirements that they must adhere to. General duties require employers to:

- Make sure that equipment is suitable for its intended use.
- Take into account the working conditions and hazards in the workplace when selecting equipment.
- Ensure that equipment is adequately maintained.
- Give adequate instruction, information and training.
- Provide equipment that conforms with EC product safety directives.

The specific requirements of these regulations cover such items as the guarding of dangerous parts of machinery, stability of equipment, warnings and markings, to name but a few.

Manual handling of loads

The incorrect handling of loads causes large numbers of injuries and can result in pain, time off work and sometimes permanent disablement. The Manual Handling Operations Regulations came into force on 1 January 1993, and replace patchy, old fashioned and largely ineffective laws with a modern, ergonomic approach to the problem.

They apply to any manual handling operations that may cause injury at work. Such operations should have been identified by the risk assessment carried out under the Management of Health and Safety at Work Regulations 1992.

Employers have to take three key steps:

1 Avoid hazardous manual handling operations where reasonably practicable.
2 Assess adequately any hazardous operations that cannot be avoided.
3 Reduce the risk of injury as far as is reasonably practicable.

The regulations are backed up by general guidance, which can help to identify the more serious risks within any work situation.

Workplace conditions

The Workplace (Health, Safety and Welfare) Regulations 1992 replace a total of 38 pieces of old law, making safety in the workplace a much easier topic to understand and making it clear what is expected of employers.

The regulations set general requirements in four broad areas.

1 *Working environment*:
   - Temperature in indoor workplaces.
   - Ventilation.
   - Lighting.
   - Room dimensions and space.
   - Suitability of workstations and seating.

2 *Safety*:
   - Safe passage of pedestrians and vehicles.
   - Safe opening, closing and cleaning of windows and skylights.
   - Use of safety materials in transparent doors and partitions.
   - Safety devices on doors, gates and escalators.
   - Construction and maintenance of floors.

3 *Facilities*:
   - Toilets.
   - Washing, eating and changing facilities.
   - Clothing storage.
   - Drinking water.
   - Rest areas, including arrangements to protect people from the discomfort of tobacco smoke.
   - Rest facilities for pregnant women and nursing mothers.

4 *Housekeeping*:
   - Maintenance of workplace, equipment and facilities.
   - Cleanliness.
   - Removal of waste materials.

Employers must ensure that any workplace within their control complies with the regulations. Existing workplaces have until 1996 to be brought up to scratch.

Personal protective equipment (PPE)

The Personal Protective Equipment at Work (PPE) Regulations 1992 replace parts of over 20 old pieces of law. PPE includes most types of protective clothing, and equipment such as eye, foot and head protection, safety harnesses, life jackets and high visibility clothing. Employers must supply PPE free of charge to their employees, and have a duty to:

- Make sure that the PPE issued is suitable for the risk involved.
- Maintain, clean and replace PPE.
- Provide storage for PPE when it is not being used.
- Ensure that PPE is properly used.
- Give training, instruction and information to staff on the use and care of PPE.

Display screen equipment

Unlike some of the other regulations described above, the Health and Safety (Display Screen Equipment) Regulations do not replace old legislation but cover a new area of work activity for the first time. Work with display screens is not generally high risk, but it can lead to muscular and other physical problems, eye fatigue and mental stress. Problems of this kind can be overcome by good ergonomic design of equipment, furniture, the working environment and tasks performed.

Under these regulations, employers have a duty to:

- Assess display screen equipment workstations and reduce risks which are discovered.
- Make sure that workstations satisfy minimum requirements.
- Plan display screen equipment work so that there are breaks or changes of activity.
- Provide information and training for display screen equipment users.

Display screen equipment users are also entitled to appropriate eye and eyesight tests by an optician or doctor, and to special spectacles if they are needed and normal ones cannot be used. It is the employer's responsibility to provide tests and special spectacles if needed.

Implications of the new health and safety regulations for the leisure and tourism industry

Any leisure and tourism organisation is likely to be affected by one or more of the new regulations, and, as we have seen, those employing five or more staff will be involved in recording health and safety information which is open for inspection by HSE staff. While each sector of the industry will have to respond to the regulations in its own particular way, there are some general implications that will need to be considered by all organisations:

- The Financial implications of implementing the new regulations may be severe, particularly for those leisure and tourism organisations that have perhaps not given health and safety a high priority in the past. Even those organisations that have implemented previous health and safety law will be faced with the extra resource implications of the new regulations covering display screen equipment. Tour operators, airlines and travel agencies, all of whom make extensive use of VDUs, will have to find extra resources in order to be able to comply with these new regulations properly.
- Staffing implications will occur with both existing and new staff. Current staff will need training in certain aspects of all the new regulations, again with financial implications. All new staff taken on will need careful induction into the health and safety procedures of the organisation and may require protective equipment and clothing or special furniture to comply with the regulations covering display screen equipment.

Other legislation affecting leisure and tourism

Fire precautions

Any objective analysis of risks to health and safety in many leisure and tourism facilities would confirm that fire is one of the most serious risk factors. There is plenty of evidence to show that outbreaks of fire have often been the cause of fatalities in this sector. The friends and relatives of the 56 people who died at Bradford City Football Club in the tragedy of 1987 bear witness to this fact.

The Fire Precautions Act 1971

One of the main requirements of the Fire Precautions Act is the need for certain leisure and tourism establishments to apply for a Fire Certificate from the local fire authorities. The Act requires that any premises providing entertainment, recreation or use of a club or association, where there are more than 20 employees on the ground floor or more than ten above ground floor level, must apply for a Fire Certificate. If, after an inspection by the local fire authority, they are satisfied that all necessary conditions have been met, a Fire Certificate can be issued. The kind of conditions contained in the Certificate include:

- Keeping means of escape clear.
- Providing employees with fire safety training.
- Limits to the number of people allowed on the premises.
- Fire drills at specified times.
- Keeping records relating to fire safety matters.

Hotels and other serviced accommodation also fall within the scope of the Fire Precautions Act. As a general rule, a Fire Certificate will be needed if the accommodation sleeps more than six guests at first floor level or just one at either second floor level or below ground.

First aid and accident/incident reporting

The HSW Act and its associated regulations place a duty on employers to provide adequate first aid for both employees and non-employees, which, in the case of leisure and tourism, would include guests, visitors, spectators, customers and contractors. From 1 January 1993, the new health and safety at work regulations require employers to carry out risk assessments; clearly the provision of adequate first aid cover appropriate to the particular leisure and tourism activity is a crucial part of any such assessment.

The law relating to accident/incident reporting is contained in the Reporting of Injuries, Diseases and Dangerous Occurrences Regulations (RIDDOR) 1985. Under the regulations, any employer, self-employed person or individual in

Health and Safety Executive

Health and Safety at Work etc Act 1974
Reporting of Injuries, Diseases and Dangerous Occurrences Regulations 1985

Report of an injury or dangerous occurrence

Spaces below are for office use only

- Full notes to help you complete this form are attached.
- This form is to be used to make a report to the enforcing authority under the requirements of Regulations 3 or 6.
- Completing and signing this form does not constitute an admission of liability of any kind, either by the person making the report or any other person.
- If more than one person was injured as a result of an accident, please complete a separate form for each person.

A Subject of report *(tick appropriate box or boxes) – see note 2*

| Fatality 1 | Specified major injury or condition 2 | "Over three day" injury 3 | Dangerous occurrence 4 | Flammable gas incident (fatality or major injury or condition) 5 | Dangerous gas fitting 6 |

B Person or organisation making report (ie person obliged to report under the Regulations) – *see note 3*

Name and address –

Post code –

Nature of trade, business or undertaking –

If in construction industry, state the total number of your employees –

and indicate the role of your company on site *(tick box)* –

| Main site contractor 6 | Sub contractor 7 | Sub contractor 8 | Other 9 |

If in farming, are you reporting an injury to a member of your family? *(tick box)*   Yes   No

Name and telephone no. of person to contact –

C Date, time and place of accident, dangerous occurrence or flammable gas incident – *see note 4*

Date   day month year   19   Time –

Give the name and address if different from above –

Where on the premises or site –

and Normal activity carried on there

ENV

Complete the following sections D, E, F & H if you have ticked boxes, 1, 2, 3 or 5 in Section A. Otherwise go straight to Sections G and H.

D The injured person – *see note 5*

Full name and address –

Age   Sex (M or F)   Status *(tick box)* –

| Employee 10 | Self employed 11 | Trainee (YTS) 12 |
| Trainee (other) 13 | Any other person 14 |

Trade, occupation or job title –

Nature of injury or condition and the part of the body affected –

continued overleaf

F2508 (rev 1/86)

E Kind of accident – *see note 6*

Indicate what kind of accident led to the injury or condition *(tick one box)* –

Contact with moving machinery or material being machined 1	Injured whilst handling lifting or carrying 5	Trapped by something collapsing or overturning 9	Exposure to an explosion 12
Struck by moving, including flying or falling, object 2	Slip, trip or fall on same level 6	Drowning or asphyxiation 10	Contact with electricity or an electrical discharge 13
Struck by moving vehicle 3	Fall from a height* 7	Exposure to or contact with a harmful substance 11	Injured by an animal 14
Struck against something fixed or stationary 4	*Distance through which person fell (metres) 8	Exposure to fire 11	Other kind of accident (give details in Section H) 15

Spaces below are for office use only.

F Agent(s) involved – *see note 7*

Indicate which, if any, of the categories of agent or factor below were involved *(tick one or more of the boxes)* –

Machinery/equipment for lifting and conveying 1	Process plant, pipework or bulk storage 5	Live animal 8	Ladder or scaffolding 13
Portable power or hand tools 2	Any material, substance or product being handled, used or stored 6	Moveable container or package of any kind 9	Construction formwork, shuttering and falsework 14
Any vehicle or associated equipment/machinery 3	Gas, vapour, dust, fume or oxygen deficient atmosphere 7	Floor, ground, stairs or any working surface 10	Electricity supply cable, wiring, apparatus or equipment 15
Other machinery 4	Pathogen or infected material 7	Building, engineering structure or excavation/underground working 12	Entertainment or sporting facilities or equipment 16
			Any other agent 17

Describe briefly the agents or factors you have indicated –

G Dangerous occurrence or dangerous gas fitting – *see notes 8 and 9*

Reference number of dangerous occurrence

Reference number of dangerous gas fitting

H Account of accident, dangerous occurrence or flammable gas incident – *see note 10*

Describe what happened and how. In the case of an accident state what the injured person was doing at the time –

Signature of person making report   Date

Fig 2.2 Form F2508 *(Crown copyright. Reproduced with the permission of the Controller of Her Majesty's Stationery Office)*

control of a work situation has a duty to inform the relevant authority of:

- Any fatal injuries to employees or other people in an accident connected with the business.
- Any major injuries to employees or other people in an accident connected with the business.
- Any of the dangerous occurrences listed in the regulations.

In the case of leisure and tourism organisations, the incidents should be reported to the local environmental health department. The regulations stipulate that a particular form (form F2508) should be used for reporting injuries and dangerous occurrences (see Figure 2.2).

Hazardous substances, electricity and noise

Most leisure and tourism facilities and premises will use chemicals of one sort or another for cleaning and disinfecting, all will have electrical installations and some may have machinery and equipment which generates significant noise. In all these three areas, regulations with the force of law have come into operation since 1988.

Control of Substances Hazardous to Health Regulations 1988 (COSHH)

These regulations add to the employer's duties concerning the use of harmful substances as laid down in the HSW Act. Under the COSHH regulations, employers must assess likely exposure to all hazardous substances and initiate control measures and monitoring procedures as appropriate. The definition of 'hazardous substance' is given in the regulations; it may be classed as 'toxic', 'very toxic', 'harmful', 'irritant' or 'corrosive'. It can be in solid, liquid, gaseous, vapour, dust or fume form. The following chemicals commonly found in leisure and tourism facilities fall within the scope of the regulations:

- Chemicals for the treatment of swimming or leisure pool water.
- Cleaning and disinfecting chemicals such as bleach.
- Chemicals for the marking and management of sports fields.
- Chemicals for the control of insects and vermin.
- Chemicals for the management of grassland in parks and open spaces.

Figure 2.3 shows advice on COSHH from the Butlin's Staff handbook.

Electricity at Work Regulations 1989

These regulations, which came into force on 1 April 1990, expand previous legislation relating to factories and building sites, to include all places of work, including leisure and tourism premises. They cover:

- Strength and capability of electrical equipment.

CONTROL OF SUBSTANCES HAZARDOUS TO HEALTH ACT (1988)

Some of you will be handling chemicals every day and you will be specially trained in using them, but all of you will come into contact with chemicals at some time, so for your own safety and for the safety of your colleagues and our customers, bear the following points in mind:
You should keep this book handy for future reference.

- Read the label before you use any chemicals

- Store chemicals in their original containers and keep them upright

- Don't eat, drink or smoke while using chemicals, and always wash your hands to prevent contamination

  - Always wear protective clothing

- If you do spill any of the chemical on yourself, wash it off with water immediately. See medical advice

  - Never leave chemicals unattended, or within reach of children

- If there is a large spillage inform your Team Leader immediately

- Maintain good personal hygiene, wash your hands regularly, keep cuts covered with a waterproof dressing

ASK BEFORE YOU USE!
REMEMBER TO ALWAYS BEWARE OF CHEMICAL HAZARDS

34

Fig 2.3 Advice to COSHH in the Butlins' staff handbook
(courtesy of the Rank Organisation)

- Adverse or hazardous environments, e.g. swimming pools, outdoor arenas, beer and spirits storage areas, special events, etc.
- Insulation protection.
- Earthing.
- Connections.
- Protection from excess current.
- Isolation of supply.
- Work precautions.
- Competent staff for electrical work.

The management of leisure and tourism facilities have to follow a clear programme of action to minimise risks from electrical plant and installations; this includes such items as regular equipment inspection, training for appropriate staff and troubleshooting.

Noise at Work Regulations 1989

These very technical regulations came into force on 1 January 1990. Put simply, the regulations define three 'action levels of noise' above which certain measures, including the wearing of ear defenders, must be taken. Management must monitor levels of sound within leisure and tourism facilities and if noise levels become too high initiate measures to control the situation. In a leisure centre, for example, which may have hundreds of swimmers in the pool at any one time, or a disco with loud music, alternative means of communicating with the public must be available should the normal public address (PA) system become inaudible.

Food Hygiene Regulations

The preparation, serving and sale of food is important in so many areas of leisure and tourism as a way of generating income, either as the principal activity, in the case of a restaurant, for example, or as a supplement to another activity, perhaps a leisure centre providing snacks for customers. Any leisure and tourism organisation involved in any way with food that is offered for sale to customers or visitors, must now work within the Food Hygiene Regulations introduced under the Food Safety Act 1990. The regulations lay great emphasis on cleanliness and sanitation, as well as the proper storage and preparation of food. Local authorities enforce the Food Hygiene Regulations through inspectors with far-ranging powers. These powers cover hotels and restaurants as well as clubs and other leisure and tourism facilities offering food for customers.

An inspector has the right to enter the premise at any reasonable hour of the day to check whether the regulations are being adhered to. Penalties for breach of the regulations are severe, including heavy fines for the original offence, and additional daily fines for each day the breach continues. In exceptional circumstances, the facility could be banned from serving food altogether until measures to rectify the situation are completed. Figure 2.4 shows advice to staff on food hygiene regulations at Butlin's.

Occupiers' liability

Under the Occupiers' Liability Act 1984, the 'occupier' of a leisure and tourism facility, who will be either the owner or the person who operates it, owes a legal duty to all people who use it, including visitors and spectators, to make sure that the facility is reasonably safe for the purpose for which the people are entering. This would include, for example, ensuring that seating for spectators is safe. As well as a duty to those on the premises, the occupier also has a duty to their neighbours and others living nearby. For example, a golf ball that strikes a pedestrian

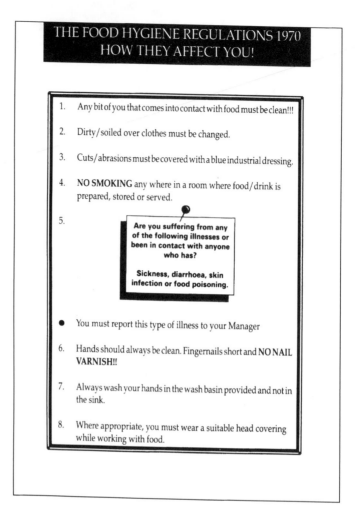

THE FOOD HYGIENE REGULATIONS 1970
HOW THEY AFFECT YOU!

1. Any bit of you that comes into contact with food must be clean!!!

2. Dirty/soiled over clothes must be changed.

3. Cuts/abrasions must be covered with a blue industrial dressing.

4. **NO SMOKING** any where in a room where food/drink is prepared, stored or served.

5.

Are you suffering from any of the following illnesses or been in contact with anyone who has?

Sickness, diarrhoea, skin infection or food poisoning.

● You must report this type of illness to your Manager

6. Hands should always be clean. Fingernails short and **NO NAIL VARNISH!!**

7. Always wash your hands in the wash basin provided and not in the sink.

8. Where appropriate, you must wear a suitable head covering while working with food.

Fig 2.4 Advice to Butlins' staff on food hygiene regulations
(courtesy of the Rank Organisation)

walking on a public footpath alongside the 18th fairway of a golf course is likely to result in a successful claim for negligence against the owner of the course if the incident could reasonably have been foreseen.

Public order

However much a leisure and tourism organisation may feel that its activities are adding to the amenity of a particular area, there may be neighbours who think otherwise. We have just seen how a golf course may be faced with a claim for negligence if injury is caused to passers-by; another way in which the law protects the public is by providing legal restraints against private or public nuisance, principally under the Public Order Act 1986. Aggrieved neighbours may decide to pursue an action in the courts against, for example, noisy speedway events, firework displays, rock concerts, etc. For the action to have any chance of success, there must be continuity of nuisance, i.e. it must occur more than once over a reasonable period of time. Neighbours may get a faster result by complaining to their local environmental health department.

Where to go for advice on health and safety matters

The Health and Safety Executive (HSE) has a network of regional offices covering England, Scotland and Wales with staff who can advise on all issues relating to health and safety at work (Northern Ireland has a Health and Safety Agency that, although independent of the HSE, liaises closely with it on matters of mutual interest). The HSE produces a wide range of leaflets on health and safety and will advise on the implementation of the HSW Act and the new regulations produced as a result of the recent EC Directives on health and safety.

For fire safety information and advice, there are two main sources. First, the local fire authority, which is responsible for issuing Fire Certificates, can give advice on safety matters and the purchase and use of fire safety equipment. Second, the local council Building Control Department can give advice on the building regulations, many of which contain instructions on the use of certain building materials and techniques to reduce fire risks.

The local authority Trading Standards Department is a good source of advice on such issues as noise pollution and control, food hygiene and safety, the EC Package Travel Directive and COSHH.

Some large organisations are employing consultants to advise on the growing amount and complexity of legislation concerning health and safety, particularly in relation to the new regulations brought about by the EC Directives. Consultancies vary enormously in size and style of operation, but there are certain points that an organisation must bear in mind when selecting a consultant, such as competence and cost. The HSE can supply an information leaflet on the subject, entitled 'Selecting a Health and Safety Consultancy'.

Certain professional bodies and quangos are helpful in providing advice and publications relating to health and safety. Examples include the Sports Council, Institute of Sport and Recreation Management (ISRM), ILAM (Institute of Leisure and Amenity Management) and the Regional Tourist Boards.

Universities and colleges often put on courses concerning health and safety issues and may offer consultancy services themselves.

Some industries have training boards, e.g. ABTA National Training Board and the Agricultural Training Board (ATB) who are active in assessing training needs in health and safety and organising courses.

As with any legal matters, solicitors, the CAB (Citizens' Advice Bureau) and local legal advice centres can give advice on the legislation relating to health and safety.

Section 2 Health and safety hazards in leisure and tourism facilities

Identifying health and safety hazards

It is a basic fact of safety management that accidents are caused rather than just happen. Careful investigations of accidents show that many could have been prevented if somebody had taken the time and care to examine the risk potential of the particular building or facility. It may be something as simple as the replacement of a broken floor tile or cracked window pane. Under the new Management of Health and Safety at Work Regulations 1992, examined in Section 1 of this unit, employers have a duty to carry out risk assessments that should highlight potential health and safety risks and lead to positive action to put matters right and so reduce the number of accidents in leisure and tourism facilities.

According to the Leisure Accident Surveillance System (LASS), the Department of Trade and Industry (DTI) estimates that there were in the region of 180,000 leisure-related accidents during the six-month period May–October 1989. These figures indicate the scale of the problem and show why any work carried out to identify hazards in leisure and tourism facilities will go a long way towards keeping accidents to a minimum.

This section will identify some of the main hazards that are likely to be found in all sectors of the leisure and tourism industry.

Visitor attractions

We saw in Unit 1 that the term 'visitor attraction' can be defined very broadly, and can include theme parks, heritage attractions, museums, stately homes, sports facilities and the like. Even the smallest attraction will need to give attention to the health and safety needs of staff and visitors. Bad publicity given to poor (or non-existent) health and safety procedures leading to accidents involving members of the public can have disastrous effects on visitor numbers. The management at Disney resorts believes that accidents and Disney do not mix, and make sure that all staff are rigorously trained in emergency first-aid techniques.

Potential hazards for visitors to attractions include:

- Unguarded or unsupervised machinery and equipment.
- Fast-moving rides and monorails.
- Accidents involving animals.
- Slippery or broken walkways.
- Loose or broken wiring.

- Poor lighting indoors and outside.
- Leaks of steam, water, gas or oil.
- Blocked aisles.
- Fire hazards.
- Water hazards.
- Poor signposting.

Sports and leisure centres

Sports and leisure centres are used for a whole range of activities by many different customers, including school groups, individuals, senior citizens, the disabled and sports teams. The variety of types of activity and types of customer, when coupled with heavy usage at peak times, places a particular emphasis on the need for strict health and safety measures, including the identification of potential hazards. If we think of a typical leisure centre, it is likely to include the following areas:

- Dry sports areas, e.g. squash courts, sports hall, etc.
- Wet sports areas.
- Toilets.
- Changing rooms.
- Showers.
- Spectator seating areas.
- Refreshments areas.

The hazards associated with each will include:

Dry sports areas
- Slippery floors.
- Unguarded light fittings.
- Low-level obstructions.
- Damaged sports equipment.
- Inadequate or insufficient storage for equipment.
- Poor lighting and ventilation.

Wet sports areas
- Poor quality water, e.g. unclear or with objectionable odour.
- Slippery surfaces around pools.
- Inadequate depth markings.
- Inadequate number of life savers.
- Unsafe diving and other equipment.
- Untrained staff.

Figure 2.5 shows the wet-side facilities of Utopia Leisure Centre, East Sussex.

Fig 2.5 Health and safety is paramount in wet-side facilities
(courtesy of Utopia Leisure Centre, East Sussex)

Toilets
- Unhygienic condition.
- Broken tiles and mirrors.
- Damaged doors and fittings.

Changing rooms
- Insecure fixtures and fittings.
- Broken tiles and mirrors.
- Damaged doors.
- Litter on floors.
- Slippery floors.
- Inadequate storage for cleaning materials.

Showers
- Damaged tiles on walls and floor.
- Water too hot or too cold.
- Insecure fixtures and fittings.

Spectator seating areas
- Damaged seats.
- Insecure steps and handrails.

- Blocked emergency exits.
- Poor lighting.
- Poor signs.

Refreshments areas
- Slippery floors.
- Food storage areas at wrong temperature.
- Litter on floors.
- Damaged tables and chairs.

Any special events that take place at the leisure centre, such as a swimming gala or Caribbean disco evening, will entail special health and safety measures appropriate to the occasion.

Hotels and other accommodation

Accommodation for business and leisure travellers comes in a vast range of sizes, styles and types; anything from a sixteenth-century half-timbered country house hotel in Herefordshire to a modern 30-storey city centre hotel. Indeed, the range of accommodation on offer in Britain is one of its strong selling points, particularly to overseas visitors. Nor must we forget about self-catering accommodation, including cottages, chalets, villas, camping and caravanning, so popular with families who enjoy the flexibility and value for money that this type of accommodation offers.

From a health and safety point of view, the wide range of accommodation on offer makes a standardised approach to analysing and eliminating risks quite impossible. The sixteenth-century country house hotel quoted above will have very different health and safety risks associated with it when compared with, say, a caravan site with over 200 pitches.

Potential hazards in both serviced and self-catering accommodation include:

- Fire (particularly important in high-rise buildings).
- Worn or damaged floor coverings.
- Faulty wiring and electrical appliances.
- Faulty air conditioning.
- Poor ventilation.
- Glass doors, screens and windows.
- Poor lighting.
- Blocked corridors.
- Suspicious packages.
- Poorly maintained lifts and elevators.

The risk assessments, which are now an essential management function under the new health and safety at work regulations, should highlight such risks and hazards and prompt urgent action by employers. Self-catering accommodation, where by definition the owner or manager of the property may not be on-site, needs very careful attention when it comes to health and safety issues. (See Figure 2.6 for fire safety advice from the Butlin's Staff Handbook.)

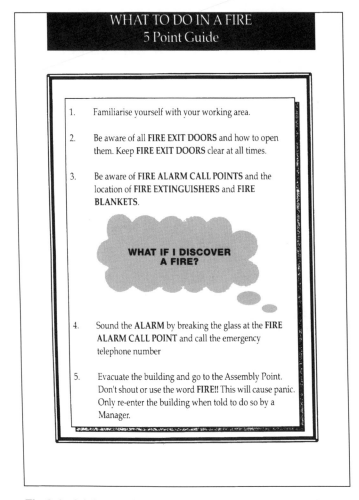

Fig 2.6 Advice on fire safety from the Butlins' staff handbook
(courtesy of the Rank Organisation)

Travel agents and tour operators

Most travel agents' and tour operators' work will be office based, including dealing with clients, raising invoices, checking availability of flights and holidays, filing and such like. Many of the 'normal' health and safety risks and hazards associated with office premises will apply, including:

- Fire.
- Blocked corridors and aisles.
- Poor ventilation and air quality.
- Faulty electrical equipment.
- Fumes from certain felt pens and correction fluids.
- Poor lighting.

One area of travel agents' and tour operators' work which has been causing concern with individuals and their trade union representatives for some time is the extensive use of visual display units (VDUs) and their harmful effects on users. Both travel agents and tour operators (together with airlines, coach operators and hotel reservation staff) use VDUs in all aspects of their work. The potential harmful effects of excessive use of VDUs has now been formally recognised with the introduction of the new Health and Safety (Display Screen Equipment) Regulations, which came into effect on 1 January 1993.

It is important to remember that travel agents and tour operators are often acting on behalf of other sectors of the leisure and tourism industry, for example hotels and transport companies, over which they have no control. The travel agents and tour operators must be convinced that the health and safety procedures of all companies they deal with are as good as their own. Working across continents and in different languages can make this a very difficult task.

Catering and hospitality

Catering and hospitality is a very diverse sector of the leisure and tourism industry. It includes:

- Catering for large functions.
- Catering in hotels.
- Contract catering for airlines, ferry operators, etc.
- Independent restaurants and cafes.
- Restaurants and eating places that are part of large multinational companies, e.g. Harvester is part of the Forte group.
- Catering associated with sports events.
- Catering at entertainment complexes.
- Corporate hospitality events.

There are potential health and safety hazards both for those working in this sector and their customers and clients. Particular examples of risks are:

- Unguarded machinery and kitchen equipment.
- Food stored at the incorrect temperature.
- Dangerous practices involving food preparation.
- Contaminated water supplies.
- Inadequate storage for potentially dangerous cleaning materials.

- Poor lighting.
- Inadequate ventilation.

The Food Safety Act and its associated Food Hygiene Regulations (see page 2.15) have come about to protect both workers and the public in this area of concern for health and safety.

Entertainment

Entertainment venues are often able to accommodate large numbers of people at any one time, e.g. cinemas, theatres, outdoor and indoor arenas, casinos, discos, etc. This puts a particular emphasis on the need for strict health and safety procedures to protect the public and those employed in the venues. Potential hazards include:

- Fire.
- Overcrowding.
- Blocked exits.
- Excessive noise.
- Harmful lighting effects.
- Poor ventilation.

Education

Schools, colleges and universities have long been used by people in their leisure time for evening, day and weekend courses. The recent severing of ties between schools/colleges and their local education authorities has increased the need to generate additional income from premises that are not usually fully occupied over a 12-month period. This independence has led to an increased awareness of the importance of health and safety procedures, both while the 'normal' pupils/students are on-site and while the premises are being put to 'different' uses, e.g. conferences and conventions, meetings, trade fairs, etc.

Leisure in the home

We saw in Unit 1 that home-based leisure was a significant growing part of the total leisure and tourism industry. When looking at health and safety hazards in leisure and tourism, we must not forget that leisure in the home has risks associated with it. The DTI's Home Accident Surveillance Survey (HASS) compiles national figures from 13 accident and emergency departments on accidents in the home. It shows that a quarter of a million accidents a year (14 per cent of all home accidents) happen in the garden. The top eight gardening accidents involving equipment in 1989 were:

Lawn mower:	6,300 accidents.
Garden fork:	4,300 accidents.
Deck chair/sunbed:	4,000 accidents.
Hedge trimmer:	3,900 accidents.
Spade/shovel:	3,300 accidents.
Wheelbarrow:	2,000 accidents.
Flower pot:	2,000 accidents.
Secateurs:	1,900 accidents.

With the projected increases in home-based leisure up to and beyond the year 2000, accidents in this area are likely to increase unless manufacturers and users alike are aware of potential risks and hazards.

Reducing health and safety risks

We have looked in detail at many sectors of the leisure and tourism industry and have identified potential health and safety risks and hazards in each. Recent UK legislation on health and safety, primarily put in place to satisfy new EC directives, has focused the minds of those managing leisure and tourism facilities on the importance of health and safety at all levels of an organisation.

When it comes to reducing health and safety risks and hazards in the workplace, the motto has to be 'prevention is better than cure'. If a leisure and tourism organisation takes a close look at its operation with a view to identifying and eliminating hazards, rather than waiting for accidents to happen, then it will reap the benefits in a number of ways:

- *Better staff morale* – involving members of staff in the planning and implementation of health and safety matters at an early stage will not only reduce incidents but also improve morale. Asking them to 'pick up the pieces' after an accident that they may have had nothing to do with, is not effective management.
- *Reduced costs* – a carefully planned and costed health and safety strategy will help to cut out major incidents that may put a strain on the financial resources of the organisation.
- *Improved image* – if customers see that a leisure and tourism organisation is taking health and safety seriously, its image will be enhanced, and through word of mouth as much as anything business will increase. If health and safety is poorly handled, the adverse PR generated may have a serious effect on visitor attendances.

How can health and safety risks be reduced?

Probably the single most important factor in helping reduce health and safety risks is management attitude. If the senior management of a leisure and tourism organisation is not committed to providing a safe and controlled environment, it is unlikely that the organisation as a whole will succeed in its efforts to reduce hazards. A committed senior management will inspire and involve its staff, suppliers, contractors and even its customers to achieve a safer environment.

Management can influence the improvement in health and safety procedures in a number of ways.

Safety audits

Many leisure and tourism organisations have, as a matter of course, been carrying out safety audits for years. As we have seen, the process of identifying potential risks has become more formalised of late with the introduction of the new EC-prompted health and safety regulations with their duty on employers to carry out risk assessments. Safety audits are invaluable in pinpointing potential hazards, but can only be fully useful if any highlighted risks are attended to.

Staff training

A management that is committed to providing a safe environment for all who enter its premises will put a high priority on staff training in the area of health and safety. New staff should be given, as part of their wider induction programme, details of the organisation's health and safety policies and practices. There should be regular updating for all staff in health and safety matters and specific training for those working in particularly hazardous areas. Staff in leisure and tourism need to be alert, responsible, calm and collected when it comes to health and safety.

Implementing legislation

The many different laws, regulations and codes of practice relating to health and safety are all based on sound common sense principles. Any leisure and tourism professional will consider it essential to become familiar with health and safety laws and implement them within the organisation for the benefit of all.

Seeking advice

Section 1 of this unit looked in detail at the many sources of help and advice available on health and safety issues (see page 2.17). Seeking advice from the experts will help to ensure both the identification of potential risks and hazards and their elimination.

Having systems in place

As well as all staff being familiar with everyday health and safety matters, such as first-aid procedures, it is essential that there are systems in place to deal with any emergencies that may arise, e.g. bomb scares, major equipment failure, major accidents, etc. Management is responsible for drawing up contingency plans to deal with such occurrences and informing all staff accordingly.

Customers with special needs

All staff should be constantly aware of potential hazards and risks not only to the able-bodied but also to those with special needs, e.g. the disabled, very young and older customers.

Budgeting for health and safety

Leisure and tourism organisations must be sure to budget for health and safety matters in the same way as other elements of their operation need resourcing. Health and safety cannot be regarded as an optional extra; it should be seen as crucial to the success of the business.

Essential maintenance

A programme of regular maintenance of equipment and machinery will help reduce accidents. All areas must be kept clear of litter and other debris and there needs to be adequate storage for such items as potentially dangerous chemicals and other cleaning materials.

Visitor and traffic management

Good signposting to help people and traffic circulation will contribute to a safe and controlled environment. Particular hazards should be identified with clear warning signs.

Section 3 Security in leisure and tourism

Security – a growing concern

British people are concerned more than ever with security in their lives. We have seen in the 1980s and early 1990s an upsurge in criminal activity; theft from houses and flats, theft of and from cars, assaults and aggressive behaviour seem to have escalated out of control in many areas of the country. It is not just run-down inner city areas that are experiencing the growth in crime; rural areas too are being targeted by criminals for robberies, and youth crime in many country areas is at an all-time high. It is not the concern of this book to investigate the causes of this rising tide of crime, if indeed the causes can be accurately pin-pointed. What we are concerned with, however, is the effect that this criminal activity is having on trends in leisure and tourism generally, as well as specific security measures that can be put in place to improve the security of individual organisations.

The reaction of many British people who now see their security threatened by increased crime has been to adapt their life-styles to improve their own particular circumstances. Some people, of course, will choose not to be deflected from their normal daily activity, but an ever increasing number of people are deciding to make their own lives more secure. Individuals are:

- Installing burglar alarms and other security devices on their houses and flats to protect themselves and their families.
- Fitting alarms and immobilisers to cars or choosing to buy cars that already have them fitted.
- Carrying less cash and using safer forms of payment, e.g. credit and debit cards.
- Being careful when, where and how they go out of their homes. Certain parts of urban areas are undoubtedly more dangerous than others and taking measures to avoid such areas makes sense.

Security in leisure and tourism

The leisure and tourism industry has also felt the effects of this rise in criminal activity in a number of ways:

- It has become increasingly difficult to attract people to events and facilities in certain inner city areas, e.g. to evening classes and sports activities.
- Travel patterns to countries and areas experiencing political instability or

terrorism have been altered. The obvious and tragic example of this has to be the complete destruction of the tourist industry in the former Yugoslavia. Northern Ireland's tourism industry has also suffered over a long period of time, and Florida is considered by many British people to be a 'dangerous' state following the recent murders of UK holidaymakers.

- The rise in importance of home-based leisure, which we looked at in Unit 1, is in part due to people looking for more entertainment in the comfort and, perhaps more importantly, the security of their own homes.
- Visitors to hotels, sports centres, tourist attractions, airports, events and other leisure and tourism facilities are no longer surprised to see security staff on duty; in fact, they expect to see them and would feel rather uncomfortable in certain circumstances if they were not there.

Legislation to protect the leisure and tourism consumer

As well as individuals altering their leisure habits and increasing their personal security, the law-makers in Britain and the European Community have been developing and passing legislation to help the security needs of those using leisure and tourism facilities and services. We looked in detail in Section 1 of this unit at the legislation affecting the health and safety of staff and visitors in leisure and tourism. There are, however, one or two important laws concerning consumer rights which directly influence the security of the product that the leisure and tourism customer is buying.

Trades Description Act 1968

This Act protects customers against false descriptions by those who are selling or providing services, including leisure and tourism services. Any description of, for example, a hotel or leisure club must be truthful at the time it was written (if circumstances subsequently change, then the operator must inform the customer of the nature of the changes). This places a duty on owners and operators of leisure and tourism facilities to produce brochures and other promotional materials that are not intended to deceive the customer.

Sale of Goods Act 1979

This Act applies particularly to one sector of the leisure and tourism industry, namely tour operators. The Act puts a duty on businesses such as tour operators to exercise care and attention when selecting all the elements of the packages they are putting together. Once they have done this, they cannot be held responsible under this Act for the day-to-day running of the services they have contracted. However, the newly introduced EC Package Travel Directive puts a slightly different emphasis on this, and other, aspects of the security of the holiday product that the customer is buying.

EC Package Travel Directive

The Package Travel, Package Holidays and Package Tours Directive came into operation on 1 January 1993 in all 12 Member States of the European Union (formerly EC). Its main aim is to give people buying package holidays more protection and access to compensation when things go wrong. The Directive places a number of duties on the organisers of packages, namely:

- Providing information to customers on who is responsible for the package they have booked. That person or organisation is then liable in the event of failure to deliver any elements of the package.
- Providing clear contract terms.
- Giving emergency telephone numbers.
- Providing proof of the organiser's security against insolvency and information on any available insurance policies.
- Giving immediate notification with explanation of any increase in prices permitted within the terms of the contract.
- Providing a variety of compensation options if agreed services are not supplied.
- Producing accurate promotional material including brochures.

The EC Package Travel Directive has come as something of a shock to the UK tourist industry since the directive covers domestic as well as outbound packages. This means that hotels, tourist information centres, resorts, conference organisers, coach operators and even school trip organisers have found that they may well fall within the scope of the directive. There has also been much debate about what exactly constitutes a 'package', with Trading Standards Officers, the people given the job of policing the directive in the UK, appearing to have different views depending in which part of the country they are located. The travel industry generally fears that the extra insurance needed by tour organisers to cover against claims under the directive is bound to put up the cost of holidays.

Enhancing security in leisure and tourism

Any security measures in an organisation will have been put in place to provide protection against all forms of loss arising from a number of different sources. The term 'security' in leisure and tourism covers:

1 Security of people.
2 Security of property.
3 Security of money.
4 Security of information.

Security of people

When looking at the wide range of security concerns confronting the industry, the welfare of people must be the prime concern for the leisure and tourism professional. 'People' will include:

- Staff.
- Visitors (invited or uninvited).
- Others (contractors etc.).

All employers have a legal duty under the Health and Safety at Work, etc. Act 1974 to ensure the health, safety and welfare at work of their staff (see page 2.3). We have looked at the various health and safety risks and hazards that may confront staff in leisure and tourism, but providing a safe working environment that is free from any violence is becoming an increasingly important concern for employers. The Health and Safety Executive working definition of violence is:

> *Any incident in which an employee is abused, threatened or assaulted by a member of the public in circumstances arising out of the course of his or her employment. (HSE 1992)*

Being a service industry involving a high degree of contact between staff and customers, those working in leisure and tourism can expect to encounter uncomfortable and sometimes violent incidents during the course of their work. Verbal abuse and threatening behaviour are the most common types of incident. Physical attacks are comparatively rare.

Both employers and employees have an interest in reducing violence in the workplace. For employers, violence can lead to low morale and a poor image for the organisation, making it difficult to recruit and retain staff. It can also mean extra costs, with absenteeism, higher insurance premiums and possible compensation payments. For employees, violence can cause pain, suffering and even disability or death. Physical attacks are obviously dangerous but serious or persistent verbal abuse or threats can also damage employees' health through anxiety and stress.

The HSE recommends the following seven-point plan to tackle violence in the workplace:

Step one: Find out if there is a problem. It may seem obvious, but many employers are not aware of a problem until they ask staff directly.

Step two: Record all incidents. By using a simple report form (see Figure 2.7), an organisation can begin to build up a picture of the problem.

Step three: Classify all incidents. Incidents that involve serious injury will be easy to classify, but those involving, for example, verbal abuse will need careful discussion with the staff involved.

Step four: Search for preventative measures. The way jobs are carried out can help reduce the risk of violence. For example, if a leisure and tourism organisation needs its staff to work late, it should arrange for them either to have a safe place to park their car or provide transport home; many nightclubs and pubs do this already, particularly for female staff. Changing from using cash to accepting cheques, credit cards or tokens can help reduce attempted thefts.

Step five: Decide what to do. A mixture of measures usually works best, and particularly if the employees are fully involved in deciding what needs to be done. It is often a question of striking a balance between the fears of the staff and the needs of the public. For example, many busy tourist attractions provide entertainment for customers who are forced to queue to get in. This helps to diffuse what can sometimes turn into a threatening situation for staff on duty.

Step six: Put measures into practice. Whatever measures are decided upon, the policy for dealing with violence should be included in the organisation's safety policy statement, so that all employees are aware of it.

Step seven: Check that the measures work. It is important to check how well the measures are working. If the problem persists, it may be necessary to go back and repeat steps two and three.

It may be that violence among customers is identified as a problem for an organisation. Similar steps to those above can be put in place to help deal with the situation. A typical incident report form is shown in Figure 2.7.

Security of property

Security of property in leisure and tourism involves:

- The fabric of the building itself, including fitments.
- The contents of the building.

Security of buildings

Buildings used for leisure and tourism purposes can be under many different types of threat. One of the most obvious and costly is robbery, but other threats include wanton damage, often carried out by youths, and daubing with graffiti. There are some fundamental rules for securing any type of property, including:

- Fitting security locks to doors and windows, and window bars to high risk areas such as equipment stores and bar areas.
- Using closed circuit television (CCTV) or employing security personnel to monitor large areas including car parks.
- Fitting intruder alarms that, for large organisations, should be capable of alerting a central monitoring station which operates 24 hours a day.

date of incident	day of week	time

EMPLOYEE

name   address
job/grade
department
what activity were you engaged in at the time of the incident?

DETAILS OF ASSAILANT(S)	WITNESS(ES)
name(s)	name(s)
address(s)	address(s)
age	age
male/female	male/female
other details	other details

WHAT HAPPENED

give an account of the incident, including any relevant events leading to the incident

OUTCOME

Injury? Verbal abuse? Anti-social behaviour? Damage to personal/other property?

                                                    time lost

                                                    legal action?

DETAILS OF LOCATION OF INCIDENT

provide sketch if possible

any other relevant information

Fig 2.7 A typical incident report form (source: HSE)

- Introducing card access control using PIN systems to identify which parts of a building are for staff access only.
- Installing security lighting particularly in high risk areas.

Security of the contents of the building

The contents of any leisure and tourism facility which are potentially at risk could be:

- Equipment, e.g. computers, sports equipment, catering equipment, furniture, museum artefacts, etc.

- Stock, e.g. wines, beers and spirits, food, sports clothing, etc.
- The personal possessions of the staff.
- The personal possessions of the customers.
- The personal possessions of any other people, such as contractors, who are on-site.

Most visitors will expect a facility to guard their possessions in exchange for a ticket, whether or not any payment is involved. This service is all part of making the visitor relaxed and in a better mood to enjoy their experience, be it a game of squash or a visit to an art gallery. Where visitors are not allowed to take possessions with them for security reasons, e.g. cameras are not allowed in certain museums and galleries, secure storage must be provided by the leisure and tourism operator.

Some of the techniques mentioned under 'security of buildings' above will help protect equipment and possessions inside the building. Over and above these technical measures, all staff must be vigilant and alert at all times to suspicious characters and circumstances. As well as ensuring a pleasant experience for all visitors, it is the job of staff and management to safeguard visitors' possessions.

Security of money

Leisure and tourism is a multi-million pound industry often revolving around cash transactions. It is usual to pay for many leisure and tourism products and services with cash rather than cheques or credit/debit cards, for example:

- Buying drinks in a nightclub.
- Paying for rides at an amusement park.
- Booking a court at the local leisure centre for a game of badminton.
- Gambling and betting.
- Buying food and drink in pubs and cafes.
- Visiting tourist attractions.
- Paying for transport, e.g. taxi, bus and train.

Having an industry that relies heavily on cash transactions places a particular emphasis on operators to make sure that their security systems in this area are as good as possible. Where practical, leisure and tourism operators should introduce more secure means of payment such as cheques and cards to reduce the risk of theft and fraud by visitors and staff. Employees who handle cash will need careful recruitment and training in the rules and procedures of the particular organisation, including:

- Authorised keyholders for offices and safes.
- Methods of paying in and receiving cash.
- The use of burglar and attack alarms.
- Locking up arrangements.

Security of information

We have seen that leisure and tourism is an increasingly competitive industry. The introduction of CCT (see page 1.32) has extended the notion of competition beyond the private sector and into public bodies and agencies. Particularly in times of recession, when many people have only limited disposable income to spend on leisure and tourism, it is essential for organisations to safeguard their business by having secure means of storing information. All organisations will have a wealth of records about their customers, the profitability of the organisation and their employees.

The two main security hazards associated with records are fire and theft. Twenty years ago, all business records would have been held entirely on paper; nowadays, information is held on a variety of other formats including microfiche, computer disks, photographic materials and audio/video tapes. These are all vulnerable to the twin threats of fire and theft and do not inherently offer any greater security than paper. Computers, however, do give the option of storing information on 'floppy disks' which can be stored securely away from the main computer terminal, thus reducing the risk of losing information in the event of theft or fire. All computer and other sensitive information should be routinely locked in fire-proof data protection cabinets kept in controlled access rooms.

The storage of information on computers raises the issue of the Data Protection Act 1984. This Act was introduced to safeguard the public from problems relating to the inaccuracy of any information held about them on computer records. In leisure and tourism, the recording of customer information on computer is widespread, and includes:

- The names and addresses of hotel guests.
- Details of travel agents' clients.
- Theatre booking lists.
- Membership lists for sports and social clubs.
- Names and addresses of visitors to exhibitions.

Under the Data Protection Act customers are entitled to see any information held about them on computer and can challenge inaccuracies with the organisation concerned (see Unit 6 for more information on the Data Protection Act).

Assignment 2

Situation

In your role of Development Assistant with a Regional Tourist Board, you have been asked by a consortium of 12 local authorities in the West Midlands to prepare a report on health, safety and security matters in the leisure and tourism facilities in their areas. The recent introduction of the new EC Directives has raised the profile of health and safety issues in the local authorities.

Tasks

Working as part of a small team, you are to research and prepare a report on health, safety and security issues in one facility chosen from the following list:

- A private hotel.
- A tourist information centre.
- A restaurant or other catering establishment.
- An entertainment or sporting venue.
- A travel agency.
- A sports or leisure centre.
- A health and fitness studio.
- An educational establishment.

Your report should set the scene concerning current legislation in health and safety matters and then look in detail at:

- Existing health and safety hazards in the facility.
- Measures already implemented to reduce the risks from health and safety hazards.
- Recommendations for new measures which need to be implemented.
- Timescale and resource implications of your proposed measures.
- Proposals to enhance the security at the facility.
- Sources of help and advice on health, safety and security matters.

Your report should be no more than 1,500 words in length and should be written for the chairman of the consortium of local authorities. Diagrams and statistics should be included as appropriate.

Revision test questions

1 What are the aims of the 1974 Health and Safety at Work, etc. Act?
2 What does a common law 'duty of care' mean in the case of leisure and tourism?
3 What are 'codes of practice' in health and safety legislation?
4 What are the three duties that the Health and Safety at Work, etc. Act places on employees?
5 Does the Health and Safety at Work, etc. Act apply only to employees?
6 What is the role of the Health and Safety Commission?
7 How and by whom is the Health and Safety at Work, etc. Act enforced?
8 Name three of the areas covered by the new health and safety regulations which came into force on 1 January 1993 to implement the new EC Directives.
9 What is a 'risk assessment'?
10 What do the initials PPE stand for?

11 Give two examples of the implications of the new EC Health and Safety Directives on the leisure and tourism industry.

12 What do the initials COSHH stand for?

13 Give two examples of health and safety legislation that a person opening a new restaurant will need to take into consideration.

14 Give five examples of organisations that can give advice on health and safety matters.

15 List five potential health hazards in a visitor attraction.

16 Give five particular health and safety hazards likely to be found in a leisure centre.

17 What are the particular safety hazards associated with hotels?

18 Give three benefits to a leisure and tourism organisation of adopting a policy of reducing health and safety hazards in the workplace.

19 Give three specific steps that management can take to improve the health and safety procedures in its organisation.

20 What is the principal aim of the 1968 Trades Description Act? Give two examples of when it may be implemented in the leisure and tourism industry.

21 Why was the EC Package Travel Directive introduced? What are its main features?

22 What measures can management put in place to improve the security of its information?

23 What are the main points of the HSE's seven-point plan to tackle violence in the workplace?

24 How can the security of leisure and tourism premises be improved?

25 How can the management of a leisure centre help stamp out theft of money and possessions?

Unit 3
CUSTOMER SERVICE IN LEISURE AND TOURISM

Section 1 The need for excellence in customer service

Introduction

The UK leisure and tourism industry has experienced dramatic changes over the last 10–15 years, from the boom days of the early 1980s to the recession of the late 1980s and early 1990s. The high levels of investment in new facilities and services seen in the 1980s have all but dried up. CCT (see page 1.32) has forced local authorities to examine the facilities they offer to their increasingly discerning visitors. The English Tourist Board has seen its government funding severely cut, putting into question the whole concept of a 'national' tourist organisation.

It is against this background that we will look at the importance of customer service in the leisure and tourism industry. It is fair to say that the expansion of facilities and services mentioned above was not matched by investment in the human resources of the industry – its staff. Except for some notable exceptions, the message that customer service and customer care are vital to the very survival of leisure and tourism has not been widely practised within the industry. It is true that many organisations have nailed their colours firmly to a 'putting customers first' strategy, but in times of financial cutbacks the resources needed for customer service training have often been sadly lacking.

Many people would argue that investing in a customer service approach is more important in times of recession since competition for customers and their reduced disposable income is even fiercer. A leisure and tourism organisation that advocates excellence in customer service is sure to survive a recession better than one that gives the subject little attention.

What is a customer?

Many organisations that are striving to improve customer service use statements similar to the following to answer this question:

Customers:

- Are the most important people to our organisation.
- Are not dependent on us – we are dependent on them.
- Are not an interruption of our work – they are the purpose of it.
- Are not people to argue with or match wits against.
- Are not statistics but human beings with feelings and emotions.
- Are the people who bring us their needs. It is our job to handle these profitably for them and for ourselves.
- Are always right!

Developing a customer service approach

We will begin this section with a quote from Peter Drucker, an authority on management practices:

> There is only one valid definition of business purpose: to create a customer.
> It is the customer who determines what a business is.
> (The Practice of Management, Butterworth-Heinemann, 1989)

This simple definition shows that without customers there would be no business. It is only when organisations begin to put the customer at the centre of all activity, that a true customer service approach has begun.

The key issues to be addressed by any organisation committed to a positive approach to customer service include:

1 *Identifying customer needs* – knowing what your customers want is fundamental to the success of any business. In Unit 4 'Marketing in Leisure and Tourism' we will look in detail at the various techniques that can be used to gather customer information. It is important to remember that the gathering of data is often relatively easy; what is often more difficult is putting into action the recommendations the information suggests.

2 *Developing the right products and services* – having found out what its customers' needs are, the organisation can begin to develop products that match these requirements to make sure they are offered at the right price, in the right place, at the right time and at a profit.

3 *Measuring customer satisfaction* – customer service is a constant process to strive to be as successful as possible in satisfying customer needs. The products and services will need careful monitoring and adjusting to meet any changes demanded by the customers.

4 *Developing internal systems* – customer service isn't just about satisfying the customers 'on the other side of the counter'. Many leisure and tourism organisations, particularly large employers, will need to give attention to the needs of the 'internal customer', i.e. the staff working within the organisation. Mechanisms to improve internal communications, including regular meetings, social events and internal newsletters, are all part of improving the overall level of customer service.

5 *Staff training* – training in customer service handling and attitude is vital for all staff in leisure and tourism organisations, not just those whose work brings them into daily contact with customers. Staff working 'behind the scenes', perhaps in kitchens or on maintenance duties, need to appreciate also that they have an important role to play in customer service.

Developing a customer service approach is all about creating the right culture within the organisation. Sometimes referred to as a quality culture, TQM (total quality management) culture or customer culture, the end result should be the same; customers who enjoy their experience, come back again and tell their friends! Some names commonly used to identify customer service approaches include:

- Putting customers first.
- Quality pays.
- Profit through service.
- Caring for customers.
- Service first.
- Excellence in service.

CASE STUDY

Customer service approach – British Airways

BA is the world's largest international passenger airline, with a scheduled network covering some 155 destinations in 72 different countries. It serves more leading international markets than any other European airline. According to the 1992–3 annual report, its mission is:

> *To be the best and most successful company in the airline industry.*

It lists seven specific goals which it is striving towards in order to fulfil its mission, including:

- *To provide overall superior service and good value for money in every market segment in which we compete.*
- *To excel in anticipating and quickly responding to customer needs and competitor activity. (British Airways PLC Annual Report 1992–3)*

BA's customer service approach was started in earnest in the mid-1980s under the direction of Sir Colin Marshall, then Chief Executive and now President of British Airways. To create a clear competitive advantage, the company recognised the importance of adopting a more customer-centred approach to its activities. In 1984 a new corporate identity was introduced across all aspects of the airline, from the colour and design of staff uniforms, through changes to stationery and promotional material to the aircraft themselves. Market research was carried out with a view to establishing both customer expectations of the standard and level of service, and the staff's perception of their role within the company.

The outcome of the market research was the development of a corporate training programme under the banner 'Putting the customer first – if we don't someone else will'. The programme was launched with a series of corporate events for staff entitled 'Putting people first' aimed at fostering a spirit of teamwork and co-operation amongst employees. A parallel programme for managers was also introduced at the same time, with the title 'Managing people first', which encouraged a more open management style.

Subsequent advertising highlighted the excellence in customer service offered to all who chose to fly with BA.

BA obtains regular feedback from its customers via its market research department which uses a variety of data collection methods.

Quality in customer service has now become an essential part of the working practices of all British Airways management and staff. Individual departments have begun to introduce their own quality initiatives and individual members of staff are encouraged to put forward new ideas for improving the level of customer service. One of the major themes of BA's current work in this area is the need to sustain high levels of customer service and provide consistency throughout the company.

The factors that have led to a customer service approach

There may be many reasons why a leisure and tourism organisation decides to strive for excellence in its customer service strategy. As the British Airways case study above shows, the factors that drive a customer-centred approach are either external or internal to the organisation.

External factors

Changing customer expectations

Customers in Britain today have far greater expectations of service quality than was the case even 10–15 years ago. In leisure and tourism today it is very much a 'buyers market', where organisations have to compete not only on price but also on quality of service in order to win their share of customer spend. Service is no longer seen as peripheral as was the case in the recent past. There is considerable evidence to show that customers, although not always willing to complain openly about poor standards of service, will take action to show their disapproval. The US Office of Consumer Affairs, for example, quotes the following:

- 96 per cent of dissatisfied customers never complain.
- But 90 per cent of them will not return in the future.
- One unhappy customer will tell at least nine others.
- 13 per cent of unhappy customers will tell at least 20 others.

Changes in customer expectations have been brought about by such influences as:

- Exposure to life-styles from around the world via TV and other mass media.
- More foreign travel with exposure to foreign customer service standards.
- Changing eating patterns and food choices.
- Increased educational opportunities.
- Greater mobility.
- Changing work patterns.

The outcome of these influences is a new breed of customer who, in leisure and tourism, is demanding improvement in both product quality and the level and standard of customer service; customers who are looking for *en suite* facilities in their hotels, who want to be able to play a game of squash at 9.30 in the evening, who want a particular newspaper with their freshly-ground coffee at breakfast, who want to party until the early hours of the morning and who want to see the latest movies in plush surroundings. In a word, customers who want service excellence.

Competition

Leisure and tourism is a fiercely competitive business. Organisations survive and prosper by having a competitive edge over the opposition and by winning customers from the competition. Because leisure and tourism is such a diverse industry, there is competition within sectors as well as between companies in the same marketplace. Competition within sectors means that the money an individual spends on leisure could be spent on any number of different leisure activities or products, e.g. a person could go to the cinema, an amusement arcade, go swimming, go to the pub or put the money towards a week's holiday in Greece. Competition between companies is commonplace with, for example, travel agents, tour operators, health and fitness clubs, theatres, etc. In such a competitive environment, excellence in customer service is vital for the survival of many organisations.

Some leisure and tourism organisations have realised that they cannot compete on price alone. A number of tour operators, for example, have seen their profit margins reduced to such a level that their long-term survival is put in serious jeopardy. Many have decided to develop superior customer service strategies to help single them out from the masses. The race to attract and retain business customers in the airline industry has led to emphasis being placed on such factors as in-flight catering and personal service.

The rise in consumerism

Following hard on the heels of customers across the Atlantic, British consumers are becoming more vocal in their opinions of product and service quality (indeed many British people will have picked up the habit of speaking their mind in such places as the USA where customer complaints are not frowned on but used as a form of market research to be built upon). The introduction of television and radio programmes devoted to the cause of consumerism, e.g. 'That's Life' and 'You and Yours', is evidence that people are no longer willing to accept poor service and will 'vote with their feet'.

The rise in consumerism has accelerated the emergence of customers who place quality of service, in its widest sense, above all other factors when making purchasing decisions in leisure and tourism. People are, of course, still sensitive to the price of the products they are buying. There is, however, a growing belief that customers will pay a higher price for a higher quality product, delivered with the highest levels of customer service.

Changes in the economy

We have experienced in the UK a shift from a manufacturing economy to one based on service industries, such as banking, insurance, financial services, and leisure and tourism. It is estimated that about half of the country's GNP (gross national product) comes from the service sector. By the turn of the century, economists estimate that three out of every four jobs in Britain will be in service industries. These fundamental changes have brought about a climate in which customers are dealing with staff in the service sector, either in person, over the telephone or in writing, on a much more regular basis than was the case in the past. This has led in turn to organisations having to respond to higher levels of customer expectation in the area of quality of service.

Privatisation, the moving of previously state-controlled industries into the private sector was heavily promoted in the 1980s under the Conservative government. This too has led customers to demand a higher standard of customer service from the newly privatised companies.

Internal factors

Benefits to the organisation

The principal benefits to an organisation of implementing excellence in its customer service are shown in Figure 3.1.

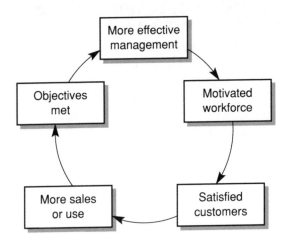

Fig 3.1 *The benefits of developing a customer service approach in leisure and tourism*

The figure shows that the benefits are part of a cyclical process starting with increased management effectiveness, which in turn will lead to a more motivated workforce. The positive attitude of the staff will ensure that customers are happy with the service they are receiving and will hopefully tell others. This will lead to increased sales or use, depending on whether the organisation is in the private, public or voluntary sector. This will help the organisation to achieve its particular objectives, be it profit maximisation or providing a service for the local community.

Other tangible benefits of introducing excellence in customer service are likely to include:

- Fewer complaints.
- Improved co-operation between departments.
- Reduced absenteeism by staff.
- Lower turnover of staff.
- Improved security.
- Less waste (of materials, time, money, etc.).
- Improved quality in other aspects of the organisation's work.
- Reduction in marketing budget (by holding on to existing customers better).

Most of all, the carrying through of a customer-centred service approach will ensure that the organisation will achieve its objectives and that all who have a stake in the business, whether they be shareholders or council-tax payers, will benefit.

Obstacles to good customer service

Customer service, in all its forms, is a highly skilled task. It requires effort, motivation, commitment and support from both management and workforce. Introducing a customer service philosophy into an organisation will inevitably involve change; change in attitude, change in work practices and change in the way that staff are rewarded. The majority of human beings are resistant to change and feel threatened when it happens to them in the workplace. By adopting a positive customer service approach, leisure and tourism organisations must be mindful of these fears on the part of their staff and may have to deal sensitively with a number of obstacles that can hinder the successful implementation of the strategy.

Lack of commitment

We are all familiar with the 'take it or leave it' attitude that is still evident in certain sectors of the leisure and tourism industry today; the restaurant waiter who gives the impression that he would rather be at home watching the TV or the sports centre attendant who is less than helpful when you try to hire some equipment. Thankfully, this negative attitude is being tackled in many organisations through management and staff training. It is the job of management to:

- Discover any underlying problems that are causing the lack of commitment.
- Put in place measures to deal with the problems, perhaps via staff training.
- Provide a supportive environment in which staff can flourish.
- Involve all staff in customer service improvement.

Lack of knowledge

Some staff, particularly those new to their job, will take time to settle into their role and gain the knowledge and experience necessary to carry it out to the full. Induction training followed by detailed training on the services, products and systems of the organisation should give these staff the confidence needed to sustain a high level of customer service and feel a valued member of the team. Figure 3.2 gives details of the qualifications and skills that British Midland Airways looks for when recruiting customer service staff.

BRITISH MIDLAND

**QUALIFICATIONS AND REQUIREMENTS FOR
CUSTOMER SERVICE STAFF**

The following is for information only and does not form part of a Contract of Employment.

Education: 4 GCSE/O Levels including English Language and Mathematics.

Desirable qualifications: Experience in dealing with the general public, as well as being able to relate to other members of staff, as team spirit is a necessity. Own transport is essential.

Appearance and personality: Smart personal appearance with weight in proportion to height. Applicants should be able to work calmly and effectively under pressure, and to maintain a friendly and reassuring manner when dealing with passengers and members of the public.

Hours of work: Basic hours of work average 37.5 per week, consisting of shift work on a rota basis. Overtime may be worked as and when required.

Holiday entitlement: Permanent staff are entitled to 18 salary days, increased by one day for each year of service, to a maximum of 23 days per annum. In addition to holiday entitlement, staff will be granted 8 bank/public holidays, with pay, during the year.

Duties: Customer Service Staff are employed for the assistance and benefit of our customers and, whilst on duty, they may be called upon to carry out many varied tasks, which may include, all, or any, of the following: completion of customer documentation, i.e. airline tickets, baggage labels, excess baggage charges; escort customers to and from the aircraft, through airport controls, Immigration and Customs; assist customers with all enquiries which may be by telephone or in person. It is occasionally necessary to provide relief staff cover at other bases.

Salary: Will be paid in accordance with the Company's current salary scales.

Fig 3.2 Qualifications and requirements for customer service staff, British Midland Airways (courtesy of British Midland)

Product knowledge is vital within any leisure and tourism organisation since it can help staff to:

- Inform customers of prices and features.
- Suggest alternatives if the client's first choice is not available.
- Give detailed information of particular services; in leisure and tourism it is often 'the little things' that either make or break the total experience for the customer.
- Raise the general level of awareness of other services and facilities that the organisation can offer.

Poor communication

Lack of communication is often the biggest single barrier to implementing a successful customer service strategy. It causes resentment among staff, frustrates managers and is often picked up by customers who are sometimes put in embarrassing situations. Managers can help to break this vicious circle by:

- Briefing all staff fully on their respective roles.
- Using simple language and communications methods that everybody can understand.
- 'Walking the job', i.e. taking the time and trouble to talk to staff about their jobs and concerns.

An organisation which looks after its staff is likely to be one that looks after its customers as well.

Lack of co-operation

We saw at the beginning of this section that everybody working in a leisure and tourism organisation has 'customers', whether or not they deal face to face with the general public. 'Internal customers' are people working in the same organisation, e.g. clerical staff, maintenance staff, receptionists, etc., who you come across in the normal daily course of events and on whom you rely for services and support. Good customer service requires a team approach and a recognition that it is not just the customers 'on the other side of the counter' who need respect and consideration, but that colleagues within the organisation need to be dealt with in the same supportive manner.

Good and bad service

Defining what is 'good' and 'bad' service is not an easy matter. One person's idea of good service in a restaurant, for example, may be thought of by somebody else as poor. Whether a person is happy or unhappy with their service is essentially a personal experience; no two people have the same perception of what good or bad service means to them.

The very personal nature of the customer service experience needs to be accepted by staff working in leisure and tourism organisations right from the outset. If customers are not treated as individuals, they will become disenchanted with the service they are getting and may choose to take their business elsewhere.

Although it is not always easy to define exactly what constitutes good service, we are all familiar with circumstances when the level of service we have received is either very good or very bad. In leisure and tourism, the following examples give a flavour of what a good customer service approach is all about:

- *In a restaurant* – an example of good service would be when the management remembers that an evening booking is for a couple's first wedding anniversary and provides a complimentary bottle of champagne. Bad service is when you telephone in advance to make a booking, only to find when you arrive that the waiter has no record of the booking and all the tables are full.
- *In a hotel* – good service would be when the receptionist remembers the name of a guest's child and the hotel provides a box of toys for her to play with. Bad service would be not attending to a broken shower in a guest's room immediately.
- *In a leisure centre* – an example of good service would be providing free use of armbands for all the under fives in the swimming pool. Bad service would be the temporary receptionist telling a telephone caller that he (the receptionist) is not sure of the cost of hiring the indoor bowls hall for the day as he is new to the job and only comes in on Saturdays.

Dealing with difficult situations

From time to time, even the best trained and most professional members of staff will find themselves having to deal with awkward situations involving customers; two of the most common are handling complaints and dealing with 'difficult' customers.

Handling complaints

In general, British people are rather reluctant to complain. When they do, however, staff in leisure and tourism organisations must know how to handle the situation and even turn the complaint to positive advantage. Handled correctly, complaints can be thought of as another type of feedback that gives the organisation a second chance to put things right and satisfy the customer.

Why do people complain?

All people are individuals and so the reasons why they complain are many and varied. Some of the most common reasons can be broadly categorised into:

- *Bad products or service* – to the customer there is a strong link between quality of products and quality of service. If he or she has poor service in getting advice on buying, for example, a set of golf clubs, the quality of the product itself tends to be put in doubt. Poor service, whether it be in person, on the telephone or in writing, is one of the main reasons why people complain.
- *Waiting* – people hate waiting around for attention and wasting their valuable time. The longer the wait the more likely customers are to complain. Mechanisms can be put in place to reduce conflict when a certain amount of waiting or queuing is unavoidable; entertainers are sometimes employed to keep the crowds happy outside London theatres and TV/video screens or the

use of music can sometimes have a positive effect.

- *Being patronised* – nothing is guaranteed to turn frustration into fury quicker than a patronising tone of voice on the part of the member of staff dealing with a customer. It is wise to assume that the customer has some knowledge of the product or service being bought and staff should be trained not to take a 'we know best' attitude.

Specific examples of situations in leisure and tourism when customers are prone to complain include:

- Having the time of the flight changed on their package holiday at the last minute.
- Not being able to get through to the information department of a tourist board as the line is constantly engaged.
- Finding that a hotel room has not been properly prepared for new guests.
- Not be able to find a parking space in a leisure centre car park.
- Being served a meal that has gone cold by the time it reaches the table.
- Being served cloudy beer in a nightclub or pub.
- Booking a window seat on a coach tour only to find that all the window seats are taken when you get on the coach.

What to do when people complain

1 Listen attentively so that you get the whole story first time.
2 Thank the customer for bringing the problem to your attention.
3 Apologise in general terms for the inconvenience but do not grovel.
4 Provide support for the customer by saying that the matter will be fully investigated and matters put right immediately.
5 Sympathise with the customer and try to see the situation from their point of view.
6 Don't justify the circumstances that led up to the complaint and go on the defensive.
7 Ask questions if you are not clear on any points of the customer's complaint.
8 Find a solution to the problem.
9 Agree the solution with the customer.
10 Follow through to make sure that what you promised has been done.
11 In future, try and anticipate complaints before they happen.

'Difficult' customers

One step on from somebody who has a justifiable complaint is the customer who is intent on 'causing a scene'. Just like handling complaints, there are tried and tested ways of dealing with these 'awkward' individuals:

1 Try not to let them get you down or get under your skin; the fact that they wish to cause a fuss may be a sign of their own insecurity.

2 Never argue with them. It can often get the member of staff into deeper trouble.

3 Never be rude to the customer, however rude they are being to you!

4 Try not to take any remarks personally. You may have had nothing to do with the alleged incident but are simply the nearest member of staff.

5 Let the customer do the talking and listen to what they have to say.

6 If in any doubt, seek help from another member of staff or senior management.

Customer care in action – HavenWarner

Part of the Rank Organisation PLC, HavenWarner operates some 60 caravan and chalet parks in the UK, offering self-catering and half-board holidays under the Haven and Warner brand names. European holidays are offered through the Haven France and Spain brand using around 40 parks in Europe.

HavenWarner employs over 1,000 permanent staff and up to 6,000 seasonal staff at the height of the holiday months. All staff are trained in the importance of customer care through a series of training events focusing on:

1 Why customer care is important.

2 How individuals can provide better customer care.

3 How to handle complaints smoothly.

4 Using the telephone effectively.

5 Providing quality service.

All employees are given a staff guide to customer care as part of their training. The guide explains the benefits to members of staff who provide high quality customer service, including:

- Your job becomes more enjoyable.
- You acquire pride in what you are doing.
- You develop skills which make you more valuable to your employer.
- The skills you develop will be valuable wherever you go.
- You become more successful as more opportunities open up at HavenWarner.
- You become an important member of a team whose success *you* have helped to create.

Under the heading '*How you can provide better customer care*', the HavenWarner staff guide mentions:

The right attitude

Employees with the right attitude are:

- Able to create a great first impression.
- Positive in outlook.
- Clean, neat and well groomed.
- Welcoming to customers – use their names if you can and remember a smile costs nothing.

- Proud of doing their job as well as they can.
- Ready to take the initiative.
- Friendly and sincere.
- Willing to act promptly and effectively.
- Ready to take extra trouble and make extra effort to give the customer what they need.

The right information

Informed employees are up to date on:

- The facilities, services and activities on the Park.
- Where the key people are located, e.g. Duty Manager, First Aiders.
- The surrounding area, e.g. places of interest, public transport, key telephone numbers.
- Health and safety procedures.
- What to do in case of an emergency.

Teamwork

No one person achieves quality service for the Park. That needs teamwork. Everybody is part of the 'team' and everybody must adopt common standards of service for the 'team' to succeed.

So be **flexible**:

- Help your colleagues where necessary.
- Think about the effect your action will have on the rest of the team.
- Keep your colleagues informed.

Remember – it doesn't matter what job you do, to the customer you are the HavenWarner representative.

In the section of the staff guide concerning handling complaints, staff are advised:

Some 'do's'
- Show interest.
- Show empathy.
- Listen.
- Restate the complaint.
- Agree a solution.
- Thank the customer.
- Turn the complaint into a compliment.

Some 'don'ts'
- Don't be defensive.
- Don't 'pass the buck'.
- Don't give commands.
- Don't make unrealistic promises.

(Information courtesy of the Rank Organisation PLC)

The importance of keeping the customers you already have

Many leisure and tourism organisations talk about 'increasing market share' and 'targeting new customers' but sometimes overlook the importance of providing a quality service to the customers they already have. While new customers are always welcome in any organisation, existing clientele provide a higher profit contribution and provide a much firmer base from which to develop further business. Statistics from the USA tell us that:

> 'It takes five times as much effort, time and money to attract a new customer than it does to keep an existing customer'
> (Source: US Office of Consumer Affairs).

If an organisation in leisure and tourism can develop repeat and multiple business relationships with its existing customers, it is more able to maximise its resources and achieve its ultimate objective. Creating excellence in customer service is obviously a crucial element in retaining loyal and valued customers.

Over and above developing a positive customer service attitude, there are many ways in which leisure and tourism organisations try to hang on to the customers they already have, including:

- Giving existing clients first choice of bookings before being launched to the general public.
- Offering preferential rates for products and services to existing customers.
- Offering incentives to existing customers to do repeat business, e.g. frequent flyer programmes in the airline industry.
- Hosting events that are only open to existing customers.

It is usual for customers to be categorised according to their volume of business with the organisation, with those at the top receiving maximum incentives to remain loyal.

The importance of existing customers is shown in diagrammatic form in Figure 3.3.

The figure demonstrates the power that existing customers can have on the success or otherwise of any leisure and tourism organisation. It shows that existing customers generate repeat business and can attract new customers to help the organisation to flourish. When linked to a planned programme of improving customer service, reputation is enhanced and all customers reap the benefits of an organisation determined to give excellence in customer service.

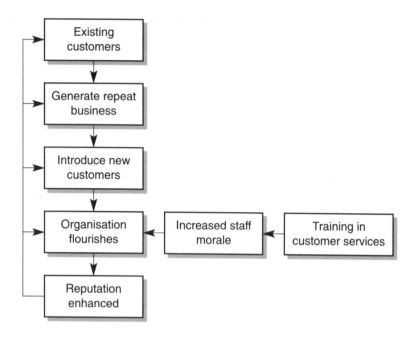

Fig 3.3 The importance of existing customers in leisure and tourism

Introduction

We will see in Unit 4 that identifying customer needs is an essential first stage in the whole process of marketing in the leisure and tourism industry. If identifying needs is considered as the foundation on which all marketing activity is built, then customer care can be thought of as one of the more important 'bricks' that go to make up the total experience being offered to the customer. To take the building analogy a little further, some people would identify customer service as the 'mortar' that holds all elements of the organisation together.

The term 'customer care' is on the lips of so many professionals in the leisure and tourism industry today that we might be persuaded that it is a concept that is totally new to the industry. This is far from the truth as any study of the high standards expected by travellers in the heyday of Victorian Britain would quickly show. What is new is the almost universal acceptance that customer care is an integral part of any successful leisure and tourism organisation.

The previous section of this unit has shown that adopting a positive customer service approach is essential to the survival of many leisure and tourism organisations. Customer care is a vital element of any customer service strategy since it focuses on the crucial interaction between customer and member of staff, and, if planned and executed effectively, will help the organisation achieve its overall objective. There are, however, a number of 'ground rules' that need to be explained before any customer care programme can be implemented.

Ground rules in customer care

There are many considerations an organisation will need to take into account before embarking on a customer care programme for its staff. Some of the more important, which we will look at in more detail, include:

- Always start at the top!
- Involve all staff.
- Have clear aims and objectives.
- Be realistic as to what can be achieved.
- Put yourself in your customers' shoes!
- Integrate customer care with other marketing efforts.
- Be prepared to invest time and money.
- Monitor the programme and measure results.

Always start at the top!

Every individual in the organisation must be committed to carrying out a customer care programme if it is to succeed. This means starting with the highest levels of management, whether it be the chairman of the board, the chief executive, the head of personnel or the director of leisure services. Without their enthusiasm and support the programme will be doomed to failure. Some senior managers sometimes need convincing of the benefits of a customer care programme before they commit resources to it, and this is where an individual from outside the organisation can sometimes play an important role in presenting an objective view of the situation.

Involve all staff

It is no good putting just 'front line' staff through a customer care training programme with the hope of saving a little time and money. This piecemeal approach will not achieve the aim of promoting a customer-centred approach throughout the organisation. All staff, whether on reception or in the plant room, will need some training in customer care and their role in helping to give the customer excellence in service. It is important also to involve staff in the planning and design of the programme, recognising that they have valuable experience and expertise to offer. Any programme that is seen to be 'imposed from above' will create hostility and not help staff to relate to the benefits of good customer service.

Have clear aims and objectives

Any leisure and tourism organisation should be asking itself the questions, 'why are we planning a customer care programme and what do we hope to get out of it?'. Unless management is clear on its aims and objectives for the programme, it will be difficult to measure whether anything has actually been achieved. The aims of the customer care programme will vary between organisations and even between different departments of the same organisation. Private sector leisure and tourism companies will equate customer care with increased profitability while the public and voluntary sector providers will invest in customer care to provide enhanced levels of service to their customers.

Be realistic as to what can be achieved

Management will need to be aware of not setting unrealistic targets for the customer care programme, since staff will feel they have 'failed' if the aims are not met. Management should be in the best position to know what resources of time, money and equipment the organisation can devote to the programme and any limitations or constraints that may exist. Outcomes should be framed within any limiting factors and should be planned over a reasonable time-scale; it is always better to have achievable aims that staff will feel good about having met, rather than unrealistic outcomes that could lead to demoralised employees.

Put yourself in your customers' shoes!

Taking the time to look at your organisation from the customers' perspective will pay dividends in helping to develop a customer care programme that is truly customer focused. Managers and staff can become complacent and overlook problems that may be obvious when looked at from the customers' viewpoint. All customers have particular needs, including:

- *Attention* – customers do not like being ignored or being given only partial attention.
- *Control* – they like to feel in control of the situation and feel good about themselves and what they are doing.

- *Understanding* – customers value friendliness and acknowledgement.
- *Fairness* – they want to feel they are being treated with fairness and honesty.

Integrate customer care with other marketing efforts

Customer care should not be seen by staff and management as a 'bolt on' to other marketing and promotional work being carried out in the organisation. Rather it should be viewed as an important part of the total marketing plan. Staff who are striving to achieve excellence in customer care should be confident that:

- Effective market research has been carried out to determine customer needs.
- The products and services offered by the organisation reflect these customer demands.
- The products and services are effectively promoted to their intended audience.

Only when customer care is integrated with all marketing activity will it achieve its full potential for the organisation.

Be prepared to invest time and money

Planning and implementing a customer care programme will have financial implications both in the long and short term. Short-term costs will revolve around releasing staff from their normal duties in order to be able to attend training sessions, and employing a trainer to see the programme through. The trainer need not necessarily be a consultant employed on a contract basis from outside the organisation; an existing employee with the right skills and attitude could be asked to do the job. However, many institutions that have used 'in-house' staff have found that their knowledge of employees and procedures within the organisation sometimes acts as a barrier to fully achieving the objectives of the customer care programme.

The organisation may well be faced with longer-term financial costs, since the customer care programme may highlight procedures, systems or equipment that may need to be changed in order for the staff to fully implement what they have learnt as part of the programme.

Financial help and advice for implementing customer care programmes may be available from such sources as the Department of Trade and Industry (DTI), under its 'Marketing Initiative' scheme, and the Employment Department.

Monitor the programme and measure results

All the effort and expense of seeing through a customer care programme will have been wasted if measures are not put in place to measure its effectiveness. This is why it is important to have specific objectives and outcomes against which to measure success. Techniques for receiving feedback from customers must be maintained to check whether there are measurable gains from the programme, such as the expected increase in sales or the predicted rise in positive customer response shown in a questionnaire survey.

Customer care in action – the 'Welcome Host' programme

Welcome Host is a training programme devised by the Wales Tourist Board (WTB) with the help of the Training and Enterprise Councils (TECs) in Wales. The programme's aim is to raise the standard of service and hospitality offered to visitors to Wales. Under Welcome Host, staff from a whole range of companies and organisations that come into contact with visitors are given the opportunity to improve their customer service skills and so help the long-term future for tourism in Wales. To date, those who have attended the training seminar include staff from:

- Hotels and guesthouses.
- Restaurants.
- Petrol stations.
- Retail outlets.
- Tourist attractions.
- Leisure facilities.
- Car hire companies.
- Tourist information centres.

The key objectives of Welcome Host are professionalism and pride. The training concentrates on raising the level of communication when dealing with customers and visitors, and focuses on the tourism attractions of the local area. More skill and more knowledge lead to a greater level of professionalism and enjoyment at work.

The WTB considers that the benefits of the Welcome Host programme will be felt not only by those attending the training sessions, but also by the community as a whole. For the community, Welcome Host should:

- Provide increased and improved services for residents and visitors.
- Encourage visitors to stay longer in the community.
- Stimulate repeat business.
- Encourage more spending in the local area.
- Increase visitors' local knowledge and appreciation of heritage and culture.

For local businesses, the Welcome Host programme is designed to:

- Provide better service standards for local consumers.
- Generate increased profits and repeat business.
- Tie into a high profile programme which is nationally recognised.
- Lead to heightened employee pride and sense of responsibility.

- Lower staff turnover and raise staff morale.

During the first 16 months of the programme, over 11,000 people attended Welcome Host training sessions, a number that far exceeded the WTB's target of 4,000 for the first year of operation. Feedback from participants clearly showed that they had found their awareness of the need for offering good customer care had been raised as a result of undertaking the training.

Source: WTB

Establishing a customer care programme

Having investigated the ground rules underlying the introduction of a customer care programme, we must now turn to the detail of the programme itself and the stages that must be gone through in order to ensure success. Figure 3.4 shows the principal stages in carrying through a customer care programme.

We will look in detail at each stage in order to understand how it contributes to the overall success of the programme.

Organisational policy

One of the ground rules we looked at was making sure that the commitment to the customer care programme started at the top of the organisation, in other words it must be embedded into its policy. All organisations nowadays seem to spend a great deal of time developing mission statements setting out the reason for their very existence. This trend seems to be evident in all sectors of leisure and tourism, whether private, public or voluntary sector. Some mission statements are very short; British Airways', for example, is:

> *To be the best and most successful company in the airline industry.*
> (BA Annual Report 1992–3)

The mission of the Wales Tourist Board is somewhat longer:

> *The Board seeks to develop and market tourism in ways which will yield optimum economic and social benefit to the people of Wales.*
> (WTB 1988–93 A Record of Achievement)

British Waterways' mission statement is as follows:

> *Our business is the efficient management of the inland waterways system for the increasing benefit of the nation. We seek to expand business on the waterways by pursuing a commercial approach, providing a safe and high quality environment for customers, staff and local communities, and aiming for excellence in every aspect of our work. The waterways heritage and*

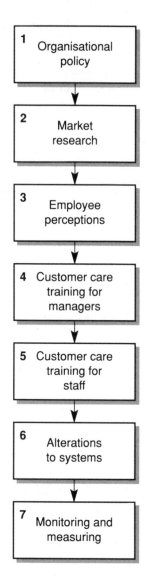

Fig 3.4 Stages in implementing a customer care programme

environment will be conserved, enhanced and made more viable for future generations. (British Waterways Leisure & Tourism Draft Strategy 1992)

Mission statements are important in that they give an indication of what an organisation is trying to achieve; the mission is often followed by specific objectives that will detail how it is to be achieved. Any leisure and tourism organisation committed to excellence in its customer relations should say so in its mission statement and associated objectives. In this way, staff at all levels within the organisation will be sent a clear message on the importance of positive customer relations, and customers will know what to expect.

It is not enough just to develop a mission statement and then forget about it. The mission is a clear public statement that should be used as the basis for future activities by the organisation. It is also essential that the mission is communicated to all staff and that they understand what the organisation is trying to achieve.

Market research

Once the leisure and tourism organisation has developed a mission statement that clarifies its commitment to excellence in customer care, the next stage of the customer care programme, namely market research, can be put into action. It is essential to identify customer needs if we wish to provide them with a high level of customer care. Without market research, management will not have a clear and unbiased view of who its customers are and what it is they are wanting.

Unit 4 looks in depth at identifying customer needs and the techniques that can be used to collect the data. The collection of information on customers invariably involves a survey of some sort, which will collect both factual data (age, sex, employment status, etc.) and customer opinions on the facilities and services they use. Some organisations may wish to know why people do not use their services and may carry out themselves or commission a non-user survey. This may reveal interesting information on why people choose to use rival facilities and services and may prompt management into making changes to its own activities.

It is important to spend time and money on getting the right information on customers; using inaccurate or incorrect information at this early stage of the customer care programme will put into jeopardy all that takes place from this point on.

Employee perceptions

Market research on customers will generate very useful information on their needs, habits and opinions. Just as important to any leisure and tourism organisation striving for excellence in customer care is to know what its own staff think about the organisation and their place within it. If staff feel undervalued and overlooked in their job, it will be difficult to inspire them in any activity aimed at improving customer relations. Depending on the size of the organisation, there are different approaches that can be adopted to discover staff perceptions. A large company or public sector organisation will probably carry out an employee attitude survey. This will often be filled in anonymously so that staff can express their feelings freely without threat of reprisal. A smaller organisation may wish to interview all staff about their work attitudes or conduct a small-scale survey.

Employee attitude surveys should not be filled in just by 'front line' staff but by management as well. A survey may reveal that although the majority of staff are very keen on the idea of improving customer care systems and practices, some senior managers may not be convinced of the merits of the idea. This may highlight the need for changes in management style, which will need to be implemented if the whole drive towards a customer-centred organisation is going to be a success.

Customer care training for managers

Whether or not the surveys of staff attitudes have indicated a need for changes in management style, all managers will need to be trained in their role in implementing a customer care philosophy. Once the initial programme has finished, it will be the job of management to inspire the staff and ensure that the initiative is a success. Although there will undoubtedly be delegation of tasks, they will also be responsible for the monitoring of the programme and its constant refinement. Management will need updating in leadership qualities and team-building techniques to ensure that the customer care programme is a success. The manager will need to be comfortable with people in their workplaces, be a good listener, trusting, open and fair. Management must keep staff fully informed of what is happening and why, which can be done through a combination of short meetings, newsletters and social events.

Customer care training for staff

We have mentioned earlier in this unit that it is a mistake to train only 'front line' staff in customer care improvement; all employees need to feel part of the drive for excellence. There are likely to be two main aims of the customer care staff training in leisure and tourism organisations. The first aim will be to focus all staff on the new company attitude towards its customers, and the second will be to equip staff with the appropriate skills in dealing with customers. The latter will include such things as:

- Communication skills.
- Listening skills.
- Dealing with difficult situations.
- Telephone technique.
- Body language.
- Dealing with customers with special needs.

The training should deal with both internal and external customers and should not be a 'one-off' event; it is important that training in customer care is seen as a continual process. Some organisations use a technique known as 'cascading', with senior management being trained first, then middle management who are in turn responsible for passing on the training to junior managers and staff.

Fig 3.5 Customers expect a high standard of service (courtesy of Eurocamp Travel)

Alterations to systems

All leisure and tourism organisations will have systems in place to handle the day-to-day management issues. A commitment to improving customer relations and the establishment of a customer care programme may expose weaknesses in existing systems which will need amendment. The systems will need to be customer-orientated and not developed solely because they bring benefits to the organisation. Looking at how customers are dealt with from their point of view, will help the management put in place systems that are far more likely to succeed.

It is at this stage in the customer care programme that management may consider pursuing external certification of its systems by going for BS5750/ISO9000 or 'Investors in People'. Having these certificates may give the organisation a 'marketing edge' over the competition, but they require a great deal of dedication, hard work and money to put in place. The British Standard BS5750, for example, will involve the organisation in extensive auditing and documentation of procedures, practices, processes and personnel related to any aspect of quality within the organisation. Some leisure and tourism organisations, regardless of whether they wish to apply for full certification or not, use relevant parts of the BS5750 guidelines when developing customer care systems.

Developing customer-orientated systems for a leisure and tourism organisation can only be totally successful when whoever is doing the development work has an in-depth understanding of the organisation, its mission and its customers. It is only when considerable time has been spent on these three points that the actual development of the systems can take place. Once developed, the systems will need embedding in the organisation and constantly updating to take account of internal changes and improvements.

Monitoring and measuring

Once the customer care programme is up and running, it will need careful monitoring to ensure that a customer focus is being maintained. Left to its own devices, any programme will wither and die. Part of the development of systems mentioned above should be the means to measure the tangible benefits that the programme has generated, e.g. increase in profits, improvement in customer attitude, etc. The whole subject of the monitoring and evaluation of customer care programmes will be dealt with in more detail in the last section of this unit.

Customer care in action – Center Parcs Ltd

Center Parcs originated in Holland 25 years ago when Dutchman Piet Derksen hit on the deceptively simple idea of 'a villa in a forest', where city dwellers could escape from the stresses of everyday life and find real relaxation. The idea was so successful with the Dutch that Center Parcs expanded rapidly and now has 12 sites across Europe, with more in the pipeline.

Center Parcs opened its first UK village in Sherwood Forest in 1987, followed closely by a second at Elvedon Forest near Cambridge. A third village is being developed at Longleat in Wiltshire and is due to open in 1994. The Center Parcs' concept is based on a high quality holiday or short break that cannot be spoiled by the weather (both UK sites have covered leisure pools with controlled temperature and atmosphere). The recipe certainly seems to work, with all villages enjoying over 95 per cent occupancy and 365 days a year opening.

The company's customer care strategy is centred on its mission statement, which is:

> To give our guests a truly unique short break holiday experience which far exceeds their expectations.

In order to achieve its mission, the company has established a number of primary goals, which focus on:

- A visionary approach to creative management.
- Continually striving for the highest standards of product available.
- Having an approach to guest service which is second to none.

- A genuine recognition of its own employees.
- Investing in the business and the personal development of all staff.
- Stimulating repeat business.
- Optimising profitability.
- Maintaining its position as market leader.

The company gives staff training a high priority, with all staff attending a three-day 'caring for people' course, which aims to enable those attending to take personal responsibility for the delivery of excellent guest care. By the end of the course all staff should be able to:

- Understand their contribution to the reputation and success of their department and Center Parcs as a company.
- Identify and utilise the skills necessary to create good guest relations.
- Communicate a professional, approachable image.
- Increase their personal confidence and self-esteem.
- Utilise the skills of promoting/selling the product and service.
- Identify and utilise the skills necessary to effectively handle guest complaints.

Further customer care training deals with issues such as:

- Interpersonal skills.
- Written and oral communication.
- Problem solving.
- Team building.
- Managing people.
- Target setting.

It is clear from the above initiatives that Center Parcs takes customer care training very seriously and is committed to the growth of a culture that stresses excellence in customer relations through individual personal development.

Section 3 Evaluating customer care programmes

Introduction

There is always the danger when a leisure and tourism organisation is implementing a customer care programme that the staff will think their work is over when the programme is finally put in place. In reality, this is far from the case and is likely to be when the hard work really begins! If the staff (and management) see the customer care programme as just another campaign, it will start to falter from day one, and another campaign will need to be launched at a later date.

All those involved with the programme must realise that it is not a 'one-off' but is part of the process of creating a different culture within the organisation, one that has customers as its focus. A customer care programme is not a 'quick fix' that will sweep away all the organisation's problems overnight. Rather it is a process that will take time to achieve its objective of excellence in customer service.

Customers' needs and expectations are constantly changing in the leisure and tourism business, so that any customer care programme must be flexible enough to meet the requirements of an increasingly discerning public.

All of these factors point to the need for constant monitoring and evaluation of the customer care programme to ensure that it is meeting the aims set by the organisation. Monitoring and evaluation is the last link in the chain of customer care, which begins with setting objectives, investigating customer needs, moves through training of staff and managers, and looks at alterations to existing systems. Monitoring is concerned with looking at how the customer care programme is operating in the organisation, where evaluation means measuring its effectiveness. Evaluation is important because: 'If you can't measure it, you can't manage it!'.

Why bother with monitoring and evaluation?

For the leisure and tourism professionals who take quality to their hearts, customer care can become a way of life, even a crusade. Following the route to excellence in customer service may change not only the way they operate at work, but also their whole attitude to life in general, with a greater degree of openness and fairness. Sadly, not all staff within a leisure and tourism organisation may share this same zeal. For example:

- Pressures on senior management may force it to move its commitment away from customer care to some other function.
- Staff may become sceptical about the benefits of a customer-orientated approach.
- There may be breakdowns in communications within the organisation.

It is because of these sorts of problems, which arise when a customer care programme is put into place, that it is essential to monitor and evaluate its effectiveness. Measuring effectiveness allows an organisation to do a number of things:

- Increase customer service awareness.

- Estimate where it stands according to certain criteria.
- Identify strengths and weaknesses.
- Focus efforts.
- Develop training.
- Monitor progress.
- Quantify achievements.
- Reward staff accordingly.

In practice, most organisations use monitoring and evaluation to achieve a mixture of the above points.

The type of questions that should be asked include:

- Are the original objectives of the programme still valid?
- How does performance to date measure against the established criteria?
- What are the successes of the customer care programme?
- How can the organisation build on these successes?
- What are the weaknesses of the programme?
- Have the customers' expectations of service quality changed?
- In which areas do improvements need to be made?
- What are the major priorities for action to put things right?

How is a programme evaluated?

There are three main elements to the evaluation of any customer care programme:

1 Setting performance standards/criteria.
2 Measuring to see if the standards are being met.
3 Putting in place measures to rectify any shortcomings.

1 Setting performance standards

When leisure and tourism organisations strive for excellence in customer care, it soon becomes clear that it is not enough simply to encourage staff to 'treat the customers well'. There comes a point when the management has to define just what 'well' means. Employees need to know the standards against which their performance will be measured. Staff will need both a clear job description and a set of performance standards or performance criteria for each of the tasks they are responsible for.

Many organisations talk at great length about their excellent customer service, but few are prepared to put in place the necessary performance standards to measure objectively just how good their service really is.

Devising and implementing performance standards is a very time-consuming task and one which, if done properly, will call for an investment of financial resources from the organisation. Large leisure and tourism organisations, with extensive personnel and training departments, may well carry out the task themselves. Smaller organisations are likely to appoint a consultant to devise the standards on their behalf or use criteria already available through professional bodies and other industry organisations.

The following example of typical performance standards that could be used in a restaurant, hotel or any catering outlet, show the detail needed for the exercise to be a success.

Example: Typical performance standards in customer service

Staff role: Waiter/waitress.

Task: Serving a light meal or snack to a customer.

Step One: Greeting the customer.

Standards: – Smile pleasantly while you wish the customer a pleasant good morning/afternoon/evening.
– Ask for the customer's order courteously.
– Use the customer's name if you know it to add a touch of warmth.
– Offer the customer a menu if he or she doesn't have one.

Step Two: Taking the customer's order.

Standards: – Be familiar with all items on the menu.
– Ask the customer for his/her order.
– Answer any questions the customer may have precisely and courteously.
– If something is requested which is not on the menu, suggest an alternative.
– Accept any special orders graciously.
– Thank the customer for his of her order and let them know how long the meal will take to prepare.

(Note: This is only a small section of a typical performance standards system)

Superimposed above any detailed performance standards for specific job tasks will be the overall objectives of the customer care programme, which again must be specific and detailed. Examples of objectives of customer care programmes in leisure and tourism could be:

● To achieve a 5 per cent increase in memberships sold for a golf club.
● For a hotel to achieve a 10 per cent increase in bednights sold to customers.
● For a leisure centre to achieve a 10 per cent reduction in the number of complaints.

- To achieve a 10 per cent increase in the 'excellent' category for responses to a customer satisfaction survey.

Using the objectives of the customer care programme and specific performance indicators as the yardsticks against which the effectiveness of the programme can be measured, the organisation is now in a position to consider the most appropriate ways in which the measurement can take place.

2 Measuring to see if the standards are being met

Leisure and tourism is very much a service industry. Whereas a company in the manufacturing sector can reasonably easily set standards for the quality of its products, and measure to see if the standards are being met, this process is much more difficult in an industry so heavily dependent on customer service. However, although a difficult task, it is essential that any leisure and tourism organisation committed to improving customer care must develop systems and procedures to measure the effectiveness of its activities.

Some of the main techniques for measuring to see if standards are being met are:

- Surveys.
- Observation.
- Recording informal feedback.
- Checking financial figures.
- Analysing customer data.

Surveys

Surveys are the most common method of monitoring levels of performance in customer care. An organisation will use a survey as part of a customer care programme to see if the targets it set itself are being achieved in reality. A survey provides a 'snapshot' of an organisation's health at a particular point in time. Surveys are important to management since they measure the satisfaction levels within the organisation and provide crucial information on which decisions can be made.

Surveys as part of a customer care programme can be directed at:

- *Customers* – a survey of visitors at a tourist attraction or a customer satisfaction survey at a leisure centre will provide valuable information about how the customer perceives their leisure experience; how they feel about the standard of service, the attitude of the staff, how any queries have been dealt with, etc.
- *Staff* – it is important to continually seek and act on the views of staff at the 'sharp end' of customer care. Without their continuing support, the programme will not succeed. An employee attitude survey will give them the chance to have their ideas and concerns formally noted. Management will be able to see

if particular concerns are being expressed by more than one individual and act accordingly.

- *'Internal customers'* – we have seen that all staff in an organisation have 'customers', whether or not they deal with the public face to face. Internal customers are colleagues in the same organisation, who may be in a different department, but whose co-operation and support is vital if the move towards excellence in customer care is to be successful. Surveys can be a useful way of establishing whether all departments are happy with the progress of the customer care programme.
- *Management* – the managers in the organisation should be surveyed routinely to see if they are clear on their role in achieving total customer satisfaction. If the management are unclear or unhappy about the culture of the organisation, these fears may be transmitted to other staff and even customers.
- *Non users* – it may be useful to find out why people are not using your facilities but are choosing to spend their money on competitor products and services. Such a survey, which is normally carried out in the street or door to door, may highlight aspects of poor customer service that could be put right.

Observation

Observing what people do and say, whether they are customers, managers or staff, can provide useful feedback on the effectiveness of any customer care programme. It is common for an employee, who has been given clear performance standards to achieve, to be observed in the workplace by his or her line manager. Indeed part of the evaluation process of the programme may be a manager observing his or her staff and recording their progress over a period of time. Staff in certain leisure and tourism organisations may also be tested from time to time by management on such matters as pricing and product knowledge.

Customers may be observed as well as surveyed in order to get a fuller picture of their satisfaction levels. Staff may be given the task of 'mingling' with customers to listen to their views; people are often more open with their comments if they know their answers or reactions are not going to be recorded on a questionnaire. The sectors of the industry where observation of customers is a particularly useful technique include visitor attractions, restaurants and cafes, museums and art galleries.

Recording informal feedback

Any leisure and tourism organisation striving to improve its customer care will go out of its way to seek customers' views in a variety of ways. To give the whole programme credibility in the eyes of the customer, it is vital that their views are listened to and acted upon. There are many occasions in the course of a normal day when staff in leisure and tourism will have the opportunity to receive informal comments from guests, clients and visitors. It is important that staff have the chance to 'pool' this feedback since it can be an invaluable management aid. It may be that staff discussion groups could be held once a week when the informal feedback could be discussed and perhaps recorded. Alternatively, customer feedback sheets could be issued to all staff for them to record the information as it happens.

Checking financial figures

If one objective of the customer care programme is financial, e.g. for a hotel to achieve a 5 per cent increase in conference business within 12 months, measuring to see if this has happened should be a relatively straightforward affair. A check on sales figures should provide the evidence.

Analysing customer data

Data on customers, such as the volume of repeat business, frequency of bookings, satisfaction levels, customer spend, etc., is available both from surveys and internal records. Analysing such information, either manually or with the help of a computer-based system, will allow managers to see if performance standards and specific objectives of the customer care programme are being met.

3 Putting in place measures to rectify any shortcomings

If the process of measuring actual performance against the performance standards shows that targets are not being met, measures to rectify the situation will need to be implemented as soon as possible to maintain the impetus of the customer care programme. The measurement exercise may highlight the need for more training for staff or management, or perhaps alterations to systems in order to improve matters. Once the measures have been put in place, the process of monitoring and evaluation will continue using a mixture of the techniques described above.

Maintaining the momentum

We have seen that the planning, implementation and evaluation of a customer care programme in leisure and tourism is a very complex and time-consuming process. Any faltering on the part of management or staff could lead to the whole exercise failing to meet its objectives. One of the most important tasks for management is to make sure that the momentum of the programme is maintained throughout. Some managers adopt a 'campaign' approach to this by involving staff in devising slogans, having T-shirts, posters and pens printed with the slogans, and arranging extra social and sporting activities within the organisation. Such an approach is particularly useful in the early stages of the customer care programme to build staff loyalty to the scheme.

Managers and staff should not be afraid of publicising achievements within the programme; perhaps a performance standard has not only been met but exceeded. Newsletters and noticeboards should be used to communicate such examples to all staff to help maintain the momentum.

Above all, managers should appreciate what their staff are doing to achieve excellence in customer care and reward them accordingly.

Assignment 3

Situation

You are the newly-appointed Leisure and Tourism Assistant at LeisureTech International, a UK consultancy specialising in customer care in the leisure and tourism industry. LeisureTech has just won the contract to prepare and deliver a customer care training package for the management and staff of Chortlewood District Council Leisure Services Department. The Council has a rapidly expanding leisure and tourism provision for the local community, including:

- A joint-use leisure centre open from 8am until 10pm every day.
- An 18-hole municipal golf course.
- Football and rugby pitches (15 in total).
- Two tourist information centres, open all year round.
- A dry-ski slope attached to the leisure centre.
- A series of countryside leisure areas, one designated a Country Park.

The Head of Chortlewood's Leisure Services Department has recently joined the Council from the private sector and is keen to improve the department's standard of customer service to the community, hence the contract to prepare and deliver the customer care training.

Tasks

Your boss is keen that you become involved in the Chortlewood contract and has asked you to research and prepare a training booklet to be distributed to ALL management and staff in the Leisure Services Department. The title of the booklet is: 'Customer care – how can I help?'.

Your booklet should seek to explain the importance of customer care in the leisure and tourism industry generally, plus the various skills and techniques which will be needed by staff working in the different facilities offered by the Council. The particular needs of different types of customers should also be highlighted.

Revision test questions

1 Who are a leisure and tourism organisation's 'internal customers'?
2 What is a 'customer'?
3 Why is it important to identify customer needs in leisure and tourism?
4 Should staff training in customer service be confined to 'front line' staff only?
5 Give three examples of organisations in leisure and tourism which have invested heavily in customer service training.
6 Give three external factors that have led to an increase in the importance of a customer-centred approach to managing leisure and tourism organisations.
7 What tangible benefits can a leisure and tourism organisation hope to achieve when it embarks on improving its standard of customer service?
8 Give three of the main obstacles to good customer service in leisure and tourism.
9 Give three specific instances in leisure and tourism which may lead to customers complaining.
10 What are the main points to remember when dealing with a complaint?
11 Give three examples of techniques that a leisure and tourism organisation can use to help retain its existing customers.
12 Why is it important to hang on to your existing customers?
13 What are the main 'ground rules' in customer care?
14 Why is it important to look at your organisation from the customers' point of view when planning a customer care programme?
15 What are the main resource implications of planning and implementing a customer care programme?
16 What part can market research play in developing a customer care programme?
17 Should senior management be involved in customer care training?
18 Why is it important to monitor and evaluate a customer care programme?
19 Why is it important to develop performance standards as part of the monitoring and evaluation process?
20 Having set up a customer care programme, how can the management ensure that the staff involved maintain their enthusiasm and commitment?

Unit 4
MARKETING IN LEISURE AND TOURISM

Section 1 Understanding the concept of marketing

What is marketing?

There are many myths in existence concerning the concept of marketing:

- *Marketing is the same as selling* – false! It is true that selling is a vital part of marketing, particularly in leisure and tourism, but it is just that, a part of a much wider process.
- *Marketing is advertising* – false! Advertising is also a very important part of marketing and, since it is the most conspicuous part of the process with millions of pounds spent on TV and press adverts every year, it is understandable that confusion between the two exists.
- *Employing staff with lively personalities will ensure marketing success* – only partly true! A lively personality is a good starting point for training in the promotional aspects of marketing, but activities such as market research, while perhaps not so glamorous, are equally vital to successful marketing.
- *Marketing is only for the private sector* – false! It is now widely accepted that marketing is just as important in the public and voluntary sectors of leisure and tourism; like private sector operators, they too have 'customers'.

The Chartered Institute of Marketing defines marketing as: 'The management process for identifying and satisfying customer needs profitably'.

Let us look at this definition in a little more detail:

1 Being a management process means that marketing ranks alongside personnel,

finance and other management functions in terms of the structure of an organisation. The importance given to marketing within an organisation will depend in part on the nature of the business and the attitude of the management.

2 Identifying customer needs is absolutely crucial for any leisure and tourism organisation that is serious about what it is trying to achieve. Different types of market research activity can be used to find out the likes and dislikes of existing and future customers.

3 Satisfying customer needs is all about developing products and services that the customer will want to buy or use and the various techniques that can be employed to promote their sale or use.

4 Carrying out points 1–3 profitably will ensure that the organisation can survive and indeed grow. As we have seen in Unit 1, private sector leisure and tourism companies will primarily be concerned with making a profit, whereas the public and voluntary sectors will have more social objectives. Marketing must be carried out with the objectives of the organisation very much in mind.

The marketing process can be explained with the help of Figure 4.1.

Fig 4.1 The marketing process simplified

Figure 4.1 shows us that:

1 Any good marketing strategy (the process by which your marketing plans are put into action) should start with the customer as its focus. Knowing who your customers are, where they come from, what they want from your facility, how much they are willing to pay, whether they are satisfied with the service you offer, and so on, provides an invaluable information base on which to make your marketing decisions.

2 Once you know the characteristics of your customers, it is much easier to develop products and services that they will want to use. By giving attention to such matters as pricing and location/accessibility of facilities, you will be able

to give the customer what he or she wants, at the right time, in the right place and at the right price.

3 There are many ways of promoting products and services to the customers, including advertising, direct mail, sponsorship, sales promotions and public relations activity.

4 Marketing is not something that an organisation does once and then forgets about. It is a dynamic activity that reflects the ever changing tastes and fashions of the general public. It is essential, therefore, that all leisure and tourism organisations evaluate what they are doing at each stage of the marketing process, by asking such questions as:

- Are our customers the same today as they were three years ago?
- Does our mix of activities meet their needs today?
- Is our promotional work reaching its intended target?
- What are our competitors doing?

It is only by constantly monitoring events that the marketeer can be sure of success.

What's special about marketing in the leisure and tourism sector?

Much of the early development of marketing theory was carried out in the USA, based predominantly on 'products' rather than 'services'; the FMCG sector (fast-moving consumer goods, e.g. food) and the marketing techniques developed around it, formed the basis of much of the early work. It is only in the last 25 years or so that study of the marketing of services has taken off, with insurance and financial services to the fore. The lessons learnt from these sectors were applied to tourism initially, reflecting the private sector nature of much of the industry, and eventually to leisure which was perceived as being public sector orientated and, therefore, 'not really concerned with marketing'; much has changed since the early days!

Being a service industry, the marketing of leisure and tourism has similarities with marketing in other sectors, notably retail. However, leisure and tourism has certain characteristics that are specific and which, when taken together, give marketing within this sector a special character. To begin with, leisure and tourism products are perishable (a 30-minute slot on the squash court not sold today, cannot be resold tomorrow). Also, much activity is seasonal, which poses a particular challenge to the leisure and tourism marketeer. Above all, however, leisure and tourism marketing differs from so many other service sectors in that it is often all about 'selling dreams'. We shall see later in this unit that many products are intangible; you are not actually buying the holiday, for example, when you hand over your money to the travel company, but an expectation of what you hope to experience on that holiday.

Market versus product orientation

We have seen the importance of putting the customer at the heart of the marketing process; this is known as market orientation (as opposed to product orientation, which focuses on the products being developed rather than their intended buyers). Organisations within leisure and tourism must adopt this notion of market orientation at all levels if they are to be successful in keeping their existing customers and attracting new ones. Companies such as British Airways, Virgin and Mecca Leisure all adopt practices that put the customer first, while public sector providers, including British Rail, train many of their staff in improving customer service.

Marketing objectives

Different organisations will have different aims and objectives, and their marketing style and practice will tend to reflect this (the size of the marketing budget will also influence what is done and how it is carried out). A large multi-national hotel chain, for example, may make extensive use of various 'aggressive' sales techniques (telesales, for example) in order to achieve maximum capacity in its hotels. A travel agent is likely to take a more 'low key' approach to selling by perhaps sending a quarterly newsletter to all existing clients. A leisure centre run by the local council, whose primary aim is the provision of a service to the local community, will use local newspapers, leaflet drops and local radio to get its message across. Voluntary groups may be able to secure the services of well-known personalities free of charge to help their promotional work and they may be able to get 'free' editorial coverage in the local and national press.

Strategic versus tactical marketing

Strategic marketing is marketing activity that is planned well in advance and has clear medium- and long-term objectives, e.g. becoming the number one tour operator from the UK to the USA or increasing the use of a sports centre by 50 per cent within 12 months. Tactical marketing is marketing activity that is unforeseen and unplanned and carried out in response to a particular problem or action by a competitor. Examples of tactical marketing activity include the need for extra advertising, promotional and public relations work that Townsend Thoreson was obliged to undertake following the Herald of Free Enterprise tragedy, and the relaunch of brochures by a tour operator that suddenly finds its prices have been undercut by a rival company. In an increasingly competitive marketplace, tactical marketing has to be used extensively by leisure and tourism organisations simply to hold on to their existing market share.

The changing business environment

Some people say that the only constant thing in life is change! Leisure and tourism organisations today operate in highly complex environments where the pace of change is quicker than it has ever been. This makes the role of marketing within leisure and tourism even more important since it involves understanding this changing environment and mobilising the organisation's resources to deliver the goods and services that the customers want.

For ease of understanding, the business environment is sometimes divided into the internal (micro) environment and the external (macro) environment.

Internal (micro) environment

This concerns those influences and factors that are close to an organisation and over which it has some degree of control. For example:

- *Customers* – customers can be influenced, to some degree, in their purchasing habits but, at the end of the day, if they are unhappy with the product on offer or the level of service they receive, they may not come back again.
- *Staff* – in the service sector, the role of staff is vital in determining success or failure. Given the right management style, adequate training, a supportive environment and fair pay, most staff will rise to the challenges to be found in abundance in the leisure and tourism sector.
- *Suppliers* – these may be suppliers of food products for the catering side of an operation, suppliers of services such as printers, trainers or cleaners, distributors or wholesalers. They must be made aware of how their product or service fits into the overall structure of the organisation and of the importance of quality and customer care.

External (macro) environment

There are certain influences outside the control of most leisure and tourism organisations but which are likely to have a direct bearing on how they survive and expand. These external factors include:

- *Competitors* – although its competitors are usually well-known to an organisation, having any control over their activities is difficult if not impossible in our democratic society. A competitor may be somebody offering exactly the same facility as yours. On the other hand, competition may come from another facility within the leisure and tourism sector, e.g. a city centre cinema will be in competition with local restaurants to try and attract customers during their leisure time. In a wider sense, spending on leisure goods and services is in direct competition with other household expenditure, such as spending on food, clothing and energy.

- *Demographics* – these are factors concerned with the age structure and other characteristics of the population as a whole. In general, people in Britain are living longer, fewer couples are having children and women are having children later in life. All such factors are important in the marketing of leisure and tourism products.

- *Economics* – the state of the economy is one of the most important influences on leisure and tourism spending. In a recession, patterns of buyer behaviour change; for example people eat out less but spend more on 'convenience' foods to eat at home. It is the marketeers job to respond to these variations.

- *Politics* – factors such as taxation policy, regional grants and political stability will all influence the leisure and tourism sector and affect demand.

- *Environment* – recent growth in the concern for, and interest in, the environment is a powerful influence on customers' habits and spending patterns and must be taken into account by marketing personnel.

- *Technology* – rapid developments in technology in leisure and tourism mean that the customer expects instant decisions on such things as bookings and availability of services and products.

SWOT analysis

One of the most common ways for an organisation to establish exactly where it stands in the business environment is to carry out a SWOT analysis (**S**trengths, **W**eaknesses, **O**pportunities, **T**hreats). One example from each of these categories for a typical local authority leisure centre might be:

Strength – the only centre in the locality with a wave machine.

Weakness – only half of the staff have had formal training in customer care.

Opportunity – to develop fitness training sessions for a new Japanese company recently located in the area.

Threat – council budgets may have to be cut by 5 per cent overall next year and the leisure services department may have to bear the brunt of the savings.

A SWOT analysis will indicate where an organisation is and the direction it must take in order to be successful.

Section 2 Identifying customer needs

Introduction

In Unit 3, we saw how vital it is for any leisure and tourism organisation to put the customer at the centre of all its activity and to develop a market- or customer-orientated culture. Organisations that fail to understand or implement this concept will not flourish in the highly competitive leisure and tourism sector of the economy.

In order to be able to put the customer as the hub of all activity, the organisation will need to have certain basic information on the characteristics of its customers, such as:

1 How many are there?
2 What ages are they?
3 Are they male or female?
4 How far do they travel to get to you?
5 What level of income do they have?
6 What is their attitude to your facility?
7 How long do they spend at the facility?
8 How much money do they spend at the facility?

Why is this sort of information important?

Without this basic data, any leisure and tourism organisation, be it a leisure centre, museum, art gallery, country house hotel or visitor attraction, will be basing its management decisions purely on guesswork; sometimes referred to as 'seat of the pants' management! Decisions on pricing, design of promotional material, advertising media used and choice of menus can only be carried out effectively with accurate knowledge of present and future customers.

Customers and markets

In the leisure and tourism industry, the term 'customer' means different things to different people. In the private sector, customers are quite obviously those individuals and groups who buy leisure goods and services; anything from a meal in a restaurant to a two-hour bingo session or a two-week holiday in the USA. In the public and voluntary sectors, the definition of a 'customer' is not quite so easy. Those who pay to use a local authority leisure centre are certainly customers, but so are those who use services for which there is no charge, such as the playground at the local park. Although there may be no direct charge for the playground, the people will have indirectly contributed to its cost by paying central and local taxes. Members of voluntary bodies, such as the RSPB or YHA, are again 'customers' of their particular organisation. They too must be treated with courtesy and respect, since without them, the organisation would not exist.

Businesses often talk about the market for a particular product; this is the total number of people who currently buy or use a particular product or service (potential market is the number of people who could consume, given the right circumstances). In the private sector, the total market is usually expressed in financial terms. For example, Table 4.1 shows the estimated values of selected UK markets in 1988.

Table 4.1 Estimated value of selected UK markets 1988

Item	£ million
New motor cars	17,000
Beer	9,793
Cigarettes	7,001
Casinos	1,722
Instant coffee	573
Ice cream	486
Disposable nappies	330
British people's spending on holidays	12,880
Overseas visitors' spending in the UK	7,065
Spending by British on all leisure activities	76,060

Source: Various, including Leisure Consultants and Social Trends

The table shows that large sums of money are spent by people in Britain during their leisure time. Examples and data given in Unit 1 suggest that spending on leisure is set to go on increasing up to and beyond the year 2000.

The size of the market for a particular facility, for example a theme park, can be calculated reasonably accurately by using population statistics readily available to the general public. Census data will indicate numbers of households and numbers of people by age groups. By calculating the population within different travel time zones, the attraction will have a good indication of its total market.

Private sector operators in leisure and tourism are constantly trying to increase, or at least maintain, their market share in an increasingly competitive environment.

Are all customers the same?

If we start from the point of view that everybody is unique, then the number and range of customers for any leisure and tourism product is immense. The characteristics of customers (e.g. their age, social class and income level) will be different at different leisure and tourism facilities and their habits, tastes and even moods will change constantly over time and in different locations (generally most British people feel better when in a sunny climate). Customers' expectations will also differ depending on, for example, their education, religion and cultural background.

An important group of customers are those with special needs; the elderly, young children, disabled people and ethnic minorities, will all need particular attention.

Because customers are so different, a number of attempts have been made to classify them or put them into different categories in order to simplify the process of providing data for marketing purposes. Three of the best-known classification techniques are:

1 Socio-economic classification.
2 Life cycle classification.
3 Lifestyle classification.

We will look at each of these in a little more detail.

Socio-economic classification

For many years, this JICNARS (Joint Industry Committee for National Readership Surveys) classification based on 'social class' was the only one available to marketeers. Individuals were placed into one of six categories according to the occupation of the head of the household (see Table 4.2).

The underlying principle of the socio-economic classification is that those in each category will have similar values, display similar patterns of buyer behaviour and have similar levels of disposable income. It is assumed, also, that those at the top of the scale will have the highest level of disposable income. Clearly, there are a number of anomalies in this classification system:

- It is too much of a generalisation to expect all those in a particular category to have similar characteristics. For example, a surgeon (social grade A) may choose to read the *Daily Mirror*, a newspaper read mostly by working class people (social grade D).
- If the Managing Director of a large PLC loses her job, she will immediately move from social grade A to social grade E.
- Many skilled manual workers (C2) may well have a higher disposable income than those in the C1, B or A social grades when payment for items such as private education and private health care are taken into account.

Table 4.2 Socio-economic classification

Social grade	Social class	Typical occupations
A	Upper Middle	Higher managerial, admin. and professional (e.g. judges, surgeons)
B	Middle	Intermediate managerial and admin. (e.g. lawyers, teachers, doctors)
C1	Lower Middle	Supervisory, clerical, junior management (e.g. bank clerk, estate agent)
C2	Skilled Working	Skilled manual workers (e.g. joiner, welder)
D	Working	Semi- and unskilled manual workers (e.g. driver, postman, porter)
E	Those at lowest level of subsistence	Pensioners, widows, casual workers, students, the unemployed

- When the whole social fabric of the nation is changing so rapidly, it is even questionable who the head of household is. Today, the heads of many households will be unemployed and in receipt of state benefits.

Life cycle classification

The shortcomings of the socio-economic classification led marketeers to investigate if there wasn't a better way of categorising segments of the population. The life cycle concept puts an individual into one of nine categories, which are based not on income but on where that person is on his or her life cycle. The categories, with an indication of their likely demand for leisure and tourism products, are:

1 *Bachelor stage* – young single people with few ties and a reasonable level of disposable income. Likely to frequent clubs, discos, bars and buy CDs and tapes.
2 *Newly-wed/living together* – possibly a higher disposable income with leisure pursuits such as going to the cinema, eating out and going to clubs.
3 *Full nest 1* – young marrieds/living together with youngest child less than six. Beginnings of family-orientated leisure including visits to the park, tourist attractions and family holidays.
4 *Full nest 2* – as above but youngest child over six. Falling disposable income, less spending on leisure.
5 *Full nest 3* – older couples with dependent children, perhaps still studying. Disposable income low. Leisure centred on the home.
6 *Empty nest 1* – older couples, childless or children all left home. Level of disposable income likely to be restored. Demand for short breaks, overseas travel and active leisure.

7 *Empty nest 2* – older couples, chief breadwinner retired. Income again restricted. Avid watchers of the television and listeners to the radio.

8 *Solitary survivor 1* – single/widowed person in work. Home and garden likely to provide most leisure activity.

9 *Solitary survivor 2* – as above but retired. Little spare cash for leisure.

Lifestyle classification

A further refinement of the process of categorisation came with the introduction in Britain during the 1980s of the concept of lifestyle classification, a technique which had been previously used in North America. One of the first British companies to test the concept was Young and Rubicam, a well-known advertising agency, who developed a lifestyle classification known as the '4 Cs'; four classes of people who were categorised according to their innermost needs into one of the following:

1 *Mainstreamers* – people who are looking for security and who live a conventional lifestyle. They usually buy well-known brands of products, such as Heinz, Daz and Fairy Liquid, rather than 'own brands'. Mainstreamers do not want to 'stick out from the crowd'. They are by far the largest of the four groups, accounting for around 40 per cent of the British population. Their leisure habits are rather conventional including reading, gardening, knitting and walking in the country.

2 *Aspirers* – these are people looking for status and who like to be thought of as being 'at the cutting edge' of society. They buy status symbols such as fast cars and expensive jewellery and generally like the good things in life. They are risk-takers and many aspirers run their own businesses. Leisure interests include hang-gliding, motor sports, power boating, karate and listening to hi-fi music.

3 *Succeeders* – these are people who have already achieved status and who ultimately like to be in control of their lives. They have no need for status symbols but value quality in all that they purchase. Leisure interests include gardening, entertaining, taking short breaks and playing golf.

4 *Reformers* – these are people who consider that 'quality of life' is more important than status and status symbols. They are the best educated of all four groups and tend to join groups to influence decision making in society. They buy many natural products and 'own label' products; they are sometimes referred to as 'the Sainsbury shoppers'! Leisure is often family orientated and includes camping, walking, cycling, reading and playing games.

Why do we need to classify people at all?

This technique of subdividing the market into different groups who share similar characteristics is known as market segmentation. One of the main benefits of segmenting the market for a particular leisure or tourism product, for example, is that it allows an organisation to target particular individuals or groups within the segment. These people then become the focus of all the marketing effort, with the design and promotion of products and services that they will want.

Segmentation within leisure and tourism happens at a number of different levels:

1 The whole leisure and tourism industry can be segmented into a range of different sectors, e.g. tourism, sport, arts, entertainment, community recreation, heritage, etc.
2 An individual sector can be segmented, e.g. tourism can be divided into accommodation, transportation and attractions.
3 Individual elements of a sector can be further segmented, e.g. accommodation can be broken down into serviced and self-catering.
4 At a fourth level of segmentation, serviced accommodation can be divided into hotels, guesthouses, inns, motels, etc.
5 Further segmentation of hotels by the type of guests, e.g. business clients, groups, short break clients, conference delegates, overseas visitors, etc.

Market segmentation is, therefore, a tool that the marketeer can use to satisfy the requirements of his or her particular customers. Being concerned with the needs of customers, however, does mean that segmentation relies heavily on market research to help match the product exactly to the clients' needs.

Market research

What is market research?

Market research is the collection and analysis of data about customers and its use for management purposes. The term marketing research has gained favour in recent years and is an all-embracing phrase to include product research, promotion research and price research. Research into customers, which is the subject of this particular section, is rightly called market research, and this is the terminology which will be used.

Market research data, from whatever source, is invaluable to the manager in providing a sound base on which effective marketing decisions can be made. All leisure and tourism organisations need feedback from their existing customers and many will want to know why people are not using their facilities but prefer what a competitor is providing. It is the job of market research to provide such data in as objective a form as possible, in other words with no bias. This is why many leisure and tourism organisations will employ outside specialists to carry out the research on their behalf. Not all market research activity is a costly or elaborate affair. The proprietor of a small hotel will constantly get informal feedback from his guests on their opinion of his facilities and service level and will make the necessary adjustments. What he doesn't always know, of course, are the opinions of the people who say nothing; the British are notoriously reticent about complaining, so that an anonymous questionnaire or suggestions form may produce more reliable and honest information.

Types and sources of market research information

There are many different sources of market research data available to those managing and planning leisure and tourism facilities, some of it very general, such as statistics on trends in the population structure, and some specific to particular sectors of the industry, for example data on the number of visitors to tourist attractions.

Material that is already available, through many different published sources, is known as secondary data. If the particular information is not available from existing sources, then it will be necessary to collect primary data. Figure 4.2 shows the different types of primary and secondary data available within leisure and tourism.

Secondary Data	
Internal Sources	*External Sources*
Membership lists	Census data
Visitor information records	Professional bodies, e.g. ILAM
Sales returns	Trade directories
Gate receipts	Trade associations, e.g. ABTA
Customer database	Annual reports, e.g. BTA,
	Sports Council, Arts Council

Primary Data
Conducting a survey
Observation
Focus groups

Fig 4.2 Market research sources in leisure and tourism

Much of the information that an organisation needs for marketing purposes may already be held within its various departments; this is what is meant by internal sources. Information found outside the organisation (external sources) is useful in giving a general picture of the state of a particular market or sector of the market. Collecting primary data about customers in leisure and tourism generally involves either direct observation, such as counting traffic or observing visitor flow patterns at a tourist attraction, or conducting a survey of one kind or another, e.g. asking hotel guests to complete a questionnaire to find out if they were happy with the facilities and service.

The collection of primary research data

If an organisation wishes to collect information not already available, or wants to update previous information, it will need to collect primary data, either through observation, by carrying out a survey or through the use of focus groups.

Observation

Observation is a very useful, and often neglected, form of primary data collection in leisure and tourism. It does not always involve people actually watching what others do and recording the details systematically. Nowadays, there are sophisticated techniques available for counting and recording customer and traffic flows, such as time-lapse photography, closed circuit television (CCTV) and electronic tally counters. Particular examples of the use of observation in leisure and tourism include:

- A tourist information centre using an electronic tally counter to record the number of people using the TIC.
- A large visitor attraction using CCTV to record visitor flows around the site.
- A museum using time-lapse photography to examine visitor movements.
- A large sports complex installing an electronic traffic counter to help traffic management and ease congestion.

Clearly, such equipment can be very useful for security purposes as well.

When people are employed to carry out observation, rather than relying on electronic means of collection, they are often able to collect useful information on customer attitudes to a particular facility by 'mingling' with them but not revealing their identity or purpose.

Carrying out a survey

There are three main types of survey used to collect primary data, all of which involve the recording of responses on a questionnaire:

1 *Face-to-face interview survey* – this is usually the most effective way of gathering information on customers. As its name implies, a trained interviewer will ask

questions of a respondent (the person being interviewed) and record the responses on a questionnaire. Although one of the best methods for getting in-depth information, since the interviewer can prompt the respondent if he or she is unclear as to the meaning of a particular question, face-to-face interviewing is very labour intensive and, therefore, expensive. The interviews can take place in a number of different locations:

- At home.
- In the street.
- At the facility (e.g. at a tourist attraction).
- *En route* to a facility (e.g. on board ship).
- At work.

Leisure and tourism organisations will often employ specialists to carry out an interview survey on their behalf so that any bias is kept to a minimum.

One of the most useful face-to-face interview surveys, which is used exten-sively in leisure and tourism facilities, is the visitor survey. Leisure centres, hotels, tourist attractions, catering outlets and entertainment complexes all use the information from visitor surveys to help develop products and services that will appeal to their customers. By asking the relevant questions, a visitor sur-vey can also indicate which media to use in promoting the facilities.

2 *Self-completed questionnaire survey* – this is a cheaper method of data collection since respondents are asked to fill in the questionnaires themselves, meaning that there is no need to employ and train interviewers. A self-completed ques-tionnaire does have the disadvantage, however, that if the respondent is unclear about a particular question, there is nobody to prompt him or her. With this type of survey, there are again different locations and methods by which the data is gathered:

3 *Postal survey* – this is a very common method in leisure and tourism involving the posting back of a completed questionnaire that may have been distributed in a number of ways:

- Through the postal system – some tour operators mail a questionnaire to clients soon after they return home.
- Given out on the return journey from a holiday, perhaps on the flight home.
- Picked up 'on-site', e.g. at a sports centre, hotel or tourist attraction and posted when completed.

4 *Full 'on-site' survey* – this is the cheapest self-completed survey of all since the respondents are asked not only to complete the questionnaire while they are at the facility, but also to leave it behind, often in a sealed box, before they leave. Cost is minimal as there are no postal charges involved.

5 *Telephone survey* – while not widespread in leisure and tourism, telephone sur-veys are growing rapidly as a way of getting a quick response to an event or activity. In the leisure and tourism industry they are most commonly used in the commercial sector and often on a business-to-business basis. For example,

the organisers of the annual British Travel Trade Fair (formerly MOOT) use the technique to contact exhibitors and trade visitors immediately after the event to gauge their reactions and comments. Hotels and other conference venues will often use telephone surveys to get feedback on the standard of service and facilities at a particular venue.

Focus groups

Focus groups are the bringing together of a small group of individuals under the guidance of a facilitator, often trained in psychology. It gives the facilitator a chance to delve into people's innermost thoughts and values with a view to exploring the influences that affect their purchasing decisions, e.g. what makes them go to restaurant A rather than restaurant B, and so on. Focus groups often produce very valuable information that cannot easily be gathered from either a face-to-face interview or self-completed questionnaire. British Rail used the focus group technique in the early 1980s to investigate ways of improving its Inter City rail services.

Survey methods

There are a number of important points that relate to how surveys are carried out using any of the methods just described. These include:

1 *Qualitative versus quantitative data* – an organisation must be clear about what it hopes to achieve by carrying out a survey. If it is only interested in factual (quantitative) information (how many visitors, how far have they travelled, how much have they spent, etc.), then a simple visitor survey based on a self-completed questionnaire would be sufficient. If, however, more in-depth opinions (qualitative) are sought, face-to-face interviews and focus groups would be more appropriate.

2 *Sampling* – in most cases it is not feasible to survey everybody who uses a particular leisure and tourism facility or buys particular products. It is, therefore, necessary to select a proportion of the total number known as a sample. Large samples produce more accurate results than small ones, but the increase in accuracy becomes less and less significant as the sample size is increased. Sophisticated statistical procedures are used to ensure that the sample is representative of the whole group and that there is no bias in selection.

3 *Questionnaire design* – we look in more detail at the task of designing questionnaires in Unit 10, but it is important to remember that it is an acquired skill best left to the professional! Questionnaires generally include a mix of factual and opinion questions and a number of 'profile' questions (age, sex, marital status, occupation, etc.) to give a clearer picture of the respondent.

Where to now?

Having made the decision to adopt a culture that puts the customer at the heart of all its activity, any leisure and tourism organisation, whether private, public or voluntary sector, will be well aware of the need for good customer feedback using one, or a mixture, of the market research techniques described above. Once it has this data, it can then begin to develop products that satisfy customer need, and it is this area of leisure and tourism products that we shall look at next.

Section 3 Products in leisure and tourism

In Unit 1 we looked in detail at the main UK leisure and tourism products and how each fits into the often complex 'jigsaw' of the leisure and tourism industry. We saw that products where either naturally-occurring or man-made, and provided in the private, public and voluntary sectors.

This section will put leisure and tourism products into the wider context of an organisation's total marketing activity by looking first at the marketing mix.

The marketing mix in leisure and tourism

The marketing mix is one of the most important concepts in marketing today. It is commonly referred to as the 'four Ps':

- Product.
- Price.
- Place.
- Promotion.

Just as the ingredients must be in the correct quantities to make a successful cake, so the four ingredients of the marketing mix must be in the right proportions to make an organisation's marketing activity successful. Different leisure and tourism providers will vary the emphasis between the four Ps to meet their particular objectives. For example:

- A newly-opened hotel will spend a lot on promotion to attract customers.
- A tour operator who has just discovered that a major competitor has undercut its prices by 5 per cent may restructure its prices in order to remain competitive.
- A visitor attraction which notices that it is receiving 50 per cent more school

parties than it had anticipated may need to look again at its product to see if the needs of this important sector are being met.
- Market research for a major leisure company shows that there is an upsurge in electronic games played at home. It decides to shift resources from its chain of fast-food outlets into home-based leisure to exploit this demand.

The above examples show that emphasis on the elements of the marketing mix will vary over time, as well as between the various sectors of the industry.

We shall now look in more detail at the four components of the marketing mix.

Product

The leisure and tourism 'product' is very different from many other products that we buy and use. The term 'product' is something of a misnomer since leisure and tourism is a service industry; it is true that a set of golf clubs, a garden spade or football shirt are all products in the strict sense of the word, but the bulk of the leisure and tourism sector is concerned with the customer's experience and how the many elements of the sector are delivered to the customer. Below are a few examples of leisure and tourism products:

- Short breaks.
- Leisure centres.
- Nature reserves.
- Sports facilities.
- Museums.
- Holidays.
- Art galleries.
- Sports equipment.
- Events.
- A 30-minute session on the squash court.

As you can see, some products are tangible, i.e. you can touch sports equipment and see a leisure centre and its facilities. However, many leisure and tourism products cannot be seen and are, therefore, intangible. You can't, for example, see or touch a session on the squash court or a short break holiday, but you can experience it. It is this aspect of intangibility which makes leisure and tourism products so different.

It could be argued that the tangible products, such as hotels, leisure centres, tourist attractions, etc., are simply the facilities in which the intangible products are experienced; for example, the session on the squash court may well take place in a leisure centre, and the short break may well involve staying at a hotel.

As well as being intangible, leisure and tourism products are also perishable; an airline seat or ticket to an event not sold today cannot be resold tomorrow.

Leisure and tourism products are also non-standardised. In other words, it is difficult to guarantee the same experience every time. A tour operator, for example, does not have control over all the elements of a package holiday. This highlights the importance of quality control in leisure and tourism.

Products in leisure and tourism also tend to be unpredictable and fragile. A customer treated badly in a leisure centre, for example, may 'vote with his feet' and go elsewhere. Training in customer care is, therefore, essential for a successful organisation.

Branding

Many leisure and tourism products are given brand names, e.g. Reebok, Slazenger, Thomson, Happy Eater and Harvester, to name but a few. A brand name gives a product a certain identity, which, when coupled with promotional activities such as advertising and direct mail, helps persuade the customer to buy that particular product. Many customers show brand loyalty, meaning that they will only buy a particular brand above all others. Branding is often linked to the concept of segmentation, with brands being developed to meet the needs of a particular segment of the market. One of the best examples of this is the wide range of products on offer from Thomson Holidays. Their brands range from 'Small and Friendly', through 'Thomson Cities' to 'A la Carte'.

The product life cycle

All products, whether they are in the leisure and tourism sector or the consumer goods market, have a lifespan. There will come a time when the product is no longer in demand at all, or needs remodelling in some way to keep its customers. We are all familiar with the rise and fall of products such as the 'chopper' bike and ten-pin bowling. The product life cycle concept argues that all products go through similar stages during their useful life, as shown in Figure 4.3.

The figure shows that the five stages in the product life cycle are:

1 *Launch* – the product is launched with heavy promotional effort, which hopefully results in encouraging sales (or encouraging use in the case of a non-commercial activity).
2 *Growth* – sales grow steadily with increasing profits for the commercial organisation.
3 *Maturity* – sales begin to decline. Perhaps competitors are offering a product with greater benefits. It is often at this point that the organisation will need to decide to either let the product die, remodel it or increase marketing support to generate more sales.
4 *Saturation* – sales have reached a plateau.
5 *Decline* – sales are dropping off quickly.

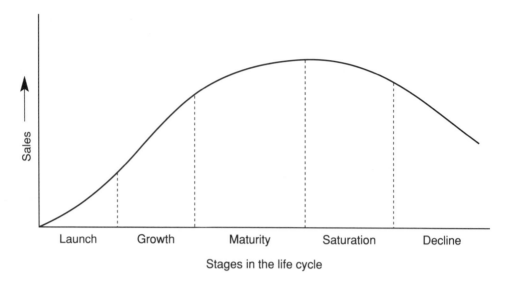

Fig 4.3 *The product life cycle in leisure and tourism*

The product life cycle – holidays to Majorca

The way that the number of visitors to Majorca has evolved since the mid-1970s is often thought of as a classic example of the product life cycle concept. After 15 years of steady growth, Majorca began to see a drop in its number of overseas visitors in the late 1980s, with a 6 per cent fall between 1988 and 1989. Many people thought the island had reached 'maturity' on the product life cycle. The main reasons for this were given as:

- An overdependence on UK and German markets, who account for 70 per cent of all overseas visitors.
- Greater competition from Eastern Mediterranean and 'long haul' destinations, e.g. the Caribbean, Far East and Australia.
- An over dependence on the package tour market (high volume/low yield).
- Lack of investment in infrastructure.
- An excess supply of one- to three-star accommodation when people were demanding four-star facilities.
- Poor image, e.g. overcrowded, too British, 'lager louts', noisy, etc.
- Deterioration of the environment particularly through unplanned hotel construction.

The public and private sector have put forward a number of solutions to try and hold on to the visitors they have and begin to tempt new customers. Among these are the following:

- Widening the 'customer mix' by extra promotion in countries such as The Netherlands, Scandinavia, Italy and Spain itself.
- Advertising campaigns highlighting 'the other Majorca'; the island is more than one or two lively resorts and can offer a relaxing holiday in natural surroundings, with activities such as walking and birdwatching
- More controls on hotel development.
- Improving the quality of the product; £8 million spent in Palma Nova/Magaluf alone on environmental improvements.
- New golf complexes aimed at high-spending tourists.

The next 5–10 years will show whether these improvements will have the desired effect of halting the drop in overseas visitors to Majorca.

Programming

Programming is an often overlooked element of marketing within the leisure and tourism sector. It is most commonly associated with leisure and sports centres, but is equally applicable to theatres, local community centres or a concert hall. In tourism, tour programmes are devised to meet particular customer needs.

Programming is all about making sure that a facility is used to its full capacity at all times and, certainly in the public and voluntary sectors, is used by as wide a cross-section of the local community as possible. It involves planning, scheduling, timetabling and implementing action and should take into account not only the needs of customers but also the availability and expertise of staff and the physical resources at the organisation's disposal. Figure 4.4 shows the programme of usage at Pond's Forge International Sports Centre in Sheffield.

Programming will help to eliminate any problems concerning the competition for use of facilities by clubs or societies and use by individuals. It will also allow better off-peak use of facilities by those customers with flexibility in their leisure time.

Price

The pricing of products and services is a crucial aspect of the marketing mix. Price is just as important as place, product or promotion; if the price is wrong, no amount of advertising or other promotional work will make the customer buy the product. Getting the price right in leisure and tourism is no easy task. The fact that it is a service industry and that most of its products are intangible makes pricing difficult. It is an industry where it is customary to charge different amounts for the same product at different times of the year and even different times of the day. An all-inclusive family French camping holiday with Eurosites, for example, will cost nearly £500 more in August than the same package in late September. Similarly, a round of golf at the local municipal course may well cost more on a Sunday morning when compared to a Tuesday afternoon. Pricing in leisure and tourism, therefore, is often related to demand.

PONDS FORGE INTERNATIONAL SPORTS CENTRE : INTERNATIONAL HALL

		SIDE 1 - SEATING					SIDE 2 - SCOREBOARD						
SESSION		**1**	**2**	**3**	**4**	**5**	**6**	**7**	**8**	**9**	**10**	**ROTUNDA**	**FUNCTION SUITE**
1	8.45 - 9.30am												**A**	**B**
2	9.30 -10.15am	SCHOOL BOOKINGS					ACTIVE LIFESTYLE (Women's day)					EQUIPMENT SET UP		
3	10.15 -11.00am													
4	11.00 -11.45am											EDUCATIONAL GYMNASTICS		
5	11.45 -12.30pm	AERO STEP												
6	12.30 - 1.15pm						PUBLIC BADMINTON						Business Bookings	
7	1.15 - 2.00pm	BADMINTON												
8	2.00 - 2.45pm	SHEFFIELD UNIVERSITY STUDENTS UNION					SHEFFIELD UNIVERSITY STUDENTS UNION					EDUCATIONAL GYMNASTICS		
9	2.45 - 3.30pm													
10	3.30 - 4.15pm													
11	4.15 - 5.00pm													
12	5.00 - 5.45pm	BADMINTON					BADMINTON							
13	5.45 - 6.30pm	ADVANCED AEROBICS/ CIRCUIT TRAINING					CORPORATE 5@ SIDE BOOKINGS					KARATE		
14	6.30 - 7.15pm													
15	7.15 - 8.00pm													
16	8.00 - 8.45pm													SELF DEFENCE FOR WOMEN
17	8.45 - 9.30pm	PUBLIC BADMINTON										FENCING CLUB		
18	9.30 - 10.15pm													

Fig 4.4 A typical programme at Ponds Forge International Sports Centre, Sheffield *(courtesy Ponds Forge)*

Price is also closely allied to value, a concept that is notoriously difficult to define since it varies so much between individuals. Some people put a very high value on a particular leisure pursuit, while others will not be interested at all and it is clearly of little value to them. Value will also fluctuate according to particular circumstances; windsurfing on a local lake in high summer will have a greater value than the same activity taking place in the freezing temperatures of February.

Pricing is clearly a far more complex subject than simply adding up all the costs associated with providing a product or service, then adding a small margin of profit. The idea of what something is worth to the individual comes into play, a feature that will influence the amount he or she is willing to pay.

Before we look at some of the methods used to price leisure and tourism products, it is important to understand some of the factors that influence pricing.

● *Costs* – it is important for the organisation to be aware of the costs of providing a particular product or service when deciding on its price. This may, however, only be the starting point of a much more complex pricing policy revolving around many of the concepts discussed above.

- *Demand* – we have shown that the same product can command a higher price at different times according to customer demand. People will often pay high prices for exclusivity, e.g. a trip on the Orient Express or a flight on Concorde.
- *Competition* – in the highly competitive leisure and tourism industry, an organisation will need to be aware of what competitors are charging and adjust its own prices accordingly.
- *State of the economy* – in times of recession, products may be reduced in price in order to gain revenue, e.g. hotel rooms are heavily discounted, particularly at weekends when the use by business clients is low, on the assumption that it is better to get a little income for the rooms rather than nothing at all if they are left empty.
- *Objectives of the organisation* – clearly a private sector company will need to maximise revenue and will try to set prices which help achieve this objective. Public sector and voluntary bodies may be able to offer more concessionary prices to achieve their social aims.

Pricing policies in leisure and tourism

From the many different pricing policies in use in leisure and tourism, the following are some of the most common:

1 *Skimming* – when a high price is charged initially for a new product that is unique and that attracts people who are willing to pay the high price for status reasons. The pricing of virtual reality facilities is an example of market skimming.
2 *Cost-plus pricing* – sometimes known as 'accountant's pricing', this is the rather simplistic approach that totals all fixed (buildings, machinery, etc.) and variable costs (wages, energy costs, postage, etc.) and adds a small profit margin to come up with the price to charge. It assumes that an organisation can calculate its costs accurately, something that a large leisure complex, for example, may find it difficult to do.
3 *Penetration pricing* – this is used by organisations wanting to get into a new market where there are existing suppliers of the same product or service. The price will be set sufficiently low to persuade customers to switch their allegiance (sometimes known as a 'loss leader'). It is important that this pricing method is seen as a long-term strategy since customers will resent an early rise in price.
4 *Competitive pricing* – sometimes referred to as 'the going rate', competitive pricing assumes that where products or services are similar, the organisation will charge the going rate, i.e. will match the price of competitors. This method often leads to very low margins and, in the long run, the collapse of some organisations, e.g. tour operators, who find their profitability is too low.

Place

Place, in the context of the marketing mix, is concerned not only with the location of where leisure and tourism activities are undertaken, but also with how they are made available to the customer, sometimes referred to as the chain of distribution. We shall look at each of these in turn.

Location

The right location can often mean the difference between success and failure for a leisure and tourism facility. A farm guest-house, for example, which is deep in the countryside and well off the beaten track, will not benefit from 'passing trade' and, unless the proprietor is skilled in marketing, will struggle to attract guests. A travel agency, on the other hand, in a busy high street location should attract a constant stream of clients. For a leisure development company looking for a suitable site for a new theme park, the prime location is likely to be close to a major centre of population. Location, therefore, is closely linked to accessibility, at the local, regional and national level. In the public and voluntary sectors of leisure and tourism, accessibility is not just about physical access to buildings, although this is important when it comes to catering for those with special needs. In these sectors, accessibility is also about providing facilities for the whole community and giving everybody equal access.

Chain of distribution

When we think of the distribution of products, images of huge container lorries full of chilled food or fashion garments driving up and down the motorway come to mind. This has little to do with how leisure and tourism products are bought or used (except perhaps if the food is destined for a restaurant chain and the fashion garments are 'leisure wear'!). It is true that some tangible leisure products, such as sports goods, CDs and computer games, will pass through standard channels of distribution. The difference with many leisure and tourism products, however, is that they are consumed at the point of production so there is no need for distribution channels of any sort. For example, a round of golf takes place on the golf course, just as a game of tennis is played on a tennis court. In cases such as these, the important point is to make sure that the facilities are made accessible to the customers and that they are promoted effectively to the intended audience.

The way that holidays are sold in Britain is a good example of distribution channels in the service sector. Figure 4.5 shows the stages in the process.

The figure shows that the tour operator assembles the 'raw materials' of a typical package holiday by buying in bulk such items as hotel rooms and airline seats. Taking on the role of the wholesaler, these are then divided into smaller proportions, the package holidays themselves, and are offered for sale through travel agents (the retailers) to the customers. While this is the usual method of selling holidays, there are certain companies that specialise in selling direct to the customer without using the services of travel agents. Some of the best-known of these 'direct sell' operators are Tjaereborg and Portland Holidays, which profess to being able to offer the public cheaper holidays because they don't have to pay commission to travel agents.

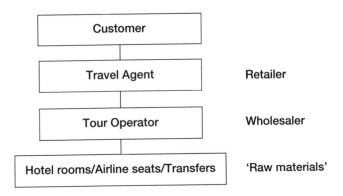

Fig 4.5 The channels of distribution in selling holidays

Promotion

Once the leisure and tourism product has the right features, is correctly priced and offered for sale in the right place, the fourth element of the marketing mix, promotion, comes into play. The next section of this unit will look at the many ways in which leisure and tourism organisations promote their products and facilities.

Section 4 Promotional activities in leisure and tourism

In the dynamic world of leisure and tourism, promotion is the most visible of the four Ps. Promotion is used:

● To make customers aware of the availability of leisure and tourism products.

- To inform customers of the benefits of one product over another.
- To stimulate demand for products.
- To provide incentives to purchase or use products.
- To remind customers of the existence of a product.

The leisure and tourism industry uses a number of different promotional techniques (sometimes referred to as 'the promotional mix'). The most important are:

1 Advertising.
2 Direct marketing.
3 Public relations.
4 Personal selling.
5 Sales promotion.

Advertising

Advertising is the most obvious of all the promotional techniques in use today. We are all subjected to advertising on our TV screens, on buses and trains, on commercial radio, at the side of the road and in newspapers and magazines. These are known as advertising media; the precise choice of media will be dictated partly by cost (a 30-second commercial on TV in peak viewing time can cost as much as £30,000) and partly by the type of product. A new museum aimed at local people is unlikely to use national TV advertising but will rely on advertisements in the local press.

Advertising in leisure and tourism is directed either at the customer (consumer advertising) or at those working in the industry (trade advertising). *Travel Trade Gazette* and *Leisure Management* are two examples of trade magazines that carry advertisements.

Many people believe that leisure and tourism organisations put nearly all of their promotional effort, and budget, into advertising, over and above other types of promotional activity. This is far from the case, since many small- and medium-size organisations find it hard to justify the expense of advertising campaigns. They rely much more on methods such as direct marketing and public relations, which can be just as effective with less investment.

Direct marketing

While advertising is sometimes criticised for not always hitting its intended audience (a product geared specifically to the needs of men will be of little interest to women watching a TV advertisement, for example), direct marketing is able to target particular customers very successfully. Direct mail is the best-known method of direct marketing, a technique used extensively in leisure and tourism. Using a mailing list, which may have been bought, borrowed or compiled from its own records, a leisure and tourism organisation can mail existing and prospective customers with a personalised letter or brochure giving details of its facilities. If planned carefully, a direct mail campaign can bring excellent results for a whole host of leisure and tourism organisations, ranging from hotels, leisure centres and travel agencies to tour operators, visitor attractions and art galleries. Direct mail is one of the fastest-growing types of promotional activity in leisure and tourism today.

Telemarketing (direct selling over the telephone) is a growing method of direct marketing in the UK. Already widespread in the USA, its use in this country in leisure and tourism is fairly new, and is limited to activities such as selling time-share and selling services to businesses.

Public relations

Public relations, or PR as it is often known, is used a great deal in leisure and tourism. Organisations sometimes think of it as 'free publicity', particularly when associated with a newspaper or magazine article that features its facilities. In reality, there is usually a price to be paid for such editorial coverage, even if it is just the cost of entertaining the journalist who wrote it!

Public relations is more than just keeping the media informed of your organisation, however, although this can undoubtedly pay dividends. PR is also about making sure that all staff and functions of an organisation which come into contact with the public, e.g. promotional literature, telephone technique, staff at reception, uniforms, etc., are well managed so as to gain maximum publicity and goodwill. PR is also about leisure and tourism organisations helping in the local community and getting involved in work for local and national charities. As well as providing much-needed cash, sponsorship can also bring PR benefits to leisure and tourism organisations. The image of a football club, for example, can be enhanced by being sponsored by a company that is regarded as successful in its own particular field.

Personal selling

Being a service industry, leisure and tourism relies heavily on the selling skills of those employed in order to achieve success. Selling is all about helping people to buy rather than selling them something they don't really want. Training in selling techniques is important for leisure and tourism staff, particularly in the commercial sector. Planning prior to a sales interview is essential as is being able to recognise buying signals, such as nodding of the head and signs of agreement from the customer. Closing the sale can be achieved by the taking of a deposit, credit card details or simply noting the customer's name and address.

Sales promotion

There are many different sales promotion techniques used in the leisure and tourism business. Some of the most common are:

- Discount vouchers and coupons (often in newspapers and magazines).
- Brochures and leaflets.
- Price cuts and 'sale' offers, e.g. 10 per cent off all brochure prices of summer holidays.
- Extra product, e.g. a 'three for the price of two' offer at a restaurant.
- Free gifts, e.g. free sports bag with every ten aerobics sessions booked.
- Prize draws.
- Competitions.
- 'Giveaways', e.g. free carrier bags, pens, balloons, hats, T-shirts, stickers, etc.
- Free demonstrations, e.g. of sports and fitness equipment.
- Free membership of a new club in the area.
- Displays and exhibitions.

The main features of all sales promotion techniques is that they are temporary and aim to stimulate demand in the short term. The fast-moving nature of leisure and tourism means that managers are constantly having to react to fluctuations in demand from customers on a daily, weekly or seasonal basis. Unlike advertising, direct marketing and public relations activities, which are essentially long-term promotional tools, sales promotion gives an organisation the flexibility needed to be able to respond quickly to such changes.

Sales promotion techniques are not limited just to members of the general public; it is common for many staff working in leisure and tourism, especially in the private sector, to be offered incentives and rewards for achieving predetermined sales targets. Travel agency counter staff, for example, may be given Marks & Spencer or Boots vouchers by tour operators in return for selling a certain number of holidays. Indeed, incentive travel is a growing sector of leisure and tourism. Started in the USA, incentive travel is the reward of, say, a fortnight's holiday in Florida for an employee who has achieved sales success within his or her organisation.

Fig 4.6 An imaginative travel exhibition display
(courtesy of Discover Islington)

Section 5 **Evaluating promotional activities**

In Section 4 of this unit we looked at the many promotional techniques available to the leisure and tourism professional to stimulate demand for products and facilities. Rather than using any single promotional tool, an organisation is likely to develop a 'promotional mix' that includes elements of all the techniques described. The exact proportions of each in the mix will vary over time and in response to internal and external influences.

Planning promotional campaigns and putting them into action are two important stages in the process of stimulating customer demand. However, without a third crucial element, namely evaluation of the promotional activity, a marketing professional may say that the whole process has been a waste of time and money. The results of any promotional work must be capable of being measured; only then can the organisation say with any degree of certainty that the time and money invested in the promotional activity was worthwhile.

Promotional objectives

Before being able to measure whether a particular promotional campaign has been successful or not, the organisation must ask itself the question 'what were we hoping to achieve from the promotion?'. In other words, promotional objectives will need to have been developed and it is against these aims that success, or the lack of it, is measured. Such objectives should be:

1 *Specific* – it is pointless having vague objectives as this will make the task of deciding success or failure all the more difficult. For example, an objective such as 'the promotional work should increase the number of guests staying at the hotel' is not specific enough. Will just one extra guest mean that the promotion has been a success? A much better objective might be 'the promotional work should result in a 5 per cent increase in the number of guests staying at the hotel'. Some managers shy away from setting such specific objectives since they may not feel comfortable about achieving them.

2 *Time constrained* – all objectives should be set within a particular time span so as to determine whether they have been achieved. Using the hotel example in 1, the objective may be developed into 'the promotional work should result in a 5 per cent increase in the number of guests staying at the hotel within the next 12 months'.

3 *Realistic* – all objectives must be realistic and capable of being achieved by the organisation and the staff working within it. Setting wildly unrealistic aims and targets is counter-productive and wasteful of resources. Going back to our hotel example, it would be pointless to set a target of, for example, achieving a 50 per cent increase in the number of guests within a three-month period. When the target was not met, staff would feel demoralised and the future success of the hotel would be put in doubt.

The promotional objectives are likely to reflect the overall objectives of the organisation, which, as we saw in Unit 1, are many and varied, depending on which sector of the leisure and tourism industry is being studied.

Measuring the effectiveness of promotion

A leisure and tourism organisation that uses just one type of promotional activity, for example newspaper advertising, will find it relatively easy to measure how effective it has been in attracting customers. Unfortunately, such a situation is very rare, and when it comes to measuring the effectiveness of a whole range of promotional techniques it is a much more complex task.

If we take the example of a newly-opened local authority leisure centre, which is reviewing its operation after its first 12 months, the management may be quite happy with the overall level of usage of the centre and will attribute much of the success to its promotional work, which could include:

- Advertising in the local press.
- Mailing of leaflets to local districts.
- Press releases to local newspapers and local radio.
- Local radio advertising.
- Promotional items such as pens, badges, carrier bags, T-shirts, etc.
- Free demonstrations of fitness facilities.
- Discounts for squash club membership.
- Incentive bonuses for staff to encourage sales of memberships.

As you can see, the centre has used the five main types of promotional activity, namely:

- Advertising.
- Public relations.
- Direct marketing.
- Sales promotion.
- Personal selling.

While the management may be quite happy with the overall promotional plan, certain elements of the plan may not have been successful and money may have been wasted on these. Unless there are systems in place to monitor the effectiveness of each activity, management may be unaware of any weaknesses. If the information is readily available, funds can be taken away from the weak activity and channelled into more effective promotion.

How can the effectiveness of promotion be measured?

Measuring promotional effectiveness is harder in some activities than in others.

1 Advertising effectiveness is relatively easy to measure, especially press advertising, which can include a coupon with a particular code written on it denoting which newspaper or magazine it is in. Look at coupons in newspaper advertisements and you will probably see a code such as DM17/9, which could mean

that the coupon was in the Daily Mail dated 17 September. Television and radio advertising are a little more difficult to measure, and are often used for image-building purposes anyway, i.e. to create or sustain a product's image in the minds of the viewer or listener.

2 The effectiveness of public relations activity can be very difficult to measure. PR too is about image-building, and attributing success to any particular part of a PR campaign is not easy. One area that is relatively easy to measure, however, is editorial coverage, i.e. articles and features in newspapers and magazines. The editorial usually stems from either a press release or complete article sent out by the leisure and tourism organisation or a visit by the journalist, some-times referred to as a familiarisation (fam) trip. Such visits are common in leisure and tourism, particularly in the travel sector. The coverage, either in col-umn inches in the case of press articles or 'air time' if the feature is on radio or TV, can be easily measured and a calculation as to how much the same cover-age would have cost in paid advertising can be made.

3 The effectiveness of direct marketing is fairly easy to measure because of its very targeted nature. Mailings to households can include coded coupons or tickets that can be traced to see which particular district a customer lives in. Telephone selling can be carried out in a very structured fashion with the sales-person logging customer details.

4 Personal selling skills should be relatively easy to measure, particularly if indi-vidual staff members are given targets to reach. Incentives can be introduced to increase sales effort and reward the high achievers. Training can be introduced for those staff not yet meeting their targets.

5 Because of their very temporary and short-term nature, sales promotion activ-ities are generally easy to measure. They often demand a firm commitment from the customer in return for which a discount, free gift or similar incentive can be gained.

Techniques for measuring effectiveness

Figure 4.7 gives some examples of techniques that can be used to measure the effectiveness of certain promotional activities.

The figure shows that not all promotional objectives are necessarily concerned with increasing profits. Certainly in the public and voluntary sectors of leisure and tourism, promotional activities may be put in place to increase the participa-tion of a particular section of the community. Even in the private sector, a company may wish to change its customer profile by perhaps going 'up market', which may not always involve increased numbers of visitors to a facility and sometimes quite the reverse.

Promotional Target	Measuring Technique
10% increase in number of visitors to a visitor attraction	Tally counter Electronic counter
5% increase in sales of caravans	Financial accounts
Improved customer attitude to facility	Visitor survey
Wider customer base	Visitor survey
Visitors to a one-off event	Tally counter Vehicle counter

Fig 4.7 Techniques for measuring promotional effectiveness

Assignment 4

Situation

You are employed as a trainee Account Executive by a leading London advertising agency responsible for a number of leisure and tourism accounts. The agency has been selected by Forte to carry out a promotional campaign concentrating on its London hotels. Like many independent and chain hotels, Forte have relatively low occupancy rates in their London hotels at weekends, when they are not used by businessmen and women. The company wants your agency to design and implement a promotional campaign that will increase the use of its London hotels at weekends by leisure rather than business clients.

Tasks

Your task as Account Executive is to plan, within budget, a promotional campaign using the full range of promotional techniques available. Your budget is £150,000 and the campaign is due to run in the period January to Easter.

Working as a member of a small team, you will be asked to make an initial presentation of your ideas to the Marketing Director of Forte. He will expect to see draft costings, a schedule and samples of creative work. Based on the outcome of the first event, your final presentation will show final budgets, schedules and artwork for the campaign. You must be able to justify why you have chosen particular themes and promotional ideas. Your team will be assessed on the originality of its ideas, the realism of the proposals and the quality of the presentation.

Revision test questions

1 What do we mean when we say that leisure and tourism products are 'perishable'?
2 What is the difference between strategic and tactical marketing?
3 When considering the business environment in which a leisure and tourism organisation operates, the terms internal and external environment are sometimes used. What do they mean?
4 Give five examples of factors in the external business environment which will influence an organisation's marketing activity.
5 What is a SWOT analysis? When would an organisation carry out a SWOT analysis?
6 Why is it important for a leisure and tourism organisation to put its customers at the centre of its marketing activity?
7 What is 'market share'?
8 Give three examples of customer classification techniques in use today.
9 What is 'disposable income' and why is it important when considering leisure and tourism products?
10 What are 'empty nesters'?
11 What do you understand by the term 'market segmentation'?
12 What is market research and why is it so important in leisure and tourism?
13 Explain the difference between primary and secondary data for market research purposes.
14 Give three examples of primary data and three examples of secondary data in leisure and tourism.
15 What use can be made of an organisation's internal records when planning a marketing campaign?
16 Who is the 'respondent' in an interview survey?
17 Explain the difference between quantitative and qualitative data.
18 What are 'the four Ps' in marketing?
19 Give five examples of leisure and tourism products.
20 What are the main advantages of branding in leisure and tourism?
21 List five factors which influence the price of leisure and tourism products.
22 What is cost-plus pricing?
23 Give two examples of direct sell tour operators in the UK.
24 What are the main promotional techniques used by leisure and tourism organisations?
25 What is PR?
26 What is the function of a press release?
27 What is direct marketing?
28 What is incentive travel?
29 What do you understand by the term 'promotional mix'?
30 Give five examples of sales promotion techniques used in leisure and tourism.

Unit 5
PLANNING EVENTS

Section 1 Events explained

Introduction

Indoor and outdoor events are an important part of the leisure and tourism scene in Britain today; not that events themselves are anything new. Informal gatherings for religious, cultural or sporting purposes have existed since the beginning of time. The first Olympic Games was held in 776 BC and religious festivals and events were commonplace in the Middle Ages. In the mid-nineteenth century, Thomas Cook was building his reputation as a travel entrepreneur by organising excursions to the great exhibitions in London and Paris, some of the grandest events of their day.

What has changed in recent times is the frequency, themes and locations of events. Whereas in the past, events were put on to celebrate a specific happening, today events can be generated in order to meet specific objectives; their scope has gone well beyond purely recognising the cultural importance of a particular date in the calendar. Organisers are forever dreaming up new ideas and themes for their events with the hope of catching the attention of a public that is becoming increasingly sophisticated in its leisure habits. Access to private transport and new technology equipment means that events can be staged very quickly in response to changing tastes and fashions.

We have already seen that leisure and tourism is an immensely broad industry. The range of events taking place within the industry is equally wide:

- Swimming championships.
- Athletics summer school.
- Mexican evening in a restaurant.
- Beer festival.
- International soccer festival.
- Firework display.
- Town carnival.
- Sponsored walk.
- Holiday show.
- Olympic Games.

- Craft fair.
- Opera festival.
- Music workshop.
- Festival of transport.
- Fitness demonstration.
- Air display.
- Caravan rally.
- Travel trade exhibition.
- Garden party.
- World Chess Championships.

While by no means exhaustive, this list gives an indication of the types of events that can be organised. What it does reveal is the vast differences in size between different events; at one end of the scale, a representative of British Gas may give a cooking demonstration to a handful of members of a local Womens' Institute, while at the other end, the World Athletics Championships will have an audience of millions both at the event and watching on television worldwide.

A definition of an event would include the fact that it is a 'one-off', or at least occurs infrequently, and that it is another opportunity for the public to enjoy its leisure time while at the same time allowing the organisers to achieve their objectives. An event may also have a theme and be celebrating a special anniversary.

Events occur in all sectors of the leisure and tourism industry, as can be seen from the list above. Travel and tourism, sport and recreation, accommodation, catering and hospitality, and entertainment and education, all use events as a part of their strategy to win customers. Events can be local, regional, national or international in their significance.

Why have events?

By their very nature, events are outside the normal activities of most leisure and tourism organisations. While this undoubtedly creates opportunities for the organisers, it can also lead to problems, particularly if the event is poorly planned or badly managed.

Opportunities

The reasons why people organise events are as many and varied as the types of events themselves. There are, however, certain opportunities which can be grasped regardless of the nature of the event itself. Events can:

- Introduce people to new activities, e.g. a young person going on an outdoor pursuits weekend for the first time.

- Publicise a destination, e.g. the Sidmouth Folk Festival has helped put this small Devon town on the international map.
- Provide world-class facilities once the event is over, e.g. Sheffield played host to the World Student Games in 1991 and now has some of the finest sports facilities in the country, thus attracting further events and activities.
- Play an important part in the economic regeneration of an area, e.g. a series of events in Mid Wales every year attracts visitors and local people and helps the local economy.
- Improve knowledge and skills, e.g. a local quilters' guild running a weekend workshop on patchwork quilting.
- Promote a cause, e.g. a local hospital organises a fun-run to raise funds for a new scanner.
- Make a profit, e.g. the Los Angeles Olympic Games.
- Increase visitor numbers, e.g. as part of an overall promotional strategy.
- Increase community participation, e.g. in sport and recreation.
- Give enjoyment and fun!

CASE STUDY

Olympic Games 2000 – the Manchester bid

Although Manchester was not successful in attracting the Olympic Games in the year 2000, all the hard work and effort that went into the preparation of the bid has contributed to an increased desire on the part of the people of the city to invest and build for the future. If nothing else, the whole bid process has been the catalyst for future growth.

Underlying the complex development plans that Manchester drew up was the need to attract investment and to build a prosperous local economy. The success that Barcelona enjoyed during and after the 1992 Games gave Manchester the inspiration to forge ahead. To achieve its vision, Barcelona planned an eight-year programme of rebuilding and the clearance of derelict areas of the city. Manchester also developed its own eight-year plan, which included the redevelopment of Victoria Station and the 80,000 seater Olympic stadium planned for the east of the city.

Manchester's excellent transport links were always thought to be one of its strongest points in its quest for the Games. It is served by excellent road and rail networks, has an efficient Metrolink tram system and one of the busiest airports in the world.

While the city has lost out on the dream and potential financial windfall of actually staging the Games, all is not doom and gloom. The pride of the people of Manchester shone through even in defeat, some of the planned facilities are being built (a new cycling velodrome for example) and the city will benefit from increased inward investment, all as a result of bidding for the Games.

Manchester, along with Sydney, the eventual winner, and all the other bidding countries, certainly felt that the benefits such an event would bring to the city far outweighed all the time, effort and money that went into putting the bid together. Los Angeles proved that the Olympic Games could make a profit and encourage investment in the local economy.

Problems

If organised well, events can be a source of great enjoyment and pride both for the organisers and those who attend. If they are done badly, they can have a serious impact on the credibility of the organisers, the sponsors (if any), the location where the event is held and any other organisations or individuals who lend their names to it. The sort of problems that occur from time to time include:

- Not setting clear objectives for the event.
- Having inadequate funding to see it through.
- Not having the right staff to plan and manage the event.
- Having insufficient time to plan the event properly.
- Lack of a team effort on the part of those organising the event.
- Overspending the budget.
- Lack of, or poor, promotional activity.
- Little regard for health and safety matters.
- Lack of consideration for those affected by the event, e.g. neighbours.
- Poor communication between staff and outside organisations.

Many problems occur because of the unique nature of an event. It is not something that management and staff in a leisure centre or hotel, for example, are used to dealing with on an everyday basis. There is no established routine for the event which will automatically make it a success. Whether the event is organised by a local council, a major company or a voluntary sector organisation, it will test the planning and management skills of all involved. There is nothing guaranteed to create ill-feeling and bad publicity quite as much as a badly organised event.

Success or failure?

Having looked at the positive opportunities an event can exploit, as well as some of the problems that can hinder progress, it should be possible to draw up a checklist of what needs to be done to make sure that any event is a success. Such a checklist would include:

1 Setting clear objectives.
2 Securing funding at an early stage.
3 Allowing sufficient time for planning.
4 Establishing a promotional strategy.
5 Recruiting and training staff.
6 Liaising with all interested parties.

7 Establishing a health, safety and security policy.
8 Having a contingency plan.
9 Carrying out the event according to the plan.
10 Reviewing the event and preparing a report for future use.

However, even if all of these points are carried out, there is still no guarantee that the event will be a success. There are many unknown factors that can tip the balance between success and failure; the weather, the location, the promotion, the pricing, the theme, the choice of staff and the audience itself are all difficult to control. Planning well in advance can, however, minimise the risks associated with any event in leisure and tourism.

Resource implications of events

Deciding to stage an event is not something that should be entered into lightly. However large or small events demand a great deal of effort, hard work, determination and confidence on the part of the organisers. Make no mistake about it, organising events is a risky business, fraught with pitfalls for the unsuspecting. An organiser of an event needs to be somebody who can combine flair and imagination with a methodical approach; a rare combination, particularly when nerves of steel are often needed as well! Because these talents are seldom found in one individual, event organisers usually adopt a team approach to getting the job done, trying to match the natural skills of team members to particular tasks.

Whether an event is organised by one individual or a team approach is adopted, the event itself will have resource implications for the organisers, including:

- Finance.
- Staffing.
- Premises.
- Disruption to other activities.
- Health and safety considerations.
- Environmental constraints.

Finance

The finance needed to stage an event will vary in direct proportion to the scale of the event itself. A small village fête may need very little funding to get it off the ground. In contrast, the city of Birmingham is estimated to have spent £2 million on its attempt to win the 1992 Olympic Games, while the British Government pledged £55 million to Manchester if its bid for the Games in the year 2000 was successful. Whatever their size, nearly all events will need a degree of financial support to start the ball rolling. Organisers can look to voluntary contributions, local or central government funding, or the private sector for help. Sponsorship and help 'in kind' often smooth the path of event planning. Once up and running, the finances of the event will need careful monitoring using accepted accountancy practices. A leisure and tourism organisation which is planning an event over and above its normal activities, must be aware of the extra burden that the event will have on its finances, and budget accordingly.

Staffing

We have seen that events call for a rare mix of qualities in those who take on the job of organisers. All staff, whether paid or volunteers, will need careful selection and training in their particular role in the event. Teamwork skills are particularly important if the event is to prove successful. Not all staff working in an organ-isation that decides to stage an event for the first time will necessarily feel happy at the prospect of getting involved with something outside their normal duties and responsibilities. Management should respect this feeling and only involve those staff who feel comfortable with the particular qualities and skills that events demand.

Premises

Depending on the scale of the event, premises may have to be hired, built, adapted or even demolished! The staging of a major event such as the Olympic Games will involve all of these to a greater or lesser degree. The necessary per-missions from local or national authorities will need to be obtained if major alterations or changes of use of premises are envisaged. Time and cost factors will need to be built into the overall event plan if premises that have been altered in some way to accommodate the event have to be reinstated to their original condition.

Disruption to other activities

Events by their very nature occur infrequently and can, therefore, be something of a headache for organisers since they will disrupt the normal operations of a leisure and tourism organisation. Unless the organisation is solely concerned with organising an event or series of events, management must accept that some disruption to other activities is inevitable and seek to minimise the impact of the event on the everyday functioning of the establishment. There must also be a recognition that the event may disrupt not only those within the organisation but may have an adverse impact on the public in general. Take, for example, the organisation of the Great North Run on Tyneside. The organisers have to be very sensitive to the needs of the local people on the route of the run, since roads have to be closed and traffic diverted. Prior warning, advanced information and a sensitive approach will ensure that local people feel involved in the staging of the event and react positively to the organisers and runners.

Health and safety considerations

Every event, no matter how small, must give serious consideration to matters such as health, safety and security. As well as any statutory requirements that may affect the event, the organisers must remember they have a common law duty of care to those attending and those assisting on the day. Unit 2 looks in detail at health, safety and security measures in leisure and tourism, but the specific laws and regulations that event organisers are likely to come across include:

- Health and Safety at Work, etc. Act.
- The new regulations (from January 1993) needed to implement EC Directives.
- Food Safety Act and the Food Hygiene Regulations.
- Public Order Act.
- Occupiers' Liability Act.
- Licensing Act.
- Trades Description Act.

This list is by no means exhaustive and each event will have its own peculiarities that may require the organisers to take account of other specific legislation. Medical advice and back-up at the event will be particularly crucial; organisers may choose to employ staff with relevant first-aid qualifications, engage the help of voluntary organisations such as the Red Cross or St. John Ambulance, as well as alerting the emergency services. In practice a combination of all three approaches will give the best result.

Environmental constraints

We have seen that events can cause disturbance to neighbours and others who may be involved with them; noise, congestion, traffic problems, road closures and disruption of normal activities are common causes of complaint. The environment too may be harmed during an event or in its build-up or dismantling phases. Events can attract large numbers of people who are often concentrated in a small space for a short period of time. Organisers need to be aware of the environmental problems their event could generate and put in place measures to minimise the impact. Typical environmental concerns that may need addressing include:

- Pollution of rivers, streams, lakes or other water courses.
- Build up of litter.
- Physical erosion of a site by feet and vehicles.
- Air pollution from vehicles often stationary with their engines running.
- Damage to wildlife, trees and flowers.
- Excessive noise.
- Disposal of toxic substances.

Organisers of a well planned event should anticipate potential environmental problems and not be left to find solutions on the day of the event.

Where to get help and advice

Every event will have its own unique set of circumstances, which cannot always be predicted in advance. Organisers should not be afraid to make use of the extensive network of individuals and agencies who have experience of event management. The organisers of successful events, whether in Britain or elsewhere in the world, are only too happy to pass on advice and tips on what, and what not, to do. Although every event is unique, there are certain basic principles that apply to all events to a greater or lesser degree. An event organiser who may 'volunteer' for the position needs to be aware both of these basic points as well as those special to his or her event.

As well as the help that can be given by fellow organisers, advice, support and information relating to the management of events is available from a number of different sources:

Event management companies

There are in Britain today companies that specialise in planning and staging events; at a price! Increased recognition of the role of events as part of a total promotional package has led to a demand from both the private and public sector for the services of such companies. They are often very small concerns, sometimes just one person, and tend to be people who have been involved in events management for larger organisations and have taken the decision to 'go it alone'. Their advice and expertise can be invaluable, particularly for large and prestigious events.

Professional advice

There are a number of areas where the help of professionals is vital if success is to be achieved. No matter how large or small the event, the following specialists are likely to be needed:

- Solicitor.
- Accountant.
- Insurance agent.
- Emergency services staff.
- Maintenance staff.
- Marketing and PR expert.
- Environmental health officer.

A local event may be able to use the services of many of the above specialists free of charge as their contribution to the event. Some organisers have found, however, that it is sometimes better to pay for the services of the professionals, who then feel more inclined to provide their usual level of professionalism. Major events will set aside significant proportions of their budget to pay fees to professionals and consultants.

Information sources

Public libraries, and libraries of colleges and universities, are good sources of information on events management in general. Some may be able to provide organisers with case studies of how successful events have been planned and managed. Collecting promotional literature on events can be a useful way of learning from others. Local authorities sometimes have events officers, who may be housed in the recreation, leisure or tourism department. General books and periodicals on leisure and tourism management may include articles on the management of events and give ideas for further reading.

Understanding events – the NutraSweet London Marathon

The first London Marathon was held in 1981 and was the brainchild of former British athlete Chris Brasher, now the Chairman of the London Marathon Company, which organises the annual event. The idea came out of seeing other city marathons operating around the world, most notably the New York Marathon. London has hosted a marathon every year since 1981 and the 14th event was held on 17 April 1994. Between 6,000 and 7,000 people ran the first London Marathon in 1981, but such is the appeal of the event that it now attracts between 65,000 and 80,000 entries every year. The course is unable to cope with this number of runners, meaning that the number of starters is restricted to 35,000, made up of club runners, individuals and a field of 'élite' competitors.

Aims of the event

One of the main objectives of the event is to generate a surplus of funds, which can be used within the London Boroughs to create or improve recreational and leisure facilities for the local people. Approximately £250,000 was distributed after the 1993 event for this purpose. Projects that help those with special needs are particularly supported; for example, one of the recent projects involved installing a hoist for disabled people in a swimming baths. The London Marathon also aims to help British marathon running and to give competitors the opportunity to enjoy themselves. Because the London Marathon is organised by a limited company, it has short-term aims that are similar to any commercial sector leisure and tourism organisation, namely to ensure that the company continues to exist and continues to generate a working surplus.

Funding

The London Marathon Company has an annual turnover of approximately £2 million. Sponsorship is vital to the existence of the Company and, therefore, the event; without sponsorship, there would be no London Marathon. Total funds from sponsors amount to around £1 million. The event has attracted a number of major sponsors since it began back in 1981; the first was Gillette, followed by Mars, then ADT and finally NutraSweet, which originally signed a contract for two years, but is now negotiating an option to extend beyond this time period. In addition to the main sponsor, there are many 'suppliers' who contribute to the funding of the event in return for publicity. For 1994 these included the sports clothing and footwear company ASICS, Citizen Timing and a host of other companies supplying everything from drinks to cars. The Company aims to maximise revenue from sponsors and suppliers in order to make the surplus available for distribution to charities and worthy causes as large as possible.

Management structure

Ultimate responsibility for the organisation of the London Marathon lies with the General Manager, who is supported by a number of full- and part-time staff, including:

- A Marketing Consultant.
- A Press Officer.
- An Administrator.
- An Entry Co-ordinator.
- A Course Director.
- An Accountant.
- The Start Co-ordinator.
- The Finish Director.

There are three committees, which oversee different elements of the organisation:

1 The Organising Committee – which meets once a month for most of the year.
2 The Executive Committee.
3 The General Purposes Committee – which meets three times per year and includes representatives of the police, fire authority, local boroughs, etc.

On the day of the Marathon itself, nearly 5,000 voluntary helpers recruited from clubs and societies help with all the tasks needed to ensure the success of the event. Team leaders are identified and are asked to attend a two-day briefing session where their roles are clarified. Because of the scale of the event and the logistics involved in making it happen, the organisers use volunteers who have worked with the Marathon before, in order to give continuity and help develop the essential teamwork skills as quickly as possible. There is no dress rehearsal of the event; it has to be right first time!

Fig 5.1 The view from Tower Bridge on the Nutrasweet London Marathon

The planning cycle

The first stage in the planning cycle is fixing the date for the Marathon, which is finalised some 18–20 months in advance. In deciding on a date, the organisers have to consult widely so as not to clash with other events of equal significance. This involves consultation with:

- The Royal Diary (from 1994 the start and finish of the London Marathon will be in the Mall, close to Buckingham Palace).
- Television companies.
- The athletics calendar.
- The British sporting calendar.
- The police and security forces.

Once the date has been fixed, detailed planning for the event can begin in earnest.

Community liaison

The organisers of the Marathon keep local communities up to date with the planning and staging of the event. A representative of the London Marathon sits on committees of all seven London Boroughs through which the route passes. Every house and car on the route is given a leaflet twice before the day of the event to let people know that it is taking place. Local newspapers and radio are kept informed of road closures and other relevant information about the Marathon. Local people are encouraged to join in with the spirit of the event perhaps by organising a street party or other celebration.

Health and safety

There are 30 St. John Ambulance stations on the course with trained first aiders and support staff. The emergency services are on hand in case of serious illness or injury. All competitors are sent a detailed training schedule four to five months before the event itself in order to be as fit as possible on the day. Those who fall ill just before the Marathon are encouraged to defer their entry until the following year.

Marketing

Much of the marketing effort surrounding the Marathon is concerned with attracting potential sponsors and suppliers. In order to attract sponsorship, organisations are offered advertising space in official programmes and magazines, on vehicles and along the route. There are also VIP hospitality facilities on race day which the sponsors can use. Television coverage is a major incentive when it comes to attracting sponsors; the event is shown live in the UK and Japan, and is distributed to another 50 countries world-wide. In addition to the work on sponsorship, the organisers have to spend time and money to attract the 'ordinary' members of the public who do not read running magazines or who are not members of a running or athletics club. As this group accounts for 50 per cent of all applications to run, the task is by no means an easy one. Local and regional newspapers and local radio stations are used to alert the general public when applications for the Marathon are being accepted.

(Information courtesy of the General Manager of the NutraSweet London Marathon)

Section 2 **Planning an event**

Introduction

Contrary to popular belief, events don't just happen! They are the result of a great deal of enthusiasm, effort, time, money and commitment on the part of many individuals and organisations, sometimes over a long period of time. Above all, what distinguishes a good event from a bad event is excellent organisation. Without an organised and methodical approach to all aspects of the staging of an event, it will not reach its full potential or, even worse, will fail miserably, with all the negative publicity and bad feeling that accompany failure.

There are five key phases (see Figure 5.2) which will need careful attention to ensure that an event has the best possible chance of success:

1 The pre-feasibility phase.
2 The feasibility study.
3 The planning phase.
4 The event itself.
5 The evaluation phase.

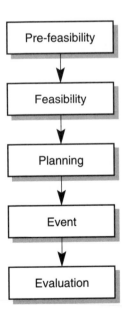

Fig 5.2 *The five key phases in successful event management*

The pre-feasibility phase

This is the point at which an individual or an organisation has an idea for an event, which may or may not prove viable. Many of the people who work in leisure and tourism are very good at formulating ideas for new events which they believe can't fail to attract visitors in huge numbers. The aim of the pre-feasibility phase is to look objectively at any proposal to see if the event really has the potential to be a winner. In many respects, the pre-feasibility phase is the most important of all; the decision to commit staff, time and money to a full feasibility study will be taken at this stage. The sorts of questions that will need careful attention are:

- Why stage the event?
- Does it meet the organisation's mission or objectives?
- When will it take place?
- Is there a suitable location?
- Can staff be made available or extra people employed?
- Does it have the backing of senior management?
- Will funding be made available?
- Does the organisation have the confidence to stage the event?

It is important at this stage to take soundings from people within the organisation and from respected individuals and organisations outside, remembering always that a degree of confidentiality will be necessary. Their views and concerns will help to answer the question 'is the idea a good one?'. Depending on the scale and nature of the proposed event, it may be felt necessary to seek the views of national governing bodies, professional organisations and local or regional groups.

If reactions to the idea are positive and those canvassed consider it worthy of further investigation, it will be necessary to begin to 'put flesh on the bones' by carrying out a feasibility study.

The feasibility study

The aim of the feasibility study will be to evaluate the idea as objectively as possible and to determine whether it is practical in an operational and financial sense to stage the event. The written study should include information on:

- The aims and objectives of the event.
- Details of the nature of the event.
- The benefits to the organisers.
- How the event fits into the overall mission of the organisation.
- The resource implications – finance, staff, time, premises, equipment, administration, etc.
- The 'track record' of those proposing the event.

- Possible problems and their solutions.
- The timescale for planning the event.

The feasibility study should be circulated to key decision makers for their comments. If they are convinced by the study that the proposed event is viable and will bring benefits to the organisation, then the real work can begin! The commitment from senior management is crucial and should preferably be in the form of a written response to the feasibility study. An endorsement in writing will signal the go-ahead for the event and the detailed planning can begin.

If senior personnel are not convinced that the event has potential, it is better that it is stated at this point rather than half way through the planning phase. They may either think that it is a non-starter altogether or may consider that with a little fine-tuning it could be made to work. Far better that any doubts are raised at this point in order to save valuable time and money later.

The planning phase

Having received the approval to proceed, the detailed planning to ensure that the event is a success can begin in earnest. The key stages in the planning process are:

- Make the decision to go ahead widely known.
- Appoint a co-ordinator.
- Assemble a committee or steering group.
- Create an organisational structure.
- Clarify objectives.
- Set timescale targets and deadlines.
- Set budgets.
- Devise contingency plans.

Make the decision widely known

It is important to publicise the fact that the event is to go ahead for a number of reasons. First, making it generally known when and where your event will take place should ensure that other organisers don't choose the same date and venue; in reality, it is practically impossible not to clash with other events taking place on the same day, but it should be possible to avoid events of the same kind on the same day, thus ensuring a good attendance. A second reason for publicising the event at this stage is to create interest from the general public and, if it is a sports event for example, to give them the opportunity to start training. A third reason is to signal to those who may be interested in helping the event in some way, to get in touch.

If there are a number of options as to when the event could take place, it is important to give some thought as to the most appropriate date, bearing in mind who it is you are trying to attract. Knowing the dates of school holidays is important if the event is aimed at families; it is also a good idea to avoid meal times for the same reason. It may be important to bear in mind the dates when British Summer Time begins and ends, if the planned event is to be staged close to either of these two dates.

We have already mentioned that one of the reasons for publicising the fact that the event is going ahead is to avoid other events occurring on the same day. Equally important is the need to be aware of any other international, national or local events already planned to take place. It would be disastrous if the sponsored walk for the local soccer team was inadvertently organised on the same day as the World Cup Final! Thankfully, the dates of major events are set well in advance.

It is interesting to note the power that television is having over the staging of major events, particularly sporting events. The timing of events often has to be planned so as to fit in with TV schedules. One of the disadvantages Sydney faced in its bid to host the Olympic Games in the year 2000 was the fact that many of the events would be taking place in the middle of the night European time, because of the time difference between Europe and Australia. As things turned out, Sydney was successful in its bid and will be liaising closely with TV companies to ensure maximum coverage of events to satisfy sponsors and those paying to advertise on television.

Appoint a co-ordinator

Getting the right person to co-ordinate the planning of the event is crucial. Time taken at this stage in drawing up a list of qualities that the ideal co-ordinator should have, and then finding somebody who matches most closely these qualities, will pay dividends in the long run. An ineffective co-ordinator can be a liability in the quest for success in the planning of the event. Although every event is unique, there are basic skills and qualities that any good co-ordinator should have:

- Excellent leadership qualities.
- An excellent communicator.
- A good organiser.
- The ability to delegate.
- Somebody not afraid of hard work.
- A motivator.
- Somebody with creativity and flair.
- A persuasive negotiator.

The event co-ordinator should be appointed with the full confidence of the senior management of the organisation, and should be given the necessary resources, authority and support to do the job properly. All those involved in the planning of the event need to be clear where the power and responsibility lie. There should be delegation downwards whenever possible so that paid staff and volunteers feel involved in making the decisions that will ensure that the event is a success.

However good the event co-ordinator, he or she will not want to operate in isolation, but will want to be involved in the selection of individuals who will collectively take the detailed decisions on planning the event: the committee.

Assemble a committee or steering group

Although it is feasible for a single person to organise an event, particularly if it is small and local, most events will be organised through a committee (sometimes called a steering group by people who think the term 'committee' sounds rather stuffy!). For very large events, it may be useful to agree a constitution, the rules by which the committee will operate; this is often carried out for events that happen every year or have national or international significance.

The committee will have a number of functions:

- To oversee the smooth planning of the event (together with the co-ordinator).
- To divide the necessary work amongst individuals and sub-groups.
- To free the co-ordinator from routine tasks.
- To take executive decisions on matters relating to the event.
- To agree an organisational structure for the event.
- To ensure that finances are managed appropriately.
- To ensure that the necessary permissions to stage the event are obtained.
- To develop a promotional plan for the event.

The membership of the committee is important. The event co-ordinator should ideally be the chairperson and be involved in deciding who is invited to sit on the committee, which will be made up of key people who are willing to give the time and effort to the job in hand. If the event is part of the activities of an existing leisure and tourism organisation, whether in the public, private or voluntary sector, the committee will include staff from within the organisation and, depending on the event's size and importance, people from outside as well. It is often prudent to invite on to the committee, individuals from professional bodies, sponsors, local authorities and the like, whose support for the event is seen as vital to its success. Depending on the size and type of event, it may be necessary to form sub-committees to deal with particular aspects of the planning of the event.

Every event committee will need a chairperson, treasurer and secretary plus others with special responsibilities peculiar to the particular event being organised. These could include individuals with responsibility for:

- Promotion and marketing.
- Fund-raising and sponsorship.
- Staffing and staff training.
- Entertainment.

- Catering.
- Equipment.

If it is thought that the committee is becoming too large and unwieldy, an executive committee may be set up to take decisions in the absence of all committee members. The executive committee will be made up of a small group of key individuals, including the co-ordinator, who should be present at every meeting.

The event organiser will need to use all his or her skills of persuasion and negotiation to ensure that the organising committee doesn't become just 'a talking shop' but takes on the role of a working group. Committees are all about fairness and democracy in decision making, but the process can be painfully slow at times. The committee will need to meet regularly to review progress, but members should not be afraid to cancel a planned meeting if there is little to discuss at that particular time; holding a meeting just because a date has been set is time wasting and can lead to frustration in committee members. Specialists can be co-opted on to the committee from time to time to help with particular aspects of the planning of the event. It is sometimes thought to be a good idea to invite a well-known person to be a figurehead by appointing him or her as president of the committee. This patronage can help promote the event and lend a welcome degree of credibility to proceedings.

Create an organisational structure

The event co-ordinator, in conjunction with the organising committee, must now begin the task of developing a structure that will ensure that all aspects of the planning of the event are carried out meticulously. One of the first jobs will be to identify 'unit' areas, which are broad areas of work, each of which will have a set of tasks associated with it. For example, an event such as a farm open day, will have the unit areas and tasks shown in Figure 5.3.

Once the unit areas have been identified, the next job of the co-ordinating committee is to assign an individual or team to develop the detailed tasks associated with the unit and accept the responsibility for making sure that the work in this area is correctly planned. The size, nature and significance of the event will determine whether an individual or team approach is needed. Those assigned to this work will report to the event organiser and organising committee.

At this stage it may be useful to draw up an organisation chart showing the linkages between the different unit groups and how they relate to the event organiser and the organising committee. By putting the structure on paper, the lines of communication and flow of responsibilities are made clear. It will help to resolve any problems or areas of overlap between individual unit areas. For major national and international events, it is often necessary to produce an organisational handbook, incorporating an organisation chart, to explain in detail the process by which the event is being organised.

Unit area 1: Site preparation and management

Tasks: (1) Public and vehicle access
       (2) Car parking
       (3) Signposting
       (4) Interpretive materials
       (5) Equipment
       (6) Admission

Unit area 2: Event promotion

Tasks: (1) Production of promotional literature
       (2) Advertising
       (3) Media liaison
       (4) VIP guests
       (5) Ticket sales

Unit area 3: Staffing

Tasks: (1) Recruitment
       (2) Training
       (3) Payment
       (4) Facilities for staff

Unit area 4: Finance and legal

Tasks: (1) Budgetary control
       (2) Fund-raising and sponsorship
       (3) Banking
       (4) Production of accounts
       (5) Legal permissions
       (6) Health, safety and security

Unit area 5: Support services

Tasks: (1) Catering
       (2) First aid
       (3) Toilets
       (4) Lighting and public address (PA) system
       (5) Staff communication system
       (6) Cloakroom
       (7) Facilities for disabled visitors
       (8) Entertainment

Fig 5.3 Unit areas and tasks for a typical farm open day

Clarify objectives

Now that the event co-ordinator, co-ordinating committee and unit leaders are in place, it is as well to clarify exactly what it is the whole team is trying to achieve. This will be a two-stage affair, concentrating first on the overall objectives of the event, as explained in the feasibility study, followed by the specific objectives for each unit leader and his or her team. This is best achieved by the event co-ordinator calling a meeting of all event personnel and setting the scene before the work in earnest begins. The work of the unit teams will concentrate on:

- Establishing the tasks within their particular unit area.
- Setting the dates and deadlines by which each of their tasks must be completed.
- Setting expenditure limits (and income targets, if applicable) for each task in their unit.
- Establishing what level and type of staffing they will need.

Set time-scale targets and deadlines

The co-ordinator will need to ensure that all unit leaders set their timetables and deadlines within an overall event time-scale plan, which will need constant monitoring and refining in response to unforeseen circumstances. It is very helpful to have a flow-chart or critical path analysis detailing the unit areas with key time targets and deadlines incorporated for each one. It is usual practice to work back from the day of the event when deciding on time deadlines. It is as well for event personnel to remember that things often take longer than expected to happen, so it is a good idea to allow extra time for 'contingencies'. It is also sound advice to allow plenty of time at the initial planning stage, so that the systems and procedures adopted can be implemented with as few changes as possible.

Event organisers invariably work from check-lists, either ones they have developed themselves or adapted from a reference source (there are a number of good books on event management which give example checklists). The detailed planning process for the event co-ordinator will involve matching the items on his or her check-list with the deadlines being developed by the unit groups, to produce an overall event planner giving the full picture of unit areas, tasks and deadlines for completion.

Set budgets

It is important to be as specific as possible when estimating the likely income and expenditure for the event, and the budgets (if any) needed by the different unit groups. Accounting for income and expenditure is particularly important when funds from external sources are being used, for example in the form of sponsorship or a grant from a local authority or voluntary trust. They will want assurances, and evidence, that their investment is being prudently managed. Unit leaders will need to account for their particular expenditure, while the responsibility for overall budgeting and finance lies with the event co-ordinator and the treasurer on the co-ordinating committee.

Different events will have different financial objectives. The main reason for a local authority staging an event is not likely to be to make a profit, but perhaps to make its leisure and tourism facilities and services better known to the local population; an event put on by a commercial organisation, however, may well be expected to create a healthy profit. While public sector events may well be subsidised by the local authority, it will none the less be made clear to the organisers that they should aim to minimise expenditure, maximise income and, hopefully, at least break even financially on the event. It is important that the event organiser and the organising committee know what the financial objectives are for their particular event; are they permitted to make a loss, and if so, how much? Should they aim to break even? Are they expected to make a surplus, and if so, how much? Without knowing the financial aims within which they must work, planning the finances for the event will be impossible.

Whether or not the event being planned is a money-making venture or has a non-profit objective, the importance of carefully setting expenditure limits for each unit area and methodically recording what is actually spent is just the same. Even small events in the local community will have costs associated with them and the idea that local authority events are 'free' is far from the truth. Local people will have contributed to the cost of organising the events through their local and national taxes.

Income generated by the event can be from a variety of sources, such as:

- Donations.
- Grants.
- Low interest loans.
- Sponsorship.
- Sale of advertising space.
- Ticket sales.
- Raffles and other competitions.
- Car parking fees.
- Income from concessions (businesses given the authority to trade at the event).
- Income from television or radio companies.
- Sale of merchandise.
- Sale of food and drink.

Income targets (if any) for each unit area should be realistic and agreed by the unit leader and his or her team from the outset. Estimating income is notoriously difficult, particularly when an outdoor event is at the mercy of the weather, and any event is competing with other leisure and tourism activities for customers.

Devise contingency plans

Murphy's Law applies just as much to events as it does to other leisure and tourism facilities and services, so 'if anything can go wrong it will!'. Some things that happen to test the nerve of even the best-prepared event organiser can truly be said to be unforeseen, but many can be predicted and contingencies or alternatives devised. In Britain, the weather must be one of the least predictable factors surrounding any event, be it in summer or winter. Organisers can reassure the public that an outdoor event will go ahead 'whatever the weather' by publicising this fact from the outset and giving an alternative venue should the worst happen. A cold spell or sudden downpour can also affect attendances at indoor events, with people choosing to stay in the comfort of their own homes rather than venturing out.

Other occurrences that will need contingency plans include:

- Failure of power supplies (is a back up alternative source of supply needed?).
- Non-arrival of key staff or personalities (have 'extras' on hand).
- Heavy traffic (consider an alternative point of entry for key personnel).
- A major accident (make sure that all emergency services have been told of the event and means of entry and exit worked out).
- Parts of the site waterlogged (have alternative areas available to move into).

There are occasions when an event will have to be called off altogether, often for reasons outside the control of the organisers. Although very disappointing for both organising staff and the visitors, the same degree of professionalism that was in evidence for the planning of the event must be maintained to deal with this situation. The organiser will need to make the decision to either cancel or postpone until a future date. Whatever is decided must be communicated as quickly as possible to the general public; an excellent way of doing this is by contacting the local radio station, which will gladly broadcast regular information so as to let as many people as possible know. There must be a method by which any advance payments can be returned in the event of cancellation, or tickets can be reused if the event is only postponed. Those responsible for press and public relations will need to handle the situation sensitively and have their own contingency plan for dealing with any adverse publicity.

The event itself

Assuming that all the prior planning has gone smoothly, the day of the event itself should be as enjoyable for those who have been involved in its organisation as for the visitors who support it. It is a good idea to hold an eve of event briefing session to go over the final details, iron out any last minute hitches and confirm any alterations to schedules. It may be that some parts of the event, perhaps the opening and closing ceremonies, will need a final rehearsal. Regardless of the size of the event, there are one or two important points that should be remembered:

- *Give the co-ordinator a 'roving brief'* – he or she should not be given specific tasks to carry out on the day itself, except perhaps welcoming and entertaining VIPs, but should be allowed to circulate around the event helping with any difficult situations that may arise and generally maintaining a positive and professional approach.
- *Stress the importance of customer care* – whether the event is free or customers have paid to enter, it is important that all staff involved in any way with it are mindful of the need to give customers the attention they need so that they can enjoy the event to the full. Visitors with special needs will warrant particular attention.
- *Keep to any published times* – there is nothing more frustrating for visitors than to turn up at a particular point to see something that doesn't happen. If changes to the schedule have to be made, make sure the message is conveyed to those attending the event.

If these points are remembered, and all the prior planning has achieved its objectives, then the event should be a memorable celebration for all concerned.

The evaluation phase

It is true to say that we all learn from our mistakes and experiences; there is invariably something we would have done in a different way if we had the chance again. The process of looking back and evaluating is just as important in event management as in any other sector of the leisure and tourism industry. Any evaluation of an event should try to answer the following questions:

- Did the event achieve its objectives, both financially and operationally?
- Was the organisational structure workable?
- Were all eventualities covered?
- Were the sponsors (if any) happy with the outcome?
- Were the customers satisfied with the event?
- What changes would be made if the event was to be staged again?

The event organiser and the organising committee should hold a debriefing session with staff, at which the above points should be considered while still fresh in their minds, before a final report on the event is prepared for distribution to interested individuals and organisations, with one copy being retained for future reference. If the event takes place over a number of days, is very large, or is split into discrete activities, more than one debriefing session may be needed.

Information that may be helpful during the evaluation phase of an event can come from a number of different sources, including:

- *Records* – any information or data about the event which has been recorded will help in the evaluation. Items such as financial accounts, attendance figures, ticket sales, receipts, photographs, video clips and media coverage can be used to reflect on the event and draw conclusions.
- *Customer feedback* – this can be both formal and informal. Formal feedback can be from surveys carried out during, and sometimes immediately after, the event. As well as information on the profile of customers attending the event, the organisers can use visitor surveys to discover attitudes and opinions. All staff should be trained to register informal feedback, in the form of comments, complaints and suggestions from customers, since this is often as valuable as the formal data.
- *Comments from observers* – the organisers of larger events often appoint observers whose role is to look at how the event has been organised and, more importantly, observe how the event comes across 'on the day'. It is useful to have the views of respected individuals who lie outside the organisational framework of the event, and whose comments can help the evaluation process.
- *Comments from staff* – whether staff are paid or are working in a voluntary capacity, they will have useful ideas of their own as to how their particular role could have been improved. The event organiser should take the time and trouble to interview key staff and feed their comments into the evaluation process.

Probably the best question to ask at the evaluation stage is, 'was the event worth all the hard work, money, time and effort that went into its planning and staging?'. If all concerned can answer yes to this, then the event can truly be said to have been a success.

CASE STUDY *Event planning – Mid Wales Festival of the Countryside*

Launched in 1985 as a contribution to the World Conservation Strategy, the Mid Wales Festival of the Countryside has grown into a pioneering model of responsible rural tourism. The Festival is a series of events (some that have been in existence for some time, some new) which take place in the countryside, towns and villages of Mid Wales from June to December. Its aim is to show that informed concern and respect for the environment can go hand in hand with economic development, in an area of Britain which is working hard to attract inward investment, create new jobs and improve the social fabric for the local people. Spearheading this work is the Development Board for Rural Wales (DBRW), a government-funded quango (see Unit 1), which considers that high quality tourism can play a significant role in the economic development of the region.

The DBRW is one of the major sponsors of the Festival of the Countryside, along with the Countryside Council for Wales and all eight local authorities in the area. It is staffed by a part-time director, two full-time assistant directors, and associates brought in for specific functions including research and compiling the Festival's annual magazine. An avid supporter of the Festival of the Countryside is leading environmentalist David Bellamy, who visits Mid Wales every year to take part in events (see Figure 5.4). He said of the Festival recently,

> *It's the only place I know where the people who have gold chains round their necks and who sit in committees are actively working with conservation to make their landscape wonderful for ever and ever.*

Fig 5.4 David Bellamy in the mid-Wales countryside
(courtesy Michael D. Smith)

The Festival, with its base in Newtown in the heart of Mid Wales, acts as an 'umbrella' organisation for marketing purposes and as a catalyst for the development of events, linking with individuals, voluntary groups and the private sector.

The aims of the Festival of the Countryside are:

1 *Environmental education* – to convey, in an interesting and coherent way, the messages of the countryside and conservation.
2 *Enjoyment of the countryside* – to help satisfy the varied recreational demands of residents and tourists.

3 *Socio-economic development* – to stimulate the rural economy, support providers of rural attractions and to involve the local community in culturally-acceptable ways.

In seeking to achieve these aims, the Festival has had notable success and is now spreading its message through links with rural areas in Europe and beyond. Training for event organisers has been provided through periodic information seminars and local group work, as well as a residential business development course held in 1992. A handbook of good practice in responsible rural tourism has been prepared for use throughout Europe.

(Information courtesy of Mid Wales Festival of the Countryside)

Section 3 **Staffing an event**

Introduction

Success or failure in planning and staging an event often hinges on the quality of the personnel given the responsibility of completing the task. Depending on the size and nature of the event, personnel will fall into one of the following categories:

- *Senior management* – these are the people responsible for setting the framework and policy within which the event will be developed. In the case of the Olympic Games, this function is carried out by the IOC (International Olympic Committee) with representatives of all the competing nations. An event of national or regional significance, such as the Great North Run, will normally have an organising committee working with an individual event co-ordinator to oversee the planning work. The management of small, local events is sometimes left to a single individual who will make all the necessary decisions. A more usual practice, however, is to form a committee or steering group to ensure fairness and democracy in decision-making; often this is made up of only a chairperson, secretary and treasurer.
- *Middle management* – working to the policy set by the senior management team will be 'middle managers' who will take on responsibility for specific functions of the staging of the event, for example publicity, staff training or health and safety matters. We saw in Section 2 of this unit that most events will be divided into unit areas, and unit leaders appointed to co-ordinate the staff working in the unit and carry out the necessary tasks associated with the unit.

- *Employees and helpers* – once the fact that an event is going to take place is publicised, there will be many people and organisations willing to get involved and
help in whatever way they can. Existing employees may be 'seconded' from
their normal duties to help plan or stage the event. Extra staff may need to be
employed, particularly if the event is very large. Volunteers may be needed
regardless of the size of the event; the NutraSweet London Marathon, for example, uses 5,000 volunteers to help on the day.
- *Support staff* – as well as the staff under the direct control of the event organisers, other support and ancillary staff may be associated with the event, for
example security personnel, concessionaires, volunteer medical back-up, crèche
workers and maintenance staff.

Recruitment and selection of staff

Organisers of local events may not have the necessary resources to be able to pay
staff, and may have to plan the whole thing from start to finish with the help of
volunteers. Where an event is of national, regional or even international significance, key staff will need to be appointed and offered an attractive remuneration
package; the more significant the event the more attractive the package will need
to be. As we saw in the last section, finding the right person to take on the role of
event organiser is crucial. To be considered for the job of an organiser for a major
event, the individual is likely to have a good 'track record' in events management
and considerable experience of the leisure and tourism industry. An organiser
may well be 'head-hunted', i.e. approached by an organisation to see if he or she
is interested in the position, rather than making an application themselves.

Staff for events can be found in a number of ways:

- By advertising in the appropriate newspapers and magazines.
- By contacting voluntary organisations.
- By sending press releases to newspapers and magazines.
- By 'word of mouth'; local councils, youth groups, colleges and voluntary
groups may well know of people willing to get involved.

If organisers are in the fortunate position of having more applications than there
are positions to be filled, then a standard recruitment and selection procedure
should be operated involving members of the organising committee (see Unit 9
for more information on the recruitment and selection of staff). Particular attention should be paid to the employment of staff who will be working with
children. There are published guidelines on this matter and the advice of the
local Social Services Department should be sought at an early stage. It may also be
able to help with the recruitment of staff with experience of dealing with disabled
visitors and those with other special needs.

Staff training

Where staff are paid to take on a specific role in the organisation of an event, taking part in the necessary training can be incorporated into their job specification. When using volunteers, however, it may not be feasible to expect them to give up time, over and above their involvement in the event itself, to attend training sessions. In practice, therefore, tasks that involve a large amount of training will normally be given to paid employees, e.g. health and safety procedures. Volunteers can be issued with written notes related to their particular tasks.

The organiser and organising committee will need to get across to all staff involved in the planning and staging of the event the importance of working as part of a team to achieve the objectives of the event. Larger events may be able to consider separate training sessions in team-building and teamwork (see Unit 7).

Briefing sessions will be an important part of the training element of an event and should be made available to all staff.

It may be possible to obtain funding for staff training through a local college or TEC (Training and Enterprise Council) if the event can be seen to be contributing to the economic or social well-being of the area.

Looking after the staff

All staff must be made to feel a valued part of the organisation that has taken on the job of setting up the event. This is when the event co-ordinator and unit leaders have a vital role to play in managing the staff under their control. The particular circumstances of volunteers will need careful and supportive action; pushed too far, they may well lose interest in the event. Important ways in which organisers can help staff feel more involved include:

- Listening to their ideas and suggestions.
- Thanking them for their help and support throughout the event.
- Paying them a fair rate for the job.
- Giving volunteers a 'reward' for their efforts, e.g. a small gift or contribution towards their travelling expenses.
- Having clear communication channels.
- Having clear health, safety and security procedures in place.
- Giving adequate training and briefing.
- Providing refreshments and a rest area.
- Holding a social event for all staff.

Above all, management must make it clear that without the help of all staff, the event would not have taken place; they are the most valuable resource.

Assignment 5

Situation

You live in an northern industrial city with few natural or man-made tourist attractions. The City Council, however, is determined to attract more visitors as a way of increasing its revenue from leisure and tourism and thus creating more employment. A small steering group of private and public sector organisations has been formed to plan and carry through a promotional strategy based on a series of events for the city. Initial thoughts are to exploit the city's historical and cultural connections, which include:

- William Shakespeare was believed to have stayed in the city while writing 'A Midsummer Night's Dream'.
- The city is twinned with Le Mans in France.
- Britain's first coal mine was opened just outside the city boundary, but was closed ten years ago.
- The City Museum houses the finest collection of impressionist paintings in the north of England.
- The city is the home of the world's oldest bicycle factory.

Tasks

You have been asked by the steering group to put forward two possible events for their further consideration. You are asked to produce a feasibility study, which should include:

- The objectives of the events.
- The resource implications of each.
- Details of expected revenues and costs, to include funding sources.
- Organisational strategies for each event.
- Health, safety and security considerations for the events.
- Promotion of the events.
- A timetable for planning and implementation of each event.

Your feasibility study should be written in the form of a report and should be approximately 1,500 words in length. An indication of your opinion as to which of the two events featured is likely to be the most successful and why, should be included in the report.

Unit 6
MANAGEMENT INFORMATION SYSTEMS IN LEISURE AND TOURISM

Section 1 MIS – an overview

Introduction

Information is the key to effective management. Without reliable data, on profitability and facility usage for example, managers in leisure and tourism are not able to carry out their many functions with any degree of certainty and are liable to make incorrect assumptions and poor decisions. The provision and use of management information systems in many leisure and tourism organisations is not given a high priority, due in part to insufficient resources and partly because of a lack of awareness of the capabilities of the resources that do exist. The fact that the industry is still in its early stages of evolution is another reason why systems are still under development.

Systems for gathering information in one form or another have existed since the beginning of human enterprise. A glance at any history textbook will produce countless examples of military campaigns and power struggles that relied heavily on the establishment of systems to ensure a flow of information to the decision makers. The same principles still apply today, the only difference being the rapid rise in technology and communications that have expanded both the amount and variety of available information, and the speed with which it can be accessed, processed and communicated. Since the introduction of the computer, information systems have been revolutionised, with many mundane tasks previously carried out manually being transferred to automated systems. Sophisticated computer systems can now give managers a whole host of information, from occupancy rates in hotels to break-even points for new leisure and tourism projects.

What is a management information system?

It is difficult to find a universally-accepted definition of a management information system applicable to the leisure and tourism industry, because of the vast range of activities that go to make up the industry and the very different information needs that the management in each sector has. The owner of a small seaside hotel, for example, has quite different information needs to, say, the manager of a local authority leisure centre; the information needed by the administrator of an art gallery will not be the same as that required by the manager of a high street travel agency, and so on.

There are, however, areas of common need and similarity of approaches that could be applied to all of the above examples, and a definition of a MIS that could encompass the whole of the leisure and tourism industry is as follows:

> *A management information system is a mixture of manual and automated resources which is concerned with the collection, collation, storage, retrieval, communication and use of data for the purposes of an organisation's sound management and forward planning.*

Not all management information systems are computer based. Smaller organisations may prefer to continue with a manual information system that has served them well for many years. A small hotel, museum, café, restaurant or tourist information centre can function quite well with a system based on card indexes, charts or files. The type of system, whether manual or automated, should not be a prime concern when setting up a MIS; far more important is deciding exactly what information is required, in what form and at what speed. If the answers to these questions point to a manual system, then a manual system should be used. Too many organisations make the decision to computerise their information system for the wrong reasons, quite often persuaded by sales staff with an eye on their commission rather than the needs of the client. Many organisations find that, rather than cutting down on paperwork, computers actually create more paper, and sometimes fail to provide the information needed for effective decision making.

Information needs

Deciding what information is required from a MIS is crucial to its success; get it wrong at this stage, and all that follows will be rendered useless. Some managers overestimate the quantity of data they think they will need and are often confronted with reams of computer printout, which they have no time to read, let alone use for management purposes! Decisions as to what is needed should start with basic data and finish with more elaborate statistics. The fundamental question to ask at all stages is, 'will this data really help in decision making?'.

Information needs should be primarily determined by the decisions that need to be made, which in turn are determined by the objectives of the organisation. This relationship between information, decisions and objectives is shown in Figure 6.1.

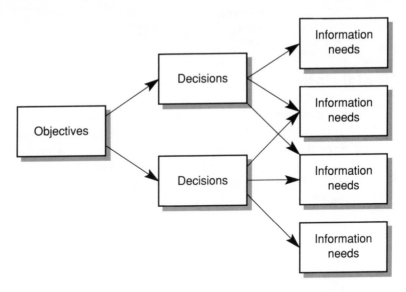

Fig 6.1 Information and its relationship to decisions and objectives

Let us look at the case of British Airways as a simple way of explaining the relationship shown in Figure 6.1. BA's goal is 'to be the best and most successful company in the airline industry' (BA Annual Report 1992–3). In order to reach this goal, BA has a series of objectives ranging from being a safe and secure airline to being a global leader. To be successful in achieving its objectives, the airline employs managers to make decisions that will effect change and thus secure its aims. To be sure that its decisions are sound, BA will need the sort of information on finance, operations and the 'market', which we discuss below.

Every leisure and tourism organisation has different information needs, meaning that every MIS will have different characteristics. There are, however, common features that should apply to the information produced by all management information systems. The information should be:

- Reliable.
- Consistent.
- Appropriate.
- Accurate.
- Timely.
- Precise.
- Clearly understood.
- Regular.

The information needed by managers in leisure and tourism organisations is likely to fall into one of three broad categories:

1 Financial data.
2 Operational information.
3 Market information.

1 Financial data

Many management information systems are introduced in the first instance to provide accurate financial data so that managers can monitor performance and plan for the future. Details of income and expenditure for the organisation as a whole or for specific sections can be made available from the MIS and trends can be plotted over time and against 'industry averages' or competitors' performance. Income figures can be produced in a number of different ways, and in the case of a leisure centre could include:

- Income related to type of customer, e.g. adult, child, senior citizen, groups, off-peak, concessions, etc.
- Income related to type of activity, e.g. squash, badminton, basketball, indoor football, aerobics, etc.
- Income related to facility used, e.g. swimming pool, sports hall, bar, catering, sports shop, all-weather pitch, fitness suite, equipment hire, etc.
- Income related to time of use, e.g. weekdays, weekends, different times of day, different months of the year, etc.

Income and expenditure information can be organised into revenue centres (income) and cost centres (expenditure). In a typical hotel, for example, revenue centres, i.e. activities that generate income, are likely to be:

- Rooms.
- Conference and banqueting facilities.
- Food and beverage.
- Telephone and business services.
- Valet services.
- Retail operations and vending.
- Special events.

Cost centres, which make it easier to analyse performance, are likely to include:

- Staffing.
- Food and beverage purchase.
- Marketing and publicity.
- Laundry.
- Maintenance and equipment purchase.
- Telephone and postal costs.

- Energy costs.
- Administration costs.

The arrival of CCT (see page 1.32) in local authority leisure services has introduced more managers in the public sector to the notion of financial ratios and performance indicators, which have been widespread in private sector leisure and tourism for some time. The range of financial ratios that can be calculated by a MIS is very broad, and could include:

- Total income: staff costs.
- Total income: number of admissions/visitors.
- Total income: operating expenditure.
- Income per facility: staff costs per facility.
- Income per facility: costs per facility.

As well as these ratios which are of use to those managers involved in day-to-day management of facilities, other financial ratios for senior management can be produced by the MIS, including:

- Net profit: sales.
- Overheads: sales.
- Gross profit: sales.
- Fixed assets: sales.

These ratios will give the policy makers the necessary information to be able to plan effectively for the future, as well as making any modifications that the figures suggest.

2 Operational information

As well as information relating to financial performance, leisure and tourism organisations need data concerned with the use and operation of their facilities, for example:

- *Occupancy and usage rates* – a hotel will want to know what percentage of its available bedspaces are occupied, a holiday centre will need to know how many of its self-catering units are let and a leisure centre will need information on the use of the facility as a whole and the take-up on individual activities. Tourist attractions, tour operators, airlines and travel agencies will also need basic data on the use of their facilities and services.
- *Stock control* – leisure and tourism organisations that operate retail outlets will use their MIS to check availability of stock, for example equipment in a sports centre shop, food in a cafeteria and drink in a bar. Many computer-based POS (point of sale) systems will automatically update stock availability figures as goods are sold or used.
- *Personnel records* – any organisation will need to keep information on its staff,

their conditions of employment and record of performance. Subject to confidentiality, this information can be held on a MIS, which can also handle the payroll function, providing an automated system for the calculation and payment of wages and salaries. The MIS can also give information on staff turnover and the uptake of staff training.

3 Market information

We have already seen in Units 3 and 4 that an effective leisure and tourism organisation must have detailed information about its customers in order to be able to provide them with the facilities and services they want, and to do so with attention to their desire for a good standard of customer service. A management information system is invaluable for providing such information on the 'market' and can help highlight under-exploited opportunities or areas of an organisation which need more promotion. A theatre's database, for example, may indicate that residents of a particular area of a city do not visit the theatre in anything like the same proportions as those who live in other areas. The management may investigate why this is so, and may feel it worthwhile to mount a publicity campaign in the under-represented area in order to increase attendance.

As well as these types of information on its 'internal' market, an organisation may use its MIS to store data on the market outside its own organisation; the 'external' business environment. For example, details of competitors and their performance, government statistics and specialist reports may be part of the MIS. Such data will give the management an idea of its position in the marketplace relative to other organisations and will be an invaluable aid in planning and decision making.

Components of a MIS

In the early days of computer-based management information systems, organisations followed a task-by-task approach to solving their information needs, often starting with specific financial data concerning income and expenditure analysis. Having satisfied one particular need for information, the organisation would move on to another data problem to solve. It is only in the last 15 years or so that UK leisure and tourism organisations have begun to commission integrated management information systems that can perform many tasks and provide a multitude of management information from a single source.

In his book on information systems in management, KJ Radford identifies five separate sub-systems, which together form the MIS. These are:

- *Administrative and operational systems* – these are the components created to support the routine functions within the organisation which revolve around the processing of data. Typical functions served by these systems are:

- Personnel records.
- Pensions details.
- Payroll.
- Accounting ledgers.
- Internal audit.
- Maintenance of inventories of equipment.
- Purchasing.
- Maintenance schedules.
- Market research databases.
- Sales planning and promotion.
- Production of documents.

- *Management reporting system* – the function of this system is to provide managers at all levels of an organisation with the necessary information on which to base their decisions. These 'reports' will be concerned with either the control of the use of resources, the efficiency of operations or the effectiveness in achieving goals and objectives; depending on which level of management has requested the reports, it may be a mixture of all three.

- *Common database* – this is the 'hub' of the MIS to which all the other sub-systems are connected. It acts as a storage compartment for information accessed by more than one department or individual in the organisation. The accessible nature of the information in the common database means that security of data is an important concern for management. The database is continually updated and altered, as the organisation goes about its normal operations. Choice of hardware for the MIS will play an important role in the operation of the common database, since, with inappropriate equipment, the expansion of the database will result in a slowing down of the speed of response of the MIS. This can be to some extent overcome by the establishment of an 'archive', a separate system into which is transferred data that is not current but may be required at some time in the future.

- *Information retrieval system* – this has a similar function to that of the management reporting system (MRS) described above, the main difference being that while the MRS provides structured reports for use by managers in their day-to-day tasks, the information retrieval system gives them the opportunity to receive information from the system on demand, and in a form that is not structured in advance. The manager of a leisure complex, for example, may be asked by a senior executive to give her up-to-date figures on the usage of one of the facilities immediately; an effective information retrieval system should be able to handle such information requests speedily.

- *Data management system* – this is the part of the MIS which arranges and controls the flow of information between the other components of the system. Its major functions are supervising the capture and updating of data on the common database, the accessing of the common database by the other sub-systems, generating reports in the formats required by management and providing security for the data in the database against accidental damage, intentional malice or inquisitiveness.

The concept of 'front office' and 'back office'

The design of any MIS for a leisure and tourism organisation will need to take into account the growing trend for organisations to divide their functions into 'front office' and 'back office'; in simple terms, the 'front office' (sometimes referred to as 'front of house') refers to the reception area of any leisure and tourism facility, the point at which the customer first makes contact with the organisation. The 'back office' (also known as 'back of house') refers to the organisation's functions that take place behind the scenes, e.g. accounting, which the customer is unlikely to be aware of. There must always be a strong link between front and back offices for a management information system to be truly effective; for example, when a guest books into a hotel at reception (the 'front office'), information must be conveyed, possibly manually but more likely via a computer system, to the other departments that need to know, such as housekeeping, accounts, food and beverage, laundry, marketing, etc.

The concept of front and back office is widespread in the leisure and tourism industry. As we have seen, hotels operate on this basis, as do leisure/sports centres, travel agencies, visitor attractions, educational establishments, transport providers, catering outlets, entertainment venues and tourist information centres. The division into front and back office allows management to focus resources on particular functions and train staff in these areas. The selection and training of staff to work in the 'front office' is particularly important since it provides the visitor with his or her first impressions of the organisation. Staff with an understanding of customer needs and expectations and who are committed to providing excellence in customer service should be chosen to work in this high-profile area. The environment in which the 'front office' is positioned also needs to be carefully planned, and should provide a clean, warm, efficient, welcoming and friendly atmosphere.

The different functions carried out by front and back office staff in leisure and tourism organisations are shown in Figure 6.2.

The use of computers in leisure and tourism

The dynamic and responsive nature of the leisure and tourism industry has meant that it has always been at the forefront of developments in new technology. The travel industry, including retail travel agencies, tour operators, airlines and other

Front Office Functions	Back Office Functions
Welcoming visitors	Cash and credit control
Taking bookings	Accounting
Selling services	Membership systems
Providing information	Stock control
Handling cash, cheques, cards	Maintenance
Controlling entry	Marketing and publicity
Promoting services	Analysis of management data
Answering enquiries	Staff training
Issuing equipment	Personnel
Maintaining records	Health and safety
Passing information to back office	Food preparation

Fig 6.2 Front and back office functions in leisure and tourism

transport providers, has been particularly noteworthy in its willingness to take on-board new developments in computers and telecommunications equipment. The leisure sector has also adapted quickly to the rapid growth in the demand for leisure, sport and recreation services by installing computer systems to handle many financial and operational aspects of the business.

Why have a computer system?

The principal reason for installing a computerised MIS will be that it will increase the efficiency and improve the effectiveness of the organisation in which it operates. More specific reasons for choosing a computer system will vary enormously between the different sectors of the leisure and tourism industry but could include:

- As a means of expanding the organisation – a small company may wish to expand its number of customers but realises that its manual system will not be able to cope with the extra information.
- To make better use of staff resources – it is unlikely that a computer system will actually reduce the number of employees once it is introduced, but it will enable the same number of people to do much more, thus improving staff efficiency.
- As a way of accessing a remote database – a leisure and tourism organisation may introduce a computer system so that it can gain access to data from other organisations. A travel agent, for example, will be able to access information and make bookings with tour operators and airlines directly via a computer link. In the same way, a public sector leisure centre may set up a direct link with its local authority mainframe computer in order to transfer and process data.

- In order to provide a better standard of service to its customers – a computer system is likely to speed up the processing of such items as bookings, membership details, cash handling, credit transfers, invoicing, letters and mailing of publicity materials.
- To provide information for management purposes, which is regular, accurate and in a form that is easily understood.

Microcomputers in leisure and tourism

In addition to large-scale, integrated computer management information systems, which can handle complex data management functions, microcomputers have grown rapidly in popularity in the leisure and tourism industry over the last ten years or so. It is becoming increasingly common to find these personal computers (PCs) not only on the desks of administrative staff but also on the desks of the managers themselves. Modern business computers, most of which conform to the standards established by the IBM personal computer, will run word processing, spreadsheets, database and DTP (desk-top publishing) programs, depending on the type of software used. Smaller leisure and tourism organisations are able to provide acceptable levels of management information with a MIS based solely on the use of microcomputers.

Security of the MIS

With so much confidential, personal and commercially sensitive information being held by leisure and tourism organisations, the question of security of the MIS must be taken very seriously by management. Loss of any part of the system may affect the viability of the whole MIS. The system must be secured against:

- Accidental interference.
- Inquisitiveness.
- Theft.
- Fraud.

Loss of part of the information contained in the MIS will be particularly acute if its loss results in an advantage to a competitor organisation; industrial espionage, involving the deliberate and unlawful entry into a system by unauthorised personnel, is not unheard of in the highly competitive leisure and tourism industry.

Simple security measures can give good protection against theft and wilful damage to components of the MIS. In the case of computer-based systems, these include strict control of access to processing facilities and data storage, and careful screening of the staff who are given access to these facilities. Steps can be taken to prevent or at least minimise damage resulting from fire, flood, power failure and civil disorder, including the provision of secure premises and storage facilities designed to combat these threats. Special measures are necessary to protect data in the MIS and to enable the management to reconstruct files from archive material stored in a different location, should the need arise. Issues concerning security of data are particularly important when employing consultants and staff from computer bureaux; rigorous screening of such companies and their personnel is vital.

The Data Protection Act 1984

Since 10 May 1986, all organisations that hold personal data about individuals on automated systems have been required to register with the Data Protection Registrar and to comply with the Data Protection Act (DPA). The exact definition of an 'automated system' is open to debate, but in general terms information held on computer falls within the scope of the Act and that which is processed manually does not. Indeed, some organisations choose to store certain data on manual systems in order that it is not covered by the DPA. The Act seeks to regulate the way in which data is gathered, stored and disclosed to third parties. The extent to which computers are used throughout leisure and tourism means that the Act has important implications for the industry.

The Act establishes eight Data Protection Principles with which data users must comply (data users are defined as individuals, corporations or other agencies that control the automatic processing of data). The eight principles, which in reality are a set of points of good practice to which data users should aspire, are as follows:

1 That the information held on computer shall be obtained and processed fairly and lawfully. Data would be said to have been obtained unfairly if the provider was deceived or misled about the purpose for which the information was being obtained.
2 That personal data shall be held only for one or more specified and lawful purposes. A contravention of this particular principle would, for example, be when an organisation holds personal information for staff training purposes but chooses to use it for the selection of staff for redundancy.
3 That data shall not be disclosed to persons other than those named in the registration document, nor for any other purpose than that registered under the Act. A tour operator, for example, which collects information on its customers to offer them discounted holidays, cannot then sell the data to another company without contravening this principle.
4 That personal data held for any purpose or purposes shall be adequate, relevant and not excessive in relation to the registered purpose. An organisation that holds data unrelated to the purpose for which it is registered or is clearly holding far more than is needed to satisfy the purpose will be in breach of this principle.

5 That personal data shall be accurate and updated as and when necessary. If an organisation, for example, holds a list of customers who have exceeded their annual credit limit, but the organisation makes no attempt to update the list when further payments are made, it is likely to be considered as having contravened this principle.

6 That personal information held for any purpose or purposes shall not be kept for longer than is necessary. A leisure centre that holds a prize draw and uses a computer to store the names and addresses of those entering, should destroy this data at the end of the promotion.

7 That an individual shall be entitled, at reasonable intervals and without undue delay or expense, to know whether information is held on him or her and to have access to any data that does exist; also to have any data corrected or erased as appropriate.

8 That the data user shall take reasonable security measures to guard against unauthorised access to, alteration, disclosure, accidental loss or destruction of the personal data.

Under the Act, individuals who have data held on them have a range of rights in civil law, including:

● Rights of access to the data.
● Rights to compensation for inaccuracy of data.
● Rights to compensation for loss, destruction or unauthorised disclosure of data.
● Rights to apply to have any inaccuracies in the data rectified and, in certain circumstances, rights to have the information erased.

We have seen earlier in this unit that leisure and tourism organisations are avid users of computers and other automated information systems. Membership lists, databases for marketing and promotional work, guests' accounts in hotels, travel agencies and tour operators, to name but a few, all involve the collection and storage of personal data on individuals. As such, managers need to be aware of the principles of the Data Protection Act and the extent to which it affects their own particular organisation.

MIS evaluation

Much of the early development work with computerised management information systems in leisure and tourism proved disappointing when it came to examining their cost-effectiveness. This was a result of a lack of clarity in terms of defining management information needs coupled with inadequate and inefficient hardware and software. The last ten years has seen great strides in the reliability and capabilities of the technology and an almost universal acceptance of the computer as a useful management tool. This has led to improvements in price/performance ratios of the various systems in use in leisure and tourism organisations; in other words, an evaluation of the benefits of the MIS when compared with its costs has given favourable results. While it is sometimes difficult to fully evaluate all the benefits of a system, since some may be intangible and therefore hard to quantify, it is important that evaluation of the system once it is operational is seen as an important element of the introduction of the MIS. Formal and informal feedback from staff, customers and managers themselves will prove invaluable in making the system as effective as possible.

On the negative side, an evaluation of the MIS may highlight actual or potential problem areas, which could include:

- Lack of adequate terminals or work stations.
- Insufficient storage capability of the system.
- Lack of operational support, including training and maintenance.
- Bottlenecks in interfacing.
- Lack of awareness of capabilities of the system.
- Inadequate security of the system.
- Inadequate expansion capability.

If the process of choosing the MIS has been objective, planned and thorough, it is to be hoped that many of these problems will have been anticipated and that the system will function according to the specification drawn up by the purchasing organisation.

Section 2 MIS in leisure organisations

Leisure centres

Irrespective of whether a leisure centre is in private or public sector control, it will need to be effectively managed, with the assistance of an efficient management information system. In the UK today, this will invariably mean the use of a computer-based MIS. Leisure centres need reliable information to be able to control costs and provide value-for-money services and facilities for their current and future customers. A good computer system can handle a great deal of tedious administrative work, can provide a database of users, membership lists for promotional work and will enable the centre to handle its finances far more effectively. The management of the centre will be able to track its performance over time, identify trends and compare performance against targets.

The introduction of CCT in local authority leisure services has hastened the need for very detailed information on income, expenditure and usage, both for the operators (known as the 'contractors') of the centres and the 'clients', the local councils themselves. Figure 6.3 shows the type of detailed information that the contractor of a hypothetical local authority leisure centre would be required to provide under the terms of the CCT contract.

The example in Figure 6.3 is just one small element of what will be needed to satisfy the demands of most CCT contracts concerning the management of leisure centres. As well as detailed data on income, the contractor will have to provide information on a regular basis, covering:

- Levels of usage of the facility as a whole and by categories of users.
- Total attendance and demand for individual facilities.
- Expenditure levels.

In addition, the management of the leisure centre will be required to furnish information concerning:

- Staffing.
- Cleaning.
- Maintenance.
- Publicity.
- Health and safety.
- Plant and equipment.
- Operational issues.

The collection of this information, and its subsequent checking by the 'client' (the local authority officers), is all part of the process of monitoring the CCT contract to see if the operator of the leisure centre is meeting the performance standards set out in the specification and is providing the level and quality of service demanded.

The need to collect this detailed management information, which has been common practice in private sector providers for many years, has resulted in an increased demand from leisure centre managers for computer systems that can provide the information both in the detail and format required by the local authority and at the intervals laid down in the CCT contract. The difficulty that has faced many such managers is how to go about choosing the 'right' MIS for the job. This is the subject we will look at next.

Choosing a computerised MIS

There are countless numbers of stories heard about computer systems costing many thousands of pounds which have failed to live up to the claims of those who provided them in the first place; systems that can provide complex management information but can't handle the basics, systems that are too slow in many of the routine operations they are asked to perform and systems that 'crash'

Facility:	Betterworth Vale Leisure Centre
Contractor:	Betterworth Leisure DSO
Client:	Betterworth District Council Leisure Services Department
Subject:	Income Analysis of the Leisure Centre

(1) Total Income   £

    Entry fees   _____
    Hire charges   _____
    Fees for courses   _____
    Fees for special events   _____
    Promotional events   _____
    Sales of sports goods   _____
    Catering sales   _____
    Vending machines   _____
    Video games/amusements   _____
    Grants   _____
    Sponsorship   _____
    Miscellaneous income   _____
                 TOTAL INCOME   _____

(2) Income by facility

    Sports hall   _____
    Squash courts   _____
    Swimming pool   _____
    Fitness room   _____
    Indoor bowling hall   _____
    All-weather pitch   _____
    Snack bar   _____
                      TOTAL   _____

(3) Income by category of user

    Adult peak rate   _____
    Adult off-peak   _____
    Junior peak rate   _____
    Junior off-peak   _____
    Leisure card concessions   _____
    Senior citizens' concession   _____
    Schools   _____
    Courses   _____
    Special events   _____
    Spectator charges   _____
    Clubs/organisations   _____
    Complimentary users   _____
    Miscellaneous users   _____
                      TOTAL   _____

Fig 6.3 The type of information required under the terms of a CCT contract

with alarming regularity. If you add to these tales of woe, the fact that many good systems can be out of date by the time they are 'on-line', then it is no wonder that leisure centre managers exercise a great deal of care and attention when it comes to installing or updating a computerised MIS.

There are four basic steps in deciding on a system and its supplier:

1 Decide exactly what information is required.
2 Write a specification based on the stated information needs.
3 Invite tenders from prospective MIS providers.
4 Choose the company that best meets your needs.

Decide exactly what information is required

This is no easy task, since it involves a methodical appraisal of everything that happens in the centre at the moment, as well as an attempt to predict what additional information may be needed in the future. All the centre's facilities and services will need to be itemised, and all procedures, both formal and informal, will need to be documented. If the system is being introduced as a result of winning a CCT contract for the management of the centre, the process may be somewhat easier, since the operator will have a specification contained in the contract to which he or she will be expected to work. This will list the information that the client will expect to see and will form the basis of the MIS under consideration.

Write a specification based on the stated information needs

The written specification will be used by the companies that submit tenders, and will give them a detailed picture of the centre's needs and requirements. The secret in writing the specification is to clearly express what the management of the centre expects from the MIS, while at the same time not making it so specific that any of the tendering companies would have to devise a completely new system in order to comply with it, with all the added expense this would involve. The specification is likely to include detailed information on the following items:

- The objectives of the system – the general principles on which the system must be based.
- Details of the facilities, activities and services which the system will have to cope with.
- Front office operations – what goes on in the reception area.
- Back office functions – for example programming, cash control, etc.
- Membership systems.
- Point of sale (POS) systems, including stock control.
- Format of the management information required.
- Security of the system.
- Support and training needs.
- Hardware requirements – capability of expansion, portability, flexibility, etc.

Invite tenders from prospective MIS providers

Once the specification for the system has been agreed, the process of inviting tenders can begin. Advertisements can be placed in relevant leisure magazines such as *Leisure Week*, *Leisure Manager* and *Leisure Management* asking interested parties to request a specification and tender application form. Details may also be distributed direct to other organisations that may have worked for the organisation before or are known to have carried out similar work at other centres. The need for impartiality, however, must be paramount, particularly in the case of local authority centres where public money is involved. The information sent out must indicate the latest date by which the completed forms should be returned.

Choose the company that best meets your needs

The evaluation of the tenders that come in needs to be a very thorough and methodical process carried out in an objective a manner as possible. A company's 'track record' will be an important consideration; it will be necessary to establish whether any companies new to leisure centre systems, although they may have worked in another business sector for some time, are looking for a 'guinea pig' on which to try out their ideas. On the positive side, however, such a company may be willing to offer a very good deal if it is new to leisure, and, if it is open in its negotiations, it may secure the contract on a lower tender price than a more established company.

It will be necessary to establish what proportion of the specification each company can meet without having to make major changes to its 'base' system. It is unlikely that any company will be able to meet all the details on the specification without some adjustments, but it is important to find out how long each modification will take and if it will incur extra costs.

Cost is likely to be a significant factor in the selection process, although it should not be assumed that the company that submits the lowest tender will get the contract. Cost must be considered along with all the other variables such as experience and expertise. The companies should be asked to itemise the various costs involved in supplying the total system and providing an on-going support and maintenance service.

Another important consideration when comparing tenders is the support that the company can give, both before installation and once it is on-line. Training for staff will be a vital part of this support, as will updating to software and hardware, and on-site maintenance and repair.

Having evaluated the tenders, a short list of possible suppliers should be drawn up and the companies invited to make presentations to managers and staff, and council representatives in the case of a local authority centre. The companies should formally present their systems and state how they will meet the requirements listed on the specification. Site visits to look at systems in action may also be part of the 'sifting' process.

Although the process of choosing a supplier for the MIS is planned to be as objective as possible, it is sometimes the case that there are two or three companies that could equally well carry out the job. In these circumstances, the company that eventually is successful in winning the contract may be the one that the management and staff of the leisure centre felt most comfortable with or the one that came across as having the most confidence in being able to get the job done to the necessary specification and in the agreed time-scale.

Pubs, bars and catering outlets

When it comes to management information systems, there is something of a mini-revolution going on in pubs, bars, restaurants, fast-food outlets and cafés all over the UK. Driven by the constant need to reduce costs, increase revenue and provide the high level of customer service that today's consumers are increasingly demanding, these leisure outlets are introducing new technology systems at a frantic rate in what has always been a highly competitive sector of the leisure market. Many operators have replaced their old-fashioned tills with sophisticated electronic cash registers, pre-programmed with prices for food and drinks. Most large organisations are now giving serious consideration to full-scale EPOS (electronic point-of-sale) systems, the sort that have long been used in retail outlets to help control stock and cash.

EPOS

Electronic point-of-sale (EPOS) systems are being introduced in ever increasing numbers to many leisure sector premises, especially pubs, clubs, bars and fast-food outlets. The only way the customer is likely to know that a facility has an EPOS system is when the staff use their 'touchpads' or 'scatterpads', the small touch-sensitive panels located behind the bar or counter, sometimes on the cash register itself. The benefits of EPOS are:

1 It gives the management control over cash transactions.
2 It improves stock control.
3 It frees staff to concentrate on improving customer care rather than having to calculate prices and issue bills.

As well as performing all the normal functions of an electronic cash register, an EPOS system will log all transactions with time, date, items served, cost, method of payment and the member of staff who dealt with the customer. This not only reduces the possibility of fraud by staff but also allows management to introduce incentives for staff who are meeting and exceeding their sales targets. The system will also mean that the busiest times can be better anticipated and allow better management of staff generally. The detailed management information given by EPOS will mean that stock levels can be monitored more closely enabling the outlet to hold much smaller levels than would otherwise be the case.

The public house MIS network

A very good example of state-of-the-art management information systems in the leisure industry is the introduction of a fully integrated system by Bass Taverns into its public houses throughout Britain; Bass is the UK's largest brewer and the fourth largest in the world. By using a front office system combining 'scatterpads' and touch-screen tills, flowmeters that automatically monitor how much beer is drawn from the kegs and a back office system that can review stocks and cashflow, Bass can monitor the operation of all pubs on the system from a central control.

The system begins with staff entering transactions using a scatterpad and touch-screen tills. As a security measure, each till only operates with the electronic identity card of a member of the bar staff. Flowmeters located on the kegs measure the amount of beer used and input data into the network. Each pint pulled is recorded by the flowmeters, which measure to the nearest quarter pint how much beer has been dispensed, while the till is automatically alerted by the flowmeter to expect a payment. If no payment is received, the system sends a warning to the pub manager who operates the back office system. Here, he or she monitors transactions and prepares data for the network. The data is downloaded to the network control in Birmingham which supervises the operation of more than 2,000 pubs.

All 3,000 of Bass's pubs were scheduled to be on this integrated MIS network by the end of 1993, less than two years since the start of the project in January 1992. Every pub manager will have a networked PC in his or her office, linked to the network control so that stock details, work rates and cash takings can be downloaded during the night. Using this sophisticated technology, managers at network control have an exact up-to-the-minute picture of what business it is doing in which areas. Regional managers are able to supervise more than 100 pubs in an area by simply connecting a PC or notebook computer to the central network and calling up the data. The system has enabled Bass to manage its public house operation more effectively and has given individual pub managers the chance to use their resources, particularly staff, more efficiently.

Bass plans to integrate an automatic delivery system in to the network to further refine the operation. By analysing the stock control data downloaded every night, the system will automatically activate deliveries of beer to the individual pubs. The system will be linked to the brewing arm of Bass in order that demand for beer can be estimated more effectively and wastage can be kept to a minimum.

Looking to the future, Bass sees this as only the start of a revolution in pubs and

the way they are managed. There is likely to be even greater use of new technology equipment to monitor, for example, energy use and to offer other services
such as cash machines and ordering of theatre tickets.

Theatres and other entertainment venues

There have been great strides in the development of management information
systems for theatres, large and small, and the indoor and outdoor entertainment
venues that exist throughout the UK, e.g. Wembley Stadium and Wembley Arena,
GMEX in Manchester, Sheffield Arena and the Royal Albert Hall, to name but a
few. Most venues serving a regional catchment, and quite often many catering
only for their local population, will have a computerised MIS controlling front
and back office functions. The national venues employ sophisticated systems that
can handle the large volume of enquiries and sales they attract.

The functions carried out by staff in the front office of such venues are in many
respects similar to the work carried out by reception staff in leisure centres. The
one big difference, however, is that theatres and other entertainment venues sell
most of their tickets in advance, rather than taking casual bookings on the day.
The main functions are:

- Selling tickets – either in person, by telephone, by post or by fax.
- Providing information.
- Cash and cards handling.
- Controlling entry and exit.

The front office or reception of an entertainment venue will almost certainly have
a VDU (visual display unit) showing a seating plan, seat availability and the
prices in the various parts of the venue. This system will include a ticket printer
to issue tickets automatically and speedily. The front office system will be connected to a back office computer, responsible for:

- Accounting.
- Sales analysis.
- Promotion and marketing.
- Personnel.

Many venues make extensive use of their database of customer details to market
their services. Customers can be targeted according to their tastes and preferences;
for example, a person who books a seat at the snooker championships in the
Wembley Arena will automatically be sent details of the same event the following
year via the database. Separate files can be created according to different types of
performances, e.g. opera, comedy, music, drama, light entertainment, sport, etc.,
enabling customers to be sent promotional material suited to their interests.

Leisure complexes

Leisure complexes, including country clubs, health resorts and golf courses, are a growing part of the leisure industry in the UK today. Offering facilities for individual and business (corporate) clients, they need fully integrated management information systems that link all the elements of their operation. Effective systems must provide a fast and efficient service for customers and allow staff to concentrate on developing the highest levels of customer service. Figure 6.4 gives an example of an integrated leisure management system developed by Baron Systems, which has worked with companies such as Gleneagles Hotel, the Belfry and Champneys Health Club in London.

Like many systems available for leisure complexes, the Baron MIS offers three integrated 'modules', covering membership, bookings and point-of-sale systems (see Figure 6.4), all of which can be tailored to the requirements of an individual resort. This modular approach offers the management, staff and customers a system through which all operations can be channelled for enhanced administrative and financial control.

The membership system is often at the heart of any leisure complex and needs flexibility, speed and accuracy of operation. The Baron MIS can record subscription information to speed up renewals (see Figure 6.5) and members' account spends can be controlled by levies or credit controls. The ledger module ensures an efficient storage of transactions and allows the collection of finance at regular intervals.

The membership system can be used for marketing purposes with the capability of producing personalised letters for mailing direct to clients.

The bookings system can control all the bookable functions at the complex, including tennis, squash, sauna, spa treatments, golf courses, etc. Figure 6.6 shows part of the Baron MIS, which lists details of golf course bookings for a particular day.

Good booking systems should offer the facility for bookings to be taken at more than one point in the complex and enquiries for bookings to be made at multiple locations. Various options within the bookings module of the Baron MIS allow the recording of information on hired equipment and the control of members' use of facilities, via magnetic strip cards.

The point-of-sale system is specifically designed for shops within complexes and clubs. It ensures control of all aspects of the shop's operation, including stock movements, stock taking and stock control (see Figure 6.7).

The POS system gives the option to barcode all items giving a faster method of recording sales and stock control information. Analysis of sales can be made under a number of categories, including by supplier, by location, by category of goods, by colour, by size, etc.

One of the most important points about each of the three elements of this MIS, bookings, membership and POS, is that reports can be generated from all three modules for use by management. Information on usage and financial performance can be generated by the system.

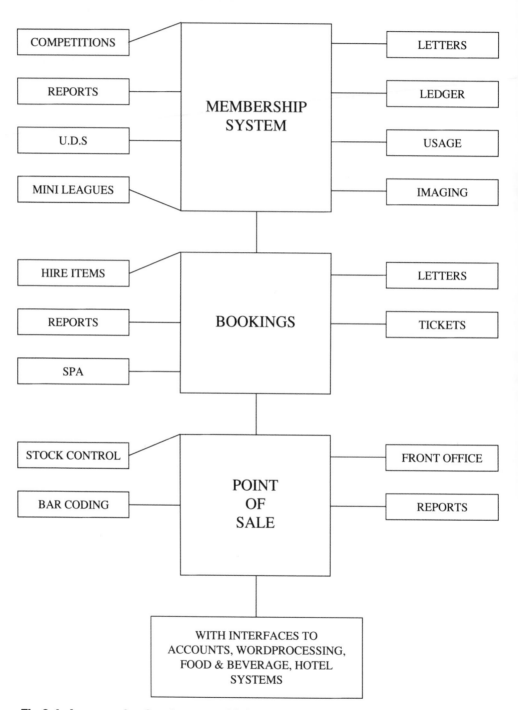

The Baron Leisure Management System
The Modular Approach

COMPETITIONS		LETTERS
REPORTS		LEDGER
U.D.S	**MEMBERSHIP SYSTEM**	USAGE
MINI LEAGUES		IMAGING

HIRE ITEMS		LETTERS
REPORTS	**BOOKINGS**	TICKETS
SPA		

| STOCK CONTROL | | FRONT OFFICE |
| BAR CODING | **POINT OF SALE** | REPORTS |

WITH INTERFACES TO
ACCOUNTS, WORDPROCESSING,
FOOD & BEVERAGE, HOTEL
SYSTEMS

Fig 6.4 *An example of an integrated leisure MIS* (courtesy of Baron Systems Ltd)

6.22 Management information systems in leisure and tourism

Baron Manor CC

Payment Notice

* * *   Your Subscription is Due on 10.09.93   * * *

Mr I Mitchell
Member Number   1

Total Gross Subscriptions   2271.54
Total Amount Due   2136.54

In 11 instalments of 189.30 and one instalment of 189.24

To: Mr I Mitchell
11 Brooksfield
South Kirby
PONTEFRACT
West Yorkshire
WF9 2JP

Tel No: 0987 453422

Remittance To Baron Manor CC

Mr I Mitchell   FULLPLAY 1510.25
Miss P L Mitchell   FULLPLAY   465.00

                          Total Subcriptions   1975.25
                          Total VAT at 15%   296.29

                          Gross Subscriptions   2271.54
                          Less Amount Paid   135.00

Fig 6.5 Typcal subscription information on the Baron MIS
(courtesy of Baron Systems Ltd)

Demonstration System ONLY
Time: 17:37:13   Page No: 1

Date: 03.07.90

Monday 2nd July 1990

Facility: Old Course 1st Tee   Times: 7.30 to 7.30   Number: 32

Name/Organiser: RICHARD/ICI UK Ltd

Main Account/Credit Card No: 4936 552 6728 123
Comments: Other details – IMPORTANT PEOPLE FRIENDS OF MD
OTHER DETAILS:
Morning Coffee: 11 am in the Conference Room One – Rich Tea biscuits and the cake as brought in by their staff. Papers to be laid on as normal.
Afternoon Tea: 3 pm there will be double the numbers as guests are invited to attend. Earl Grey Tea must be used. If a hot day please provide Highland Spring Water and fresh orange juice. Cakes and scones have been ordered.
Lunch Details: The set meal no 6 will be adapted slightly for all the 60 members of the party. Starter to have Salmon Smoked as no 7 menu rather than the soup. Wine is to be the St Emilion no 564, Also Muscadet De Sevre et Maine no 785

Monday 2nd July 1990

Facility: Old Course 1st Tee   Times: 7.38 to 7.54   Number: 22

Name/Organiser: DAVIS/Dunlop UK

Main Account/Credit Card No: 4976 563 5738234
Comments: VERY HAPPY WITH LAST YEAR – SALES PROMOTION DAY
OTHER DETAILS:
Morning Coffee: 40 COFFEE AND BISCUITS IN THE GAMES CONF ROOM, NEWSPAPERS AND SEE NOTES BELOW
Afternoon Tea: 4 PM SCONES AND HIGH TEA NORMAL FOR 30
Lunch Details: LMENU: NO 16
                 WLIST: NO 345
Presentation Details: ARRIVE 9 AM WITH COFFEE AS BRIEFED ABOVE. A SHORT PRESENTATION WILL BE GIVEN TO INVITEES. OVERHEAD REQUIRED

Monday 2nd July 1990

Facility: Old Course 1st Tee   Times 8.02 to 8.18   Number: 4

Name/Organiser: JOHNSON/Johnson TJ

Main Account/Credit Card No: Visa
Comments:
OTHER DETAILS:
Morning Coffee: N/A
Afternoon Tea: N/A
Lunch Details: NORMAL YEARLY SOCIETY DO DITTO OF LAST YEAR
                 LMENU: NO 10

Fig 6.6 *Example of a booking system showing details of golf bookings*
(courtesy of Baron Systems Ltd)

SALES BY CATEGORY REPORT

Product Category	Description	P.L.U. Number	—01.06.91 to 21.06.91— Sales	Sales Value	—Up to 21.06.91— Sales	Sales Value
		9999999999999	2	10.00	395	4316.50
			2	10.00	395	4316.50
1	Equipment	0000000101000	0	0.00	702	259.72
		0000023464210	0	0.00	16	4.50
		0000027654280	1	0.50	22	1.00
		0000037651480	0	0.00	20	0.00
		0000047852861	0	0.00	23	3.00
		0000065035091	0	0.00	21	1.00
		0000478631562	0	0.00	33	6.00
		0000487651620	0	0.00	11	1.25
		2953700981242	0	0.00	11	2.00
		5000000000001	0	0.00	10	0.00
		5000000000002	0	0.00	10	0.00
		5000000000004	0	0.00	10	0.00
1	Equipment		1	0.50	889	278.47
2	Clothes	0000001234567	0	0.00	6312	162869.000
		0000001234568	0	0.00	105	160.00
		0000027615424	0	0.00	12	7.00
		0000276543122	0	0.00	22	7.50
		0000345218538	0	0.00	20	0.00
		0000378961342	0	0.00	20	0.00
		0000764182610	0	0.00	20	0.00
		0000785247122	0	0.00	30	0.00
		0009287541782	0	0.00	10	0.00
		2096541329091	0	0.00	20	0.00
		5000000000003	0	0.00	10	0.00
		8222935790152	0	0.00	12	12.00
		9975186521790	0	0.00	20	0.00

Fig 6.7 Shop sales report from the Baron MIS
(courtesy of Baron Systems Ltd)

Figure 6.8 is an extract from the Baron MIS showing a report on the usage of a golf course, while Figure 6.9 gives an extract of a monthly financial summary.

Fully integrated management information systems offer the leisure complex with many facilities and a mix of clientele, the opportunity to make maximum use of its resources to provide a professional service backed up with sound management practices.

Baron Manor Country Club   –   FACILITY UTILISATION REPORT   –   Date: 05.06.91   Time: 08:59:21   Page No: 1

???? Code & Name	Date	Usage	DARK	MAINTENANCE	CLOSED	MEMBERS ONLY	EARLY BIRD	NIGHT OWL	COMPETITION	2 BALL ONLY
at Course	31.05.91	59.65%	2.74%	2.74%	–	–	28.57%	5.48%	10.96%	–
at Course 1st Tee		8.22%	–	–	–	–	–	–	–	–
at Course 10th Tee		13.70%	–	–	–	13.04%	–	–	–	–
at Course	01.06.91	63.64%	4.11%	2.74%	–	–	9.59%	5.48%	17.81%	–
at Course 1st Tee		9.59%	–	–	–	–	50.00%	–	–	–
at Course 10th Tee		13.70%	–	–	–	–	–	–	–	–
at Course	02.06.91	40.00%	4.11%	1.37%	–	–	9.59%	5.48%	17.81%	–
at Course 1st Tee		9.59%	–	–	–	–	50.00%	–	·	–
at Course 10th Tee		13.70%	–	–	–	–	–	–	–	–
1st Course	03.06.91	65.00%	4.11%	–	–	–	14.28%	5.48%	8.22%	–
at Course 1st Tee		10.96%	–	–	–	–	–	–	–	–
at Course 10th Tee		31.14%	–	–	–	4.35%	–	–	–	–
1st Course	04.06.91	33.33%	–	2.74%	–	13.70%	4.11%	5.48%	12.33%	–
at Course 1st Tee		17.81%	–	–	–	–	–	–	–	–
at Course 10th Tee		23.29%	–	8.70%	–	–	–	–	–	4.35%

Fig 6.8 Facility utilisation report *(courtesy of Baron Systems Ltd)*

Date: 19.07.90

Demonstration System ONLY

Monthly Financial Summary for July 1990

Type of Ticket	Description	Sun 1	Mon 2	Tue 3	Wed 4	Thu 5	Fri 6	Sat 7	Sun 8	Mon 9	Tue 10	Wed 11	Thu 12	Fri 13	Sat 14	Sun 15	Mon 16	Tue 17	Wed 18	Thu 19	Fri 20	Sat 21	Sun 22	Mon 23	Tue 24	Wed 25	Thu 26	Fri 27	Sat 28
1/001	Members Rate	–	9	5	1	–	6	24	–	–	–	–	–	–	–	–	2	3	3	–	12	1	–	1	1	2	6	1	1
1/002	18 Holes Golf – Weekday	–	6	5	4	–	–	3	–	–	–	–	–	–	–	–	–	3	9	12	23	1	1	2	–	1	5	1	1
1/003	18 Holes Golf – Weekend	–	–	3	–	–	–	1	–	–	–	–	–	–	–	–	–	2	3	3	4	–	1	1	–	–	–	–	–
1/004	18 Holes Golf – Weekend with Mem	–	–	–	3	–	–	1	–	–	–	–	–	–	–	–	–	6	6	4	–	–	–	–	–	–	–	–	–
1/005	18 Holes Golf – Weekday with Mem	–	1	1	1	–	–	1	–	–	–	–	–	–	–	–	–	–	1	2	–	–	–	–	–	–	–	–	–
1/006	Early Bird	–	1	–	–	–	–	1	–	–	–	–	–	–	–	–	–	–	–	1	4	–	–	–	–	–	–	–	–
1/007	Night Owl	–	–	–	–	3	–	1	–	–	–	–	–	–	–	–	–	1	–	1	–	1	–	1	–	–	1	–	–
1/008	9 Holes Only	–	–	–	–	1	–	1	–	–	–	–	–	–	–	–	–	1	–	–	–	1	–	1	–	–	–	–	–
1/009	Golf Academy	–	–	–	–	–	–	2	–	–	–	–	–	–	–	–	–	–	–	–	–	–	–	–	–	–	–	–	–
1/010	Golf Special	–	–	–	3	–	–	2	–	–	–	–	–	–	–	–	–	–	–	–	–	–	–	–	–	–	–	–	–
1/800	test rates code	–	–	–	1	–	–	–	–	–	–	–	–	–	–	–	–	–	–	–	–	–	–	–	–	–	–	–	–
2/001	Members Rate	–	–	–	–	1	5	3	–	–	–	–	–	–	–	–	–	–	–	–	–	–	–	–	–	–	–	–	–
2/002	18 Holes Golf – Weekday	–	–	1	–	–	–	–	–	–	–	–	–	–	–	–	–	–	–	–	–	–	–	–	–	–	–	–	–
2/003	18 Holes Golf – Weekend	–	–	–	–	–	–	2	–	–	–	–	–	–	–	–	–	–	–	–	–	–	–	–	–	–	–	–	–
2/004	18 Holes Weekday with Mem	–	–	–	–	2	–	–	–	–	–	–	–	–	–	–	–	–	–	–	–	–	–	–	–	–	–	–	–
2/005	18 Holes Golf – Weekend with Mem	–	–	2	–	–	–	–	–	–	–	–	–	–	–	–	–	–	–	–	–	–	–	–	–	–	–	–	–
2/006	Early Bird	–	2	–	–	–	–	–	–	–	–	–	–	–	–	–	–	–	–	–	–	–	–	–	–	–	–	–	–
2/007	Night Owl	–	–	–	–	2	–	–	–	–	–	–	–	–	–	–	–	–	–	–	–	–	–	–	–	–	–	–	–
2/008	9 Holes Only	–	–	–	2	–	–	–	–	–	–	–	–	–	–	–	–	–	–	–	–	–	–	–	–	–	–	–	–
2/009	Junior – Weekday	–	–	–	2	–	–	–	–	–	–	–	–	–	–	–	–	–	–	–	–	–	–	–	–	–	–	–	–
2/010	Junior Weekend	–	–	–	2	–	–	–	–	–	–	–	–	–	–	–	–	–	–	–	–	–	–	–	–	–	–	–	–
2/011	Golf Special	–	–	–	4	–	–	–	–	–	–	–	–	–	–	–	–	–	–	–	–	–	–	–	–	–	–	–	–
5/001	Squash Court Weekday	–	1	–	14	–	–	–	–	–	–	–	–	–	–	–	–	–	–	–	–	–	–	–	–	–	–	–	–
5/002	Squash Court Weekend & Evening	–	–	2	1	–	–	–	–	–	–	–	–	–	–	–	–	–	–	–	–	–	–	–	–	–	–	–	–
5/003	Squash Coaching – Alex	–	–	–	1	–	–	–	–	–	–	–	–	–	–	–	–	–	–	–	–	–	–	–	–	–	–	–	–
5/004	Squash Junior	–	–	3	–	–	–	–	–	–	–	–	–	–	–	–	–	–	–	–	–	–	–	–	–	–	–	–	–
5/005	Squash Special	–	–	2	2	–	–	–	–	–	–	–	–	–	–	–	–	–	–	–	–	–	–	–	–	–	–	–	–
5/006	Tennis Weekday	–	–	3	–	–	–	–	–	–	–	–	–	–	–	–	–	–	–	–	–	–	–	–	–	–	–	–	–
5/007	Tennis Weekend & Evening	–	–	–	–	6	–	–	–	–	–	–	–	–	–	–	–	–	–	–	–	–	–	–	–	–	–	–	–
5/011	Snooker Day	–	–	2	–	–	–	–	–	–	–	–	–	–	–	–	–	–	–	–	–	–	–	–	–	–	–	–	–
5/012	Snooker Academy	–	–	1	–	–	–	–	–	–	–	–	–	–	–	–	–	–	–	–	–	–	–	–	–	–	–	–	–
9/100	Golf Buggies	–	14	–	–	–	5	22	–	–	–	–	–	–	–	–	–	–	–	–	–	–	–	–	–	–	–	–	–

Fig 6.9 Extract from a monthly financial summary (courtesy of Baron Systems Ltd)

Introduction

The need in the tourism industry to be able to communicate quickly on a global scale means that it is ideally suited to the use of new technology equipment and systems. Computers and sophisticated communications media enable organisations to check up-to-date information, make reservations, confirm complex fares, issue tickets and provide information for management purposes. This is not to say that manual management information systems, often using wall charts and card indexes, do not exist in the travel and tourism sector, but they are becoming very rare!

Travel agencies

Independent travel agents, and those owned by one of the well-known multiple chains such as Lunn Poly and Thomas Cook make extensive use of new technology to sell holidays and other travel products to the public. Working as the agents of the large tour operators (the 'principals'), they earn their money from commission on sales, so that access to up-to-date information on product availability is an important part of their operation. A computer system in a typical UK travel agency will be designed to handle:

- Front office functions.
- Back office functions.
- Management functions.

Front office functions

The computer terminal or VDU on the counter is now an accepted part of the furniture in any travel agency. In the hands of trained personnel, this front office system is a powerful selling tool. It can give access, via a telephone line and the correct computer software known as a 'gateway' system, to the computer reservation systems (CRSs) of major tour operators and airlines, in order to check availability of holidays and flights, check prices and ultimately make bookings on behalf of the clients. One of the first companies to offer this facility was Thomson with its Thomson On-line Program (TOP) introduced in 1986.

Back office functions

Back office systems handle the ticketing, accounting and administrative functions of the travel agency. An integrated back office can allow the staff to create client profiles and itineraries, undertake invoicing, issue tickets and generate word-processed items. The system can also build a database that can be used for marketing and promotional purposes.

Management functions

One of the main advantages that a computerised MIS has over one that is operated manually is that it can provide accurate information on the performance of the agency at the touch of a button. In times of recession when profit margins are being squeezed, it is even more important to have this regular and up-to-date management information. Reports can be requested under a number of different categories, for example:

- Level of sales by departure airport.
- Level of sales by tour operator.
- Sales volume by member of staff.
- Departures by date.
- Level of sales by client.

This detailed information will give the manager or owner an accurate picture of the financial state of the business as a whole, and accurate data on the different components of the agency's work, which will prove invaluable for decision-making purposes.

Tour operators

Unlike travel agents who sell the holidays and other travel products, tour operators actually 'construct' the holidays, putting together packages tailored to the needs of individual travellers. They play the part of wholesalers who buy hotel bedspaces, airline seats and other services in bulk, and then repackage them into the holidays that we see offered for sale through travel agents. The information needs of tour operators are, therefore, quite different from those of travel agents, which are the retailers in the chain of distribution of holidays. Tour operators will need a MIS that can provide the following information:

- Level of sales of particular holidays and destinations.
- Data on the availability of accommodation and flights (or other mode of transport).
- Financial data on agents and their sales performance.

- Feedback from clients on their holiday experiences.
- Personnel information (UK and overseas).
- Management accounts showing profit and loss, balance sheet, etc.
- Information on competitors and the market in general for package holidays.

The largest UK tour operators, including Thomsons, Airtours and Owners Abroad, all have integrated computerised management information systems operating from a central database. This can be accessed by their own reservations staff in response to enquiries or, if a 'gateway' system is in operation, agents can gain access themselves to check availability and make bookings. Small and medium-sized tour operators, which make up the bulk of companies, will often use a mixture of manual and automated systems and can sometimes use standard business software packages for accounts, data processing and database management.

Airlines

The two main types of service offered by the airlines are scheduled and charter. Scheduled services operate to a published timetable on defined routes, either domestic or international, and seats are freely available to leisure and business travellers. Charter services have developed in response to the rise in package holidays and are the services which are restricted to passengers who have bought the full package. The distinction between scheduled and charter services is becoming less clear since some charter airlines now offer scheduled services, and scheduled airlines offer charters as well. Much of this is due to the increased demand for 'seat only' sales linked to the growth in independent holidays.

The information needs of an airline are broadly similar, whether their principal business is in the scheduled or charter market. They will need information systems that will provide operational information, such as 'load factors' (seats sold as a percentage of seats available on the aircraft), route planning, timetable information and fare structures. Information relating to capital and operating costs must also be provided by the MIS, as must data concerning marketing and customer satisfaction.

Computer reservations systems have become a major force in the airline industry over the last 20 years or so. These fully integrated systems not only store accurate data on airline fares and services, but also have information on other travel services including car hire, exchange rates, excursions, sporting events, resort and country information, etc., making them attractive to travel agents. Probably the best-known system is American Airlines' Sabre CRS, but European systems including Galileo and Amadeus have been introduced to counter the powerful US threat in this highly-competitive sector of the industry.

Visitor attractions

Like any other sector of the leisure and tourism industry, visitor attractions need to compete for customers. They need reliable information on which to base their management decisions. Small attractions catering for a purely local market may not need a computerised MIS but may be able to cope with a manual system. Attractions catering for larger numbers, however, will need to give serious consideration to computerising all or part of their operation if they are to remain competitive. The top UK theme park, Alton Towers in Staffordshire, has recently spent a considerable amount of time and money on investigating its information needs and updating its MIS. The results of its work are highlighted in the following case study.

MIS in visitor attractions – Alton Towers

Around two million people a year are welcomed to Alton Towers, the UK's number one paying attraction. With such a large number of visitors, it is important that the managers of the theme park have access to detailed information on matters such as visitor numbers, costs, staffing, income and marketing. This is why it was decided to initiate a department-by-department review of its MIS in 1991. The review has resulted in the introduction of 100 terminals and PCs throughout the business, handling data concerning finance, admissions, marketing, merchandising and catering. The reorganisation of the MIS has grouped departments that were hitherto separate, for example the retail department has brought together catering, merchandising and amusements. The park's catering function has benefited from the most recent system installation. Catering accounts for 400 of the 700 peak season workforce within retail, with 76 outlets generating in excess of £6.5 million during the 32-week season.

From the outset, the rationalisation of the MIS was put into the hands of a team including a departmental head, stores manager and office co-ordinator, as well as a group IT consultant. This approach encouraged a high degree of commitment to the system and its operation. The park's managers have sought to improve the flow of management data, while at the same time recognising the need for Alton Towers to remain competitive in the marketplace and improve on its already admirable record of customer service.

(Adapted from an article in Leisureweek)

Hotels and other accommodation providers

Because of their long history of serving the needs of the travelling public, hotels have been at the forefront of developments in management information systems. The hospitality industry in general has evolved with the manual handling of guests' transactions and the production of volumes of paper documenting these activities. The development of computerised management information systems has been undertaken as an attempt to simplify the handling of an organisation's stock of information, to reduce costs, to increase speed and offer a higher degree of accuracy than was the case with manual systems. There has also been the assumption that automating many mundane tasks would give staff a greater degree of job satisfaction, which would result in improved levels of customer service.

A management information system for a hotel or similar accommodation provider is likely to have the following objectives:

- To present management with timely, accurate and comprehensive reports.
- To provide increased operational control.
- To reduce the amount of unnecessary paperwork.
- To free staff to concentrate on customer service functions.
- To enable management to monitor and control the guest experience better.
- To enable the hotel to provide an expanded range of guest services.

Hotel information systems follow the classic differentiation into front and back office functions (see Figure 6.2), but must also link with other departments, such as food and beverage, laundry, maintenance, marketing, etc.

Assignment 6

Situation

You are a consultant specialising in the design and installation of computerised management information systems for leisure and tourism organisations, in the private, public and voluntary sectors of the industry. After working for a large multinational leisure corporation since leaving college, you decided, five years ago, to start your own consultancy business. You are weathering the current recession reasonably well but were forced to make one of your three associates redundant 12 months ago.

Tasks

At a recent MIS exhibition in Glasgow, you made contact with an old school friend, George Taylor, who is now the Managing Director of a leisure company with a wide range of interests, including:

- A travel agency.
- A health and fitness club.
- A fast-food outlet.
- A pub.

George has been concerned for some time that the mainly manual systems that he currently has in place in all his outlets are proving costly to operate and that he may well be losing valuable business to competitors who run computerised management information systems. He has asked you to produce a short report explaining the costs and benefits associated with introducing a computerised MIS in any THREE of his businesses. You should give careful consideration to the information needs of the businesses you choose, as well as indicating the most appropriate systems and equipment which would best meet his needs.

Your report should be around 1,500 words in length and include relevant information on systems currently on the market.

Revision test questions

1 What is a management information system?
2 What is the relationship between information and the objectives of an organisation?
3 List five common features which an organisation should bear in mind when designing or purchasing a management information system.
4 What are the three key information needs of managers in leisure and tourism organisations?
5 What are 'cost centres'?
6 What do you understand by the term 'performance ratios' in relation to leisure and tourism organisations?
7 Give two examples of operational information that is required by the managers of leisure and tourism organisations.
8 Explain the meaning of 'front office' and 'back office' in the leisure and tourism industry.
9 List five 'front office' and five 'back office' functions in a leisure and tourism organisation.
10 Give three risks which a MIS must be guarded against.
11 Explain four of the eight Data Protection Principles that are contained in the Data Protection Act 1984.
12 Give five examples of specific data that a local authority leisure centre will need on its management information system.
13 What are the four basic steps in deciding on a computerised MIS?
14 Explain what is meant by EPOS and give three examples of its use in leisure and tourism.
15 What are the specific functions that a theatre will require from its MIS?
16 What do the initials CRS stand for in the travel and tourism sector?

17 What functions will an outbound tour operator consider when choosing a MIS?

18 How can a computerised MIS help with the management of a major tourist attraction?

19 What does an airline mean when it talks of 'load factor'?

20 What measures can a leisure and tourism organisation take to ensure the security of its management information system?

Unit 7
WORKING IN TEAMS

Section 1 Teamwork in leisure and tourism

Introduction

Teamwork is an essential part of the leisure and tourism industry, not just in the UK but throughout the world. All sectors of this very broad industry rely on teams and groups of people to get things done. There are countless examples of team situations in leisure and tourism, including:

- A team of three students carrying out a visitor survey for a local tourist attraction.
- A conference organiser and her team of two who organise business conferences and meetings at a country house hotel.
- The crew of a Britannia Airways jet flying from Manchester to Palma in Majorca with 190 holiday-makers on board.
- A small independent tour operator with a team of four sales and reservations staff.
- A school's hockey team.
- A team responsible for organising a charity event such as a fun-run.
- The cast of a major West End musical such as Cats.
- An English couple who own and run a wine bar in Benidorm.

It is a fact of life in leisure and tourism that most tasks are carried out by teams rather than by individuals. Good products, services and facilities don't just happen, but are the result of concerted effort by groups of people seeking to achieve a common goal. By the same token, the skills of teamwork are not always built into an individual's character but frequently have to be learned through training and experience. It is important to remember that teamwork is both a philosophy and a skill; it is one of the roles of the leisure and tourism manager to create the organisational culture within which teamwork is encouraged and supported, and to allow staff to develop the skills needed to operate as an effective team member.

Characteristics of teams

What are teams?

A concise definition of an effective team would include the following characteristics:

- A group of people working towards a clearly defined goal or objective.
- Is made up of individuals committed to the task.
- Is given the necessary authority to carry out the task.
- Is allocated the necessary resources to do the job properly.
- It operates in an 'open' fashion, sharing ideas and concerns.

A team may develop formally or informally. An example of a formal team is given in Figure 7.1, where the structure of a typical high street travel agency is shown. A formal team often operates within the work environment and is characterised by having a leader appointed by the organisation, in this case the branch manager.

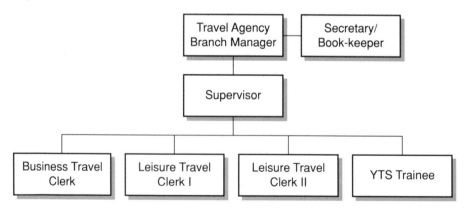

Fig 7.1 A typical formal team structure

As well as having an appointed leader, formal teams also:

- Are established to carry out specific tasks and to help achieve organisational objectives.

- Assign specific roles to each team member.
- Have clearly identified channels of communication.
- Have clear lines of authority and responsibility.

Informal teams also exist in leisure and tourism organisations. They tend to develop organically rather than through an organisational structure. They may form for social or work-related reasons. In the work situation, colleagues often find it easier to make decisions through talking informally rather than in a formal setting, such as at a meeting or group presentation. The importance of informal teams should not be underestimated, but there should be mechanisms in place to channel the outcome of informal gatherings into the more formal team setting.

Why have teams?

This may seem a rather strange question to ask, since many of the tasks carried out in leisure and tourism organisations can only be accomplished through the efforts of a team of people. Tasks such as staging a banquet for 150 guests or hosting a major swimming championships are too large and complex to be left to a single individual or workers who neither communicate with each other nor work as part of a team; in many cases, a team approach is the only solution.

Effective teamwork brings benefits both to the organisation that sets up the team and to the individual team members. Benefits to the organisation will vary depending on its size, structure and culture, but are likely to include:

- *Increased efficiency* – an example of this could be that an effective team working in the information department of a national tourist office will be able to handle more enquiries from customers.
- *Increased sales* – a teamwork approach to selling holiday insurance by telephone is likely to yield increased sales when compared with the same activity carried out individually.
- *Less staff conflict* – a team that is trained to take responsibility for its own work and decision making is likely to be better at resolving its own internal problems, thus saving valuable management time.
- *Reduced absenteeism* – staff who see themselves as valued members of a team are likely to be more content and take less time off work.
- *Increased loyalty* – teamwork instils a sense of loyalty and commitment into members of staff.
- *A more creative workforce* – team members are more likely to come forward with ideas for improving work practices, reducing costs or increasing efficiency.
- *A happier workforce* – teamwork allows individuals to work to their full potential and feel good about themselves and their work.

Above all, management is keen to see that by establishing a team to carry out a task, it is getting more than just 'the sum of the parts'. In other words, three people who previously prepared meals in a fast-food restaurant individually and were able to prepare ten meals each per hour, would be expected to deliver more than 3×10 meals per hour when working as a team.

Benefits to individual team members are:

- An enhanced sense of their worth within the organisation.
- The ability to use their talents to the full.
- Increased status within the organisation.
- The chance to be innovative and creative.
- Increased rewards for their work made possible as a result of greater efficiency, e.g. a productivity bonus or extra 'perks'.
- The support of other team members.
- More job satisfaction.

Good and bad teams

Why do some teams fail?

Selecting individuals to be part of a team is not an easy task. Leisure and tourism managers who think that building a team involves nothing more than selecting the brightest staff and locking them away in a room are in for a nasty shock! It is essential to be aware of group dynamics, i.e. how individuals relate to and interact with each other, when choosing staff for a team. A lack of awareness of group interaction is one of the main reasons for teams failing to achieve their objectives.

Another reason why teams fail is that they are not given, or do not develop, clear goals and objectives from the outset. If members of a team are unclear as to what it is they are supposed to be achieving, then their performance will suffer and their work will lack direction and purpose.

Vested interests can sometimes lead to the downfall of a team. For example, a group of local council sports development officers who have come together to mount a major county-wide sports promotion event, may be hampered in their efforts by one of their number who insists that his district must always have the last word when any decisions are made. Individuals who put their own vested interests before the 'corporate good' are of little use to a team that is trying to be as effective as possible.

Ineffective leadership can mean that a team fails to achieve its full potential. A leader who does not recognise potential in individual members, who cannot prioritise or lead by example, will lack credibility and may even become a liability to the team.

Another reason why teams sometimes fail is because of poor communication. Team leaders need to establish the mechanism by which decisions are conveyed both inside and outside the team, and develop an 'open' culture that encourages feedback, questioning and debate amongst team members.

A failure to maintain momentum can lead to a team not being able to fully meet its aims. The team leader should anticipate that after an initial period of excitement and commitment from team members, their enthusiasm may falter, and he or she will need to have ideas and mechanisms to hand to be able to generate a new tide of effort from all team members. It is a good idea to plan social events and gatherings where team members can 'let their hair down' and forget about the challenges they face at work. Changing the venue of team meetings can be another good way of maintaining momentum.

The characteristics of an effective team

Having considered some of the reasons why teams fail to meet their objectives, we can begin to think about a 'blueprint' for a successful team. Such a team would have the following characteristics:

1 Members who have a clear idea of what the team is trying to achieve.
2 An informal atmosphere within which ideas are developed.
3 A leader whose role is that of 'facilitator', i.e. creating the culture that allows others to work to their full potential.
4 Good communication among team members.
5 A commitment from all team members to the task in hand.
6 Team members selected on the basis of their skill at working with others.
7 Regular team meetings in an appropriate environment.
8 A known 'lifespan' if the team has been formed for a specific project.
9 Access to the necessary resources to achieve the task.
10 The support of senior management in the organisation.
11 A system that ensures accurate recording of decisions made by the group, with clear identification of who is responsible for taking the action and by when.

In an ideal world, every leisure and tourism organisation would like to be able to develop teams that exhibit all of the above characteristics. However, as we are all aware, the reality of working in leisure and tourism, particularly in times of economic recession, is often far from 'ideal'; budgets may not be increased or, even worse, may be cut, staff may have to be made redundant and other cost-cutting measures may need to be implemented. While these pressures will have an undoubted effect on team operation, many of the characteristics of effective teams listed above are internal to the team itself and its members. The team will, for example, be responsible for its own internal communication and for setting an atmosphere that is informal yet conducive to getting the task done. To some extent, therefore, a team can still operate effectively even in a difficult economic climate; indeed it could be argued that it is more important to develop effective staff teams when the economy is in recession, in order that an organisation remains competitive in the leisure and tourism industry.

Team leadership

The role of the team leader

In leisure and tourism the team leader must be more than just a figurehead but an effective manager as well. Good team leaders do not wallow in the glory and prestige of their position, but get involved with guiding their team to eventual success in its task. Once the decision has been taken to form a team to carry out a specific task or tasks, the choice of leader must be the first consideration. He or she must be involved in all stages of team development (see Figure 7.2).

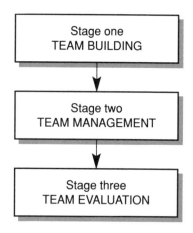

Fig 7.2 The stages in team development

In many cases, a team leader will not have the luxury of selecting a complete team from scratch. He or she will often be in the position of taking over an existing team of people who may have been together for a long period of time. Whenever feasible, the leader must be involved at the team building stage in selecting team members for a new team or one which is being reorganised. An organisation which arbitrarily selects team members over the head of the team leader is immediately undermining the leader's position.

The leader will act as a facilitator during the team management stage when the real work of the team is underway. The leader should not try to dominate proceedings but rather create the right atmosphere to give team members the best chance of success.

The leader will need to constantly monitor how the team is functioning and will need to reflect on how well it performed at the team evaluation stage. Evaluation is all about measuring team effectiveness, i.e. how well did the team perform? If clear objectives have been set for the team, it will be easier to answer this question (see Section 3 of this unit for more on evaluation of team performance).

The perfect team leader

We have acknowledged that organisations in the leisure and tourism industry often have to operate in an imperfect world; for example, a local council may be forced to make cuts in the provision of leisure services for local people, there may not be the money for the extra staff needed in a city-centre hotel, a travel agency may still be using out-dated computer equipment, which should have been replaced 12 months ago owing to a shortage of capital, or an airline may have to postpone the introduction of a new fleet of aircraft until business picks up. Against these difficult situations, finding the 'perfect' team leader, and being able to give him or her all the 'tools' to carry out an effective job, is not an easy task. When looking for a team leader, however, it is important to appoint the 'best' person for the job, whether it is somebody already working for the organisation or a candidate from outside. When looking for the 'perfect' team leader, an organisation needs to find an individual who will:

1 Accept the challenge and responsibility of leading the team from day one.
2 Be enthusiastic about the task and spread this enthusiasm to all members of the team.
3 Communicate effectively with other team members and those outside the team who need to be kept abreast of developments.
4 Plan and co-ordinate, with all team members, the strategy that the team will adopt, while keeping the objectives of the team constantly in mind.
5 Develop skills and qualities in other team members so that they may achieve their full potential.
6 Promote an 'open' style of management by discussing all matters of concern to the group and by listening to the views and concerns of all team members.
7 Adopt an action-orientated approach to making things happen, by first identifying what needs to be done in a certain situation, then stating the action that needs to be carried out, who is responsible for carrying it out and a date or time by which it must be completed.
8 Constantly promote a positive approach to solving problems and pushing the work of the team forward in a positive manner.
9 Manage the evaluation process to identify any ways in which the team could have worked more effectively or how particular problems could have been resolved.
10 Acknowledge the achievements of team members and publicise successes both internally and externally.
11 Not be afraid of admitting mistakes, but will build on them and actively work towards quality in all aspects of team operation.
12 Involve all team members in the decision-making process.

Communication and teamwork

Of all the reasons why teams fail to fulfil their objectives, poor communication is probably the most common. A team that is unable to develop an 'open' culture, with effective communication channels both within the team and outside, will not achieve its full potential. The team leader will have a crucial role to play in ensuring that effective communication takes place, and, just as importantly, takes place in a way that encourages team members to perform to their maximum; handled badly, communication can be a distinct disincentive to good performance.

Communication within a team means more than just the occasions when the team members are talking to each other in a meeting. This verbal communication, to which can be added talking on the telephone, is obviously very important, but is only a small part of the total communication process. Communication by team members can also be in written form, for example minutes of meetings, fax/telex messages or a report on a particular subject. Often as important as written and verbal communication is the way in which information is sent, received and understood by others; this is the subject known as non-verbal communication (NVC). The most talked-about type of NVC is body language, the process by which we send and receive messages without using words. A team leader who is making an important point during a meeting may well bang the table or wave his or her arms about to stress the importance of what is being said. Body language is sometimes classified as:

- *Bodily contact* – shaking hands, for example.
- *Physical proximity* – the distance we feel we need to keep between ourselves and other people, for example as a spectator at a football match.
- *Orientation* – where we place ourselves in relation to others. By tradition, a leader running a team meeting will sit at the head of the table.
- *Posture* – whether standing, sitting, lying down, walking or running, there is often something about our body posture which relays a message to those around us, either consciously or unconsciously.
- *Gestures* – we all make gestures from time to time to signal approval or disapproval, for example 'a thumbs up' to show you agree with what is being suggested.
- *Facial expression* – the face can transmit an enormous range of messages and emotions, either consciously or subconsciously. Like much non-verbal communication, facial expressions can sometime be misinterpreted.
- *Eye contact* – whether we are aware of it or not, we pay a great deal of attention to a person's eyes when they are communicating with us.

Two-way communication

Effective teams must develop good two-way communication channels. An example of two-way communication in a team situation is as follows:

> *Julie, the duty manager of a local authority leisure centre, has called a meeting of the four staff under her control to explain the introduction of a new membership system for the squash courts. Mike, a recreation assistant who has recently joined the team, asks Julie a question on prices for squash players who are under 12 years of age. Julie is able to respond to the question and give Mike the necessary information. Mike is still not clear about part of her answer and so asks a further question. Julie finally answers all Mike's points and thanks him for raising the matter.*

Both parties, Julie and Mike, are able to ask questions of each other and clarify any points about which they may be unclear. An alternative way of explaining the new membership system to staff would have been to circulate a memo; this is an example of one-way communication since it gives the person receiving it no immediate answers to any points that are unclear or could be misinterpreted. Two-way communication has many advantages, although it is initially more time consuming, and should be used whenever possible.

CASE STUDY

Teamwork in action – the British Travel Trade Fair

The British Travel Trade Fair (BTTF) is an annual exhibition that gives suppliers of British tourism 'products' the chance to introduce themselves and their organisations to potential buyers, who may be coach operators, conference organisers, tour operators, excursion organisers, the travel press, overseas buyers or travel agents. The buyers need up-to-date information on new products on offer from British suppliers and the BTTF is a cost-effective way of doing business 'under one roof'. In 1993 the exhibition was held at the National Exhibition Centre (NEC) in Birmingham, chosen for its central location and excellent road, rail and air links. BTTF attracted 380 exhibitors for the 1993 event, the first to benefit from the full support of all four UK tourist boards and the BTA. Exhibitors included:

- *Hotels and other accommodation providers* – e.g. Best Western Hotels, YHA, Consort Hotels, Forte Hotels, Queens Moat Houses, etc.
- *Visitor attractions* – e.g. Alton Towers, English Heritage, London Zoo, Wembley Stadium Tours, the World of Robin Hood, etc.
- *Destinations* – e.g. City of Bath, Black Country, Cheshire, Llangollen, City of Gloucester, Portsmouth Tourism, York Visitor and Conference Bureau, etc.
- *Tourist boards* – e.g. London Tourist Board, West Country Tourist Board, Wales Tourist Board, British Tourist Authority, etc.
- *Operators and transport providers* – e.g. Channel Island Ferries, Butlin's Holiday Worlds, Jersey European, Rainbow Holidays, Le Shuttle (Eurotunnel), etc.

- *Suppliers, services and publications* – e.g. Bus and Coach Council, Travel GBI newspaper, Conference Blue & Green Books, 'In Britain' Magazine, etc.

The organisation of the BTTF is very much a team affair. It is organised by Group Travel Trade and Events, a subgroup of the English Tourist Board (ETB) Marketing Department, in co-operation with the Scottish (STB), Wales (WTB) and Northern Ireland (NITB) Tourist Boards. The BTTF organising team is made up of:

- Exhibition Manager (ETB).
- Exhibition Operations Manager (ETB).
- Exhibition Executive (ETB).
- Events Co-ordinator (ETB).
- Press Office Manager (ETB).
- ETB Marketing Department Staff (3).
- STB Marketing Department Representative.
- WTB Marketing Department Representative.
- NITB Marketing Department Representative.

This team is given the overall responsibility for planning, staging and evaluating the event. For the duration of the BTTF, which in 1993 was a two-day event from 31 March until 1 April, the organising team is joined by 8 more ETB Marketing staff to cope with day-to-day management.

As well as attending training and briefing sessions about the event, all team members are issued with BTTF briefing notes, compiled by the organising group to give details of the roles and functions of the team members. The briefing notes cover:

- Names of the organising team.
- Categories of exhibitors (distinguished by colour-coded badges).
- Types of buyers (again given different colour badges).
- The location.
- Registration information.
- Organisers' office.
- Press office.
- 'Privilege' club (for VIP guests and buyers).
- Students' room.
- The official BTTF guidebook.
- Storage facilities.
- Catering facilities.
- Canvassing (only exhibitors are allowed to distribute printed material).
- Telephones/radios (for the team to keep in touch).
- Accommodation for the team.
- Dress (which staff wear which 'uniform').

Team operation

The rota for day one of the 1993 BTTF (Tuesday) is given in Figure 7.3, together with an explanation of the codes used in the rota.

	ELEANOR	CHRIS	SHEILA	JOHN	KIRSTY	EMMA	DAVE	JOSIE	DIANA	HELEN	DOLORES	KERSTIN	JO
TUESDAY													
0830				H	F	F	F	*	*	*	*	F	F
0900				H	F	F	F	*	*	*	*	F	F
0930				H	F	F	F	*	*	*	*	F	F
1000				H	H	H	H	*	*	*	*	H	H
1030				H	H	H	H	*	*	*	*	H	H
1100				H	H	H	H	*	*	*	*	H	H
1130				O	O	H	O	*	*	*	*	H	H
1200				O	O	H	O	F	F	F	F	H	H
1230				O	O	H	O	F	F	F	F	H	H
1300				O	O	H	O	F	F	F	F	H	H
1330				H	O	H	H	H	H	H	H	H	H
1400				H	O	H	H	H	H	H	H	H	H
1430				H	C	H	H	C	H	H	H	H	H
1500				H	C	H	H	C	H	H	H	H	H
1530				H	C	H	H	C	H	H	H	H	H
1600				H	C	H	H	C	H	H	H	H	H
1630				H	C	H	H	C	H	H	H	H	H
1700				H	C	H	H	C	H	H	H	H	H
1730				H	H	H	H	H	H	H	H	H	H
1800				H	H	H	H	H	H	H	H	H	H
1830				H	H	H	H	H	H	H	H	H	H
1900				H	H	H	H	H	H	H	H	H	H
1930				H	H	H	H	H	H	H	H	H	H
2000				H	H	H	H	H	H	H	H	H	H

STAND ROTA CODE EXPLANATION

C **Conferences . . . and Forums and Seminars and Meetings**
– Generally looking after people;
– Before: showing them where coffee is, directing them into Seminar Suites;
– During: operating roving mikes;
– After: directing them to Hall 6 (or to Coach and Bus Week Reception).

E **Exhibitor Registration Desk**
– Inserting Exhibitor badges into red badge holders; answering questions.

F **Familiarisation**
– Familiarising yourself with the British Travel Trade Fair!

H **Helping wherever needed**
– Setting up (stands; Press Office; Privilege Club; Students' Room);
– Doing stand drops;
– Being welcoming at the Welcome Reception;
– Being sociable at the Coach and Bus Week Reception/CTC Ball;
– Helping on Registration, including Exhibitor and Information desks; acting as a runner;
– Stage managing (John); poster mounting signing, and prop moving including signs upstairs and downstairs (John + Dave);
– Looking round the show; talking to exhibitors and buyers.

I **Information Desk**
– Giving directions; answering questions; solving problems.

O **Organisers' Office**
– All the time: answering telephone/fax messages; dealing with problems; ordering food and drink; keeping office tidy;
– During Build Up: registering buyers; inserting Exhibitor badges into **Red** badge holders; exchanging guides for vouchers; allocating welcome reception welcome drink vouchers;
– During Business Hours: giving callers for exhibitors the Heart of England stand Tel. 021-780 2266; sorting/counting registration cards.

P **Privilege Club**
– Being the VIP public face of BTTF (and ETB); keeping room tidy.

R **Registration Area**
– Directing visitors to the right registration points i.e.
– Exhibitors
– Buyers With Badges
– Buyers Without Badges
– Overseas Buyers
– Press Office
– Students' Room
– Assisting CES Team in selecting correct-colour badge holder; handing out carrier bags; keeping area tidy and people flowing through.

Fig 7.3 Team rota for day one of 1993 British Travel Trade Fair (courtesy of ETB)

The chart clearly identifies the role that each team member should take up at the relevant time. We can see how the rota works by looking at one of the team members, John, in detail. Between 0830 and 1100 John is covering role 'H', which we can see by looking at the code explanation means that he is generally helping wherever needed; a roving troubleshooter! Between 1130 and 1300 John is assigned role 'O', working in the organisers' office. For the rest of the day, between 1330 and 2000, he goes back to role 'H', helping wherever needed. A glance at the rest of the team members along the top of the rota will show their respective roles and duties.

After the event, the organising team holds a debriefing session where good and bad experiences are shared, with a view to making the 1994 BTTF even better.

(Information courtesy of ETB)

Section 2 **Team building and interaction**

Building an effective team

We saw in Section 1 of this unit that teamwork is an essential part of leisure and tourism the world over. Working in teams, however, is not new; since the beginning of time, man has selected individuals to form groups in order to achieve specific tasks, whether for work, social or religious purposes. Manufacturing industry in the nineteenth and twentieth centuries relied heavily on team work, and much of what was learnt in this sector is now being put into practice in service industries such as banking, insurance and leisure and tourism.

The recognition of the importance of teamwork in leisure and tourism is a recent phenomenon. While it is true that some organisations have used a team approach to providing leisure and tourism services since Victorian times, it is only in the last 20 years at best that team building and team development have been given a high priority in the management of facilities. Today's most effective and efficient leisure and tourism organisations, in the private, public and voluntary sectors, have recognised that time, money and effort spent on team building pays dividends. Using techniques and practices developed in the USA, Europe and the Far East, many UK leisure and tourism organisations have changed their structures, increased their staff training and developed a culture based on decision making by teams of people rather than individuals. These organisations have become more successful in achieving their objectives and individual employees have benefited from a more 'open' management style and a more cohesive approach to work.

There are six main stages in building an effective team:

1 Team rationale.
2 Selection of staff.
3 Resource provision.
4 Developing a team approach.
5 Encouraging team development.
6 Evaluating team performance.

Stage one – team rationale

It is important to remember that building a team is not always the most effective way of achieving a task. Managers must be skilled at deciding when a team approach to solving a particular problem or tackling a job is the best course of action. Many day-to-day management decisions are taken by individuals without recourse to a team. There are occasions when a manager will set up a team to tackle a particular issue to hide the fact that he or she is unable, or unwilling, to take on the responsibility for making the necessary decision. Senior management must be aware of this practice, which is wasteful of scarce resources.

The rationale stage of team building is concerned with whether it is necessary to set up a team to achieve a particular objective. It tries to answer such questions as, 'do we really need a team?' and 'is there a better (and cheaper) way of achieving the same conclusion?'. If an organisation is convinced that a team approach is the best way forward, it must then consider the objectives of the team and the parameters within which it will work. The parameters could include:

- The budget the team will be allocated. The team should be given at the outset the limits of any expenditure it can incur and any income targets it has to meet.
- The maximum number of staff who can be invited to join the team. In a small organisation, it may be felt that only two or three people can be spared to join the team, otherwise normal operations may be adversely affected.
- Specific individuals who cannot join the team. If the team is being established in an existing organisation, these will usually be members of staff who have a full workload at present and cannot be released. If the team is being put together for a specific event, there may be many reasons why particular individuals are not invited to join the team, ranging from confidentiality to personality clashes.
- The time-scale within which the team must operate. The team members should know how long they will be working together, and if there are any interim time targets they will have to meet for specific elements of their work.

When we come to the objectives of the team, the leader may be given a broad goal by the organisation and asked to develop with the team the specific objectives that will need to be achieved in order to reach the goal. For example, a tour operator which at present only organises holidays to Spain may set up a team with a goal 'to expand operations into long-haul holidays to West Africa'. The team will then identify specific objectives, which could include:

- To have a turnover of £5 million on holidays to West Africa within three years.
- To sell 1,000 holidays to West Africa in the first year.
- To set up contracts with 20 hotels in West Africa for the first season.
- To be known for offering a high quality product within the industry.
- To train all staff in the importance of customer service.
- To establish a network of agents to sell the holidays.

The team will organise itself to work to these objectives within the time-scale and budget given by the organisation. In some cases, specific objectives will already have been developed and the team will be asked to comment on them and suggest any modifications it may feel are appropriate.

Once the rationale for the team has been developed and everybody is clear about why it has been set up, the job of selecting staff can begin.

Stage two – selection of staff

The most important appointment to the team is likely to be the team leader. We discussed in Section 1 of this unit the characteristics of the 'ideal' leader and the qualities he or she will need to mould a successful team (see page 7.7). The team leader may be somebody already working for the organisation or may be taken on to head up a team working on a specific project or event. Unless they have very strong characters, leaders who already work for an organisation sometimes find it difficult to adapt to their new roles and responsibilities. The staff selected to join the team may also find it hard to accept that the leader has a new function in the organisation and may themselves have to change the way they deal with the leader. For these reasons, leisure and tourism organisations sometimes prefer to appoint a new person from outside the organisation to be the team leader. This person then has the difficult task of selecting team members from a pool of staff about which he or she knows very little. The leader will also need to be sensitive to the fact that some of the team members will feel insecure and perhaps uncomfortable in their new positions. A leader with great tact and diplomacy will be needed to 'win over' some members of the team.

Size of the team

There is no 'best' size of team that will apply in all circumstances. The number of people who are chosen to form the team will depend on many factors, including:

- The type of task to be undertaken – a team brought together to deal with a very technical task, e.g. involving language translation, is likely to need more 'specialists'.

- The size and significance of the task – a team formed to plan and stage an inter-national sporting event, for example, is going to need to be large in order to cover the multitude of complex tasks involved.
- The length of time it is likely to take to complete – a project that will run for months or even years may be managed by a small team who may, from time to time, change roles and responsibilities.
- The size of the organisation – the bigger the organisation, the less likely it is to suffer from team members being released from their normal work duties.
- The time of year – many leisure and tourism organisations operate on a sea-sonal basis, thus making it possible for a larger team to be formed outside the peak season, than would be the case if it was formed at the busiest time of year.
- The abilities and skills of the team members – a small team of highly experi-enced individuals may be able to achieve the same outcomes as a larger team made up of staff with less experience and training.

Research does suggest that teams can become unwieldy and difficult to control once the number of members gets into double figures. The team leader can begin to experience difficulties with communication and co-ordination when numbers go beyond ten people. A team size of six to nine members is likely to function effectively and be of a size which is capable of being managed by the team leader.

There may be occasions when the task that the team has been set is so large that no single team could be expected to cope with all that is expected. In such cir-cumstances, the leader may well decide to slit the team into subgroups and identify a group leader who would report back on progress. This is the situation that often exists in the management of hotels, for example, when a general man-ager delegates authority to section managers who control the working of a team of staff (see Figure 7.4)

In Figure 7.4, the general manager delegates authority (through an assistant manager) to the food and beverage manager who in turn organises teams to deliver the services in the restaurant, kitchens and banqueting with back-up teams in the food stores, bars and cellar.

Compatibility of team members

The mix of personal characteristics in members of a team is a major determinant of its success. Simply bringing together the individuals with the greatest techni-cal expertise, best qualifications or most experience, does not guarantee success in a team. These qualities are obviously important, but just as important is the way in which the team members interact. The most important characteristics that can affect the team's performance are:

- *Personality* – all human beings have a unique personality and will react in dif-ferent ways when in a team situation. Some will be quiet and reflective while others will be loud and try to dominate the group. It is the team leader's role to give all team members the opportunity to state their views, while building on

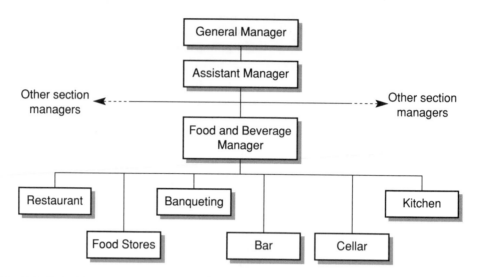

Fig 7.4 Sub-division of teamwork in a hotel

the positive characteristics of individuals. The leader must anticipate potential conflict and have measures ready to resolve any problems caused by differing personalities.

- *Background* – team members who have a similar background are more likely to gel into an effective team quickly and understand the task in hand. Differences in culture, language, education and social status, can sometimes lead to problems of team cohesion. Team members with similar hobbies or interests will have a common talking point from the outset, which will help team development.
- *Age and experience of work* – team members who are roughly the same age and with similar lengths of time in their jobs, are likely to form into an effective team on the basis of their shared experiences.

Training the team

Resources will need to be made available for staff training if the team is going to achieve its objective. Training for teams can take many forms:

- *Training in technical skills* – it is likely that some members of the team will need specific technical training in order to be able to fulfil their roles effectively. Going back to the example of the food and beverage section of a large hotel (see Figure 7.4), some members of the team working in the kitchens will need technical training in, for example, food hygiene and food storage. A team that has been developed to change the admissions procedure at a visitor attraction may need specialist training in computer spreadsheets and databases. Members of a team working on a new fitness suite for a leisure centre will need instruction and training in the technical aspects of the equipment being installed.

- *Training in administrative skills* – whether or not a team is lucky enough to have good administrative support, it is helpful if at least some team members have a grasp of basic administrative skills, such as note taking, word processing and report writing. All teams will need to process day-to-day paperwork. It is useful to have a team member who can interpret financial data and train others in the group to be able to do the same, perhaps with the help of computer software.
- *Training in inter-personal skills* – all team members will benefit from training in such matters as communication, decision making, listening skills, problem solving, working collaboratively, and a host of others. The team leader may need specialist training in, for example, managing team meetings, developing team skills, negotiation, evaluating team performance and resolving conflict. Such training can be carried out 'in-house' or with the help of an outside trainer. An increasingly popular way of learning team building and other interpersonal skills is for team members to spend time at an activity centre, where they are given physical and mental challenges to help develop management skills. One of the leading companies offering this type of training is 'The Competitive Edge', based in the Lake District (see Figure 7.5), which has worked with many well-known companies including Stakis Hotels, BMW and Laing Homes.

Stage three – resource provision

Any team that is given a specific task to do should also be given the 'tools' to do the job properly. We shall look at some of the more important resources that the team will need, starting with the physical environment it is given to work in.

The work environment

A team always functions best if its members all work in the same location or at least in close proximity to each other. Team members who share the same office, for example, are likely to form into a cohesive group. Where it is not possible for all the members of a team to be housed together, perhaps because the group is simply too large, there must be effective means of communication so that ideas and decisions can be swiftly conveyed to all staff. The nature of many leisure and tourism organisations will mean that the work environment for the team will be the facility itself, e.g. a leisure centre, hotel, museum, aircraft or outdoor activity centre. Working in close proximity to colleagues in these situations, with few physical barriers, can mean that teams perform particularly well and that a tremendous team spirit is built up. Team leaders need to be aware, however, of the potential pressures and conflicts that can arise in such circumstances and be prepared to take whatever action is necessary to manage the situation.

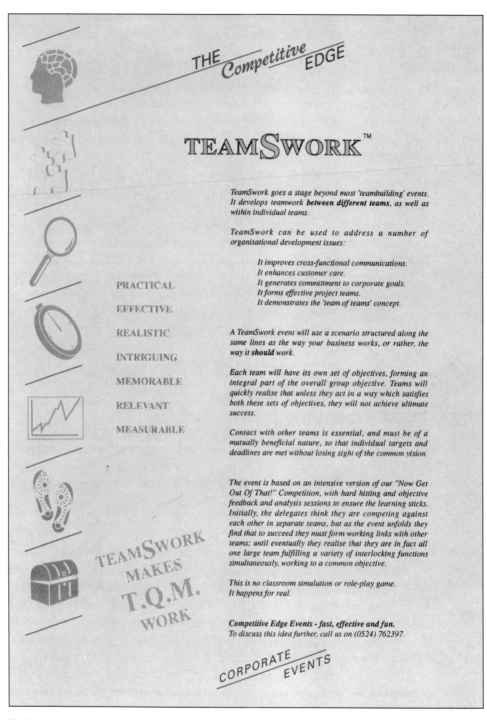

Fig 7.5 An example of inter-personal skills training offered by 'The Competitive Edge'

Equipment

Access to the necessary communications equipment and technology will be vital to the team if it is to stand any chance of meeting its objective. Depending on the nature and size of the team's task, it may need to have:

- Specialist computer software, e.g. for a CRS (central reservations system).
- Technical equipment, e.g. specialist ovens for kitchen staff.
- Communications equipment, e.g. fax machine, telex, telephones, audio-visual aids, etc.
- The use of vehicles for transporting people and equipment.

Given the right level of equipment, the team will feel comfortable about having sufficient resources to do the job it has been set.

Support staff

There will be times when the team will need the support of other people in order to function effectively. These people may be from inside the organisation, so it is important that the whole workforce is aware of the team's existence and has a feel for what it is trying to achieve. A team leader may sometimes feel that it would be helpful to employ somebody from outside the organisation to join the team, perhaps for a short period of time or for a particular task that cannot be carried out by the current team members. Consultants can be employed to take on the role of 'facilitator' or 'observer', and so give an objective view of how the team is performing and pinpoint any ways in which it could improve its effectiveness.

Stage four – developing a team approach

Once the team members have been selected and sufficient resources made available, consideration must be given to the many factors that influence the way in which a team approach can be developed, including:

- Team leadership and management styles.
- Group motivation.
- Personnel policies and practices.
- External threats.

Leadership and management styles

We have already discussed the pivotal role the team leader plays in managing the work of the team. He or she should not try to dominate proceedings within the group but rather act as a 'catalyst' who creates the right environment and conditions in which the team can operate effectively. While the leader of the team may have a very 'open' management style, he or she may be constrained by the decisions of senior management, who may appear distant and bureaucratic. For a team to be completely effective, the senior management of the organisation must also adopt an 'open' style of management and give the leader and team members the freedom to take risks in seeking to achieve their objectives. Compare, for example, the management styles of Virgin Atlantic Airways, with its charismatic Chairman Richard Branson, with that of British Rail, a state-controlled monopoly. Virgin is characterised as an organisation that is willing to take risks to achieve its objectives, and, in so doing, is committed to an 'open' style of management with team decision making in evidence throughout the organisation. British Rail, on the other hand, has a very hierarchical structure, which some say leaves little room for team innovation and swift decision making.

Group motivation

The more successful the team, the more motivated its members are likely to be, and vice versa. The leader should aim to maintain this cycle of motivation and success, which will lead to effective team performance, by praising individuals and the team as a whole when successes have been achieved. There may be times when the team deserves more than just praise from the team leader or senior management, but has earned a reward for its efforts. Rewards can act as positive motivators if handled carefully and in such a way that doesn't build resentment between those in the organisation, but outside the team, who do not receive the reward. Typical rewards for teams could include bonus payments, social events, free holidays or short breaks.

Personnel policies and practices

Policies concerned with personnel matters should reflect the importance that is given to teamwork by the organisation. It is pointless for a local authority leisure services department, for example, to say that it puts a high priority on teamwork in the management of its facilities, and then to have no budget for training in teamwork skills. Similarly, systems for appraisal, promotion and personal development should reflect a commitment to team operation and development. Personnel practices should also treat all members of teams in an equitable fashion and should not create antagonism between those members of staff who work in teams and those who do not, by virtue of the fact that members of teams are perceived as being favoured by management.

External threats

One of the most powerful factors in helping develop team cohesion is a threat from outside the team. Human nature dictates that individuals will co-operate more effectively in the face of external threats. In the world of leisure and tourism, threats could come from a number of different sources. It could be a threat from a competitor who is about to open a fast-food outlet next door to your restaurant, or an airline that is trying to get permission to fly its planes on one of your most profitable routes. Closer to home, the appointment of a new manager or new team leader may be considered a threat by some members of the team. Even if the threat is subsequently removed, team development will have been helped and a more cohesive team will result. It has been known for some organisations to create mythical threats, perhaps by circulating a rumour, in order to develop team cohesion.

Stage five – encouraging team development

BW Tuckman wrote an article in the mid-1960s which looked at the different stages of team development and the relationships that develop between team members. Tuckman's work, which is still often quoted by researchers and academics who specialise in team building, identified four stages of team development; forming, storming, norming and performing.

Forming

This is the initial stage of the formation of the group, when the objectives and team roles are being clarified. Team members are likely to feel anxious at this stage and will be trying to establish their credentials and create an impression on both the team leader and the other members of the team. The leader too may feel unclear about the capabilities of team members and be unsure about his or her own performance.

Storming

Once individual team members get to know each other, they will be more willing to enter into debate and challenge colleagues on issues they are concerned about. This should be encouraged by the team leader, since, if handled constructively, it will often lead to the team as a whole clarifying its rationale and the way in which it operates. Having a clarified purpose will also help to mould the team into an effective force.

Norming

Norming is all about setting the guidelines, standards and levels of acceptable behaviour under which the team will function. The storming stage should have united the team members and identified where each person stands on the sorts of issues to be dealt with at the norming stage. In other words, the norming stage sets the ground rules for all team members. At this stage, the team leader may feel the need to intervene when decisions made by the team could be seen as controversial or contrary to organisational policy.

Performing

Having progressed through the first three development stages, the team will now be in a position to perform the role or roles for which it was established, with a cohesive team framework allowing all team members to contribute to the attainment of their objectives.

Stage six – evaluating team performance

All team members will be encouraged to constantly monitor their individual activities and the performance of the team as a whole. Evaluation of team performance involves looking back at how effective the team was, either at the end of the project or event for which it was formed, or at clearly identified stages in its development. Evaluation is an important tool for both management and the team itself, so that lessons are learnt, excellence is rewarded and mistakes are analysed. Section 3 of this unit looks in detail at evaluating team performance (see page 7.25).

Conflict in teams

All organisations in leisure and tourism will, from time to time, have to deal with conflict in their staff. Teams, which by their very nature are made up of people working closely together, are perhaps more prone to conflict situations, particularly if the same team members are together over an extended period of time or are sharing the same workspace. A degree of healthy debate and criticism within a team is not of itself necessarily a bad thing; it is only through open discussion of issues that good decision making and problem solving can take place. Conflict, however, is a stage removed from healthy debate and discussion, and, if not managed well, can have serious implications for the organisation in which the team is working. Conflict in teams can lead to:

- Poor levels of customer service.
- Reduced profitability.
- Increased staff absenteeism.
- Reduced staff morale and commitment.
- Increased disciplinary problems.
- More management time being devoted to dealing with the problem.
- High staff turnover.

It is when conflict becomes so serious as to damage the viability of the organisation that the problem must be managed. Some organisations are of the opinion that conflict can be predicted, and there may well be occasions when potential conflict situations can be diffused before any real harm is done. Much conflict, however, is hard to predict because of its very spontaneous nature.

Why does conflict arise?

There are two types of conflict situations that may exist in leisure and tourism organisations; that which develops within the team (intra-team) and that which may exist between teams (inter-team). Intra-team conflict usually arises from a clash of personalities between one or more members of the team. An individual's personality is a very complex thing, but there are some clashes which appear frequently in team situations; for example, there may be a member of the team who is:

- *Aggressive* – often contributes unnecessarily hostile comments.
- *Cynical* – sees no point in going on.
- *Critical* – cannot think positively about the team and its work.
- *A perfectionist* – who is constantly revising decisions and ideas.
- *A liar* – is out to dismantle the team at all costs.
- *A gossip* – constantly spreads rumours.
- *A time waster* – continually interrupts with insignificant remarks.

Conflict may develop between the team leader and a member or members of the team. In this situation, senior management may well need to intervene to sort things out.

When we consider inter-team conflict, that is conflict that exists between one or more groups in the same organisation, there is often more to the problem than personality clashes alone. Inter-team conflict can result in one group becoming hostile to another, can lead to a breakdown in communication or a mistrust of one group by another. If we take as an example a large theme park such as EuroDisney, with many different teams controlling the rides, the car parking, catering, maintenance, litter and a host of other duties, a little rivalry between teams is to be encouraged in order to increase job satisfaction and team performance. Conflict could arise when one team is regarded by some of the others as being of a lower status; the staff responsible for litter collection, for example, may be considered of less value than those operating the rides. This could be overcome by rotating jobs on a regular basis, so that the rides operator in week one takes on the role of the litter collector in week two, and so on. Management must also continually stress that every member of staff is crucial to the success of the organisation.

Inter-team conflict can also arise when one team considers that it is not getting the same treatment as another team. Management must strive to treat all teams on an equal basis and, if there are reasons why one team is better rewarded than another, then an explanation is given.

Dealing with conflict

In the example of EuroDisney above, we saw two solutions to specific conflict situations, but there are some general principles that can be employed to deal with conflict.

Management style

We have compared the different styles of management employed at Virgin Atlantic and British Rail from the point of view of leadership and the development of a team approach to decision making. Management style is also very important when considering how to deal with conflict in a team. The style of management of the team leader and the organisation itself will determine how well conflict situations are handled.

In leisure and tourism organisations, management styles vary enormously. They can be categorised as follows:

- *Style one – passive management.* The passive manager will do the bare minimum in any given situation, will generally resist change and will operate with an unhealthy degree of 'slackness'.
- *Style two – committee management.* Committee managers will tend to steer a middle course on most matters and will try to remain popular with the members of the team. They will avoid open conflict and praise achievement, almost to the point of flattery.
- *Style three – administrative management.* This style of management will be carried out by the person who likes to 'do everything by the book'. The administrative manager will tend to be conscientious rather than innovative and will develop systems within the team for most operations.
- *Style four – aggressive management.* The aggressive manager is generally not a good listener but will request that everything is done his or her way, often without recourse to team discussion. He or she will give the impression of not worrying unduly about creating conflict within the team.
- *Style five – motivational management.* The motivational manager will agree goals with team members and will expect the team to perform well and achieve its aims. He or she will be supportive if staff are experiencing difficulties in their work. The motivational manager will consult widely with team members and make clear who is responsible for what.

When it comes to selecting which is the most effective management style when we are looking at how best to deal with conflict, most organisations would agree (except perhaps those that exhibit styles one to four!) that style five, motivational management is likely to achieve the most positive outcome. Displaying a management style that is 'open' rather than defensive, supportive rather than destructive, criticises in a positive rather than negative fashion, is assertive rather than aggressive, praises rather than undermines staff achievement and advocates good communication, is far more likely to resolve conflict by confronting it in a calm and logical manner.

Striving for the same goal

If conflict does develop within a team or between teams, it is important to stress to the conflicting parties that they are all striving for the same goal and are part of the same organisation. If the staff can focus on their own and their team's part in achieving the goal, then they can all feel valued members of the organisation and so be part of the 'winning team'. This message is often best conveyed by bringing the conflicting groups or individuals together and raising the level of debate above their own areas of conflict to the level of the common goal of the organisation. Management may decide to hold a series of regular informal meetings where members from all teams are given the opportunity of raising issues of concern and putting forward new ideas for team operation.

Section 3 Evaluating team performance

Teamwork in leisure and tourism is a means to an end, rather than an end in itself. It is a process, not a one-off event. Too many teams fail not because their initial planning and development lacks direction, but because they commit little, if any, time to review their effectiveness and to ensure that the gains, agreements and decisions made by the team are being implemented. Without time being set aside for evaluating performance, the team members will not fully learn from their experiences and management will not have an objective view on how well the team has performed.

Any evaluation of team performance will be trying to answer some or all of the following questions:

- Did the team as a whole achieve its objectives?
- Was the team leader effective?
- Did individual team members perform to the best of their ability?
- Were any weaknesses identified?
- Were measures put in place to rectify weaknesses?
- What were the strengths of the team and its members?
- Were there examples of outstanding performance?
- Was good performance commended or rewarded?
- Did the team identify any new directions for future work?
- Were the channels of communication effective?

Who should carry out the evaluation?

The precise methods of evaluating team performance and the personnel involved in the process will differ from one organisation to another. It is, however, generally agreed that the people who should not be left out of any evaluation are the team members themselves. They will have the most knowledge about how the team operated and will be aware of its successes and failures. Their perception of how the team performed will, of course, be subjective, i.e. their conclusions will be from their own viewpoint as members of the team. None the less, their views are critical to obtaining a valid evaluation of performance.

To arrive at a more objective view of the team's performance, the team leader may carry out an appraisal of the relative performance of each member of the team. A member of the senior management of the organisation may be allocated the job of appraising the team leader, individual team members or the team as a whole (see Unit 9 on human resource management for more details of staff appraisal). This same senior manager may be given the task of reviewing the team's performance against its objectives to see if it has, for example, achieved any financial targets it was set or reached any quotas on use by particular members of the local community, e.g. disabled people.

An observer is sometimes used to further increase the objectivity of the exercise. Usually from outside the organisation, this person will view the team's progress from the outset and be able to comment on performance and development issues. Consultants, staff from leisure and tourism departments at Colleges and Universities, local authority personnel and staff from professional bodies can be called upon to take on the role of observer to a leisure and tourism team.

Evaluation methods and techniques

Team review and evaluation

As soon as possible after the team has finished its work, or at pre-planned stages of its development, the team should carry out a review and evaluation exercise. This is likely to take the form of a meeting of all team members and will include both informal and formal feedback. Informal feedback from the team members will include their personal views and comments on their own performance and the effectiveness of the whole team, including the team leader. While informal feedback is a very useful tool for identifying broad areas of success and failure, a more formal reporting mechanism will be needed to measure team effectiveness. It is likely that the team will have identified its objectives at the start of its work. The more precise the objectives, and any associated performance criteria, the easier it will be for the team to measure its effectiveness in meeting its targets. For example, a member of a team that has been set up to introduce a new customer care programme into a museum may have been set performance criteria that could include:

- Record every complaint on an official complaint form.
- Write a letter to each person who complained apologising on behalf of the organisation and keep a copy for reference.

It will be a relatively straightforward matter to check whether these tasks have been carried out and so reach a conclusion on this element of the person's work performance.

Other recorded information that could be useful in measuring the team's performance includes customer feedback questionnaires, sales returns, ideas in suggestion boxes, wastage rates, repeat orders, numbers of returning customers, etc.

Staff performance review

Individual team members may be interviewed by either their line manager or the team leader, who may in fact be the same person, to formally assess an individual's performance in the team. This may be part of a wider staff appraisal exercise that links pay to performance. The interview will seek to identify good performance by the team member and areas where performance needs to be enhanced, perhaps by a particular type of staff development activity, e.g. going on a course that improves decision making. The outcome of the performance review should be a written development plan, agreed by both the reviewer and member of the team, which should list personal development objectives and the activities needed to meet the objectives.

Self-appraisal

Team members may be asked to formally evaluate their own performance against objectives and performance criteria by carrying out a self-appraisal, which, if undertaken in as objective a way as possible, can produce useful feedback both for the individual and his or her line manager. Such an appraisal can be fed into any wider staff appraisal exercise the organisation may undertake.

Peer appraisal

Peer appraisal involves the evaluation of a member of the team by his or her peers, i.e. the other members of the team. Formal rather than informal peer appraisal is more useful, since it can prevent the exercise becoming too personal.

If managed effectively by the team leader, however, it can be very enlightening and can help to identify strengths and weaknesses in individual team members, who can use the outcomes to identify any remedial measures that may be necessary.

Assignment 7

Situation

An important aspect of your GNVQ course is the development of skills that will help you in later life. Learning to work as an effective member of a team is essential for anybody wishing to follow a career in the leisure and tourism industry. There are few occasions in leisure and tourism when you will not be relying on the co-operation and support of colleagues.

Tasks

Working as a member of a team, you are to plan a fund-raising event for charity. It is likely that the whole of your college or school group will be involved with the planning, but you should nominate a small team of three or four to be observers. This small group will not be involved with organising the event, but will observe the larger group as it goes about its business.

The group organising the event could choose from a wide range of possible ideas, including:

- A coach excursion for a group of under-privileged children.
- A sports coaching session for disabled people living locally.
- A sponsored sports match.
- A disco or concert.

The group must work in a systematic fashion and record all meetings which take place. Responsibilities must be identified and individuals given specific tasks to perform. Careful attention will need to be paid to budgets and timescales.

The brief for the small team of observers is to monitor how the group as a whole, as well as individual members, performs. In deciding on the degree of effectiveness of the team, the observers will need to consider:

- Lines of authority.
- Channels of communication.
- Handling conflict.
- Team objectives.
- Roles and responsibilities.
- Factors that influence team effectiveness.
- Use of resources.
- Contributions of individual team members.

Once the event has taken place, a debriefing meeting should be called by the team of observers, at which they will report back to the rest of the group on how well they considered the team performed. There will be an opportunity for feedback from those involved in organising the event. The team of observers should conclude by writing a short report (no more than 500 words) on the effectiveness of the team in achieving its aims.

Revision test questions

1 Give three examples of team situations in leisure and tourism organisations.
2 List five characteristics of an effective team.
3 Explain the difference between formal and informal team structures.
4 What are the principal benefits to a leisure and tourism organisation of an effective team?
5 What are the main benefits to individual team members of working in an effective team?
6 Give five reasons why teams in leisure and tourism sometimes fail.
7 How do vested interests sometimes lead to the breakdown of a team?
8 Give five characteristics and qualities of an effective team leader.
9 What is 'non-verbal communication'?
10 What are the main stages in building an effective team?
11 What types of training are likely to help team effectiveness?
12 What effect can external threats have on an established team?
13 Why is it important to manage any conflict that arises in a team?
14 List five questions that an evaluation of a team's performance will seek to answer.
15 Who should be involved in the evaluation of a team's performance?

Unit 8
EVALUATING THE PERFORMANCE OF FACILITIES

Section 1 Organisational objectives

Setting objectives

All leisure and tourism organisations set themselves objectives or goals in order to provide a framework within which all their resources can be used to best effect and their performance measured. Objectives for individual organisations will be very diverse and will reflect the philosophy of the owners or managers, the size of the organisation, its stage of development and whether it is in the commercial or non-commercial sector. Objectives of leisure and tourism organisations will be developed and refined by all those who have an interest in the organisation, including:

- The owners.
- The managers.
- The staff.
- Visitors or users.
- Shareholders.
- Local councillors.
- Members (of a club or association).
- The local community.
- Society in general.

Owners and managers will be concerned that the objectives are realistic and achievable and provide a reward for their effort, skill and management expertise; staff will want to be sure of their conditions of employment and future prospects in terms of promotion and the growth, or otherwise, of the organisation. Visitors will be concerned with the experience they receive and whether they think the organisation gives value for money. Shareholders will be looking to the owners and/or managers to provide them with a growing return on capital invested in the organisation (the dividend). Local councillors, representing the local community, will be keen to see that public facilities are being used to the maximum, objectives are being achieved and that local authority funds are being wisely deployed. The members of a club or association will be actively involved in setting objectives and helping to achieve them. Society in general has, to a greater or lesser extent, a stake in the aims and objectives of leisure and tourism organisations. The benefits of faster travel, instant entertainment and access to a wealth of activities and facilities needs to be balanced against the wider issues and concerns of social and environmental exploitation, problems of congestion and changes in the nature of work and leisure in society.

Objectives of non-commercial and commercial organisations

Non-commercial organisations

Non-commercial leisure and tourism organisations, falling within the public or voluntary sectors of the economy, do not have 'profit maximisation' as their primary objective. They have been developed with wider social objectives in mind; a council-run leisure centre, for example, will have as a primary aim, 'the provision of a wide range of leisure and recreational services and facilities for the benefit of local people'. There are many examples of non-commercial organisations in leisure and tourism, including:

- *Local clubs and societies* – set up by local people with a specific purpose in mind, these organisations will aim to break even on their finances and may apply for some financial help from their local authority. A good example is a local photographic society.
- *Charitable trusts* – many trusts are established to conserve or preserve our national and local heritage. The most well-known and respected is the National Trust which today protects more than 600,000 acres of land in England, Wales and Northern Ireland as well as over 200 houses and parks (see case study in Unit 1). The Civic Trust, established in 1957, is a registered charity that aims to uphold high standards of environmental quality and management throughout the United Kingdom.
- *Local authorities* – local councils play a major role in the provision of leisure and tourism facilities in Britain. Without their involvement, facilities such as recreation grounds, parks, libraries, museums, leisure centres, tourist information

centres and visitor attractions would not exist. The general move towards privatisation, market testing and compulsory competitive tendering (see Unit 1), has meant that local authorities are now functioning much more like private sector operators and the distinction between commercial and non-commercial is becoming blurred.

- *Public corporations* – the main public corporation linked to the leisure and tourism industry is British Rail, offering a service to both business and leisure travellers. Privatisation has meant that the former state-owned enterprises of British Airways and the British Airports Authority (BAA) are now in private hands. BR is itself scheduled for privatisaton in the not too distant future.
- *Quangos* – these are quasi-autonomous non-governmental organisations which are primarily financed from the public purse but which have a high degree of autonomy. Examples in leisure and tourism are the Sports Council, Countryside Commission and the British Tourist Authority.

Although profit maximisation is not the primary objective of non-commercial organisations in leisure and tourism, those which are part of local government or are agencies of central government (e.g. the quangos), are expected to offer value for money and meet targets and agreed performance criteria. Many local authorities have recruited staff from the private sector and have implemented private sector management practices in order to help achieve their objectives.

Commercial organisations

The leisure and tourism industry in the UK is dominated by commercial or private sector organisations. Some of the best-known names in the industry are private companies, such as Nike, British Airways, Mecca, Forte, Thomson Holidays and Alton Towers, to name but a few. The private sector is made up of large and small organisations owned by individuals or groups of people whose primary aim is to make a profit. Many individuals rely on the profits generated by commercial organisations for a substantial part of their income. Profit maximisation is an important objective for a number of reasons:

- In order to provide resources for further expansion of the business.
- To reward risk taking.
- To enable the business to respond to the needs of its customers.
- To encourage efficiency and innovation.

Although profit maximisation is the primary objective of most private sector companies, it is by no means the only objective of all commercial leisure and tourism organisations. A lot of small businesses in the leisure and tourism industry are run by people who used to work for larger companies, but became frustrated with the high level of bureaucracy they encountered. Operating your own business in leisure and tourism can give a great deal of job satisfaction and the feeling that you have control over what decisions are made. We saw in Unit 1, however, that there are also disadvantages to being a sole trader or partner (see page 1.20). Some owners will not seek to maximise profits to the full, but may be content with a level of profit that gives them the type of life-style they are happy with; after all, why work in an industry concerned with leisure, holidays and travel and have no time to enjoy yourself and have fun!

The role of mission statements

It is currently very fashionable for organisations, whether in the public, private or voluntary sector, to develop a mission statement. The mission statement is intended to convey to all those with an interest in the organisation, be they staff, shareholders or the public in general, what business it is in and where it sees itself going. Some mission statements introduce an element of the organisation's philosophy and values.

Mission statements vary enormously in their complexity; some are very short and to the point, for example British Airways:

> To be the best and most successful company in the airline industry.
> (BA Annual Report and Accounts 1992–93).

Others go into far more detail, for example the following mission statement of the Arts Council of Great Britain:

> The aims of the Arts Council of Great Britain –
> – to open the arts to all;
> – to promote excellence among artists of all kinds;
> – to encourage innovation in the arts;
> – to keep alive our heritage in the arts; and
> – to serve as a national forum of thinking and planning in the arts
> by
> – encouraging people to recognise the contribution made by artists and those who work in the arts to the quality of life;
> – pressing the case for the arts and their public funding;
> – encouraging and supporting all other sources of arts funding;
> – using our financial resources to achieve our aims in Scotland, Wales and England;
> – collaborating with individuals and organisations who share our aims; and
> – making our own organisation open and accessible. (Arts Council of Great Britain Annual Report and Accounts 1991/92).

Some people are very sceptical about the value of mission statements and see them as nothing more than a public relations exercise. What the mission statement can do is set out in very broad terms the direction in which an organisation is hoping to progress in the future and provide a framework for the development of its more specific objectives. British Airways is a very good example of this; although its mission statement is very succinct, the Annual Report 1992–93 lists the seven detailed objectives (which it calls goals) that the company will hope to fulfil in order to achieve its mission. These are:

1 *Safe and secure* – to be a safe and secure airline.
2 *Financially strong* – to deliver a strong and consistent financial performance.
3 *Global leader* – to secure a leading share of the air travel business world-wide with a significant presence in all major geographical markets.
4 *Service and value* – to provide overall superior service and good value for money in every market segment in which we compete.
5 *Customer driven* – to excel in anticipating and quickly responding to customer needs and competitor activity.
6 *Good employer* – to sustain a working environment that attracts, retains and develops committed employees who share in the success of the company.
7 *Good neighbour* – to be a good neighbour, concerned for the community and the environment.

Mission statements were first developed in private sector companies, principally in the United States, but are now to be found in public and voluntary sector leisure and tourism organisations. Some local authorities, however, have chosen not to follow the trend of developing a mission statement and prefer to continue to summarise their work in a policy statement. A policy statement for a typical, progressive borough council would be as follows:

> *Blueridge Borough Council takes pride in the standards of service it delivers to the residents of the Borough. Our primary responsibilities are to promote services of the highest possible quality within the resources we have, at a cost acceptable to Council Tax payers, tenants and users of our leisure services. We, therefore, place great emphasis on caring for the needs of our customers and on being cost conscious and efficient.*
>
> *We aim to deliver services through an effective partnership of councillors and employees. We endeavour to ensure that our staff are well trained and are aware of the aims and objectives of the Council.*
>
> *The Council's belief is that the residents of the Borough expect a high level of efficiency in the services they use, and are looking for a dynamic and forward looking approach towards building on its services for a growing population, thus enhancing the quality of life for all.*

Hierarchy of objectives

The examples of British Airways and the Arts Council of Great Britain show that it is often sensible to think of setting objectives within a hierarchy, with the mission statement, giving the general direction and policy of the organisation, at the top of the apex (see Figure 8.1). The mission or policy will then be translated into organisational objectives, which may, depending on the size and structure of the organisation, be converted into objectives for particular departments or divisions. Targets for team or individual performance will then be developed so that measurement of success or attainment can take place.

Fig 8.1 A hierarchy of objectives

Conflicting objectives

We have seen that leisure and tourism is a dynamic industry, constantly adapting in response to changing customer expectations, new technological developments and wider changes in the nature of society in general. Leisure and tourism organisations must reflect this dynamism by constantly reviewing their objectives and methods of operation. The setting of objectives cannot be seen as a once-and-for-all operation, but as an evolving process concerning all those who have a stake in the organisation.

The process of modifying objectives can sometimes lead to conflict within organisations. A local museum, for example, funded by the town council, which has for many years offered an excellent service to local school children may be required to adopt a more commercial approach to its activities in order to provide an income to offset against its council subsidy. This change from an educational to a financial objective may not be accepted by the staff at the museum who see their job as providing an educational resource and not running a business. At a national level, questions have been raised about institutions such as the Victoria and Albert Museum and the National History Museum charging for admission. Both museums used to admit visitors for free, but decided to introduce an admission charge to offset rising operating costs. Some people fear that commercial activities at the museums will detract from the educational and conservation objectives for which they were established.

Some tourist companies are criticised for taking little heed of the negative environmental and social effects their activities can have on destinations, particularly those fragile areas new to tourism. All too often, there is a conflict between the purely commercial objective of maximising profits by selling as many holidays as possible, and the wider social and environmental objectives of disturbing places and people as little as possible.

There may be conflict when a leisure organisation says it has one objective that states it will endeavour to provide a range of facilities and services for all sectors of the community and a second that says it will be 'a good neighbour, respectful of community feelings and concerns'. If it happens to organise events that cause disturbance late into the night, there may be bad feeling in the local community, which may lead to the organisation reviewing its operation and objectives.

Management by objectives

From time to time, all managers in leisure and tourism organisations set themselves and their staff objectives in order to get results. Some organisations have gone one step further by implementing the formal technique known as MBO (Management by Objectives), which is widespread in many sectors of the UK economy. To call MBO a technique undervalues its true purpose; it is better thought of as a total management approach or management style which encourages participation by all employees and rewards openness. The basis of MBO is the involvement of managers and employees in a setting of a mutually-acceptable set of objectives. It examines the current status of an organisation, highlights areas that need improvement or amendment, specifies means of achieving the changes, and gives time limits within which they will be made. When the time limit is reached, the results are reviewed, new objectives may be set and the process is repeated. Figure 8.2 sets out the cyclical nature of MBO.

At **stage one**, a manager meets with an employee to discuss how that employee can best contribute to the overall effectiveness of the organisation by jointly agreeing objectives for the individual. The sort of objectives that may be agreed by an employee and manager working in leisure and tourism could include:

- Improving the level of customer service in a restaurant or fast-food outlet.
- Increase in occupancy, attendance or usage rates for a facility such as a hotel, tourist attraction or sports centre.

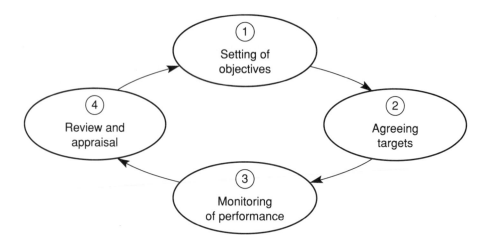

Fig 8.2 The cyclical nature of MBO (Management by Objectives)

- Reduction in staff turnover in the reservations department of a tour operator or airline.
- Control of stock levels and wastage in the catering function of a major visitor attraction.
- Increased sales in a high street travel agency.
- Increased levels of guest spending on ancillary services in a self-catering villa complex.
- Increased turnover in the shop at a golf course or fitness suite.
- Improved security in a major out-of-town entertainment venue.

Stage two is concerned with the manager and employee agreeing targets against which to measure whether or not the objectives have been met. These targets, sometimes known as performance indicators (PIs), should be:

- Easily measurable – for example, reduce the number of customer complaints by 20 per cent or increase turnover by 10 per cent.
- Realistic – a target is only an incentive to the employee if he or she considers that it is realistic and achievable. A target of reducing customer complaints to zero, for example, is totally unrealistic and therefore not appropriate.
- Specific – targets must be specific and unambiguous; general statements are unlikely to be measurable.
- Set within a time frame – for example, increase the use of a local authority leisure centre by disabled people from 1 per cent to 4 per cent within 12 months.

A central feature of MBO is that objectives and targets should not be imposed by management but rather agreed between management and employees. Staff feel more comfortable with the process if they are asked to accept responsibility for achieving targets rather than being told exactly what to do without consultation.

Stage three of the MBO process involves the periodic monitoring of the performance of the individual member of staff against the agreed targets. This is likely to be an informal process and will take the form of a manager overseeing the work of a particular employee or group of employees and giving support and advice on work methods and systems, highlighting any areas that may need adjustment or further action.

At **stage four**, manager and employee will hold a more formal review and appraisal meeting at which the performance of the member of staff will be judged against the original targets, which may have been modified as part of the monitoring process. The outcome of the appraisal may be linked to the employee's pay via a performance related pay scheme or other incentives. Stage four of the MBO process should end with a statement of objectives and targets for the next period of time, in order to continue the cycle.

Benefits and drawbacks of MBO

The Management by Objectives system has many potential benefits to the leisure and tourism industry. If it is part of a wider participative style of management which encourages openness, it can:

- Let staff know exactly what is expected of them.
- Allow management to accurately measure the efficiency and effectiveness of their organisation.
- Help management to plan for the future.
- Encourage motivation on the part of employees.
- Identify staff and management training needs.
- Highlight areas of the organisation that need further development.
- Encourage the review of the organisation's structure.
- Encourage innovation from employees and managers.
- Allow management to deploy resources profitably.

Although MBO, if properly installed, has a number of potential advantages to a leisure and tourism organisation, the system does have its critics. They point to the rigidity and inflexibility of MBO, which doesn't fit well into an industry that is by its very nature very dynamic and having to respond quickly to the changing habits, fashions and tastes of its consumers. Those who favour the MBO approach would argue that all organisations must set themselves objectives and targets, since, without them, success or failure cannot be accurately measured. A well-developed MBO system should be able to take into account the dynamic nature of the leisure and tourism industry by, for example, shortening the length of time between monitoring and appraisal meetings.

Relating objectives to performance

We have seen that the MBO system offers one way for the management of a leisure and tourism organisation to set objectives and targets and review its performance. Whichever management philosophy or system is followed, one thing is quite clear; the setting of objectives is only the first part of evaluating performance of individual members of staff and the efficiency and effectiveness of the leisure and tourism organisation generally. In order that the objectives can be realised, the organisation must translate them into workable practices and achievable targets. It is this process of linking objectives and performance that we will look at in the next section of this unit.

Section 2 Evaluating performance in leisure and tourism

Why do we evaluate performance?

Leisure and tourism organisations, whether in the public, private or voluntary sector, need to establish systems and processes to measure their performance for a number of reasons:

- To find out if the objectives they have been set are being met.
- To establish whether customers and users are happy with the service and facilities.
- To find out if financial and staff resources are being used to best effect.
- To discover how well they are performing in relation to competitor organisations.
- To identify weaknesses in management systems, including communication and decision making, and to highlight training needs.

As well as evaluating these internal operations, organisations also need to measure the impact that they have outside of their immediate environment. Depending on the size and nature of the organisation, it will need to evaluate its performance in relation to economic, environmental and social/cultural factors. A large tourist attraction, for example, will certainly have an impact on the economy of the local area by creating jobs and attracting visitors who will spend money on local goods and services. At the same time, it may have an adverse effect on the local environment and its operations will need to be constantly monitored and evaluated. If not planned carefully, the attraction may, for example, generate traffic congestion in its vicinity, thereby causing problems for local people.

The role of performance indicators

Performance indicators (PIs) are an essential feature of the evaluation of efficiency and effectiveness of any leisure and tourism organisation. By efficiency, we mean the optimum use of resources, i.e. the maximum output from the resources used. Effectiveness is a measure of how well an organisation has met its objectives. At senior management level, the most important performance indicators are those that help with the evaluation of financial and operational performance, for example the income per visitor to a museum or the number of staff employed per 1,000 seats sold in a theatre. PIs are often expressed as ratios, for example:

- Staff costs : total income.
- Number of staff : total income.
- Number of visitors : total income.
- Operating costs : total income.
- Catering spend per visitor : total spend per visitor.

Ratios give a manager an easy and quick way of comparing performance over a particular time period or between different departments or teams of staff. They are commonly used in the commercial sector of the leisure and tourism industry and are now being adopted in the public sector in response to CCT and other efficiency initiatives. The hospitality sector of leisure and tourism has long used PIs and ratios to evaluate performance and, as such, there is a wealth of information available which can facilitate performance evaluation both within a particular hotel and even between hotels with similar characteristics; the use of this industry standard data can help the management of new ventures to gauge their levels of performance. In the leisure and recreation sector, the Chartered Institute of Public Finance and Accountancy (CIPFA) publish comprehensive data and statistics on the finances and operation of leisure centres which is useful for purposes of comparison.

There are literally thousands of different performance indicators, expressed as ratios, which can be developed for any leisure and tourism organisation. It is important, therefore, to specify only those ratios that will give meaningful information and will aid management decision-making. A glance at some CCT specifications and contracts for leisure or sports centres, will clearly show a tendency to include ratios that yield little useful data. It is also important to remember that ratios and PIs are only one measure of performance of a facility or organisation and should not be treated in isolation. Performance indicators concerning queueing times at a theme park, for example, should be supplemented by direct observation of the situation in order to give a true picture of what is happening. PIs are based on information gathered over a period of time and must be used in conjunction with other management techniques to highlight where performance is average, or better or worse than expected. If the latter is the case, the PIs should trigger an investigative process to identify the cause of the poor performance and suggest ways of improving the situation.

Key aspects of performance

Having considered the part performance indicators play in the overall evaluation of performance, we now need to look in detail at the key areas of performance a manager in leisure and tourism will need to evaluate. These will vary from one organisation to another and may be implemented in a slightly different way depending on which sector of the industry is being measured. There are, however, a number of aspects of concern to all organisations, including:

- Financial performance.
- Operational performance.
- Customer satisfaction.
- Compliance with health and safety and other legal requirements.
- Environmental impact.
- Economic, social and cultural impacts.

Financial performance

If any manager in leisure and tourism is asked to comment on the success or otherwise of his or her facility, operation, department or organisation, it is very likely that the first set of statistics consulted will be those relating to financial performance. Whether we like it or not, the main criteria used to evaluate the success of a venture will be those concerned with its finances. Managers may be able to produce a whole list of positive features and statistics about their organisation, such as total numbers of visitors, amount of coverage in the local and national media, a range of glossy promotional materials or a state-of-the-art computer management information system. At the end of the day, however, if the organisation has unhealthy finances when 'the bottom line' is investigated, no amount of clever public relations activity will conceal this weakness.

The need for sound financial performance has long been important in the private sector, which is why it is commercial leisure and tourism organisations that have been at the forefront in developing a range of performance indicators and financial ratios in order to have accurate data on which to base their decisions. Put very simply, there is a limit to the amount of time that a company not making a profit can be financed, either from external sources or from other departments or companies within the same group. There will come a point at which the company will cease trading.

In the public sector, very few leisure and tourism facilities actually make a profit. They are subsidised from central and local government funds because they are considered important to the social well-being of the community and society at large. It must be remembered, however, that local authority spending on leisure and tourism, on such things as play areas, tourist information centres, swimming pools, leisure centres and museums, is purely discretionary; there is no statutory duty on a local council to provide leisure and tourism facilities and services in the same way that they are obliged to provide, for example housing and education. In reality, they all do provide a range of leisure and tourism services related to their budget allocation. Increasing pressure from central government to reduce spending on local services has meant that there have been, and will continue to be, cuts in local services, and a corresponding need for local authority leisure and tourism departments to be as efficient as possible in the deployment of their financial resources.

Assessing the financial performance of an organisation involves the management in first preparing the detailed information on which the appraisal will be based, and second having sufficient expertise and experience to be able to interpret the data. The next section of this unit will concentrate on the role of accounts and accounting conventions in the process of performance evaluation.

Types of accounting in leisure and tourism

Accounting methods used by leisure and tourism organisations mirror closely those used by organisations in many other sectors of the economy. In order for a manager to be able to make the necessary day-to-day and longer-term planning decisions about his or her organisation, financial information such as the annual accounts and interim financial statements must be readily available. Accounting in leisure and tourism can be divided into two categories:

- Financial accounting.
- Management accounting.

Financial accounting

Financial accounting is concerned with the preparation of the financial information that an organisation is required by law to produce. In the private sector these statutory accounts comprise:

1 The profit and loss account.
2 The balance sheet.
3 The cashflow statement.

The profit and loss account shows an organisation's income and expenditure over a period of time, usually 12 months, as a result of its normal trading activities.

Figure 8.3 shows the profit and loss account for the year ended 31 December 1992 of a tourist attraction in Mid Wales, the Centre for Alternative Technology, which is unusual in that it is a relatively small operation that has chosen to become a public limited company (PLC).

CENTRE FOR ALTERNATIVE TECHNOLOGY PLC

PROFIT AND LOSS ACCOUNT
FOR THE YEAR ENDED 31ST DECEMBER 1992

	Notes	£	1992 £	£	1991 £
TURNOVER	2		805,710		678,166
Cost of sales			297,609		264,271
GROSS PROFIT			508,101		413,895
Administrative expenses			(495,978)		(445,430)
			12,123		(31,535)
Other operating income	3		17,701		19,502
OPERATING PROFIT/(LOSS)	4/5		29,824		(12,033)
Interest receivable and similar income	6	8,574		40,721	
Interest payable & similar charges	7	(10,300)		(8,758)	
			(1,726)		31,963
PROFIT ON ORDINARY ACTIVITIES BEFORE TAXATION			28,098		19,930
Tax on profit on ordinary activities	8		–		338
RETAINED PROFIT FOR THE YEAR			28,098		20,268
Retained (deficit) brought forward			(70,276)		(90,544)
RETAINED (DEFICIT) CARRIED FORWARD			£(42,178)		£(70,276)

Fig 8.3 Profit and loss account of the Centre for Alternative Technology PLC
(courtesy C.A.T.)

Figure 8.3 is typical of a profit and loss account in that it starts with the turnover (sales) for the year, from which is deducted a figure for the cost of sales to produce the gross profit. In this example the net profit (or loss) is shown as the operating profit (or loss). All profit and loss accounts will show whether the organisation is carrying forward either a surplus or deficit into the next accounting period, and are useful for comparing financial performance over different periods of time.

The balance sheet for any leisure and tourism organisation is a statement of its financial position at a given point in time; a 'snapshot' of the financial health of the business on a particular day, for example. Balance sheets are constructed at least on an annual basis and often more frequently than this, depending on the financial systems of the organisation. Figure 8.4 shows a typical balance sheet for a leisure and tourism business.

As Figure 8.4 shows, the balance sheet revolves around an organisation's assets and liabilities, the difference between the two being the working capital that it has available to use for day-to-day operations. Fixed assets include buildings, machinery and equipment, while current assets represent debtors, stock and assets that will convert into cash in the normal course of trading. Current liabilities are liabilities that fall due within a relatively short period of time, usually within 12 months, such as taxation and short-term bank loans.

A leisure and tourism organisation's cashflow statement shows the flow of funds into and out of the operation for a given period of time. Figure 8.5 gives the cashflow statement of the Centre for Alternative Technology for the year ended 31 December 1992.

An organisation's cashflow statement provides a link between its profit and loss account and balance sheet. It forms part of the audited accounts and shows the funds that have entered the company, how they have been used and how any net surplus or deficiency in short- and long-term funds have been applied.

Management accounting

Whereas financial accounting is concerned with the production of statutory accounts, management accounting focuses on the provision of financial information to help with business decision making and for control purposes. The managers of all leisure and tourism organisations need accurate financial data to manage on a day-to-day basis and to plan for the future, which makes management accounting just as important in the private, public and voluntary sectors of the industry. Managers need information to be able to analyse the viability of various courses of action and to test options before making a final decision. Effective control, on the other hand, requires frequent and accurate data so that actual performance can be measured against original plans and targets, thereby allowing corrective action, if needed, to be implemented as soon as possible. Management accounts tend to be used purely within an organisation and there is no statutory requirement for them to be published.

There is a great deal of confidential and commercially sensitive information held in the management accounts, so it is important that the management information system (MIS) that stores the data is designed with security in mind and that access to the MIS is restricted to authorised personnel only.

CENTRE FOR ALTERNATIVE TECHNOLOGY PLC

BALANCE SHEET
AS AT 31ST DECEMBER 1992

	Notes	1992 £	1992 £	1991 £	1991 £
FIXED ASSETS					
Tangible assets	9		950,943		799,337
CURRENT ASSETS					
Stocks	10	54,480		66,185	
Debtors	11	37,755		21,596	
Cash at bank and in hand		77,843		229,959	
		170,078		317,740	
CREDITORS – amounts falling due within one year	12	(41,477)		(95,056)	
NET CURRENT ASSETS			**128,601**		**222,684**
TOTAL ASSETS LESS CURRENT LIABILITIES			1,079,544		1,022,021
CREDITORS – amounts falling due after more than one year	13		(71,720)		(53,045)
NET ASSETS			**£1,007,824**		**£968,976**
Financed by:					
CAPITAL AND RESERVES					
Called up share capital	16		1,050,002		1,039,252
Profit and loss account			(42,178)		(70,276)
			£1,007,824		**£968,976**

These financial statements were approved by the board of directors on ....

.... Director
Mr. R. Kelly

Fig 8.4 Balance sheet of the Centre for Alternative Technology PLC

Management accounts will provide the leisure and tourism manager with information on such items as:

- Costs of the operation.
- Total sales or turnover.
- Profit for the organisation as a whole.
- Profits for individual activities, facilities or services.
- Cash flows.

8.16 Evaluating the performance of facilities

CENTRE FOR ALTERNATIVE TECHNOLOGY PLC

CASHFLOW STATEMENT
FOR THE YEAR ENDED 31ST DECEMBER 1992

	Notes	1992 £	1992 £	1991 £	1991 £
Net cash inflow/(outflow) from operating activities	18		50,470		31,942
Returns on investments and servicing of finance					
Interest received		8,574		40,721	
Interest paid		(10,300)		(8,758)	
Net cash inflow from returns on investments & servicing of finance			(1,726)		31,963
Taxation					
Corporation tax			–	5,252	
Tax paid					(5,252)
Investing activities					
Payments to acquire tangible fixed assets		182,032		733,913	
Receipts from sale of tangible fixed assets		(623)		–	
Net cash outflow from investing activities			(181,409)		(733,913)
Net cash outflow before financing			(132,665)		(675,260)
Financing					
Issue of ordinary share capital			10,750		402,200
(Decrease)/Increase in cash & cash equivalents	18		£(121,915)		£(273,060)

Fig 8.5 Cashflow statement for the Centre for Alternative Technology
(courtesy C.A.T.)

It is vital that managers have precise information on the costs of running their organisation. Costs are generally classified as either fixed, which remain relatively static regardless of the level of business activity, or variable, which go up or down in direct proportion to the level of activity. Fixed costs include rent, interest payments or leasing charges that have to be met whether the organisation is trading successfully or struggling to survive. In service sector industries such as leisure and tourism, the biggest variable cost is nearly always that related to employing staff, both permanent and temporary. Other significant variable costs in the industry include telephone and postage charges, especially for tour operators, travel agents and airlines, maintenance charges in the visitor attractions sector, and the cost of raw materials such as food in hotels, restaurants and fast-food outlets.

Controlling the flow of funds into and out of the organisation, known as cash flow, is vital if it is to survive and expand. Maintaining a positive cash flow position is particularly difficult for new businesses or for organisations that have chosen to expand their operation by the addition of new buildings, plant or machinery. In these circumstances, banks and other providers of finance may be able to offer short-term loans or overdrafts until such time as the cash flow is stabilised. It is not always apparent to the world outside that an organisation is experiencing difficulties in its cash flow position. It may seem that an organisation is trading normally, but the true position may be that it has insufficient funds coming in to be able to meet its payments and other financial obligations. A recent case in point was the collapse of the International Leisure Group (ILG), which was best known for its Intasun tour operating subsidiary.

Interpreting financial information

The accounts of an organisation are an important source of information, which enable the management to examine and evaluate its financial performance. All leisure and tourism organisations, regardless of which sector they are in, are striving towards effective management and control, which should lead to a healthy profit and loss account and balance sheet. These statements, together with other performance indicators, should be used by managers to assess efficiency and indicate areas that may need adjustment to improve the overall outcome. It is common practice for organisations to develop ratios from the accounts, which can be used for performance appraisal.

Financial ratios

Financial ratios tend to be the most common method by which managers interpret information so as to give them an easy way of comparing performance both within and between organisations. Comparisons between one year and another, between similar organisations in the same sector or comparisons with budgeted targets, are much more useful than actual figures. It is important not to consider a single ratio in isolation or make decisions based on a single set of figures. It is much better to study a number of ratios in order to assess the state of health of the organisation. Also the ratios themselves can only be as good as the financial information from which they are compiled; inaccuracies in the original data will result in ratios that give a false picture of performance.

Profitability ratios

The most widely used indicator of the profitability of an organisation is based on the return on capital employed (ROCE), since it is meaningless to look at profitability without also analysing the resources that have been used to generate the profit. In simple terms, the ROCE is calculated as follows:

$$\text{Return on capital employed} = \frac{\text{Profit}}{\text{Capital employed}}$$

This is known as the primary ratio. It has many variations, which leads to a lack of consistency and distortion. In particular, there are a number of interpretations of resources or capital employed in a business. If we look at Figure 8.3 and Figure 8.4, which show the profit and loss account and the balance sheet of the Centre for Alternative Technology (see pages 8.14 and 8.16), and if we focus in particular on the figures for 1992, we can calculate the return on capital employed as follows:

Net profit (operating profit) before tax = £29,824
Capital employed = Fixed assets £950,943 + Current assets £170,078
= £1,121,021

By this method, the return on capital employed for 1992 is, therefore:

$$\text{ROCE} = \frac{£29,824}{£1,121,021} = 0.026\%$$

Different organisations will have different methods of determining the figure for capital employed, but, whichever is chosen, the same basis should be used from one year to the next to produce consistency.

Other profitability ratios used by leisure and tourism organisations include:

- *Net profit: sales ratio* – this is generally expressed as a percentage rather than a ratio. It will give a figure for profit (or loss) made per £ of income. The percentage profit on sales varies between different sectors, so it is essential to compare the ratio with similar businesses and also to make allowance for the prevailing economic conditions.
- *Sales: capital employed* – this ratio measures the efficiency with which an organisation uses its capital in relation to its sales. Again this ratio will vary according to the type of business; most tour operators, for example, work on low profit margins with a high turnover, whereas a country house hotel will have a higher profit margin but with a lower turnover.

Financial ratios in the public sector
Most public sector leisure and tourism organisations are subsidised from either central or local government funds and are not normally expected to make a profit. It is still, however, important to measure the ratio of income to expenditure in order to calculate to what extent the income from such items as ticket sales and admission charges can be offset against operating costs. The ratio, usually expressed as a percentage, is calculated as follows:

$$\frac{\text{Income}}{\text{Operating expenditure}} \times 100\%$$

Another useful ratio for public sector organisations is the level of subsidy per visitor or user, which is calculated as follows:

$$\frac{\text{Net operating expenditure}}{\text{Number of admissions}}$$

This ratio can be applied to a whole range of leisure and tourism facilities provided by local councils, including leisure centres, swimming pools, theatres, museums and entertainment venues.

A number of other primary ratios can be applied to public sector provision, including:

- Staff costs : operating expenditure.
- Bar gross profit : bar revenue.
- Catering gross profit : catering revenue.
- Income : number of admissions (to give spend per head).
- Bar income : number of admissions.
- Catering income : number of admissions.

The number and range of secondary ratios that can be developed for public sector leisure and tourism organisations is vast. It is important to calculate only those ratios that will contribute to the manager's decision making process. From the expenditure point of view, common ratios that could prove useful include:

- Energy costs : operating expenditure.
- Marketing expenditure : total operating expenditure.
- Cleaning costs : operating expenditure.

Ratios related to revenue include:

- Bar income : total income.
- Shop income : total income.
- Catering income : total income.

It must be remembered that whether financial ratios are being applied in the private, public or voluntary sector, they are just one of the methods by which financial performance can be measured. Decisions taken on the basis of financial ratios alone will not produce the desired satisfactory outcome.

Operational performance

In the previous section of this unit we have looked in detail at the very important area of financial performance appraisal, through such means as performance indicators and financial ratios. This financial data can be supplemented by the evaluation of operational performance, which adds a further dimension to the whole process of assessing the performance of leisure and tourism organisations, facilities and services.

The level of occupancy or usage is an important operational performance indicator for a whole range of leisure and tourism facilities. Leisure centres, swimming pools, theatres, hotels, self-catering units, coaches, aircraft, conference facilities, to name but a few, can all be appraised on the basis of the extent of their use. Occupancy ratios, usually expressed as percentages, can be calculated and compared over time and between different organisations in order to gauge performance. The occupancy ratio can be calculated as follows:

$$\frac{\text{Actual number of bookings, seats, spaces, etc., taken up}}{\text{Total number of bookings, seats, spaces, etc., available}} \times 100\%$$

In local authorities, under CCT, targets for occupancy and usage levels of leisure centres and other facilities are usually set by the client. For example, a leisure centre operator may be required, as part of the CCT contract, to achieve the following usage levels and targets over a 12-month period:

- 80 per cent use of the main sports hall.
- 65 per cent use of the squash courts.
- 45 per cent use of the fitness suite.
- 55 per cent use of the indoor bowls hall.
- Attract one national and a minimum of ten regional sporting events.
- Offer a children's activity programme during the school holidays.

Other useful performance indicators related to the operation of leisure and tourism organisations are:

- Total throughput of visitors.
- Length of stay of visitors.
- Load factor (number of seats occupied in relation to the number available).
- Total number of clients booking with a travel agent.
- Number of destinations offered by a tour operator.
- Ratio of maintenance costs : total costs.
- Ratio of cost of cleaning : area cleaned.

As can be seen, the range of operational performance indicators and ratios is virtually endless, and management must be very clear to specify only those that will help in the difficult task of performance evaluation.

Social objectives

Many leisure and tourism organisations, particularly those in the public and voluntary sectors, will have objectives that are not easily quantifiable, and which are, therefore, harder to measure. These social or community aims are very variable, but could include:

- An art gallery that welcomes school parties will be fulfilling an educational role.
- A visitor attraction may offer special rates and services for disadvantaged young people.
- A leisure centre may admit disabled visitors free of charge.
- A special event may be staged for an ethnic minority group which will achieve a community objective.

Although these, and other, qualitative objectives are sometimes difficult to evaluate, the introduction of compulsory competitive tendering and other efficiency initiatives has forced local authorities to begin to quantify them so that they can be measured along with the more conventional objectives relating to financial performance. An example of this would be a local authority museum that has as one of its objectives:

To provide the best possible educational service for all pupils in the borough.

Although this is an aim that would be encouraged by all concerned, how does the management of the museum know if it has been successful in meeting the objective? What is 'the best possible' service? In order to quantify this objective, the museum would need to draw up a list of all the services and facilities it considers are contributing to providing the educational service, for example the building itself, any worksheets and factsheets produced for the school children, the catering service, promotional literature, etc. The next step would be to devise performance indicators or targets for each of these components. For the catering service, these could include:

- To provide a food and drink service whenever the museum is open.
- To offer four different types of cold drink.
- To have no more then ten people waiting in the payment queue at any one time.

Once these targets have been set, all staff and management must be involved in making sure they are committed to meeting or even exceeding them. Quantifying aims and measuring performance in this way, will go a long way towards informing management and the local borough council if the educational objective is being met.

Customer satisfaction

One of the most important aspects of a service industry such as leisure and tourism is for operators to provide facilities and services that the customers are happy with. The level of customer satisfaction can also be a very potent weapon when it comes to evaluating performance of an organisation; get it wrong, and you won't have any customers to ask if they are happy with the service! There is a general acceptance in the industry that customers and users have increasing expectations from the leisure and tourism organisations they use, and that they are becoming more assertive in demanding higher levels of customer service (see Unit 3 for more detail on the importance of customer service in leisure and tourism).

Evaluating performance via customer feedback

Leisure and tourism organisations that are truly customer-centred will gear all their activities and operations to the needs of the customer. Customers and users will form the focus of a total management system that acknowledges they are the reason for the organisation's very existence; without them there would be no organisation. These enlightened and 'open' operations will welcome feedback from customers, both positive and negative, and will use it as a way of improving organisational performance. Feedback is seen as vital to effective management and is built in to evaluation procedures and practices from the outset, rather than being considered as an additional and onerous duty.

How is the feedback gathered?

Information from customers on their attitudes to a particular leisure and tourism organisation can be gathered either informally or formally. Informal feedback is often spontaneous, making it just as valuable as information given in a more formal manner. Indeed, many would say a customer is more likely to reveal his or her true feelings and attitudes in an unprompted chat with a member of staff, than when that same member of staff is carrying out a survey of users with the help of a questionnaire. Informal feedback can take many forms, including:

- A remark to a holiday representative about the poor standard of the food in a resort hotel.
- A member of staff overhearing customers praising the standard of service received at a golf club.
- A child heard complaining to his father about the length of time they are having to queue for a 'ride' at a theme park.

It is important that management establish a mechanism by which this informal feedback is collected and monitored. We are all well aware of the influence unhappy customers can have on the image of an organisation and thereby its success. We all like to talk about our leisure and tourism experiences, which, if unhappy, can spread very quickly by 'word of mouth'. This powerful mechanism can also be beneficial for those organisations that have provided a good standard of service.

Many leisure and tourism operators now have regular staff meetings at which employees are invited to share any informal feedback they have picked up. They are also encouraged to record comments from customers on specially designed feedback forms, so that management can monitor the situation to see if corrective action is needed in any areas. The new EuroDisney resort near Paris follows the legendary Disney management philosophy of putting the customer at the heart of the operation. All staff at EuroDisney are trained in customer service skills and have regular training sessions at which they discuss the importance of informal feedback and share their experiences with other employees.

There are a number of ways in which customer feedback can be collected in a formal manner, including:

- Customer comment forms.
- Suggestion boxes.
- Interview surveys.
- Focus groups.
- 'Mystery shoppers'.

Customer comment forms give visitors an immediate opportunity to tell the management what they think of the service and facilities they have used. Figure 8.6 shows an example of a customer care survey in use at the Low Wood Hotel in the Lake District.

This example asks guests to comment on the facilities in the hotel itself, the quality of the staff and the standard of service received. The form finishes with some questions relating to the purpose of the visit and the profile of the customer. Completed forms are monitored by the general manager and discussed at regular staff meetings. Customer comment forms are in widespread use throughout all sectors of the leisure and tourism industry, including tour operators, travel agencies, leisure centres, hotels, transport operators, destinations and tourist information centres. Figure 8.7 gives an example from a cross-Channel ferry.

Suggestion boxes are a novel way of inviting customer feedback. A simple form can be provided, which, when completed, is put into the box to be looked at by staff and management. Suggestion boxes often highlight ways in which leisure and tourism organisations can make simple alterations to facilities that will improve the customer experience. They can help in the process of monitoring customer complaints; management should aim to keep these to a minimum by setting targets for number of complaints received, which should be reduced over time.

Interview surveys are an invaluable way of gaining useful feedback from customers, both on their attitude to the facilities provided and information that can be used to build up customer profiles, which can form the basis of future product development and promotional activities. It is sometimes helpful to carry out user surveys, aimed at those customers currently using the facility, and non-user surveys that aim to discover why some people do not use the service. Carrying out interview surveys is a very skilled task, encompassing questionnaire design, training interviewers, collating the data and analysing the results.

Market research organisations are sometimes asked to assemble focus groups to look in detail at what influences people when they are deciding which product or service to buy.

OUR HOTEL

How well did we meet your expectations?
(Please tick the appropriate box)

	Excellent	Good	Fair	Poor
Finding the hotel from our literature (if applicable)	☐	☐	☐	☐
Your welcome on arrival	☐	☐	☐	☐
In Reception: Check in procedure	☐	☐	☐	☐
In the Bedroom:				
Cleanliness of room	☐	☐	☐	☐
Overall comfort of room	☐	☐	☐	☐
Standard of decor	☐	☐	☐	☐
In the Restaurant:				
Quality of food - Breakfast	☐	☐	☐	☐
Quality of food - Dinner	☐	☐	☐	☐
Standard of ambiance	☐	☐	☐	☐
In the telephone service				
Staff telephone manner	☐	☐	☐	☐
Speed of response	☐	☐	☐	☐
Leisure facilities if used:	☐	☐	☐	☐

When in the area again, what is the likelihood that you would stay with us?

Definitely ☐
Very Likely ☐
Not Very Likely ☐
Not At All Likely ☐

Any other comments: ....
....
....

OUR TEAM

How would you rate our team overall in terms of:
(please tick the appropriate box)

	Excellent	Good	Fair	Poor
Friendliness	☐	☐	☐	☐
Efficiency	☐	☐	☐	☐
Reliability	☐	☐	☐	☐
Anticipating your needs	☐	☐	☐	☐
Ability to resolve problems	☐	☐	☐	☐

We operate a bonus scheme for staff who go out of their way to make your stay enjoyable. If there is someone you would like to mention, please do so below:

Name: ....

Any other comments: ....

OUR SERVICE

How would you rate the service given.
(Please tick the appropriate box)

	Excellent	Good	Fair	Poor
Reception	☐	☐	☐	☐
Porterage	☐	☐	☐	☐
Lounge & Bar	☐	☐	☐	☐
Restaurant	☐	☐	☐	☐
Housekeeping	☐	☐	☐	☐
Leisure Club	☐	☐	☐	☐
How do you rate the hotel in terms of value for money	☐	☐	☐	☐

Some general points:
What did you most enjoy about your stay:
....

What did you least enjoy about your stay?
....

Any other comments:
....

Was this your first visit to the area?   Yes ☐ No ☐

What was the primary purpose of your visit?
Business ☐
Pleasure ☐
Conference ☐
Weekend Break ☐

Finally, please, a few details about yourself.

Your age:
Under 25 ☐
25 - 35 ☐
36 - 45 ☐
46 - 55 ☐
Over 55 ☐

Are you Male? ☐
Female? ☐

Number of nights stay ....

Your Room Number ....

What other hotels have you stayed at in this area?
....

Was the service they gave you:
Much better ☐
Better ☐
The same ☐
Worse ☐
than the service you received with us.

Name: ....

Address: ....

Please place this questionnaire in the box at reception.
Thank-you once again for your time.

Fig 8.6 A typical customer comment form (courtesy of Low Wood Hotel)

SEALINK STENA LINE

SOUTHAMPTON•CHERBOURG

GENERAL ASPECTS SURVEY

Dear Passenger,

We would be obliged if you could find time during your trip to fill in this simple survey and give us your opinion of the general aspects. This will allow us to improve our quality of service.

Once you have filled in the survey please hand it to a member of staff or put it into the special box provided at the Information Desk.

Many thanks for your assistance!

GENERAL ASPECTS	☺	☺	☹	☹	☹
Overall impression					
Car deck organisation (motorists only)					
Car deck environment (motorists only)					
Reception on board					
Finding things on board					
Information desk					
Standard of cleanliness - outside					
Standard of cleanliness - inside					
Children's play area					
Staff attitude - friendliness					
Staff attitude - professionalism					
Seat availability					

With the exception of the journey you are making, how often have you travelled with Sealink Stena Line on this particular route over the past 12 months?

Not at all ☐ 0   Once ☐ 1   Twice ☐ 2   3-4 times ☐ 3

5-6 times ☐ 4   7-10 times ☐ 5   More than 10 times ☐ 6

Age:

-14 ☐ 1   15-19 ☐ 2   20-24 ☐ 3   25-34 ☐ 4   35-44 ☐ 5

45-54 ☐ 6   55-59 ☐ 7   60-64 ☐ 8   65+ ☐ 9

Sex: Male ☐ 1   Female ☐ 2

Nationality:

British ☐ 1   French ☐ 2   Spanish ☐ 3   German ☐ 4

Italian ☐ 5   Other ☐ 6   *Please specify* _____

Fig 8.7 A customer comment form used on a cross-channel ferry *(courtesy of Stena Sealink)*

A small number of customers who already use a particular product, or those with specific social and economic characteristics, are invited to spend a couple of hours with a trained interviewer, employed by a company or group of companies to help them increase their market share. Although not widespread in the leisure and tourism industry, there are examples of airlines holding focus group sessions with business travellers and some conference and business organisers are known to use the technique.

A 'mystery shopper' is somebody who is employed by an organisation to anonymously visit a facility or use a product or service, and report back to management on his or her experiences. It can be used to gain information on the performance of staff, for example, in the management's own organisation or to look into the service offered by competitors. The technique is widely used in the commercial sector of leisure and tourism, most notably in airlines and travel agencies.

Compliance with health and safety and other legal requirements

The vast amount of legislation covering health and safety and other legal aspects of running a leisure and tourism organisation means that managers are constantly being monitored, and their performance evaluated, by public agencies outside of their own organisation. Although the present government has set itself the aim of reducing to a minimum the amount of 'red tape' surrounding organisations, there is still a great deal of legislation that starts its life in Brussels through the European Union (formerly the European Community). Legislation and codes of practice covering health and safety at work, food hygiene, the control of hazardous substances, workplace conditions and fire precautions, to name but a few, all place a duty on the owners and managers of leisure and tourism organisations to carry out audits or risk assessments to highlight any problems they may have. Once highlighted, procedures must be put in place to deal effectively with the problems.

Environmental impact

The performance of organisations in relation to the impact they have on the environment is becoming a major issue for the 1990s. No leisure and tourism organisation can operate without having positive and negative effects on its immediate natural environment and, in some cases, on the environment thousands of miles away. Western societies are becoming increasingly concerned about the threats to the environment posed by many leisure and tourism developments. The 1980s saw the growth of the 'green consumer' who not only looks for environmentally sound products in the supermarkets, but also for leisure and tourism products developed in harmony with the environment. Many tourism developments in particular have been criticised for their lack of concern for environmental issues, while many argue that the whole of the tourism industry is, by its very nature, environmentally destructive.

Evaluating environmental performance

The rise in the awareness of, and concern for, the environment has meant that leisure and tourism organisations are becoming more involved in measuring their environmental effects. This is often as a direct result of a national or local government regulation linked to the planning and development process. It is now very common for large leisure and tourism projects to be asked to carry out an appraisal of the costs and benefits of the development from an environmental point of view. The most common technique for carrying out such an evaluation is the environmental impact assessment (EIA), which can be applied to a wide range of planned developments in leisure and tourism. The EIA is a structured process which aims to:

- Identify the costs and benefits of a particular development.
- Establish who will lose and who will gain if the development goes ahead.
- Examine alternative courses of action and their likely impacts.
- Consider ways of reducing impacts if the project is given the green light.

For leisure and tourism enterprises already in existence, the technique of environmental auditing is gaining in popularity. Some pioneering work by the Inter-Continental Hotel Group, which has resulted in a manual of procedures giving consideration to the environmental consequences of all its business activities, has led to many large hotel companies, airlines and tour operators looking at their activities and processes from a different angle. Some organisations have used their concern for the environment as a marketing tool, hoping to tap into the growing market for leisure and tourism products and services that are truly respectful of the world we live in.

Economic, social and cultural impacts

We have seen that leisure and tourism organisations are beginning to evaluate the impact they are having on the environment, both close to home and further afield. An equally important concern is their effect on the social and cultural fabric of local communities and society in general. Leisure and tourism can bring enormous benefits to people, by providing leisure facilities locally, by giving them the chance to travel widely, by boosting economies with the provision of jobs and income, and by introducing them to new people with different cultures and traditions. There are, however, disadvantages at the local, national and international levels.

There will be many occasions when an organisation is asked to quantify the benefits and costs of its activity in relation to, for example, its local community. It may be seeking financial help from central or local government in the form of a grant or a loan, or may be trying to obtain permission to expand its operations by building new premises. Economic points are always much easier to quantify and evaluate than benefits relating to social and cultural factors. Some new projects are now being asked to provide an impact assessment concerning these factors in the same way that they may be asked for an EIA.

Assignment 8

Situation

You have recently taken up a post as Leisure and Tourism Assistant with a well respected firm of management consultants, Knox, Bennett and Fryth, which have carried out work for private and public sector leisure and tourism organisations, both in the UK and overseas. It is a specialist in evaluating the performance of facilities and personnel in a whole range of service sector industries.

Tasks

Your specific job with the firm of consultants is to work in its public sector division, which currently has contracts with local councils, quangos and the Department of National Heritage. Working to the senior partner, Mrs Penelope Knox, you have been given the job concerning the evaluation of performance at two leisure centres operated by Meadsdown District Council. Your task is to draw up an action plan concerning the evaluation of the performance of the leisure centres, which will be studied by the members of the Leisure Services Committee at Meadsdown, before final approval is given to go ahead with the appraisal. Your action plan should indicate to the non-specialist members of the Leisure Services Committee exactly how the evaluation will take place. In detail, they will want to know:

- Which aspects of performance you will be evaluating and why?
- How the evaluation will take place?
- What sources of data you will need access to?
- How the action plan will be presented to the Committee?
- What it is likely to cost?
- How much Meadsdown management and staff time will be involved?
- The timescale for implementation?

You are free to use whatever form of presentation you feel is the most appropriate for the action plan, but it should be the equivalent of approximately 1,500 words.

Revision test questions

1 List the individuals and organisations that are likely to have an interest in developing the objectives of a local authority leisure centre.

2 Give three specific objectives of non-commercial leisure and tourism organisations.

3 Is profit maximisation the only objective of all private sector leisure and tourism organisations?

4 What is a 'mission statement'?

5 Give two examples of conflicting objectives in leisure and tourism organisations, one in the private sector and one in the public sector.

6 What do you understand by the term 'management by objectives'?

7 Why is it important for a leisure and tourism organisation to have clear objectives?

8 What are 'performance indicators' in leisure and tourism?

9 Give three types of performance which a manager in leisure and tourism will need to evaluate.

10 What is the difference between management accounting and financial accounting?

11 What is the purpose of an organisation's balance sheet?

12 Explain the difference between fixed and variable costs.

13 What do the initials ROCE stand for?

14 What is the difference between primary and secondary financial ratios?

15 How can customers be involved in the evaluation of an organisation's performance?

16 What is an environmental impact assessment (EIA)?

17 How can informal feedback from customers be used in the evaluation process?

18 Give five examples of performance indicators which would be useful to the manager of a large hotel.

19 Give five examples of performance indicators which could be used in local authority leisure centres.

20 How could an outbound tour operator measure its performance in terms of social and cultural impacts?

Unit 9
HUMAN RESOURCE MANAGEMENT IN LEISURE AND TOURISM

Section 1 The personnel function in leisure and tourism

The importance of human resource management (HRM)

We saw in Unit 1 that leisure and tourism is a major employer. Tourism alone accounts for over 118 million jobs world-wide, and is set to become the world's biggest industry by the year 2000 (WTO estimates). Figures for Britain, show that leisure and tourism employs around 1.5 million people, principally in the private sector. Add to this the 200,000 or so entrepreneurs who have set up their own businesses, and are officially classified as self-employed, and you can see that leisure and tourism is a significant force in employment creation.

Leisure and tourism is very much a 'people business'. Like all organisations in the service sector, it relies to a very great extent on the performance of its staff and management to achieve overall success. Quite simply, the staff are the most important resource in any leisure and tourism organisation. The quality of the customers' experience is dependent not only on the skills of the employees but also on their attitude and personality. What sets leisure and tourism apart from most other service sector industries is the fact that the staff are an integral and essential part of the 'product' the customer is buying. This holds true whether we are talking about an overseas holiday, when the client will deal with a range of staff from a travel agency clerk, airport check-in assistant to an overseas representative, or a 40-minute game of squash in the local leisure centre, when the attitude and efficiency of the staff will again influence the overall quality of the experience the customer receives. As Butlin's Holiday Worlds state in their hand-book for all members of staff:

> We are a holiday home to many thousands of families each week. Families like your own who have been saving and looking forward all year to their visit to us. They rely on you and fellow members of your team to make their visit enjoyable. We need to ensure that they will receive five-star care.

Leisure and tourism is a very labour-intensive industry, characterised by a number of distinct features:

- A high proportion of unskilled staff.
- A large proportion of seasonal workers.
- Many part-time staff.
- High staff turnover in many sectors.
- Low rates of pay in some sectors.
- Employees who need to be mobile.

These characteristics of leisure and tourism employment place particular pressures and challenges on the personnel departments of many organisations.

Is HRM the same as personnel management?

It is difficult to argue that there is a clear distinction between human resource management and personnel management. There are many examples of leisure and tourism organisations that have simply changed the name of their personnel department to include the fashionable phrase, HRM, with little or no change to the internal operations of the department. Others have adopted the title of HRM department at the same time as they have carried out a major reappraisal and restructuring of the way in which they manage their human resources. Whereas the function of a personnel department could be viewed as rather mechanistic, bureaucratic and administration led, a unit that calls itself a human resource management department is signalling to those inside and outside the organisation that it is adopting a more long-term view of all aspects of employing, empowering, supporting, developing and rewarding their employees. At the end of the day, HRM is concerned with achieving a balance between the ambitions of the individual and the returns to the organisation. It is crucial that time and money is invested in getting the right balance, particularly in view of the fact that staff costs typically make up more than three-quarters of all costs for many leisure and tourism organisations.

What is the personnel function?

The personnel function in any organisation has traditionally been concerned with the 'hiring and firing' of staff. The personnel department of the 1990s, however, has to take a much more sophisticated approach to the management of its people, and is likely to become involved in a wide range of issues including:

- Recruitment and selection.
- Training and personal development.
- Staff retention and turnover.
- Staff appraisal and review.
- Employment legislation.
- Redundancy, retirement and pension advice.
- Skills training, e.g. customer care.

These issues, when combined with the more established personnel tasks, such as grievance and disciplinary procedures, negotiations with trade unions and staff associations on such matters as pay and conditions, and the general welfare of staff, demand an enormous amount of expertise, understanding and commitment from those working in personnel today. The tasks of those given the responsibility for managing staff, which in leisure and tourism will occur across all sectors of the industry, are, therefore, far more wide-ranging than they have ever been before, and the role of the human resource manager is rightly being acknowledged as a key function in the management of any organisation striving for excellence and long-term success.

Manpower planning

In a volatile industry such as leisure and tourism, which is constantly developing and innovating in response to changing customer requirements, the task of planning likely future staff needs is no easy matter. In such a competitive environment, however, the need to have just the right number of employees, in order to keep staff costs to the minimum, becomes even more important. Manpower planning gives an organisation the opportunity to look at its existing staffing levels and to forecast the mix of human resources it will need to meet its future objectives.

Although leisure and tourism organisations vary greatly in their size and in terms of the sector in which they are operating, it is possible to identify a number of stages that any organisation will have to go through in order to draw up its manpower plan. These are:

1 An examination of the organisation's strategic plan.
2 Consideration of existing staff resources in the context of the strategic plan.

3 An estimate of any likely future changes in the supply of staff.
4 The likely demand for staff in the future.
5 Development of the future human resource 'mix'.

The organisation's strategic plan will identify where the organisation sees itself at the moment, where it wants to be in the future and what it has to do in order to get there. Obviously, a key element of this strategy will be how many staff will be needed and what type of people will need to be trained. In estimating the likely supply and demand situation in relation to staffing in the future, the organisation will need to look at both its internal strengths and weaknesses, and the many external influences that affect the situation. These external influences are likely to include:

- *Demography* – this is concerned with population characteristics, e.g. the decline in the birth rate in the UK since the 1960s has led to a decline in the number of young people available for work in the 1990s (the so-called 'demographic time-bomb'). This has major repercussions for an industry such as leisure and tourism which employs a large number of people under the age of 30. Although most leisure and tourism organisations appear not to have addressed the issue to any great extent, with the exception of Eurocamp and one or two other operators which now actively seek out older staff, the supply of younger staff is likely to get worse as we lead up to the year 2000. With an ageing population generally, it makes sense from an operational point of view to consider employing more mature staff who may be able to relate more easily to an older clientele.
- *The strength of the economy* – spending on leisure and tourism is directly linked to the economic health of the country. A period of prolonged recession will suppress the demand for leisure and tourism facilities and so reduce the need for extra staff.
- *Technology* – we have seen that leisure and tourism is an industry that makes extensive use of new technology, for example a computerised reservation system in a local travel agency or a global communications network used by an international airline. Although there are many scare stories about new technology replacing people in jobs, leisure and tourism is in the fortunate position of being reliant on so much face-to-face contact, which a machine simply could not reproduce. It is considered that leisure and tourism will be one of the fastest-growing industries because it has harnessed new technology equipment and systems.

Once the staff demand and supply has been predicted, the organisation will be in a position to implement the final stage of its manpower plan, namely the development of its future human resource 'mix'. It will use all the information made available in the first four stages to estimate the numbers of full- and part-time staff, any temporary or contract appointments, training requirements and an overall manpower strategy for the future.

Personnel records

All leisure and tourism organisations will need to keep information on their current employees and people who have worked for them in the past. Some may hold on file, for future use, speculative applications from individuals seeking employment. These personnel records on individual members of staff may be supplemented by data on, for example, staff turnover on an annual basis, an analysis of staff illness patterns or details of why employees have left the organisation.

The personnel records of most leisure and tourism organisations are likely to include details of the following:

- *Personal details* – address, telephone number, date of birth, bank account number (if payment is by direct transfer), details of dependents, etc.
- *Job title and grade* – with details of annual holiday entitlement.
- *Accident and sickness record* – details of accidents at work and reasons for sickness are kept.
- *Absenteeism* – details of authorised and unauthorised absences will be held on file and, in cases where the situation is either particularly bad or good, the details may be referred to in an appraisal interview.
- *Payroll information* – current remuneration with details of any annual increments or bonus payments made or planned for the future. Details of pension arrangements and payments are also included.
- *References* – the names and addresses of people willing to give a reference or copies of actual references will be held.
- *Staff appraisals and reviews* – if the organisation has a formal appraisal or review system in place, details of any interviews or action plans arising will be held in the personnel department.

In smaller organisations, the personnel information may be stored and updated manually. If only a small number of staff are employed, this system will prove to be quite adequate. Larger organisations, however, are likely to use a computerised personnel records system, with the benefits of greater storage capacity, speed of use and accessibility to many staff at the same time. Information on employees which is held on computer, however, does fall within the scope of the Data Protection Act 1984, which provides new rights for individuals and demands good practice from those who hold personal data on individuals (see Unit 6 on management information systems for more detail on the Data Protection Act). Whether a manual or automated system is used for storing data on employees, the security of the personnel records is very important. Handling such sensitive, personal information calls for a system that allows access only to authorised staff and is housed in a safe and secure environment.

Recruitment of staff

Good staff are the backbone of any organisation in the service sector, and particularly in leisure and tourism where they are an integral part of the 'experience' the customers are buying. But how can you be sure of getting the best people for the job? A thorough approach to recruitment and selection, paying attention to detail and allowing enough time to see the process through to its completion, will pay dividends to the organisation, and in particular will go a long way towards reducing the high levels of staff turnover that are found in some sectors of leisure and tourism. Management time spent on recruitment should be regarded as a wise investment for the future; all too often, more time and attention is given to choosing a new computer system than to selecting the most important resource the organisation has, its staff.

The recruitment process

Factors such as the fall in the number of young people available for work, the number of employees who no longer see a post as 'a job for life' and the general 'skill shortages' within the UK workforce mean that the task of selecting staff can no longer be left to chance. While there will always be mistakes made when it comes to employing people, a systematic and objective approach to the process of recruitment is likely to achieve the objective of getting the best person for the job.

The recruitment process is shown in diagrammatic form in Figure 9.1.

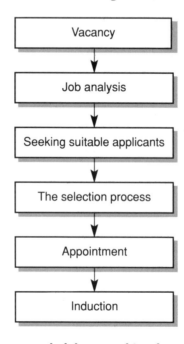

Fig 9.1 The recruitment process in leisure and tourism

Once the need for a new member of staff has been identified, Figure 9.1 shows that the recruitment process consists of five interrelated stages, which we will now look at in more detail.

Job analysis

Whenever a vacancy arises, whether it is to replace an employee who is leaving or if it is a new post, there needs to be a thorough analysis of what the job entails. If it is an existing post to be filled, simply finding a set of old job details and reproducing them without considering if they are still relevant is not good enough. The dynamic nature of the leisure and tourism industry is such that an approach of this sort will not achieve the desired objective of filling the post with the best candidate. Information to be included in the job analysis can be obtained from the existing postholder, previous records, other members of staff and by direct observation. A job description can then be compiled, detailing the content of the job and areas of responsibility. A typical job description is likely to include:

- *Basic details* – title of post, grade, post number, department/section, location, etc.
- *Summary of the job* – outlining the key objectives of the post.
- *Responsibilities* – clarifying the position in the organisational structure, detailing to whom responsible and for whom responsible.
- *Detailed duties* – a list of all the relevant duties attached to the post.
- *Conditions of employment* – general information on salary/wage, holiday entitlement, hours of work, pension arrangements, welfare and social facilities, trade union membership arrangements, training, etc.

Figure 9.2 shows an example of a typical job description for an assistant manager of a local authority leisure centre.

The job description will be sent out to potential candidates together with an application form and further details as appropriate. Some organisations prefer to ask for a CV (curriculum vitae) rather than a completed application form, while others make it very clear that CVs are not acceptable in place of an application form.

At the same time as they are compiling a job description, many organisations will also draw up a job specification, often referred to as a *person specification*, which provides a blueprint of the 'ideal' person for the job in terms of skills, character, previous experience and qualifications. Figure 9.3 is an example of a person specification for an Assistant Events Officer post with a voluntary sector organisation.

As well as indicating the type of experience and skills that the successful candidate will need to demonstrate, the example of the person specification shown in Figure 9.3 also shows how the extent to which the candidate meets the criteria will be assessed. In this case, the criteria will be assessed from the application form, at interview, by role play and by means of a writing exercise. Some person

WEALDEN DISTRICT COUNCIL

January 1991

JOB DESCRIPTION

1.	**Title of Post**	Assistant Manager
2.	**Post No.**	L053 L060 L062
3.	**Located at**	Utopia L.C.
4.	**Responsible to**	Leisure Centre Manager
5.	**Responsible for**	Leisure Centre Staff and employees in the absence of the Leisure Centre Manager and as directed by him/her.

6. **Functional Relationships:**

(1) Internal: Leisure Centre manager and Centre Staff, the administrative staff of the Leisure Services Department.

(2) External: The general public and relevant organisations.

7. **Job Summary:** To generally assist the Leisure Centre Manager in maintaining a safe and economically viable customer orientated centre, adopting a motivating approach to staff management with a commercial bias.

8. **Limits on Authority:** As defined by the Leisure Centre Manager.

9. **Main Activities:**

(1) To act as duty officer with full responsibility through the Manager's delegated authority for the operation of the Centre of shift.

(2) To carry out duties and specific projects as directed by the Manager.

10. **Special Conditions:**

(1) Arrangement of working hours will be as decided by the Leisure Centre Manager commensurate with the Centre's requirements.

(2) Arrangements of hours will involve evening, weekend and bank holiday working on such basis by rota and shift, etc., as is required. No additional payment will be made.

(3) Salary is inclusive of all other enhancements, e.g. unsocial hours, public holiday and weekend work, etc.

(4) To operate and provide cover from any of the Wealden District Council Leisure Centres as required.

(5) Flexi-time does not apply.

(6) Casual user car status.

Fig 9.2 Job description for the post of Assistant Manager of a local authority leisure centre (courtesy of Wealden District Council)

JOB KNOWLEDGE, SKILLS & EXPERIENCE	AF	I	RP	WE
Experience Required				
Working as a team member with groups of people either in the voluntary or commercial sector	x	x		
Planning, organising and managing projects	x	x		
Skills Required				
Good communication skills including listening skills and the ability to give accurate information and clear instructions	x	x	x	x
The ability to write letters and reports	x	x		x
Interpersonal skills including the sensitivity to respond to different people and situations appropriately and the ability to deal with the public in a tactful and diplomatic manner	x	x	x	x
Good organisational and planning skills including the ability to prioritise and to manage his/her own time	x	x		
Ability to work under pressure and to meet deadlines	x	x		
Sound administrative skills and attention to detail including the ability to set up and maintain accurate records and filing systems	x	x		
Willingness to undertake routine and mundane tasks		x		
Good personal presentation		x		

KEY
AF   Assessed from Application Form
I   Assessed at Interview
RP   Assessed by Role Play
WE   Assessed by Writing Exercise

Fig 9.3 Person specification for the post of Assistant Events Officer

specifications divide the qualities, experience and skills sought into those that are 'essential' and those that are 'desirable'. When drawing up a person specification, organisations must be careful not to introduce bias either in favour of, or against, one particular section of society, for example disabled people. Discrimination on the grounds of sex or race are covered by legislation under the Sex Discrimination Act and the Race Relations Act respectively.

Seeking suitable applicants

Once the job specification and person specification have been finalised, the task of finding potentially suitable applicants can begin in earnest. The task may focus solely on internal candidates or may be opened up to outside applicants. The process can be carried out entirely in-house or may be partly or wholly delegated to an outside recruitment agency. In leisure and tourism, agencies tend to be used either for very senior appointments, e.g. Director of Marketing or Head of Leisure Services, or in situations where jobs are becoming hard to fill, notably some posts in the hotel and accommodation sector. Recruitment agencies specialising in leisure and tourism advertise their services in the relevant trade newspapers and journals. There are many different methods that leisure and tourism organisations use to look for suitable applicants, including:

- Advertisements in local, regional and national newspapers, e.g. the *Guardian* has appointments covering the arts, marketing, tourism, environment and countryside.
- Advertisements in trade journals and magazines, e.g. *Leisure Management*, *Leisure Opportunities*, *Travel Trade Gazette*, *Caterer* and *Hotelkeeper*, to name but a few.
- Employment agencies.
- Job centres.
- Links with universities, colleges and schools.
- A 'trawl' through any speculative applications held on file.
- Advertisements in internal staff newsletters or equivalent.
- Vacancies circulated by Professional Bodies.

The selection process

If the job description and person description have been carefully prepared, and any advertisements, if used, are written in a clear and precise manner, the organisation is likely to keep the number of unsuitable applications to a minimum. The initial sift of application forms, letters or CVs will concentrate on matching the candidates' qualifications, experience and skills to the previously prepared person specification. This process will end with the drawing up of a short list of suitable candidates who will be invited to take part in the next stage of the recruitment process. This will usually take the form of an interview, either one to one or by a panel, at which the candidate will be given the opportunity of expanding on his or her written application and will be able to learn a little more about the people and the organisation he or she is hoping to work for. The candidate will also be asked questions during the interview and may be asked to carry out tasks, such as operating a computer or piece of machinery. Some organisations use other selection methods, including written tests and personality questionnaires.

Interviewing

Although often criticised for being too subjective, the interview is usually the central component of the selection process for any job in leisure and tourism. It has two basic aims:

- To give the organisation the opportunity to meet candidates face to face and find out more details about the applicants and their achievements to date.
- To give the candidates the chance to formulate their assessment of what the job entails and the people they will be working for and with.

Much of the criticism levelled at interviewing as a way of selecting staff is that it is by its very nature personal and, therefore, open to bias on the part of those carrying it out. In order to make the interview as objective as possible, it needs to be carefully planned in advance, with each candidate being asked exactly the same set of questions. In this way, candidates' responses can be more accurately compared and evaluated. There are a number of 'golden rules' in interviewing, including:

- Draw up a list of questions in advance of the interview.
- Take brief notes during the interview, as it is very easy to mistake one candidate for another, particularly if several are being interviewed on the same day.
- Invite the interviewees to take notes if they wish.
- Get the interviewee to expand on the information contained in the application form or on the CV.
- Be alert to the interviewees' strengths and weaknesses.
- Ask open questions that invite an answer other than 'yes' or 'no'.
- Ask for information on future career plans. A question often used at interview is 'where do you see yourself in x years' time?'.
- Give applicants plenty of opportunity to reveal all relevant information and ask any questions.
- Avoid asking personal questions.

There are occasions when, after having carried out the painstaking task of interviewing several candidates, the interview panel does not consider any of the applicants suitable for the job. This should not necessarily be seen as a failure of the selection process, but rather the fact that the process has worked well, even though no suitable candidate has been found. On these occasions, the organisation may decide to re-interview a selection of candidates or start the whole process again by seeking new applications.

Appointment

If the interviewer or interview panel are sure that a suitable person has been found, a formal written offer of appointment can be made, subject to satisfactory references and possibly a medical examination. The successful candidate will be invited to reply in writing that he or she accepts the offer of the job. Once this letter of acceptance is received, those candidates who were unsuccessful should be informed of the decision as a matter of courtesy and to maintain the organisation's professional image.

Induction

It is vital to maintain the momentum of the recruitment process by providing the successful candidate with a structured induction to the organisation. An induction programme should be designed to help new members of staff familiarise themselves with their new environment, to settle easily into their new jobs and to establish good working relationships with other members of staff. Induction is particularly important in those sectors of the leisure and tourism industry which have a higher then average staff turnover, since it can help to build relationships over the crucial first few months of a new appointment.

A comprehensive induction programme should include the following details:

- Brief information on the scope and importance of the leisure and tourism industry.
- The structure, aims and philosophy of the organisation.
- The main features of the job with an indication of lines of responsibility.
- The principal conditions of employment.
- An introduction to work colleagues.
- A tour of the facilities.
- Rules on dress, personal appearance, eating, drinking, smoking, etc.
- Health, safety and security procedures.
- Staff representation, including trade union membership and trade associations.
- Social and welfare facilities.
- Training and personal development opportunities.

An example of an induction check-list for new staff employed by Top Rank Ltd. is shown in Figure 9.4.

Some organisations identify an existing member of staff to help the new person settle in to their new surroundings, a process known as mentoring. The mentor plays an important role in the induction process, which, if planned well and carried out with enthusiasm, will give the new employee an early opportunity of becoming an effective and valued member of the team.

Staff training and development

There can be little doubt that a well-trained workforce is any leisure and tourism organisation's best asset. Offering opportunities for training and development increases staff morale and motivation, which in turn feed through into increased efficiency, productivity and output.

INDUCTION CHECKLIST

Your Manager will tick the tasks that have been completed during your induction.

1 **Show the Starter:**
   a) Main areas of the Club
   b) Position of the clocking-in machine / signing in book
   c) Position of Fire-fighting equipment
   d) Staff room
   e) Emergency exits
   f) Video "Welcome to Top Rank Ltd"
   g) Pensions Video

2 **Introduce Starter to:**
   a) Management Team
   b) Appropriate Supervisor
   c) Staff Representative
   d) Departmental Colleagues

3 **Issue to all new Starters:**
   a) Conditions of Employment Agreement
   b) Statement of Hours
   c) Uniform Receipt
   d) Wishes Letter (all employees)
   e) Disciplinary Rules & Procedures booklet
   f) Health and safety at Work Policy booklet
   g) Fire Information & Procedures booklet
   h) Legal requirements form
      (to be signed on engagement and thereafter every 12 months)
   i) Cinema Discount Card (after 6 months)
   j) Pensions
      * Gatefold leaflet "Your Pension Choice"
      * RO Pension Plan application card
      * RO Money Purchase Scheme application card
      * Disclaimer card
      * Pension booklet (as appropriate)

4 **Explain to all Starters:**
   a) Conditions of Employment (show "Employees Guide")
   b) Job Description
   c) Fire Drill & Evacuation Procedure
   d) Benefits
   e) Legal Requirements
      - Main provisions of the Gaming Act
      - Health & Safety Policy
      - Hygiene Regulations
   f) Function of the SRC
   g) Company Pension Arrangements

Fig 9.4 An example of an induction checklist for new staff
(courtesy of the Rank Organisation)

In short, training can:

- Increase profitability and efficiency.
- Improve customer service.
- Reduce staff turnover.
- Increase flexibility.
- Trigger innovation and new ideas.
- Reduce costs.

Training needs analysis

A logical starting point for any leisure and tourism organisation wanting to introduce, or improve, training for staff, is to implement a training needs analysis
(TNA). A TNA is an auditing process that aims to identify:

1 The current level of technical and management skills within the organisation.
2 The required level of technical and management skills needed to be an effective
organisation.
3 Any shortfall or surplus in the level of technical and management skills.

If a shortfall is identified, which is often the case in the leisure and tourism industry, which has generally under invested in training for its staff, the TNA should
make recommendations on the action necessary to bridge the training gap. TNAs
can be carried out by staff within the organisation or by employing outside consultants who specialise in the field. Either way, the senior management must give
full commitment to the initiative, since it will require additional resources over a
long period of time. A fully planned and costed staff training plan is not a 'quick
fix' solution, but one that will take time to achieve its aims. The TNA may well
identify the need for increasing the level of technical and management skills
through a mixture of on-the-job and off-the-job training.

On-the-job training

As its name implies, on-the-job training is when employees gain and develop
their skills and knowledge while carrying out their normal everyday duties.
Many jobs in leisure and tourism are ideally suited to this type of 'hands-on'
training, for example operating a VDU in a travel agency, working in the plant
room of a leisure centre, training to be a chef in a restaurant or hotel, working
behind the counter in a tourist information centre, to name but a few. On-the-job
training often leads to qualifications such as National Vocational Qualifications
(NVQs), SVQs in Scotland and General National Vocational Qualifications
(GNVQs), all of which give employees credit for training related to the world of
work.

Off-the-job training

Training that takes place away from the normal place of work is sometimes preferred by staff and employers as a way of achieving a specific training objective. Some leisure and tourism organisations make extensive use of 'day release' courses offered by local colleges and private training providers, often leading to industry-related vocational qualifications. Evening classes are also popular in sectors such as travel and leisure centre management. Some organisations encourage their senior staff to work towards management and supervisory qualifications, either by the traditional route of going on a course, or perhaps by following a distance-learning programme based around home study and a small amount of tutorial support. Many organisations have found that the areas of customer care and foreign language training are particularly beneficial for staff working in leisure and tourism.

 CASE STUDY

Training in leisure and tourism – Investors in People

The Investors in People standard was introduced by the government in 1990 to encourage all organisations throughout Britain to analyse their training needs and draw up plans for developing training programmes throughout their workforce; in other words, to begin to take training seriously in order to achieve their overall objectives and make best use of their most valuable asset, their staff. Although Investors in People has been developed by business people for business people, it is by no means restricted to the private sector. Local colleges, university departments, examination bodies and voluntary sector organisations are just some examples of the types of organisations now working towards Investors in People. The award is administered by local Training and Enterprise Councils (TECs) located throughout England and Wales, which look for organisations that can successfully demonstrate high quality, ongoing staff training and development programmes that work towards an overall objective of providing the highest possible standards.

Within the leisure and tourism sector, one of the first companies to achieve the standard was De Vere Hotels Ltd., which was unusual in that it received Investors in People for the whole of its chain of 25 hotels in the UK rather than for just one specific hotel. The award followed an assessment of its staff development programmes involving every member of staff in the hotels and at head office. The training needs of each individual member of staff were assessed, agreed targets were set and a performance appraisal system was implemented to monitor and reward achievements. It was implemented in all the Group's hotels from the Belfry in the West Midlands, home of golf's Ryder Cup, to the recently refurbished Oulton Hall near Leeds. All De Vere staff have been involved in developing quality standards manuals and attend frequent training sessions. An open management style has helped communication and has led to a high degree of commitment to the standard on the part of both staff and management.

Staff appraisal

The main function of staff appraisal, sometimes referred to as staff development review, is to give an employee and his or her immediate superior the opportunity to discuss current performance and to agree a working plan for the future, in relation to specific targets and objectives. The appraisal, usually taking the form of an interview between the two parties, is also likely to highlight training needs for the individual which will have time and cost implications for management. Some leisure and tourism organisations, particularly in the commercial sector of the industry, use the staff appraisal process to determine what level of bonus or per-formance-related pay the employee should receive. Others prefer to keep the two issues quite separate.

Staff appraisal has been widely used in private sector leisure and tourism companies for many years. More recently, in response to the 'privatising' of many local authority leisure and tourism services through such measures as CCT and market testing, the public sector has begun to introduce the concept of appraisal of staff performance as part of a wider process of increasing efficiency and becoming more competitive.

In order to be of maximum benefit to any leisure and tourism organisation, whether it is in the private or public sector, an effective system of staff appraisal needs:

- Careful preparation by both the supervisor/manager and the employee.
- A procedure that is clearly understood by both parties.
- A well-designed appraisal form with space for comments by both parties.
- An appraisal interview that is structured, but flexible enough to incorporate new ideas and developments.
- An objective, written summary of the key points of the interview and agreed future targets and plans.
- Feedback from employee and supervisor/manager on the effectiveness of the process.
- An informal yet 'business like' atmosphere.

Most organisations recognise the benefits of introducing a staff appraisal system, although it can have one or two drawbacks if not carefully planned. The benefits include:

- Assisting in meeting organisational objectives.
- Helping managers improve the effectiveness of their staff.

- Assisting the employee to identify his or her role in the organisation.
- Improving communication between staff and management.
- Building commitment and loyalty.
- Helping managers understand better the jobs that their staff carry out.
- Identifying training and personal development needs.

Because staff appraisal is understandably a very sensitive issue, introducing such a scheme without a supportive and positive approach on the part of management and employees can sometimes lead to problems. There is often a great deal of uncertainty and suspicion surrounding the process when appraisal is linked to pay and bonuses, which is why many organisations choose to treat the two issues separately. Managers and supervisors must be aware of the importance of confidentiality in the whole process in order to gain the confidence of the staff. Management must also be careful not to raise expectations in their staff which cannot be met; for example, promising staff training opportunities that fail to materialise. If staff appraisal is well planned and has the commitment of management and employees, it can be a very useful tool for improving performance and helping meet overall objectives.

Staff motivation

We have seen in earlier units that leisure and tourism employs a large number of unskilled, low-paid workers who are often called upon to work unsocial hours; it is a fact of life that those employed in leisure and tourism are asked to work at the very time that most people are 'at leisure'. Add to these factors the high level of direct contact that leisure and tourism employees have with their customers and we can begin to see the challenges that face managers when it comes to motivating their staff. The motivation to work well is usually related to job satisfaction, a complex issue that depends on many inter-linking factors, such as the working environment, attitude of senior management, co-operation with colleagues, pay and reward systems, terms of employment, recognition of achievements, personal circumstances, status, etc.

Leisure and tourism organisations that put people first and treat staff requirements as a high priority are likely to be rewarded with employees who:

- Attend work regularly.
- Display high morale.
- Project a good company image.
- Are happy at their work.
- Give a high level of customer service.
- Achieve greater productivity.
- Are motivated to achieve.
- Work well as members of teams.

Above all, an employee needs to feel a valued part of the organisation, recognised for his or her achievements and managed by senior staff who provide a supportive and effective environment. With all of these points in place, staff motivation will be high and the organisation will be in excellent shape to achieve its aims.

Section 2 Employment law, rights and responsibilities

Employment contracts

An employment contract is a written document that sets out the terms and conditions under which a member of staff is expected to work. Most leisure and tourism organisations will want to give every member of staff a written statement that gives details about the job, rates of pay, holiday entitlement, etc. If such points are not clarified in writing, there may be disputes at a later date about what was agreed at the time when the employee started the job. Although it is clearly desirable for all staff to be given a written contract of employment, under current British law not all employees are entitled to receive such a document. The Employment Protection (Consolidation) Act 1978 gives the following clarification as to exactly which employees are entitled to receive a contract of employment:

- Employees who work 16 hours or more per week must be given a written statement within 13 weeks of starting work.
- Employees who work less than 16 hours but more than eight hours per week have the right to a written statement after five years with an employer.
- Employees who work less than eight hours per week do not have the right to a written statement.

Contracts of employment vary between one organisation and another, but there are some basic points that should be included, namely:

- The names of both parties to the contract, i.e. the name of the employee and the name of the organisation that he or she is to work for.
- The job title.
- The date when the period of employment began.
- Details of remuneration.
- Conditions relating to hours of work.
- Holiday entitlement and holiday pay.

- Procedures relating to incapacity to work through sickness or injury including any provisions for sick pay.
- Any pension arrangements.
- Periods of notice on both sides relating to the termination of the contract.
- Details of grievance procedures.

Although, under the law, not all employees have to be given a contract of employment, every worker has a right to receive a formal written offer of acceptance from their employer confirming their appointment. This letter should include:

- An offer of work.
- Hours to be worked.
- Standard opening and closing hours of the organisation.
- Start date and time.
- Details of where and to whom the new employee should report.

There has been a general move in recent years away from permanent contracts for workers in leisure and tourism towards short-term contracts and casual working. The growth in these temporary contracts has been seen by many organisations as a cost-saving exercise in difficult economic circumstances. The wages bill is by far the biggest cost for the majority of leisure and tourism organisations, and is, therefore, a prime target for cost cutting. While temporary contracts make sense for the employer, they are not always in the best interests of employees, who may lose out in terms of job security and career progression. Temporary contracts have a specific finish date included in their terms, and are common in hotel work and any tourism employment that is seasonal. The emergence of CCT has seen a growth in subcontracting, where particular tasks are put out to tender, with contracts usually awarded to the lowest bidder. It is becoming common to find subcontractors providing the cleaning, catering and grounds maintenance services in leisure and tourism organisations in both the private and public sectors.

Redundancy

Redundancy is defined as dismissal of an employee wholly or partly due to:

1 The fact that an employer has ceased, or intends to cease, to carry on the business for the purposes of which the employee was employed, or has ceased, or intends to cease, to carry on that business in the place where the employee was so employed.
2 The fact that the requirements of that business for employees to carry out work of a particular kind, or to carry out work of a particular kind in the place where they were so employed, have ceased or diminished, or are expected to cease or diminish.

These rather lengthy definitions mask a process that can be very painful for both employers and employees. For the employers, it can be seen as the ultimate sign of failure, after what is often a long struggle for survival. For employees, it means the loss of a job that they may have held for many years, with all the financial and emotional repercussions that this entails. In simple terms, redundancies occur when an organisation ceases to trade entirely, or is forced to reduce its workforce. In leisure and tourism, one of the biggest collapses in recent times was that of the International Leisure Group (ILG), best known for its Intasun brand, with the loss of many thousands of jobs. Less publicised, although no less tragic, are the daily redundancies of employees working in all sectors of leisure and tourism, as their employers cut back on staffing levels in order to survive the harsh economic environment in Britain today.

Redundancy payments

Any employee who is made redundant cannot accuse an employer of unfair dismissal but may be entitled to compensation under the State Redundancy Payments Scheme. Claims for redundancy payments can only be made by employees over the age of 18 and under 65 years of age. The number of hours worked for the employer is also important in deciding whether an employee is eligible; those who work less than eight hours per week are not entitled to any redundancy payments, those who work between eight and 16 hours per week cannot claim unless they have worked for more than five years, and employees who work more than 16 hours each week can claim redundancy payments as long as they have worked for the same employer for two years or more. The amount that any individual receives will depend on the number of years service for the employer and how much he or she earns.

As well as access to redundancy funds, some employees who face redundancy have the right to be given time off to look for another job without loss of pay.

Dismissal

There are occasions in all industries, and leisure and tourism is no exception, when the dismissal of an employee can cause problems that may end up being resolved by way of an arbitration scheme or an industrial tribunal. Dismissal is defined as:

- The termination of an employee's contract by his or her employer either with or without notice.
- Where a fixed-term contract comes to an end and is not renewed.
- Where the employee is entitled to terminate the contract without notice by reason of the employer's conduct (constructive dismissal).

There are provisions in the Employment Protection Act 1978, as amended by the Employment Act 1989, concerning the protection of employees who feel that they have been unfairly dismissed. Under present law, not all workers can claim for unfair dismissal. Those excluded are:

- Employees over the age of 65, or the normal retirement age of their organisation if this is lower.
- Those who work for less than 16 hours per week.
- Staff who have been with their employer for less than two years.

What constitutes 'unfair dismissal'?

The most common reasons for employees to be dismissed include misconduct, a lack of capability to do the job properly, absenteeism, redundancy, ill health or a legal restriction which makes continued employment impossible, e.g. a coach driver who is disqualified from driving for 12 months following a prosecution for dangerous driving. Any reason that does not fall into one of these categories will be regarded as 'unfair' by an industrial tribunal. While there are many instances when the dismissal of a member of staff by an employer is wholly justified, for example when a leisure centre assistant continues to arrive at work under the influence of drink after repeated written and verbal warnings, there are occasions when employees are dismissed unfairly. Even if an employer is sure that the reason for dismissal is fair, there is a further requirement that states that the dismissal must be reasonable, must take the individual's circumstances into account and that the manner of dismissal must be fair, e.g. warnings must be given to the employee before the decision to dismiss him or her is made.

Any employee who is eligible to claim unfair dismissal must do so by complaining to an industrial tribunal within three months of the date the employment was terminated. If the tribunal is satisfied that the dismissal was indeed unfair, it can propose three possible remedies:

1 The employee can have his or her job back.
2 The employee can take another job with the same organisation, but not necessarily on the same terms and conditions.
3 The employee can choose compensation made up of a basic amount that is calculated in the same way as a redundancy payment, plus an amount to cover loss of earnings.

Disciplinary procedures

Most employees in leisure and tourism who are given clear guidance as to the standards of work and conduct that are expected of them will be motivated and professional enough to exercise effective self-discipline and work well with a minimum of supervision. However, it is sometimes necessary for management to take action to deal with those employees whose behaviour, work performance or absenteeism are giving cause for concern. Minor problems of this nature are best dealt with informally by the employee's immediate supervisor in the first instance, but for serious or more persistent problems, it will be necessary to implement the organisation's formal disciplinary procedures. Figure 9.5 shows an extract from the Butlins' Holiday Worlds' staff handbook outlining the company's discipline procedure.

SOLVING PROBLEMS
Discipline Procedure

Like every large company we have rules although we like to keep these to a minimum. Those we do have are strictly enforced and we ask that you comply with them.

WE'RE UNHAPPY

If you break the Company Rules, you are likely to receive a recorded **VERBAL WARNING**. If the problem is more serious you will be asked to attend a Disciplinary Interview where you will be given a chance to explain and justify your actions. You may then receive a **WRITTEN WARNING** of what will happen if the same thing occurs again or you do not improve your performance. If you continue to break Company Rules you will receive a **FINAL WRITTEN WARNING** which may lead to your dismissal.

Examples of this type of **MISCONDUCT** are:
● Poor timekeeping   ● Refusal to carry out instruction
● Offending customers/work mates   ● Failure to achieve standards expected of you.

Some things will cause you to lose your job without any notice. These are known as **GROSS MISCONDUCT**.

Examples are:
● Drinking or drunk on duty.   ● Theft or fraud.
● Assault.   ● Causing damage to or misusing Company
● Any act that risks the safety of others. Property
● Reporting for work under the   ● Using or dealing in drugs.
  influence of drugs or alcohol.   ● Misuse or abuse of fire equipment.

You can appeal if you feel you have been treated unfairly. The Personnel Department will advise you.

Fig 9.5 An extract from the Butlins' Holiday World staff handbook

In any leisure and tourism organisation, it is essential for the management to follow the disciplinary procedures to the letter, so as to ensure fairness for the employee and to reduce the likelihood of a claim for unfair dismissal being brought at an industrial tribunal. Such claims can be very costly, both in terms of staff time devoted to contesting the case and any financial settlement that may arise. Unless the problem is one of gross misconduct, which could include such matters as being drunk on duty, theft or fraud, assault, causing damage to company property or the misuse of equipment, dismissal should be regarded as the final stage of the procedure and is only considered after formal warnings and other sanctions have failed to solve the problem. Other sanctions available to management include demotion, suspension without pay and loss of promotion opportunities.

In order to be fair to all concerned, the disciplinary procedure must follow the rules of natural justice, which state that:

- Individuals must be told of the complaints against them.
- They must be given the opportunity to state their case.
- They must be given the right to be accompanied by a representative of their choice.
- Nobody should act as 'prosecutor' and 'judge' in the same case.
- They must be told clearly of the outcome of the proceedings.
- They must be given the opportunity to appeal against any decision.

It is essential that written records are kept at all stages of the disciplinary procedures. In cases of inadequate performance, the employee must be given the chance to improve and must be offered suitable training and possibly the chance to be transferred to a less demanding job. In arriving at any decision following a disciplinary hearing, it is necessary to take into account factors such as age, length of service, previous employment record, domestic circumstances, etc.

Equal opportunities

There has been a steady growth in recent years in the number of leisure and tourism organisations that publicly announce they are 'equal opportunities employers', or that they are 'working towards equality of opportunity'. Hotels, local authority leisure services departments, tour operators, airlines, visitor attractions and voluntary sector providers, to name but a few, have all followed this trend in order to enhance their image, thereby attracting and retaining the best possible staff. In the same way that an organisation may say that it is 'committed to customer care', however, there must be a firm organisational policy that puts the words into action and proves that a commitment to equal opportunities for its workforce is more than just a statement of good intent.

Such a policy should include:

- A clear statement that the organisation will avoid all forms of discrimination in its employment practices.
- A statement that it will take steps to outlaw discrimination if, or when, it is found to occur.

- What the policy means in terms of recruitment, selection, training and promotion of staff.
- How the policy will be monitored and evaluated.
- Who will be responsible for managing the implementation of the policy.

An equal opportunities policy that includes each of these elements and is implemented with the full support of both management and staff will go a long way towards allowing employees to achieve their full potential without the fear of being held back by prejudice or discrimination.

The three most common types of discrimination that employees, or those seeking employment, in leisure and tourism are likely to encounter are:

- Discrimination on the grounds of race.
- Sex (or gender) discrimination.
- Discrimination related to equal pay.

This list is by no means exhaustive and focuses on the areas of discrimination thought to be the most common in leisure and tourism. Other forms of discrimination, for example on the grounds of disability, having dependent children and related to age, are no less important to the individual who is faced with these types of discrimination.

Race discrimination

Britain is a multi-cultural and multi-ethnic society where people of all races live and work together and have the right to use their leisure time as they choose. When it comes to employing staff, the Race Relations Act 1976 states that it is illegal to discriminate against anybody on the grounds of race by treating them less favourably in areas such as recruitment, training and promotion. Any employer who does so is guilty of direct discrimination. An example of a breach of the Act involving direct racial discrimination would be an advertisement for the post of a tourist information centre manager which stated that the post was 'considered unsuitable for those of African descent'. Indirect discrimination is also unlawful under the Race Relations Act, and is when a condition is imposed on all staff, but is clearly more difficult for certain staff to comply with on account of their race or creed. If a visitor attraction, for example, made it a condition of appointment that all staff must work on a Sunday, but an employee of a particular creed was unable to fulfil this requirement on religious grounds, he or she may be able to claim indirect racial discrimination by the employer.

Sex discrimination

The Sex Discrimination Act was introduced in 1975 to outlaw discrimination on the grounds of whether a person is male or female. As with race discrimination, employers must not discriminate on the basis of a person's gender by treating them less favourably when it comes to recruitment, training and promotion. The distinction between direct and indirect discrimination also applies to sex discrimination. An example of direct discrimination would be to advertise for an assistant in a local museum and state that it was only suitable for female applicants. Indirect discrimination on the grounds of sex would include an airline setting an unnecessary minimum height requirement of 6 ft for the post of steward or stewardess; clearly such a requirement would favour male applicants and discriminate against females who wished to apply.

There are certain circumstances when discrimination on the grounds of race or sex is allowable under the law, if employers can show there is a genuine occupational qualification that demands that the applicant must be of a particular sex or race. There are many occasions in leisure and tourism when these exceptions need to be used, including:

- Where a job involves personal contact with one sex or another and may lead to embarrassing or compromising situations, e.g. an advertisement for an attendant to work in the male changing room at a leisure centre could legally ask for male applicants only.
- Where staff of a particular race are needed to provide authenticity, e.g. an Indian craft shop set within a theme park may wish to recruit only Indian workers to provide an authentic atmosphere.
- Where an actress or entertainer is playing the part of a woman, for example, and the essential nature of the job would be materially different if it was carried out by a man.

Equal pay

The Equal Pay Act was introduced in 1970 to abolish discrimination between men and women in pay and other terms of their contracts of employment. It was amended in 1983 to give all workers the right to equal pay for work of equal value, when:

- The work being carried out by both male and female employees is the same or broadly similar; the technical term for this is 'like work'. A female swimming pool attendant should be paid the same as her male colleagues, for example.
- The work of employees undertaking different jobs is of 'equal value'; for example, a hostess employed by an inter-city coach company may argue that her job is of equal value to an airline stewardess and she should, therefore, receive similar pay.
- A job evaluation study (JES) has been carried out and two jobs have been rated as 'equivalent' in terms of the demands made under various headings, including skills, decision making, effort, etc.

Employees who feel they should be receiving equal pay can apply to an industrial tribunal at any time during their employment, or up to six months after leaving.

Section 3 Remuneration for employees in leisure and tourism

If you were to ask a group of people why they go to work, the chances are that nine out of ten of them would say 'to earn money to pay the bills'. We all need money to buy food and clothes, and to provide a roof over our heads. Although surveys taken of British people show that, by and large, most workers are not very happy in their jobs, working in the leisure and tourism industry is very appealing to a great many people. They are attracted by the fact that it is very much 'a people industry', where interaction with customers and clients is an essential part of the job. Many jobs in leisure and tourism sound very glamorous and involve travel, working in the open air and are, in some cases, an extension of a sport or hobby. It is little wonder that there has been such a dramatic growth in the number of leisure and tourism courses on offer at colleges, universities and even in schools to prepare people, young and old, for working in this dynamic industry.

While the leisure and tourism industry reflects a very positive image to those seeking employment, it does have something of an image problem when it comes to pay; it is generally perceived as a low-wage industry with a high proportion of unskilled and often temporary jobs. It is still a very new industry that is working hard to develop career structures and qualifications that will project a more professional image through the 1990s and beyond. Many who work in leisure and tourism are willing, in the short term, to put up with low pay, which they consider is compensated by the travel opportunities, freedom and rapid promotion that many sectors of the industry can offer.

Salary and wage structures

A lot of people who work in leisure and tourism will be expected to work unsocial hours. The very nature of the industry means that it is necessary to work during the times that are normally associated with 'leisure', often at evenings and weekends. Staff working in leisure centres, hotels, visitor attractions, restaurants, airports, etc., will all be affected by this work pattern. For working these unsocial hours, the employees may be paid a shift allowance in addition to their normal basic pay.

Depending on which sector of leisure and tourism we are dealing with, the basic pay may be fixed solely by the employer, by the employer in consultation with a trade union or workers' association, or by a wages council (the hotel and catering sector has its own wages council).

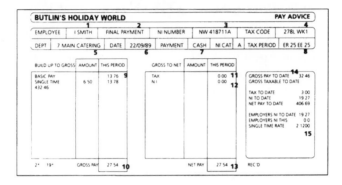

YOU AND YOUR WAGES
Explanation of Wage Slip

1. Your name.
2. Shows that this is a final payment.
3. Your national insurance number.
4. The tax code. This is from your P45. If you did not give a P45, your code will be the "emergency rate" which you can then claim back from the tax office if you have paid too much by the end of the year.
5. Department.
6. Date of wages.
7. Type of payment.
8. Tax period in which wages are paid.
9. Basic pay, amount paid at different rates.
10. Gross pay.
11. Deduction for tax.
12. Deduction for National Insurance.
13. Net pay (= Gross Pay - Deductions).
14. Shows total paid in this tax year.
15. Rate of pay.

Fig 9.6 A typical wages slip for an employee in leisure and tourism
(courtesy of the Rank Organisation)

The 'going rate' for any job will be depend on many factors, such as:

- The supply of suitable people who could do the job.
- The skills demanded.
- The qualifications necessary to secure the job.
- The level of responsibility.
- The part of the country in which the job is located (jobs in the South-East of England sometimes attract an extra payment known as a London 'weighting').
- The degree of danger or risk involved with the job.
- The experience of those applying for the job.

Some leisure and tourism organisations prefer to pay their existing employees overtime rather than take on new members of staff, when extra work becomes available. The sorts of occasions when overtime may be paid include:

- To cover for staff illness and short-term absence.
- To be employed for a special event that is not part of the normal work programme.
- To put in extra hours in response to a heavy demand on the organisation, e.g. a reservations assistant for a tour operator may work overtime in the peak booking period or a leisure centre assistant may work extra hours over a Bank Holiday weekend.
- To carry out a survey of users of facilities.
- To write up an important report or complete a tender application.

Holidays with pay are enjoyed by the vast majority of people who work in the leisure and tourism industry, although it is interesting to note that Britain is one of the few countries in the European Union (formerly the EC) where virtually no worker has a statutory right to holiday leave and pay. The majority of British workers have between 21 and 30 days paid holiday per year, excluding Bank Holidays, the actual amount depending on such issues as length of service, whether they work in the private, public or voluntary sector and the nature of the job itself.

Incentive schemes

In addition to basic pay, many leisure and tourism organisations offer their employees other incentives in order to encourage performance, such as:

- Commission payments.
- Bonuses.
- Profit-sharing schemes.
- 'Perks' and fringe benefits.

Commission payments

Commission is usually associated with sales staff who can increase their earnings by increasing the amount they sell. A commission is a payment that is usually paid in addition to a basic salary, although there are occasions when a job is 'commission only' with no basic pay at all. The commission may be a lump sum that is paid when a certain target is reached, or, more usually, a percentage of the value of the sales. The payment of commission occurs in many sectors of the leisure and tourism industry, including:

- Counter staff in a travel agency who receive extra payments according to the number of holidays and other products sold.
- An area sales manager for an airline who earns commission based on the value of flights sold by her sales team.
- A conference executive who receives part of his salary as commission based on the number of conference bed-nights sold by his company.

Commission is a very good incentive for the employee to work hard and achieve pre-determined work targets.

Bonuses

It is common in the leisure and tourism industry to pay staff a bonus at certain times of the year or in appreciation of the hard work and effort on the part of the employees in relation to a particular campaign or project. Hotel workers may receive a bonus at Christmas, overseas representatives may be paid a bonus by their tour operator at the end of the summer or winter season and a manager of a major tourist attraction may receive a bonus for a particularly successful year. Bonus payments are not normally linked to the productivity or performance of an individual member of staff but are one-off payments that will vary from time to time.

CASE STUDY

Incentive schemes – Top Rank 'Pacesetters' Programme

The Rank Organisation PLC is the leading bingo and social club operator in the UK with some 160 outlets trading under the 'Top Rank' and 'Mecca' names. In order to help staff to work to their full potential, Top Rank runs an innovative incentive programme called 'Pacesetters'. As Top Rank's managing director says in the foreword to the 'Pacesetter' booklet, 'the scheme is about sharing in the success of the company, rewarding performance and recognising outstanding individual achievement'. The comprehensive scheme is available to:

- Head office executives and managers.
- Head office controllers.
- All regional, area and head office staff.
- Regional directors.
- Regional executives and managers.
- Area executives and area managers.
- General managers.
- Support managers (deputy and assistant managers).

The 'Pacesetters' incentive scheme is based on the payment of cash bonuses for achieving pre-set performance targets. General managers, for example, will receive cash bonuses based on their achievement of a club admission target and a club profit contribution (CPC). A manager who reaches his or her quarterly CPC will be paid a bonus equivalent to 10 per cent of the quarterly salary. Providing that the CPC is achieved, bonuses will be paid according to how well the admissions target is met or exceeded, on the following scale:

Achievement of admissions target	Bonus
100%	10% of quarterly salary
101%	12.5% of quarterly salary
102%	15% of quarterly salary

The maximum payment for achieving and exceeding CPC and admissions targets will be 40 per cent of the quarterly salary.

In addition to the payment of cash bonuses, the 'Pacesetters' scheme also gives Top Rank the opportunity to recognise and reward individuals who demonstrate exceptional drive and commitment, through the élite awards and the coveted manager of the year awards. The 'Pacesetter' élite awards are made by head office directors, regional directors and area executives, and are worth up to £500 depending on the position of the recipient. Presented in the form of 'Pacesetter' cheques, the élite awards allow staff to choose their own gifts from a selection of high street retail stores, including Argos, Boots, Currys, Marks & Spencer and Next.

To be selected as manager of the year is the greatest honour that Top Rank can bestow on its employees. Gold (£5,000), silver (£3,000) and bronze (£1,500) awards are made for manager of the year, with three awards of smaller value made available to support manager of the year. The awards are made in recognition of performance versus target, customer service, promotional skills, presentation standards, staff training and development, and general management skills.

(Information courtesy of the Rank Organisation PLC)

Profit-sharing schemes

As its name implies, a profit-sharing scheme is when an employee receives an extra payment in addition to his or her basic salary, which is related to the profitability of the organisation. For example, a 10 per cent increase in profits over a 12-month period may result in an employee receiving a bonus that is equivalent to an extra 10 per cent of his or her annual salary. When an organisation is not generating any profits, perhaps because it has only just begun trading or is struggling to maintain its share of the market, the bonus will not usually be paid, although it is rare for staff to be asked to take a cut in pay in this situation.

'Perks' and fringe benefits

We have seen that many employees working in leisure and tourism are attracted to the industry by the glamour often associated with the industry and by the 'perks' that many positions can offer. 'Perks' are very common in leisure and tourism, and are seen as a way of supplementing a sometimes low basic wage or salary. One of the most widespread fringe benefits is the right to buy or use facilities and services either free or at discounted prices, for example:

- Free use of swimming pool and sports facilities for staff working in a leisure centre.
- Discounted flights for travel agents, tour operators and airline personnel.
- Free rail travel for British Rail staff and their families.
- Free entrance to visitor attractions for staff and their guests.
- Discounted rates at hotels in the same chain for employees.
- Free admittance to football matches for ground staff.

There may be certain restrictions on when staff can take advantage of these 'perks'; Center Parcs, for example, insist that employees can only use the facilities when they are off-duty, a ruling that is widespread throughout all sectors of the industry.

Other benefits to staff in leisure and tourism include discounts at selected stores, subsidised canteen services, free uniforms, private health insurance, company vehicles and free shares in the company, to name but a few. Figure 9.7 indicates the type of 'perks' available to staff employed by the Rank Organisation.

Staff working in travel agencies are offered many types of incentives by tour operators, airlines, car hire firms, coach operators, etc., to encourage them to sell their particular product. One of the most common is to give sales staff gift vouchers from major high street stores in return for selling a particular number of holiday packages or a certain value of airline flights, for example. By using this technique, sales representatives are able to influence counter staff and hopefully increase sales for their company.

Pensions

Most leisure and tourism organisations will want to help their staff in later life and will offer pension facilities that will give their permanent employees an extra income when they retire. This benefit will be in addition to the normal state retirement pension, which is available, at the moment, to men at the age of 65 and to women when they reach 60 years of age. Pension arrangements will vary greatly between one organisation and another, as well as between individuals doing the same job. This is why some organisations offer free financial and pre-retirement planning for their employees, to ensure that they receive the best possible pension

Fig 9.7 Staff benefits and discounts offered by the Rank Organisation PLC

benefits at retirement. Public sector leisure and tourism employees are likely to be members of a local authority pension scheme, which, within certain parameters, can be transferred from one public sector organisation to another, without loss of benefits.

Pensions can be either contributory, when the member of staff pays a certain amount towards the pension, or non-contributory when all pension payments are made by the employer. Even with a contributory pension scheme, it is likely that the employer will make some contribution towards payments. There has been a steady growth in recent years of private pensions as a tax-efficient way of supplementing an existing pension. The Rank Organisation, for example, operates an additional voluntary contribution scheme (known as AVC), which allows staff to make additional payments towards a supplementary pension; many public sector organisations also offer AVCs.

Section 4 Industrial relations in leisure and tourism

We have seen in this unit that there are times when even the most amiable employee will come into conflict with his or her employer, and that procedures need to be implemented to ensure equity in resolving the conflict. Put in very crude and simple terms, leisure and tourism employers seek to extract from their employees the maximum work for the minimum pay, while employees are keen to receive maximum rewards for their efforts, with as much security of employment and safety at work, as possible. In view of these differing perspectives, there needs to be a process that develops compromise and agreement between the two parties. This is what is meant by industrial relations in its widest sense. In an individual organisation, it is best seen as a bargaining process that is constantly shifting emphasis and direction.

Trade unions

The beginnings of the trade union movement can be traced back to the late eighteenth and early nineteenth centuries, when conditions of work were poor and workers were exploited by powerful employers. Staff saw trade unions as a way of protecting themselves against this exploitation through collective action, including, ultimately, the right to go on strike. Today, we see trade unions in all walks of life, from journalists to shipworkers, teachers to miners. Leisure and tourism is not a particularly 'unionised' industry, on account of its very diverse nature involving many different sectors.

The role of trade unions

Many trade unions have both industrial and political objectives. The industrial objectives include:

- To negotiate on behalf of their members with management on such matters as pay, working conditions, hours of work, pension rights, contracts of employment, etc.
- To assist individual members with any problems they may have, for example, in a disciplinary or grievance action.
- To advise on a range of legal matters related to employment, including health and safety and equal opportunities.
- To attempt to play a role in the decision-making processes of the organisation.

Trade unions have been associated with the Labour Party since their earliest days and are, therefore, keen to pursue general political issues, including:

- Full employment.
- Improved social security provisions.
- A voice in national decision making.
- Improved public services, e.g. health, education, childcare.
- Public ownership of the means of production.

Trade unions and the law

In the 100 years or so following the Trade Union Act of 1871, the trade union movement used its influence and collective power, latterly through the work of the Trades Union Congress (TUC), to grow into an important industrial and political force that could influence governments and provide a supportive environment for its followers. The 1980s brought a dramatic change to this situation, with the introduction of a host of new laws aimed at 'curbing the excesses of the unions', as the Conservative government of the day characterised the situation. The Employment Acts of 1980, 1982, 1988 and 1990, plus other related legislation, sought to outlaw the 'closed shop', when workers had to join a union whether they wished to or not, and introduced the concept of compulsory secret ballots related to the call for strike action. Many commentators consider that the union movement was mortally wounded in the 1980s and is unlikely ever to regain its former influence and power. Others point to the fact that there are still around 400 trade unions in the UK today with approximately 10 million members, and that they are still a force to be reckoned with.

Assignment 9

Situation

You work in the busy personnel department at a leading outbound tour operator. Having just joined the company after completing a two-year Travel and Tourism course, you have been given the job of updating the company's information booklet, which is sent out to young people looking for employment, both full- and part-time. So that you can approach the task with an open mind, the personnel manager has decided not to show you the existing six-page booklet, which has been distributed in response to enquiries for the past two years.

Tasks

You are to research and produce a booklet or information pack that can be sent out to young people seeking employment with the company. Although you have an open brief, there are one or two items that must be included:

- An indication of the main types of opportunities that exist within the company.
- Outline job descriptions of three typical posts.
- Details of the skills and qualities needed in each of these three posts (person specifications).
- A typical job advertisement for one of the posts, with an indication of where the company advertises its posts.
- The main types of remuneration available to employees.
- Typical staff training opportunities.

Your booklet or information pack should be designed with a young audience in mind and should be about 1,500 words in length.

Unit 10
APPLYING MARKETING AND MEDIA TECHNIQUES IN LEISURE AND TOURISM

Section 1 Market research techniques in leisure and tourism

The principles of market research

We saw in Unit 4 that successful marketing in leisure and tourism is founded on an effective market research base. All organisations need to have detailed information on their existing customers and users, as well as data with which to plan for the future, a concept known as forecasting. Identifying customer needs is an essential first stage in the marketing process, from which products and services geared to customer needs can be developed and their success monitored. Without the structured, objective and focused approach to the collection of data, which a well designed market research study can offer, decisions taken by managers in leisure and tourism are unlikely to be wholly effective.

Research may be required at any stage of the marketing process, perhaps linked to a feasibility study to investigate the expansion of an existing theme park or to consider alterations to the pricing levels at a bowling complex. Most managers would agree that market research is very important since it can help their organisations remain competitive in the increasingly competitive leisure and tourism industry. More specifically, market research can:

- Identify problems and suggest solutions, e.g. should the council of a Victorian spa town which is keen to expand tourism, spend its budget on improving infrastructure or on marketing the town and its attractions?
- Allow an organisation to plan for the future with confidence.
- Identify new market opportunities or sales outlets.

- Monitor the reaction of customers and users to a product, service or facility.
- Help pin-point business problems, e.g. why has their been a steady drop in sales for a particular product or at a particular facility?
- Monitor trends in the industry and its constituent sectors.
- Project an image of an organisation that cares about its customers and respects their views and comments.
- Reduce costs by highlighting ineffective practices and systems.

While most people would agree that market research has an important role to play in the success of an organisation, there is not universal agreement in the leisure and tourism industry that it is necessarily a good thing. Some owners and managers prefer to rely on their judgement when it comes to making decisions about their organisations, rather than giving up time and investing money in data collection and analysis. While there are undoubtedly examples of when this 'seat of the pants' approach to marketing pays off, talking to any business consultant specialising in leisure and tourism will indicate that the lack of an effective market research base is one of the most common causes of business failures.

The market research process

Although the nature of any market research carried out will vary between different leisure and tourism concerns, depending on such matters as the size of the organisation, the sector in which it operates, its turnover and the importance it attaches to the process, there are a number of clearly defined stages that any market research process needs to go through, namely:

1 *Identification of the objectives of the market research* – for example 'to seek the views of the visitors to a tourist information centre to aid further development of the products and services on offer'. A process with a clearly defined purpose is far more likely to provide information that is useful for decision making purposes. Aims that are non-ambiguous, identifiable and measurable, will not only provide a focus for the research activity, but also allow those who have commissioned the research to evaluate whether or not it has been successful in meeting its objectives.

2 *Development of a research strategy* – once the purpose of the market research has been agreed, it will be necessary to draw up a plan of how the objectives are to be met, in other words, to devise a strategy indicating which research methods are most appropriate (the methodology). The strategy will need to answer such questions as:
   – Is any (or all) of the information required to meet the objectives already available from other sources?

- What emphasis will be placed on secondary and primary research sources?
- If secondary research is needed, which sources will be consulted?
- What primary research method or methods will be used?
- Who will carry out the research?
- What will it cost?
- What is the timescale for implementation?

3 *Implementation of the chosen strategy* – it may be, for example, that a major travel agency chain that is considering opening a new city centre travel shop may decide to carry out a small-scale interview survey of shoppers in the city and a telephone survey of major businesses as its primary research, together with an analysis of economic and demographic data published by the local council planning department and local chamber of trade, plus reference to the *Travel Trade Directory*, as its secondary research.

4 *Analysis of the data* – once collected, the information will need to be collated into a form that is easily interpreted. Depending on the size of the market research project, this may be carried out manually or with the help of a computer.

5 *Reporting on the findings of the study* – in nearly all cases, a written report will be produced for distribution to those who have commissioned the study. It is helpful if the main elements of the study and its recommendations are summarised as 'an executive summary'. Nowadays, it is becoming increasingly common to supplement this written document with a formal presentation, where the people who carried out the study can be questioned in more depth on their findings and recommendations. Such an event will normally take place after the distribution of the final report, so as to allow time for the readers to look in detail at the document.

Who should carry out the research?

A market research exercise can be carried out by staff already employed in an organisation or it may be undertaken by outside specialists. The 'in-house' option has the advantage of being cheaper and under the direct control of the organisation and its management, but this could itself introduce bias and a degree of subjectivity that could make the results meaningless. Larger leisure and tourism organisations are likely to employ their own market research professionals who will be responsible for commissioning research, analysing data and reporting back to other departments. Most organisations in leisure and tourism will not be able to afford the luxury of having their own specialist staff and will look to external agencies to meet their market research needs. Such services can be provided by advertising agencies, market research agencies, universities and colleges, and market research consultants.

Sources of secondary data

Secondary data is information that is already available, usually in written form, but increasingly now made available via computers and other electronic sources. Research that uses secondary sources is sometimes also known as 'desk research'. The main advantage of using secondary research material is that it can save both time and money when compared with primary market research. In reality, most market research studies undertaken for and by leisure and tourism organisations involve a combination of primary and secondary methods.

There is a wealth of secondary data available to leisure and tourism organisations, some available from internal sources and much that exists outside its immediate environment (external sources).

Secondary data from internal sources

It is often surprising to outside observers what little use many leisure and tourism organisations make of their own internal information. A 'trawl' through existing files, databases and records to see if the information contained in them can help with the market research should be the first priority, before external sources are consulted. The following data, held by most leisure and tourism organisations, may reveal useful information:

- Past and present usage or attendance figures.
- The results of any recent initiatives to record visitor attitudes and behaviour, e.g. visitor surveys.
- Lists of names and addresses of customers.
- Details of customer profiles, e.g. age, sex, interests, etc.
- Details of any business or corporate clients and their interests.
- Formal and informal feedback from customers.
- Analysis of spend per head on catering and retail.

The advent of computer management information systems makes this sort of data so much more accessible and useful for market research purposes (see Unit 6 for more detail on MIS in leisure and tourism).

External sources of secondary data

There is an enormous amount of data available to leisure and tourism professionals from published information widely available through public libraries and specialist organisations. The government produces a great deal of general data, which, although not always specific to leisure and tourism, can be very useful in helping to forecast changes in society and the economy. This includes the Family Expenditure Survey, General Household Survey, Social Trends, the Census of

Population carried out every ten years and data published in the Employment Gazette.

Sources of data specific to the UK leisure sector are available from a wide range of private and public bodies, and include:

- *Leisure Futures* published by the Henley Centre for Forecasting.
- Data published by consultancies such as Jordan's and Leisure Consultants.
- Annual reports of various bodies including the Sports Council, CCPR, Arts Council of Great Britain, Countryside Commission, National Trust, Department of National Heritage, etc.
- CIPFA Leisure and Recreation Statistics.
- The *British Leisure Centre Directory*.
- Annual reports of private sector leisure organisations including Forte, the Rank Organisation PLC, Granada PLC, etc.
- Reports on the leisure industry under the Mintel name.
- Professional bodies such as the Institute of Leisure and Amenity Management (ILAM) and the Institute of Sport and Recreation Management (ISRM, formerly IBRM).

Information specific to the UK tourism sector can be found in:

- Annual reports of the English, Scotland, Northern Ireland and Wales Tourist Boards.
- BTA Annual Report.
- The International Passenger Survey (IPS).
- The United Kingdom Tourism Survey (UKTS).
- *Business Monitor MQ6 – Overseas Travel and Tourism* published by HMSO.
- Annual reports of commercial travel and tourism organisations including British Airways, Thomson Holidays, Airtours PLC, Thomas Cook, etc.
- Trade associations such as ABTA and IATA.
- The Statistical Office of the European Communities (EUROSTAT).
- Professional bodies such as the Tourism Society and the Hotel, Catering and Institutional Management Association (HCIMA).

Primary research

Although we have indicated that there is a good supply of relevant and up-to-date secondary data available on the leisure and tourism industry, it is highly likely that an organisation, at some stage in its development, will need to collect information that is specific to its own operations and is not already available; the collection and subsequent analysis of this information is known as primary research.

Methods of collecting primary research data

An organisation wanting to collect primary data has three main options available to it:

- Surveys.
- Observation.
- Focus groups.

Surveys

By far the most common method of collecting primary data in leisure and tourism is by conducting a survey, which involves the collection of data from a proportion of a total 'population', which researchers refer to as the sample. In this context, 'population' means the total number of people who could be interviewed. For example, the manager of a tourist attraction may decide to interview a 10 per cent sample of all visitors to the attraction on a particular day during the season. If the total number of visitors is 5,000 (the 'population'), 500 interviews (the sample) will need to be undertaken. Sampling is carried out because it is usually impractical to interview the whole 'population'. It is a very precise technique which we will investigate later in this section.

There are three main types of survey that can be used to collect primary data:

- Face-to-face interview survey.
- Self-completed questionnaire survey.
- Telephone survey.

Face-to-face interviews

A face-to-face interview survey involves an interviewer asking questions of a member of the general public, known as the respondent, and recording his or her answers and comments on a questionnaire. This type of survey is very common in all sectors of the leisure and tourism industry, from leisure centres to seaside resorts. The face-to-face interview is a very good way of obtaining both quantitative and qualitative data. Quantitative refers to factual information such as:

- Age of respondents.
- How far they have travelled.
- Their occupation.
- Mode of transport used to reach the facility.
- Amount of money spent on-site.
- How many times a respondent has visited a site.
- How the respondents had heard about a facility.

Qualitative data refers to a person's opinion or attitude to a particular facility, product or service, and provides managers with direct feedback on the views of their customers. Typical questions that would produce qualitative data are as follows:

- Which feature of the theme park did you like the most?
- How would you rate the standard of service you received at the hotel – excellent, average or poor?
- How could the facility be improved for disabled people?
- If the company was to introduce a discount scheme, would you use it?
- What is your opinion of the food in the hotel?
- What was your general impression of the resort?

Face-to-face interviews can be carried out in a number of different locations, such as:

- At the respondent's home – more in-depth interviews tend to be carried out in the comfort and privacy of the home.
- In the street – busy high street locations are often used to interview a cross-section of the general public on general issues related to leisure and tourism.
- On-site – for example, at a leisure centre, tourist attraction, hotel, resort, airport, fitness centre, etc. On-site surveys have the advantage that customers can be interviewed while they are actually taking part in the activity.
- *En route* – for example, at a frontier post, a toll booth, on a ship or at a motorway rest area.
- At work – organisations wanting information on business and conference tourism may choose to interview respondents at their place of work.

Face-to-face interviews have a number of advantages when compared with other survey methods:

- The interviewer is able to explain difficult questions.
- Visual aids can be used.
- The interviewer can prompt the respondent for further detail.
- Initial interest on the part of the respondent is aroused.

The principal disadvantages of the face-to-face interview are that it is expensive, since the interviewers have to be fully trained and the administrative load is high, and that it is time consuming when compared with other techniques, e.g. telephone interviews. It does, however, continue to be used very widely in leisure and tourism as a means of providing valuable information that can be used by management to improve its products and services.

Self-completed questionnaire surveys

A survey that requires respondents to fill in a questionnaire themselves has the benefit of being cheaper than a face-to-face interview survey since there is no need to recruit and train interviewers. Self-completed questionnaire surveys are used extensively in leisure and tourism as a relatively low-cost method for obtaining both qualitative and quantitative data on customers and usage. Many tour operators carry out a postal survey of returning holiday-makers, asking them to complete a questionnaire related to their holiday experience (see Figure 10.1).

(E)urocamp
Customer 1993
QUESTIONNAIRE

Name _____

_____

Ref No: _____

Please return to: Eurocamp Travel Ltd., Canute Court, Toft Road, Knutsford, Cheshire WA16 0NL or 40 Lower Leeson St., Dublin 2.

Win A FREE CAMERA!

SECTION 1 - GENERAL

1. How would you describe your overall level of satisfaction with your holiday? (please tick as appropriate)

Very satisfied (1)	Generally satisfied (2)	Not satisfied with certain aspects (3)	Generally not satisfied (4)

2. How did the holiday measure up to expectations? (please tick as appropriate)

Better than expected (1)	Much as expected (2)	Below expectations (3)

3. Would you: (please tick as appropriate)

	Yes Definitely (1)	Probably (2)	Possibly (3)	Definitely Not (4)
a) Go on a Eurocamp holiday again?				
b) Recommend Eurocamp to others?				

4. ACCOMMODATION, EQUIPMENT AND ON-SITE SERVICE

What is your assessment of: (please tick)

	Very Good (1)	Good (2)	Adequate (3)	Poor (4)	Not Applicable (5)
a) The Eurocamp Tent?					
b) The Eurocamp Mobile-Home?					
c) The quality of equipment provided?					
d) The standard of camp-sites used?					
e) The standard of our Courier service?					
f) Our children's courier service?					
g) The Play-mobile?					
h) The Windsurf Courier service?					

5. OUR SERVICE AND DOCUMENTATION

What is your opinion of: (please tick)

	Very Good (1)	Good (2)	Adequate (3)	Poor (4)	Not Applicable (5)
a) Our Reservations and administration service?					
b) The Eurocamp Traveller's and Country Guides?					
c) The Eurocamp Route Map?					
d) Our Local Guides?					
e) Our Junior Travel Packs?					

THERE IS SPACE FOR GENERAL OBSERVATIONS AND SUGGESTIONS ON PAGE 6

To enable us to keep our mailing list up to date we would be most grateful if you could correct any inaccuracies in the address to which our correspondence to you is sent. Should you have moved to a new address please write in the space provided.

Fig 10.1 An extract from self-completed questionnaire (courtesy of Eurocamp Travel)

The information contained in these questionnaires gives valuable feedback from clients and is often the starting point for changes to products or services. It is common to find self-completed questionnaires at visitor attractions and leisure facilities, for customers to complete and either return by post, or leave behind before they depart. Some leisure and tourism organisations provide an incentive, such as a free gift or discounted product, in order to increase the number of completed questionnaires. Although self-completed questionnaire surveys are undoubtedly cheaper than face-to-face interviews, there are disadvantages, such as lower response rates, which can sometimes be improved by sending a reminder to the respondent. Also, if a respondent does not fully understand a question, there is no interviewer to ask for clarification.

Telephone surveys

Telephone surveys are gaining in popularity in leisure and tourism, as a way of getting a fast response to an event, facility or service. They are used widely in the USA, but are largely restricted in UK leisure and tourism to business-to-business activities, such as following up enquiries from buyers who have attended trade shows such as 'Leisure Industry Week' or the 'World Travel Market'. Companies specialising in selling timeshare also use telephone surveys to target likely customers. Conducting a survey by telephone can certainly give a speedy response and, if trained operators are used, many interviews are possible in a given time period. Disadvantages include the fact that it is not possible to use visual stimulus materials and the likelihood that people will feel that they have had their privacy invaded and will be not co-operate.

Questionnaire design

As any student will tell you, designing a questionnaire is not difficult! Designing a good questionnaire that will achieve its intended aim, however, is a skilled operation. It is also a very time-consuming process, with constant checks to see that the questions are easily understood and in an appropriate order (a colleague once spent nine months designing a questionnaire for a countryside visitor survey, although most are not quite so time consuming!). Specialists in the design of questionnaires suggest the following sequence to ensure an effective finished product:

1 With reference to the objectives of the survey, make a list of expected 'outcomes'.
2 Formulate the questions that will achieve these 'outcomes'.
3 Produce a first draft of the questionnaire paying attention to question order, language style and overall layout.
4 Carry out a 'pilot' survey with a small number of respondents to check understanding and suitability of the questions.
5 Amend the first draft as necessary to produce a final version.
6 Use the final version in the survey, but be prepared to make minor adjustments if they will better achieve the 'outcomes'.

The following is a list of guidelines that should be followed when designing questionnaires:

- Always put 'sensitive' questions, e.g. age, occupation, marital status, etc., at the end of the questionnaire. Respondents will feel more comfortable about giving answers to such questions than if they appear at the beginning.
- Avoid ambiguous questions (questions with 'double meanings').
- Avoid using jargon.
- Make the questionnaire as short or as long as it needs to be; don't be tempted to include questions that, although interesting, will not help achieve the 'outcomes'.
- Simple, objective, pre-coded (agree/neutral/disagree) questions will provide clearer answers than open-ended questions.
- Avoid 'leading questions', e.g. 'don't you agree that the hotel is comfortable?' is a question that invites a positive response.
- Do not include questions that are an impossible test of the respondent's memory, e.g. 'how much did you spend on drinks per day for the first week of your holiday?'
- Use language that is appropriate to the respondent.

Sampling

It is usually impractical for a leisure and tourism organisation to interview all its existing or potential customers to gather qualitative and quantitative information from them. Unless the 'population' is very small, for example interviewing all 12 members of a party of tourists on a Himalayan trekking holiday, the organisation must rely on the responses of a proportion of the total number, known as a sample. If the selection of the sample is fair, accurate and based on proven statistical methods, the responses of the people interviewed should mirror those of the total 'population' within known limits of accuracy. The sampling method chosen must reduce bias to a minimum. For example, if a local authority leisure services department wanted to collect data on customer perception of its three leisure centres, but carried out 80 per cent of the interviews at its 'premier' centre, the results would clearly be biased and not representative of all three facilities.

Sampling may be either random or quota. For a random survey, individuals are pre-selected from a sampling frame, such as the electoral role. The interviewer is asked to carry out interviews at selected households chosen at random. Many government surveys are carried out in this way. When using the quota sampling method, the interviewer is given instructions as to the number of respondents he or she must interview in certain categories, e.g. defined by age, sex or social class.

The size of the sample will determine the level of accuracy of the data. Large samples provide more accurate results than small ones, but the increase in accuracy becomes less significant as the sample size is increased. Provided that proven statistical methods have been used to select the sample, a survey made up of around 2,000 interviews will give an accurate reflection of the public's view of general matters to a 95 per cent confidence level (in other words, 19 out of 20 surveys will fall within a stated 'margin of error'). It would be rare for a market research agency to carry out a survey with a sample size of less than 100, even if only broad impressions were needed.

Analysis of data

Once data has been collected by the most appropriate means, it will need collating, which, in the case of questionnaires, involves a process known as coding. Each response is given an appropriate numerical code to simplify the analysis, e.g. a question may have three possible answers, and will be coded as follows:

Yes	(code 1)
No	(code 2)
Don't know	(code 0)

Simple factual questions, such as this example, are relatively easy to code and may well have been pre-coded, i.e. assigned a code number at the questionnaire design stage. 'Open' questions, to which there could be an infinite number of possible responses, are still able to be coded as there are usually five or six 'popular' answers, which arise more often. Some market research agencies use a technique known as optical mark reading (OMR). OMR equipment 'reads' the pencil marks made on the questionnaires by the interviewers, so speeding up the process considerably. The data from the questionnaires or other data sheets is then analysed either manually or with the help of a purpose-designed computer programme. Computer software has the advantage of speed and the ability to examine the relationships between a wide range of variables.

Having coded the responses, counts of responses can be made and expressed as percentages, e.g. 46 per cent of those interviewed were male, 24 per cent lived within a 12-mile radius of the facility, etc. An often more relevant, and interesting, analysis of the data can be found in cross tabulations, when the responses to questions can be cross-referenced with a range of respondents' variables, such as age, sex, social class, employment, income, etc. For example, a cross tabulation of data from a visitor survey may reveal that 45 per cent of men visiting a museum were satisfied with the standard of customer service, but only 34 per cent of women gave the same response. Similar analysis in another survey may indicate that males between the ages of 25–34 were twice as likely to visit a fitness suite when compared with males in the 35–44 year category. Detailed analysis of this type is often more useful for management purposes than simple analysis of numbers of responses.

The collated data will next need interpreting for the eventual reader of the market research study. With the availability of sophisticated computer graphics software and laser printing, it is now possible to reproduce data with exceptional style and clarity, using tables, charts, graphs, histograms, pictograms and pie charts.

Reporting on the market research study

The interpretation of the data will culminate in the production of a written report, which should adhere to the following guidelines:

- It should be written in a tone and style appropriate for the intended audience.
- Jargon should be avoided wherever possible so that the report can be easily understood by a non-specialist.
- There should be an executive summary of the main points and recommendations of the report.
- Items such as blank questionnaires and interview schedules should be included where relevant, but are best put as appendices.
- Any critical comments must be fully justified.
- Any tables, maps, diagrams, charts, etc., should be reproduced to a high quality, and referred to in the main body of the report.
- Where appropriate, references and a bibliography may be included.
- Above all, any market research report that is to influence management decision making should not be written in an 'academic' style, but should be regarded as a working 'tool' that has practical applications.

The format in which the report is presented should include:

- Title, date, name of the organisation commissioning the research and name of the individual or organisation contracted to carry out the study.
- Executive summary.
- Details of the brief, terms of reference, objectives of the study and acknowledgements.
- Details of the methodology used, to include reasons for selection of methods, how samples were drawn, number of interviews undertaken, etc.
- The findings of the study.
- Conclusions and recommendations.
- Appendices.
- References and bibliography (where appropriate).

By following closely the five stages of the market research process (see page 10.2), the final report produced should summarise the key points of the study and make realistic recommendations that management should be able to implement for the good of their organisation.

Observation

As well as formally requesting information from respondents by way of a survey, some leisure and tourism organisations make use of observation as a method of collecting primary research data. It is particularly suitable for visitor attractions such as theme parks, art galleries and museums. Observation is practised in many large attractions with the help of sophisticated techniques such as closed circuit television (CCTV) and time-lapse photography, and can produce valuable information on the flow of people and traffic. Electronic tally counters are used in attractions, leisure centres and tourist information centres to monitor usage. On occasions, staff may be asked to 'mingle' with visitors or customers and to eaves-drop on their conversations without revealing their identities. People are often far more honest about their true feelings when talking in private than they would be when asked questions as part of a survey.

Observation has an important role to play in researching competitors' products. There are very few products, services and facilities in leisure and tourism that are truly unique, most having been based on an idea seen elsewhere. It is not uncom-mon for hoteliers, travel agents and airlines, for example, to use the facilities of competitors in order to pick up new tips and improve their own products. As we have seen recently with the British Airways' alleged 'dirty tricks' campaign aimed at Virgin Atlantic Airways, however, observation of the competition can be pushed too far and have serious repercussions.

Focus groups

Focus groups, or panel interviews as they are sometimes called, give organisa-tions an opportunity to discover what influences an individual's purchasing decisions; for example, why does somebody prefer to fly with airline A rather than airline B? This in-depth information is not easy to obtain from questionnaire surveys or observation, but focus group sessions give respondents the time to reflect and consider in detail why they make the decisions they do. A focus group usually consists of up to ten consumers under the guidance of a skilled inter-viewer. The interviewer will use a number of techniques to explore the innermost thoughts and values of the members of the group. The sessions are generally tape-recorded for future analysis and will often signal changes of direction in terms of product range or promotional activities. Given the intensive nature of the focus group, it is an expensive method of gaining primary research material and tends, therefore, to be used mainly by larger leisure and tourism organisations.

Section 2 Media techniques used in leisure and tourism

Introduction

We saw in Unit 4 that promotion is an essential part of the marketing process in leisure and tourism; a leisure centre, for example, may have the latest state-of-the-art equipment and facilities, but if it cannot promote itself effectively, it is unlikely to succeed. An event such as the NutraSweet London Marathon which gets its promotion wrong, will not only suffer embarrassment if it fails to meet its targets, but will also have to deal with the many sponsors who have invested their time and money in the expectation of tangible benefits.

Promotional work in leisure and tourism is concerned with communicating information and 'messages' to persuade people to use or buy particular products, facilities or services. The promotional activities of the Youth Hostels Association, for example, will be geared towards maximising the use of YHA accommodation and activity holidays. The effectiveness of their promotional efforts will have a vital role to play in the overall success of the organisation.

There are a number of communications techniques that leisure and tourism organisations can use to inform and influence their existing and potential customers. The most important are:

- Advertising.
- Direct marketing.
- Public relations.
- Sales promotion.
- Personal selling.

Advertising agencies and professionals refer to 'above the line' and 'below the line' marketing activities. 'Above the line' refers to advertising in the various media, for which the agency or individual earns a commission. 'Below the line' activities include direct mail, public relations and sales promotion, which do not attract a commission but are charged on a 'fee' basis, i.e. an agency may charge £5,000 to devise, implement and monitor a small direct mail campaign for a particular organisation.

Whichever technique is chosen, it is likely to follow the principle known as AIDA, which stands for:

- Attention.
- Interest.
- Desire.
- Action.

AIDA is just as applicable whether an organisation or agency is developing an advertising campaign, writing a direct mail letter, designing an exhibition stand or selecting sales promotion materials. In the case of a newspaper advertisement for a newly opened theme park, for example, the person responsible for writing it may choose to:

- Attract attention to the advertisement by using colour, bold headlines, a picture of a famous personality or striking graphics.
- Maintain the readers' interest by keeping the wording of the advertisement as brief as possible, including language and images that the reader can easily relate to.
- Create a desire to visit the theme park by perhaps offering a discount voucher or other incentive as part of the advertisement.
- Trigger action on the part of the reader by clearly letting him or her know what to do next, e.g. by including a simple map or directions to the park, printing the address and telephone number clearly, or displaying the opening times.

Advertising

Although advertising in general is very widespread in the UK, its use in leisure and tourism is fairly restricted. This may seem hard to understand, particularly if we think of the number of travel advertisements on the television, in the newspapers and on commercial radio around Christmas time every year. This is the peak advertising time for most travel operators when organisations try to persuade potential holiday-makers to book early. It is only the larger travel companies that have the financial resources to be able to mount expensive nationwide television advertising campaigns. Smaller operators rely on selective advertising in the classified pages of newspapers and in specialist magazines. In an industry dominated by small operators, leisure and tourism organisations have to make every promotional pound count and so devote their attention more to 'below the line' activities such as PR and sales promotion, rather than spending their limited budgets on extensive advertising campaigns.

The two main types of advertising in leisure and tourism are:

- *Consumer advertising* – when an organisation such as a tour operator or leisure centre advertises direct to the public, e.g. Hoseasons Holidays placing an advertisement in the *Daily Mirror*, or a community leisure centre advertising on local radio.
- *Trade advertising* – sometimes known as business-to-business advertising, for example when a tour operator advertises its products in the *Travel Trade Gazette* or a distributor of sports goods places an advertisement in *Leisure Management*, which is read by people working in leisure and recreation.

The choice of advertising media

The term 'media' is used in marketing to mean the various channels of communication an organisation can use to advertise its products or services (a single channel is known as a medium). It is important for leisure and tourism organisations to seek the advice of professionals before deciding which media to choose. Smaller operators will not have the experience to gauge which medium will be the most effective for their particular products and may, therefore, be wasting their money. As well as working within budget limits, media selection will also depend on the target audience, i.e. the number and type of potential customers the organisation is trying to reach (the coverage), as well as the number of times the advertiser wishes the message to be communicated to the audience (the frequency). All types of media will provide detailed data on their coverage and circulation, as well as detailed demographic and 'life-style' information on their readers/listeners/viewers. This information is usually presented in the form of a rate card.

The more an organisation knows about its existing and potential customers, the better the chance it has of selecting the right choice of media. Market research, therefore, is crucial to effective media selection.

Types of advertising media

The principal media used frequently by leisure and tourism organisations are:

- Newspapers and magazines, including trade newspapers and journals.
- Television.
- Radio.
- Cinema advertising.
- Outdoor advertising.

Newspapers and magazines

The printed media is by far the largest group of media in the UK in terms of the amount spent by advertisers. The British are avid readers and buyers of newspapers and magazines, which is why they are extensively used by organisations wishing to promote their products and services. The total average daily sale of newspapers in the UK is in the region of 15 million copies, with the *Sun* and the *News of the World* being the most popular daily and Sunday newspaper respectively at the present time. Advertisers have a choice of over 9,000 different magazines from which to choose. The main advantages of newspapers and magazines from the advertisers' point of view are:

1 They are relatively cheap when compared with other media.
2 Messages can be sent nationally, regionally or locally, depending on which publication is chosen (see Figure 10.2).

3 Specific segments of the market can be targeted, e.g. readers with an ABC1 social classification are more likely to read the 'quality' newspapers such as *The Times* or the *Guardian*.

4 Readers with specialist interests can be targeted, e.g. an organisation specialising in organising garden tours can advertise in magazines devoted entirely to the subject of gardening.

5 Reply coupons can be included in an advertisement as a way of compiling a database or mailing list.

6 Advertisements can normally be placed at very short notice so giving the medium great flexibility.

Fig 10.2 An example of an effective newspaper advertisement aimed at a regional market (courtesy of Golley Slater and Partners)

As far as disadvantages are concerned, some people point to the static nature of a newspaper or magazine advertisement, poor quality printing (although new technologies have meant that excellent results are now achievable) and the poor impact some advertisements can have, particularly if they are included among many hundreds selling very similar goods and services. An example of this would be the classified advertisements in the travel sections of the 'broadsheet' Sunday newspapers, which at certain times of the year are very crowded.

Trade newspapers and journals, such as *Leisure Week, Travel Trade Gazette, Travel News, Leisure Manager, Leisure Management* and *Hotel & Caterer*, allow leisure and tourism organisations to communicate with their fellow professionals in the industry and to inform them of new developments in products and services.

Television

Television is the most powerful advertising medium available, which is why it is the most expensive! Approximately 98 per cent of British households have a television set and audiences in the UK can exceed 20 million viewers for a single programme. With the developments in satellite technology, world-wide audiences of hundreds of millions are easily achievable. Advertisers will pay anything up to £40,000 for a 30-second 'slot' at peak viewing time across all ITV regions, and even more when the advertising is linked to a major feature, such as a British athlete running in the 100-metres final in the Olympic Games, which will guarantee a larger than average audience. These costs only represent the 'air time' that the advertiser buys; costs of producing the advertisements themselves are extra and can sometimes be as expensive, second for second, as producing a Hollywood feature film.

With costs of this magnitude, it is not surprising that many leisure and tourism organisations are not able to budget for TV advertising. Only companies such as British Airways, the Rank Organisation, Thomson Holidays, Alton Towers and Thomas Cook have the financial resources available for national television advertising. Regional TV advertising is within the reach of some smaller leisure and tourism operators, such as tourist attractions, resorts and destinations, hotel groups, leisure centres and regional airports.

When leisure and tourism organisations have the resources to be able to use TV advertising, the advantages include:

- Access to a large audience.
- High degree of creativity possible.
- Maximum impact with the use of colour and sound.
- The message is dynamic.
- The advertisement can be repeated.

In addition to cost, another disadvantage levelled at TV advertising is that it is difficult to broadcast to a particular market segment, i.e. the message will not be relevant for many of the viewers. Targeting specific segments is becoming more possible with the introduction of 'themed' satellite channels, such as MTV and SkySports.

Radio

Commercial radio is an important outlet for local news and events. It is also a useful advertising medium for leisure and tourism organisations that want to communicate with a local audience. Travel agents will use local radio at certain times of the year to publicise their services and private and local authority leisure providers will advertise their facilities. Local radio is an obvious choice for events, such as a local holiday show or a sports match, and visitor attractions will make extensive use of the medium. Its main advantages are:

- It is relatively cheap when compared with other media.
- The message can be repeated many times.
- Audiences can be targeted geographically.
- Production costs are low.
- It has the advantage over printed media in that voice and sound can be used.

The main disadvantage of advertising on commercial radio is that it is often seen as a 'background' medium, meaning that messages are not always conveyed to the audience effectively.

Cinema advertising

With the recent introduction of 'multi-screen' cinemas, and the general improvements in levels of quality and customer service, there has been something of a revival in cinema-going since the mid-1980s. This renewed interest has led advertisers to look again at the cinema as a means of conveying messages to the general public. Cinema advertising has all the advantages of commercial radio, namely the ability to promote local facilities and services, plus the impact and movement associated with the 'big screen', but it does have the disadvantage of high production costs. Cinema-goers are predominantly in the younger age groups, making it a particularly suitable medium for advertising products and services to a sector of the population that, in general terms, has a high disposable income and is motivated to buy leisure and tourism products.

Outdoor advertising

Outdoor advertising includes a much wider variety of media than just posters and billboards; flashing signs, tube trains, delivery vans, representatives' cars, taxis, advertisements on buses, sports ground advertising and fascia signs are all part of the communications process in leisure and tourism marketing. Outdoor advertising is often part of a larger advertising campaign involving many different media, acting as a reminder of a message that may already have been shown on television or included in a newspaper advertisement. Some local authorities advertise their leisure facilities at poster sites in their locality and may co-ordinate this activity with a mailing of leaflets to local residents or advertising on local buses. The London Underground is a particularly popular medium for leisure and tourism organisations, which use clever and evocative images to appeal to a 'captive' audience of commuters. The Highlands and Islands Development Board (now Highlands and Islands Enterprise) has run a very successful campaign on the tube for a number of years, extolling the virtues of clean air and breathtaking scenery (two features that the Underground is not noted for!).

While production costs are high for outdoor advertising, overall costs per site are lower than comparable coverage by television advertising.

The role of advertising agencies

It was stressed earlier in this unit that it is important for leisure and tourism organisations to seek professional help and advice when embarking on an advertising campaign. There are countless examples of organisations that have relied on their own limited experience of the industry, only to find that their advertisements have little effect and that they have wasted their money. An advertising agency is one body that can offer a range of services to help an organisation achieve maximum impact with its advertising budget. Although larger leisure and tourism organisations will use agencies as a matter of course, many small- and medium-sized concerns are beginning to realise that the fee charged by an agency may well be a wise investment for the future, given the very competitive nature of leisure and tourism. Having advertisements designed professionally gives an organisation an 'edge' over the competition and may well lead to increased business. Figure 10.3 shows the structure of a typical advertising agency offering a full range of client services.

Account executives play a key role in ensuring that an advertising campaign meets its objectives and that the clients are satisfied with the work of the agency. They are the link between the clients, known as 'accounts', and all the other specialists within the agency who will contribute to the campaign. Working with the account director, the account executive will work to meet the client's wishes and will assemble and lead an account group made up of staff from the relevant departments of the agency, who will advise on such matters as media selection, creative ideas and market research needed to support the campaign.

The creative team are the 'ideas' people in the agency, chosen for their skill in producing effective slogans and text (copywriters) or their artistic ability (artists and graphic designers). The media planner will be called upon to select appropriate media for a campaign and devise a realistic schedule for its implementation. Once the media plan has been agreed, the media buyer will liaise with printed and broadcast media to book space or airtime. Print and

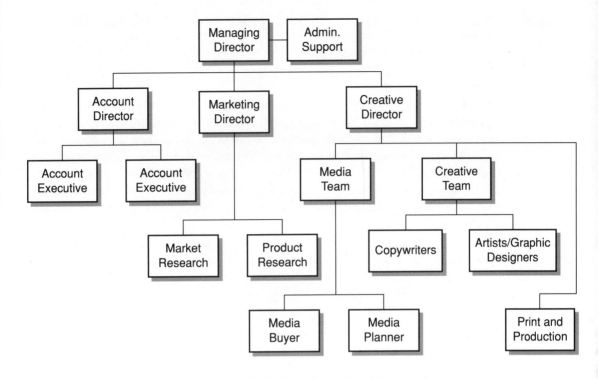

Fig 10.3 The structure of a full service advertising agency

production staff will take the creative ideas and turn them into a finished form ready for production.

The marketing director may be consulted if market or product research are needed before the campaign detail can be finalised. He or she may commission a survey or 'test market' a product or service, to provide feedback for the creative team.

Advertising agencies were originally only concerned with placing advertisements for which they earned a commission. The example of the agency we have just examined indicates that they have come a long way since the early days and are able to offer a full range of services, for which a fee is charged. While they do still earn commission, this is usually passed on to the client in the form of a reduction in the agreed fee. In general terms, if a leisure and tourism organisation is planning to spend up to £20,000 on an advertising campaign, an agency will be very pleased to do business. Even if the budget is only a couple of thousand pounds, smaller local agencies may well be able to help. Lists of agencies can be obtained from the Institute of Practitioners in Advertising or the Advertising Agency Register, both based in London.

Media techniques in action – The London Tourist Board Campaign

CASE STUDY

Introduction

In the summer of 1991, American Express, British Airways and Forte Hotels provided the London Tourist Board (LTB) with 'pump priming' funding for the production of a business plan to promote London. The plan was produced as a result of extensive consultations with LTB staff and members representing all sectors of the London tourist industry – accommodation, retail, the arts, attractions and museums. The plan suggested a three-year above and below the line marketing campaign focusing on the consumer market in the UK and USA in year one (1993).

Six advertising agencies were briefed and in January 1991, Equator (a subsidiary of Saatchi and Saatchi) was appointed to take forward the initial proposals and devise a creative strategy. A steering group was formed to monitor the progress of the campaign at each stage and to ensure that all sectors' interests were represented. The steering group comprised representatives from:

- American Express.
- British Airways.
- Forte Hotels.
- British Tourist Authority (BTA).
- English Tourist Board (ETB).
- London Arts Board.
- The attractions sector.
- The retail sector.

Strategy

The original aims and objectives of the promotion were:

1 To reinforce the positive images of London.
2 To emphasise the affordability of London.
3 To address negative perceptions of London ('Beefeaters and chips', congested, dirty, etc.).
4 To re-present London as a vibrant, modern destination offering huge variety to the consumer, in order to compete with other destinations such as Paris, Rome and Madrid.
5 To fulfil individual sponsors' requirements for increased business as early as possible.

The target audience was high-spending first time visitors to London living in the UK and USA from the socio-economic groups A, B and C1.

The campaign theme, 'It's not only Londoners who love London', has been exploited to the full in all advertising and public relations activity. The execution of the campaign in its first year included a number of activities:

IT'S NOT ONLY LONDONERS WHO LOVE LONDON

Fig 10.4 The voucher booklet used in the LTB campaign

- An 'image-building' brochure was developed as a key selling tool to promote London and all its facilities.
- Quirky, original and stylish black and white photography, featuring people involved in all facets of London life, was used in the brochure and the UK advertising.
- In the USA, the advertising featured BA flight and hotel packages that were booked directly with BA Tours in Orlando.
- Advertisements carried a direct response coupon inviting people to apply for the London brochure.
- Mailing lists from key sponsors were used in a direct mail campaign aimed at the target audience.
- A card included with the brochure was redeemable for a book of discount vouchers when recipients visited London (see Figure 10.4).
- Positive quotes endorsing London were obtained free of charge from famous personalities and used in the advertising.

The campaign in the UK

There were three elements to the UK part of the campaign:

- *Advertising* – £300,000 was earmarked for an advertising campaign to run in selected Sunday supplements.
- *Direct mail* – 40,000 brochures were mailed direct to American Express card-holders with an offer of three nights for the price of two at participating hotels.
- *Travel trade* – the campaign was launched to the UK travel trade on the LTB stand at the World Travel Market in November 1992. A series of familiarisation trips featuring the many different aspects of London life took place throughout 1993.

The campaign in the USA

The US part of the campaign comprised five elements:

- *Advertising* – Autumn 1992 and Spring 1993 campaigns were carried out using selected US newspapers and magazines which had performed well in the recent past.
- *Direct mail* – a mailing to 100,000 selected American Express cardholders took place in January 1993.
- *British Tourist Authority* – 150,000 brochures were distributed through BTA USA offices and by LTB staff at consumer shows in the USA.
- *Prodigy* – this is an IBM/Sears service linking 1.8 million US high spending, passport-holding families with personal computers to a host of features including shopping and travel related services. One page featuring the campaign was booked on Prodigy for the first 12 months.
- *Travel trade* – the campaign was launched to the US travel trade in New York in October 1992. Further travel trade work, including familiarisation visits and attending trade shows, was carried out in 1993.

Public relations

As well as the two travel trade launches mentioned above, two further PR events were held, one at the Hilton Hotel on Park Lane for UK consumer media and another, in the presence of Prince Edward, at Madame Tussauds in London for current and potential sponsors. A full PR plan was developed for the campaign which included suggested itineraries for selected US and UK journalists and a list of features for distribution to US and UK media. Blue Badge Guides have been involved in the planning and guiding of these familiarisation visits.

Staff training

An innovative aspect of the campaign has been the development of a training programme for 'front line' staff in leisure and tourism organisations in London. Funded partly by London Training and Enterprise Councils (TECs), the training programme aimed to train 3,000 staff to:

- Appreciate the importance of the tourism industry to London.
- Understand the principles of the London promotion.
- Understand the necessity of providing accurate and up-to-date information on London to visitors.
- Appreciate the benefits of consistently high standards of customer service to the visitor, the employee, the employer and London as a whole.

Effectiveness of the campaign

In a written review of the first year of the campaign, Catriona Campbell, Head of Marketing and Convention Bureau at the LTB, produced research figures to show that:

In summary, the campaign has achieved its original objectives – reaching the right target audience of ABC1 high spending individuals:

- *it has broad appeal across the age groups,*
- *it is successfully re-presenting London while continuing to focus on the traditional strengths,*
- *it has had significant impact given the size of the spend.*

The review pointed to the fact that 1,200 British Airways' London packages were sold as a direct result of the campaign. In addition, a 'conversion study' found that 69 per cent of US respondents to the advertising campaign did intend to travel to London as a result of receiving the brochure. Taking a conversion rate of 69 per cent from the media response alone (69,554), an average party size of 2.6 plus an average spend of £483 per head, this results in a yield of around £65 million from an initial budget of £2 million. A similar study of the UK campaign estimated that well over £2 million was generated as a direct result of the campaign.

(Information courtesy of LTB)

Direct marketing

One of the disadvantages levelled at advertising in the printed and broadcast media is that it is not always effective in reaching its intended audience. For example, an advertisement on local radio may be missed since it is often considered as a 'background' medium. Similarly, a small classified advertisement in the travel columns of a Sunday supplement may be hard to see in amongst many hundreds of others. Direct marketing, however, is rarely criticised for failing to reach its target audience. In fact, some people even go as far as likening the precision of direct marketing to a 'rifle', while the imprecise nature of advertising can be thought of as a 'shotgun'. Direct marketing is the term used to describe the various techniques that an organisation can use to sell its products and services on a personalised basis direct to the consumer, without the need for an intermediary. The most common direct marketing methods used in leisure and tourism are:

- Direct mail.
- Telemarketing.
- Door-to-door distribution.
- Direct response advertising.

Telemarketing is growing in importance in leisure and tourism, particularly in the business-to-business sector, where one company will provide services and facilities for another. Its use in the consumer sector of the industry is restricted to such products as timeshare and the sale of leisure products.

Door-to-door distribution is popular with hotels, restaurants, attractions and leisure facilities that want to capture a local market. A certain amount of market segmentation is possible, with particular postcode areas being targeted in terms of social class, family composition, age, etc.

Direct response advertising is widely used by leisure and tourism organisations that want to create a mailing list at the same time as distributing brochures and other promotional materials. Any advertisement, whether it is on the television, on local radio, in a newspaper, in a magazine or on a billboard, which asks the customer to respond in some way falls within the category of direct response. For example, Figure 10.5 shows a good example of a direct response advertisement inviting the reader to complete a coupon or telephone to request a brochure.

Some organisations use freephone numbers such as 0800 and 0500, reduced rate 0345 numbers or a freepost address in order to stimulate more responses.

Direct mail

Direct mail is by far the most important method of direct marketing used by UK leisure and tourism organisations. It can be very cost-effective when compared to advertising and is, therefore, ideally suited to smaller organisations. It is very flexible in terms of timing, budgets and targeting. A direct mail campaign can be actioned very quickly and aimed at particular target markets. Its uses in leisure and tourism are many and various, including:

- A seaside hotel that sends all its past guests a Christmas card.
- The Conference Officer for a major tourist city who sends a letter and leaflet featuring conference facilities in the city to the top 100 companies in the region.
- A tennis club that mails all its members with details of a tournament sponsored by a local car dealership.
- A local authority that sends out a leaflet with its Council Tax bills giving details of its leisure services.
- A newly opened sports shop that uses the membership list of a local walking club to send out a brochure and discount voucher.
- A top tourist attraction that mails details of group rates and facilities to the major coach companies in the UK every year.

One of the most important aspects of a good direct mail campaign is the mailing list, which can either be created from existing information on customers or bought in from a specialist list broker or mailing house. Lists covering all parts of the country and every conceivable interest and life-style category are freely available. Larger direct mail campaigns can make use of sophisticated computer-based systems such as ACORN, PIN or MOSAIC, to target by postcode areas the individuals or families most likely to want to buy a particular product or service. The use of these systems will ensure the best possible results and cost efficiency by avoiding wastage by mailing to consumers who are not in the target group.

The basic steps needed for a successful direct mail campaign are:

1 Decide on the objectives of the campaign – for example, do you want to promote a new attraction?; increase off-peak use of a sports centre?; promote your tour packages to overseas travel agents?
2 Determine the budget.
3 Agree the timescale for the campaign.
4 Create the mailing list.
5 Devise the direct mail package (see below).
6 Carry out the mailing.
7 Do a follow-up mailing (optional).
8 Evaluate the results.

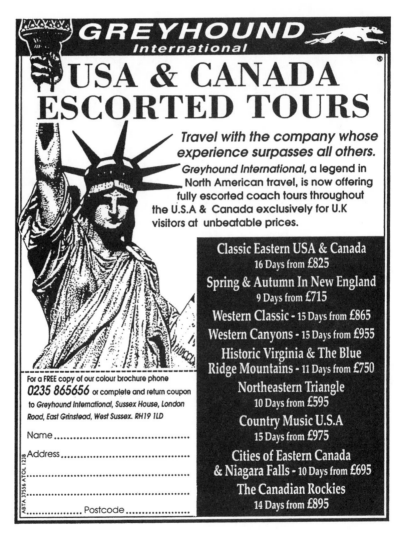

Fig 10.5 An example of a direct response advertisement

A typical direct mail package will consist of:

- A personalised letter.
- An envelope, which may be overprinted to match the letterhead (see Figure 10.6).
- A 'reply device', such as a freepost address or freephone telephone number.
- An insert, which would usually be a brochure, leaflet or discount voucher.

It takes considerable skill and experience to produce an effective direct mail letter, which will both inform and persuade the reader to buy or use the product or service on offer. As with advertising, the AIDA principle (see page 10.14) applies to the wording of the letter.

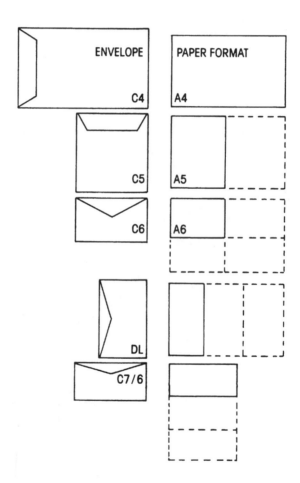

Fig 10.6 Envelope and paper sizes for use in direct mail campaigns

Public relations

The Institute of Public Relations (IPR) defines public relations as:

> . . . *the planned and sustained effort to establish and maintain goodwill and mutual understanding between an organisation and its publics.*

The last word of this definition is deliberately used in the plural, since an organisation actually has to deal with many different publics, of which its customers are only one. A leisure and tourism organisation, for example, must also maintain goodwill with suppliers, trade unions, the press, councillors (if in the public sector), shareholders (where appropriate), members, distributors, neighbours and voluntary helpers. Public relations is important at all levels and in all departments within an organisation and is not just the concern of the PR department or public relations officer (PRO).

The fact that leisure and tourism is a service industry often means that the reputation of an organisation and its products hinges on the attitude of its staff when dealing with customers and users. The highly competitive nature of the industry makes it vital that all organisations make every effort to develop and maintain a friendly and personal image. PR can play an important role in supporting and publicising this image and presenting to its customers the face of a caring and professional organisation.

As a marketing tool, PR can be far more cost effective than either advertising or direct mail. This makes it a particularly attractive medium for leisure and tourism organisations that have a small promotional budget. In fact, the smaller the promotional budget, the stronger the case for PR.

If used effectively, PR in leisure and tourism can:

- Assist in the launch of new products, services and facilities.
- Help to 'reposition' existing products, services and facilities.
- Generate interest in an organisation.
- Help publicise an event.
- Influence specific target groups.
- Defend an organisation when things go wrong.
- Build a favourable image.

Although public relations can take many forms and is important at all points where an organisation interfaces with its public, it is most often associated with press or media relations. It is in the interest of every leisure and tourism organisation to build a relationship with its relevant media, whether it be personal contact with key reporters on local, regional or national newspapers, feature editors on appropriate trade and consumer magazines, or TV and radio stations. Familiarisation ('fam') trips are frequently used in leisure and tourism as a way of giving a journalist first-hand experience of the product or service being promoted. Liaison with the relevant media will not only help the organisation gain publicity for its achievements and success stories, but also improve the chances of putting its side of the story when the news is bad. Good PR can help when a tragedy strikes or unfavourable stories begin to circulate.

The most usual method of informing the media about current news and events is by issuing a press release (see Figure 10.7). They can be sent to local radio and television stations as well as to newspapers and magazines. Editors are inundated with news releases on a whole range of subjects every day, so the chances of gaining some 'free publicity' are limited. If the release is printed, however, the information it contains appears far more credible to the reader than the same message conveyed in an advertisement. The disadvantage of press releases, however, is that the organisation has no control over what the editor chooses to include or exclude. Parts of the news release may be printed out of context and give a negative image of the organisation and its activities.

There are some basic guidelines that will increase the chances of a press release being used:

- Keep it crisp, factual and informative.
- Write from the point of view of the journalist.
- Write to suit the style of the publication.
- Answer the basic questions of who?, what?, when?, where?, why?, as early as possible in the release, preferably in the first two paragraphs.
- Get the main newspoint into the first paragraph.
- Don't make it any longer than it needs to be.
- Give a date to the release and indicate clearly if there is an embargo (a date or time before which it cannot be used).
- Respect copy deadlines (the date by which it must be with the editor).
- Include full details of a contact person at the end of the release.
- Use double spacing to allow for editing.
- Include a picture if it will help tell the story (7" × 5" black and white for preference, captioned on the reverse to explain who is doing what).

It is important to monitor PR coverage by organising the collection of press cuttings either through an agency or in-house. The PR specialist within the organisation should be encouraged to organise visits by journalists and VIPs to see facilities first hand. Also, the relevant people within the organisation should go out and speak to local groups, clubs and schools, to let them know what you are doing and why.

Sales promotion

Sales promotion describes a range of techniques designed to encourage customers to make a purchase. They usually support advertising, direct mail, personal selling or public relations activity and, in leisure and tourism include activities

Ty Brunel 2 Ffordd Fitzalan
Caerdydd CF2 1UY

Brunel House 2 Fitzalan Road
Cardiff CF2 1UY

☎ (0222) 499909
Fax (0222) 498151

**BWRDD CROESO CYMRU
WALES TOURIST BOARD**

NEWYDDION NEWS

26 May 1993

TOURISM SET TO GAIN 10,000 NEW JOBS AND
£950 MILLION BY THE YEAR 2000

The Secretary of State for Wales, David Hunt today, May 26 at 10.15am at the Park
Hotel, Cardiff, launched the Wales Tourist Board's proposed blueprint for the tourism
industry in Wales, Tourism 2000. The strategy is intended to guide the way in which this
important industry is developed and marketed in the year 2000. It is the most far-
reaching strategy ever produced by a tourist board in the UK.

Wales Tourist Board forecasts, based on an annual growth rate of expenditure by UK
and overseas visitors of 5% and 14% respectively (at current prices) estimate that
earnings from Welsh tourism could increase from £1.25 billion to £2.2 billion (current
prices) by the year 2000. A further 10,000 jobs could also be sustained by the industry
by the end of the decade, according to the Tourism 2000 strategy. Currently tourism
sustains some 95,000 jobs in Wales, representing about 9% of the Welsh workforce.
Tony Lewis, the Board's Chairman, stressed that these targets were achievable while
supporting the conservation of our natural environment and the Welsh language and
culture.

The Board's vision for tourism in Wales for 2000 is for an industry that is competitive
in terms of both the quality of facilities and customer care, and the diversity of the
holiday experience.

This vision is of:
* a country that is of appeal to the overseas visitor by virtue of its outstanding
  natural environment and its distinctive culture and history;

– 1 –

Fig 10.7 Extract from a press release (courtesy of WTB)

such as:

- *Price reductions* – it is common for leisure and tourism organisations to offer price discounts to encourage more business, e.g. a 'happy hour' in a bar when all drinks are half-price, a leisure centre offering discounted rates at off-peak times, tour operators advertising cut-price holidays if bookings are made before a certain date. Sainsbury's joined forces with British Airways in 1993 to run a promotion offering up to 40 per cent of BA flights abroad.
- *Free gifts* – a travel agent may provide a free holdall or item of clothing to all clients booking a holiday; a tourist attraction may give free badges and hats to all children who visit. In 1993, Hoover offered free flights to anybody who bought one of its vacuum cleaners. Unfortunately, the promotion was too successful and Hoover was unable to completely fulfil its promise to every purchaser.
- *Exhibitions* – are a good way of showing both the general public and the trade what's new in leisure and tourism. They are also a good PR activity, helping staff to cement relationships and make new contacts.
- *Competitions* – some organisations run competitions to encourage the public to buy their products and services. The prizes on offer may include holidays, short breaks or leisure/sports activities.
- *'Extra product'* – this is when a customer is given additional benefits without having to pay any more. For example, a hotel may provide free newspapers for all guests, a leisure centre may offer vouchers for a free beauty treatment to ladies who attend their aerobics classes, or an airline may provide a chauffeur-driven car from home to the airport for business travellers. 'Three weeks for the price of two', an offer commonly made by holiday companies, is also an example of 'extra product'.
- *'Passport' or 'loyalty' schemes* – some leisure and tourism organisations offer loyalty schemes to encourage people to stay with them and use their services in the future. Frequent flyer programmes operated by airlines are one of the best-known loyalty schemes; passengers are given points for each trip made and, when they have collected a particular number, can cash them in for free flights. Similar programmes are operated by hotel companies and car hire firms. Visitor attractions sometimes offer a 'passport' that can give free or discounted entry to the site.
- *Point-of-sale (POS) materials* – these range from window displays, posters and merchandising units to brochure racks, hanging cards and special demonstrations.

The essential feature of sales promotion is that it is a short-term inducement to encourage customers to react quickly. Many sales promotions are undertaken in response to the activities of competitors to ensure that an organisation retains its share of the market.

Although the examples of sales promotions given above are targeted at the consumer, sales promotion techniques can also be aimed at staff working in leisure and tourism in order to persuade them to sell or recommend the products or services of a particular company. Travel agency sales clerks, for example, are offered many different incentives by airlines, tour operators and hotel companies. Staff working in leisure and tourism may be offered a bonus payment, free training, the use of facilities at discounted rates, social events or entries to a prize draw, to retain their loyalty to a particular organisation.

As with other forms of marketing activity, it is important to evaluate the effectiveness of the sales promotion against its objectives. It is a relatively easy matter to measure sales or usage before and after a sales promotion and calculate a percentage increase or decrease in activity. The aim of some sales promotions is to clear current stock, for example sportswear, unsold package holidays or seats for a concert. It is difficult to measure whether a customer who has taken advantage of a special offer may well have paid the full price at a later date. In many respects, the answer to this question is irrelevant as long as the sales promotion fulfils the original objectives.

Personal selling

Many staff employed in leisure and tourism are constantly involved in some form of personal selling activity. It might be closing the sale on a two-week holiday to Majorca, booking a group into an outdoor pursuits centre or working on the reception at a leisure centre, handling cash and enquiries from customers. Personal selling involves persuasive communication between two parties, the buyer and the seller. It is important to remember that the 'buyer' does not always part with cash in order to enjoy the facilities on offer. Some leisure and tourism facilities provided by local authorities will be provided free of charge, financed from local and national sources.

In the same way that we have the four Ps in marketing, personal selling is characterised by the five Ps, namely:

- *Preparation* – staff should be adequately trained and familiar with the products, customers, competition and the market for leisure and tourism.
- *Prospecting* – this is the name given to identifying prospective customers before selling takes place.
- *Pre-approach* – this is concerned with learning about the prospective customer.
- *Presentation* – this involves active selling skills and will be based around the AIDA principle (see page 10.14).
- *Post-sale support* – following up the sale to make sure that the customer is happy helps to create repeat business.

In leisure and tourism, selling is all about helping people to buy, rather than selling them something they don't really want. Selling doesn't always come naturally to British people, so training in selling skills is vital for sales staff in leisure and tourism.

Section 3 **Devising marketing strategies**

Marketing planning

All leisure and tourism organisations have an idea of how they should market their facilities, the prices they should charge, the type of customers who are likely to use their services and how they can reach them. Some spend a great deal of time and effort in developing marketing plans, which chart the way ahead in terms of marketing activity over a defined time period. Others prefer to take an altogether more casual and reactive approach to marketing, rarely committing anything to paper. Although the latter approach may well work for a small number of gifted individuals, nearly all leisure and tourism organisations will benefit from a fully researched and carefully constructed marketing plan. Such a plan will:

- Identify the resources that will be needed to implement the plan.
- Provide a focus for all marketing activity.
- Define objectives and targets which will need to be met.
- Analyse competitor activity.
- Help forecast future trends in the industry.
- Allow measurement of marketing performance to see if the objectives have been met.

The marketing plan will help the organisation to answer a number of important questions, such as:

1 What do we want to achieve?
2 Where are we now?
3 Where do we want to be?
4 How do we get to where we want to be?
5 How do we know when we've arrived?

These five questions and the answers to them, can provide the structure for a very effective marketing plan for any leisure and tourism organisation, based on the following linkages:

Question	Section of the Marketing Plan
1 What do we want to achieve?	Mission statement or organisational policy
2 Where are we now?	Business situation (SWOT and PEST analyses)
3 Where do we want to be?	Organisational objectives
4 How do we get to where we want to be?	Marketing strategy
5 How do we know when we've arrived	Monitoring and evaluation

Strengths	Weaknesses
1. Commitment and enthusiasm from management team.	1. Recent pool closure.
2. Excellent pool facility with high usage.	2. Staffing problems/turnover/ commitment to customer care.
3. Established, balanced pool programme.	3. Ageing dryside environment.
4. Lack of immediate competition.	4. Unco-ordinated and restrictive marketing.
	5. Limited market research achieved.
Opportunities	**Threats**
1. Growing market (Uckfield).	1. New competition (Lewes Leisure Centre).
2. Press attention and interest.	2. Decrease in disposable incomes.
3. Corporate business market.	3. Local management of schools.
4. Re-launch of facilities potential.	4. Changing demographic patterns.
5. Capital expenditure controls.	

Fig 10.8 SWOT analysis for Utopia Leisure Centre (courtesy of Wealden District Council)

In devising a marketing plan, a leisure and tourism organisation will identify what it is wanting to achieve by way of a mission statement or policy statement (see Unit 8 for examples of these in the leisure and tourism industry). It will next seek to establish its current position in the marketplace with the help of a SWOT analysis (Strengths, Weaknesses, Opportunities, Threats) and/or a PEST analysis (Political, Economic, Social and Technological factors that may affect the organisation and the market). Figure 10.8 shows a SWOT analysis for a local authority leisure centre in West Sussex.

The PEST analysis will vary between organisations, but is likely to include information on:

- *Political* – government and EU (formerly EC) policy on leisure and tourism, taxation, local authority constraints, regional development, legislation, regulation/deregulation.
- *Economic* – disposable incomes, exchange rates, CCT, inflation, unemployment.
- *Social* – demographic trends, lifestyle changes, community involvement, education, changing work practices, holiday entitlement, retirement, environmental awareness.
- *Technological* – global communications, growth in home leisure, reservations systems, payment methods.

Having carried out its situation analysis, the next stage of the marketing plan is to set specific objectives, which must be clear, measurable and realistic (see Unit 8 for more detail on setting objectives in leisure and tourism).

Stage four of the marketing plan is the one that focuses on the marketing strategy, which tries to answer the question, 'How do we get to where we want to be?'. The following sections of this unit look in more detail at marketing strategies.

The final stage of the marketing plan is monitoring and evaluation, when the organisation reviews its marketing efforts and achievements against the original objectives of the plan to see if its work has been successful.

Marketing strategies

The strategy is the broad means by which the organisation hopes to meet its objectives and should not be confused with day-to-day or month-by-month courses of action, which are usually referred to as the marketing tactics, or tactical marketing. The tactics to be employed are sometimes expressed in the form of an action plan, which will include details of timing and who will be responsible for carrying out the tactics.

Examples of marketing strategies in leisure and tourism are as follows:

- To enter a new market – Airtours has recently entered the self-drive camping market with the 'EuroSites' brand to complement its other tour operating products.
- To restrict its range of products – a leisure centre may decide to discontinue its 'early bird' swimming sessions because of poor attendance.

- To change the scale of its operations – a successful fitness studio may decide to open branches in a number of nearby towns.
- To change the method of distribution – a country house hotel may choose to offer all its services for sale through travel agents, rather than dealing direct with the public.
- To change the emphasis of promotional activity – a museum that has always advertised in the national press may decide to commit half of its advertising budget to attending exhibitions.

Marketing strategies are essentially about getting the many components of the marketing mix in the correct proportion to maximise efficiency and output. We looked in detail at the marketing mix in Unit 4 and saw that it was composed of four main elements, known as the four Ps; price, place, product, promotion. In deciding the most appropriate 'mix' of these four components, a leisure and tourism organisation will need to consider:

- *Price* – discounts, commissions, surcharges, competitor pricing, demand levels, 'value for money', concessions, subsidies, disposable income.
- *Place* – distribution channels, location, accessibility, transport links, car parking, warehousing.
- *Product* – design, quality, range, 'brands', features, benefits, service, after sales support.
- *Promotion* – advertising, direct marketing, sales promotion, PR, personal selling, sponsorship, 'print'.

Types of marketing strategies

A leisure and tourism organisation has a number of different options open to it when deciding which type of strategy to adopt. It can choose:

1 *Undifferentiated marketing* – when a single marketing mix is offered to the total market. This is unlikely to succeed, since markets are made up of many types of buyers, all with different characteristics.
2 *Differentiated marketing* – is an approach that tailors specific marketing strategies to different sectors of the market. A leisure centre, for example, will have different strategies for reaching families with children and senior citizens.
3 *Concentrated marketing* – involves choosing to compete in only one sector of the market and developing the most effective mix for this sector. Many smaller operators select this option and gain in-depth knowledge of their customers and their requirements. Eurocamp is a good example of a company that concentrates on one sector of the market.

As well as deciding which type of strategy to adopt, any leisure and tourism organisation can consider the way in which the strategy will be implemented, for example they may select:

- *A defensive strategy* – these are designed to hold on to existing customers by, for example:
  - Improving the image of the organisation.
  - Increasing the standard of customer service.
  - Improving product quality.

  In recent years, the most successful leisure and tourism organisations have worked very hard on improving the quality of all aspects of their operations, notably British Airways, Forte PLC and the Rank Organisation PLC.

- *A developing strategy* – these are designed to offer existing customers a wider range of products or services by, for example:
  - Increasing the number of outlets for products and services.
  - Developing completely new products.
  - Making products more environmentally friendly.
  - Increasing the range of features and options available.

  The very competitive nature of the leisure and tourism industry has led organisations to look afresh at their products and become more 'customer focused'.

- *An attacking strategy* – these are designed to generate business through new customers. No organisation has a 100 per cent coverage of its existing market, so there is always scope for gaining extra market share from competitors. Also new customers can be found in new geographical or industry market segments, for example aiming promotional efforts at business as well as leisure travellers. Typical attacking strategies would include:
  - Changing pricing policy to 'undercut' competitors.
  - Opening new sales outlets.
  - Entering new geographical areas.

  All strategies have an element of risk attached to them, perhaps the most risky involving entering into new markets or developing new products for existing markets.

Marketing strategy 1992/93 – Utopia Leisure Centre, East Sussex

Aims

To further pursue aims and objectives identified in the business plan by optimising profit potential and offering quality, customer-orientated services and facilities.

Centre objectives

1 To continue to highlight the philosophy of concurrent use on a community multi-use site.

2 To establish and improve productive partnerships with a range of local community contacts; colleges, schools, youth and community, social services, businesses, etc.

3 To continue to heighten awareness of the centre's facilities and services as effectively as possible through promotion, publicity and advertising, reflecting a high quality image and identity.

4 To enhance customer-led philosophy by a market-driven approach to programming.

Market research

1 Wealden Leisure Survey 1991 – continued use of results and issues.

2 New non-user household survey to supplement past survey in 1991/92 to be undertaken in-house early in 1993.

3 On-going research information from Customer Comment Forms. Analysis of results April 1993.

4 Specific in-house mini-surveys, e.g. Health Suite use and feasibility.

Image/Identity

1 Continued extensive use of leisure centre logo and Utopia name.

2 Wealden Leisure logo accompanying above in all cases.

3 Use of 'elephant' for children and family advertising, publicity and information material.

Environment

1 Reception lightbox display – consideration for new facilities.

2 Increased use of moving message/selscan for information.

3 Leaflet racks – extend and planned refilling system.

4 Noticeboards – changing displays, update system.

5 Customer comment forms – new posting box site and display.

6 Standards of cleanliness/tidiness, etc. – new cleaning contract February 1993. Monitoring procedures to be reviewed.

7 Repairs and maintenance – dryside refurbishment due to commence Autumn 1992. Identify major items from condition survey for inclusion. Wetside closure December 1992.

8 Staff uniform – current uniform stocks to be utilised. Corporate uniform review due 1993/94.

Pricing

1 Increasing autonomy/control of activity/facility pricing by centre management, e.g. fitness, dance, courses, etc.

2 Core prices – squash, badminton, swimming – to be subject to a recommendation for minimal/nil price increases for 1993/94, weighted against non-members.

3 Ongoing monitoring of competitors' prices.

4 Refine trading account approach to course/activity sessions. Marginal costing techniques to review viability.

5 Promotional special for off-peak, family, seasonal activities.

Publicity Material

1 Posters and leaflets
   - Continued use of logos, clear presentation and recognisable format.
   - Explore reduction in printing costs without compromising quality; in-house graphics packages.
2 Develop reminder cards for booking/court times.
3 Customer sports/activity information scheme at reception in operation by end of 1992.
4 Extend members' mailshots on quarterly basis with newsletter and additional information – use for promotional offers.
5 Repeat direct mailshot to non-users, e.g. Chamber of Commerce re Corporate Memberships.
6 Expand distribution list for catchment area, schools, libraries, shops, halls, etc.
7 Increased use of community college for distribution, research, etc.

Advertising

1 Target local newspaper advertising for specific events/activities by use of editorial/press release deals.
2 Monitor effectiveness through special offers, vouchers, etc.
3 Use names and addresses of voucher holders for future mailing lists.
4 Continue to advertise in local annual publications, guides, etc.
5 School noticeboards scheme.
6 Marketing packs distributed through local estate agents.

Public Relations

1 General increase in use of press releases in raising profile.
2 Improvement in press relations through regular contact, invitations and information.
3 Refurbishment project – use contract period to raise awareness and expectation.

Merchandise

1 Utopia logo'd merchandise available for sale through reception, e.g. stickers, bags, bugs, T-shirts, hats, etc.
2 Use of merchandise through promotions, events, etc. Holiday programme prizes, birthday parties.

Programming

1 Market-driven approach to programme evolution – encouragement of suggestions through comment scheme, interest lists at reception. Other informal schemes to be considered.
2 Concurrent use philosophy and practicalities of joint use to be explained more fully on advertising and publicity material.
3 Uckfield Community College's timetabling to be discussed at joint meetings with a view to further enhancing flexibility for dryside facilities.

Outreach and development

1 Improvement in local community links – school visits, demonstrations, promotions.
2 Representation at local events – fêtes, carnivals, etc., use of inflatable, sponsorships, prizes, etc.
3 Liaison with Sports Development Officers – county and sports specific.
4 Introduction of *Oasis of Health* GP Referral Scheme. Staff training and initial approaches to GPs to be made during run up to new facilities in 1993.
5 Consideration to be given to formalising other existing community links with social services and voluntary groups.

(Information courtesy of Wealden District Council)

Assignment 10

Situation

A local coach operator, Waterson's Travel, which offers UK and Continental tours with a fleet of 18 luxury coaches, has ambitious plans for expansion of its operation. Your group has been contacted by Geoff Waterson, the owner of the family firm, who understands that you may be able to help him find out a little more about people's attitudes to coach tours and what they like or dislike about travelling in the UK and Europe by coach. He is convinced that sound market research is the key to a successful expansion of the business.

Tasks

Working as part of a small team, your task is to carry out a survey of a cross-section of the travelling public to investigate their attitudes to coach travel. You must carry out face-to-face interviews in order to get the depth of responses that Geoff is looking for. You should design a suitable questionnaire and run a pilot survey before embarking on the main survey of at least 50 individuals, right across the age range.

Each member of your team will be responsible for compiling a report, to include:

- The methodology adopted.
- The findings of the survey.
- Graphical presentation of the results.
- Analysis of the findings.
- Explanation of any correlation between age, sex and the responses of those interviewed.

The report, with its associated charts and diagrams, should not exceed 1,500 words in length.

Unit 11
INVESTIGATING TRAVEL ORGANISERS

Section 1 The work of travel organisers

Introduction

Travel organisers undertake a very specific function in the UK leisure and tourism industry. They make travel arrangements on behalf of individuals or groups who, for a variety of reasons, choose not to arrange their own journeys. Most travel organisers operate in the commercial world and, therefore, are looking to make a profit on the services they offer to clients. Some travel organisers in the public and voluntary sectors are not seeking to maximise their returns, but merely 'break-even', with any surpluses being used for non-commercial purposes.

Travel organisers act as intermediaries between the customer and organisations that provide travel products and services, as shown in Figure 11.1.

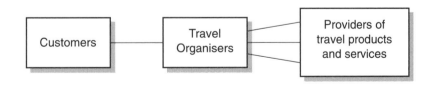

Fig 11.1 The position of travel organisers

We have seen in previous units that the providers of travel products and services, referred to in Figure 11.1, are many and varied, including:

- Hotels and other accommodation providers.
- Transport organisations, e.g. airlines, car rental companies, coach companies, etc.
- Visitor attractions.
- Destinations.
- Travel insurance companies.
- Guiding organisations.
- Entertainment venues.
- Catering outlets.

Travel organisers will liaise directly or indirectly with such suppliers in order to satisfy the needs of their clients.

Why use travel organisers?

Travel organisers fulfil a number of important functions, for example:

- They offer specialist knowledge and advice – in the same way that you might ask a plumber to fix a leaking pipe rather than trying to do it yourself, travel agents and tour operators are specialists in their field, many with years of valuable experience about countries, health requirements for travellers and the various travel options open to the client.
- They have access to up-to-date information – by using reference manuals and computer databases, they can quickly find information on travel services which is not available to members of the general public. New technology can give travel organisers direct access to the computer systems of airlines and tour operators.
- They have the ability to negotiate discounts – in return for a guaranteed volume of business with the suppliers of travel services, travel agents and tour operators can offer reduced rates to their clients, for such items as hotel and airline bookings.
- They offer security to their clients – companies registered with industry associations such as the Association of British Travel Agents (ABTA) or the Association of Independent Tour Operators (AITO) offer travellers financial security in the event of the company experiencing difficulty.
- They offer an 'after-sales service' – most good travel organisers understand that their service does not finish when the product has been sold. A travel agent, for example, may well contact clients soon after their return from holiday or a business trip, to find out if everything went according to plan. Apart from anything else this is good PR for the agency.

Types of travel organisers

The very diverse nature of the UK travel and tourism industry means there is a wide range of organisations that arrange travel on behalf of others. In terms of volume of sales, the two most important travel organisers are travel agents and tour operators. To these can be added a number of other organisations, large and small, which undertake travel arrangements, including:

- Coach operators.
- Airlines.
- Ferry companies.
- Railway organisations.
- Travel departments and individuals in private and public sector organisations.
- Schools and other educational institutions.
- Youth groups.
- Religious groups.
- Clubs and societies.
- Conference organisers.

Many of these travel organisers will deal directly with the organisations that provide the travel products and services, while others will deal through a third party that can provide specialist services; for example, a rugby team may be organising a tour to France, but will use a local travel agency to book the flights and accommodation. The local travel agent may in turn deal with the central reservation service (CRS) of a chain of hotels to make the accommodation arrangements and a number of airlines to compare fares and schedules. The CRS will then check availability with the hotels, the chosen airline will book the seats and both will confirm the arrangements with the travel agent. This example, shown in diagrammatic form in Figure 11.2, highlights the often complex nature of travel organisation.

The role of travel agents

There are some 7,000 travel agencies in the UK which are members of the Association of British Travel Agents (ABTA). There is no compulsion under UK law for an agency to join ABTA, although, until very recently, non-ABTA agents were effectively barred from selling the most popular holidays, under an arrangement known as the 'stabiliser' (see the case study on ABTA on page 11.10). Travel agencies in the UK are either independently-owned or part of a chain of agencies owned by a single company (often referred to as the 'multiples'). In recent years, there has been a shift in emphasis in favour of multiple agencies that have carried forward ambitious expansion plans at the expense of independent agents. At the time of writing, the 'big three' multiple agencies in terms of number of

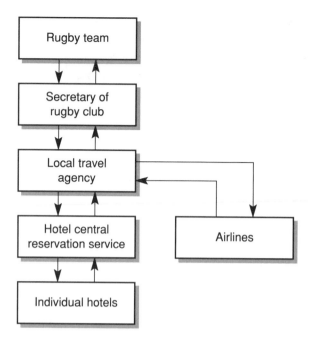

Fig 11.2 An example of the travel organisation process

branches are:

1 Lunn Poly.
2 Going Places.
3 Thomas Cook.

Each of these three multiples has a close alliance with a major tour operator, a process known as vertical integration (one company having control of more than one level of the distribution chain). Lunn Poly is owned by Thomsons, the UK's number one tour operator; Going Places, part of the Airtours group, is the new trading name for the former Pickfords and Hogg Robinson agencies; and Thomas Cook has a 'strategic alliance' with Owner's Abroad, owning 20 per cent of the tour operator's shares. Vertical integration of this sort, when a tour operator controls the sales policy of its own retail travel agencies, is thought by some people in the industry to be against the public interest, as it could lead to an anti-competitive environment. In such cases the Monopolies and Mergers' Commission can be asked to investigate if the public are indeed being disadvantaged.

Travel agency functions

Travel agencies are the retail arm of the travel and tourism industry. In the same way that a clothes shop sells products to shoppers, so travel agencies retail their 'products' to the general public. Indeed, the term 'travel shop' is commonly used to refer to travel agency premises. The one major difference between these two types of retail outlets, however, is that, unlike the clothes retailer, travel agencies do not buy in 'stock' in advance, but rather react to the wishes of their customers before contacting the holiday companies. The fact that opening a travel agency does not involve a heavy initial capital outlay is an attractive feature to many people who are considering starting up their own business in the service sector.

Travel agencies are generally acting on behalf of two parties when they undertake their work. They are agents for the customer, referred to as the client, on whose behalf they are making the travel arrangements. They are also agent for the company that is supplying the product; this company is known as the principal, and could be:

- A tour operator.
- An airline.
- A coach company.
- A hotel.
- A car hire firm.
- A ferry company.
- British Rail.
- A cruise line.
- A theatre.

Travel agents earn commission from the principals whose products they sell. The commission payment is usually expressed as a percentage and varies according to the product being sold and the commission policy of the principal. At present, average commission rates are as follows:

Package holidays	10 per cent.
Airline tickets	7.5 per cent–9 per cent.
Ferry bookings	9 per cent.
Travellers' cheques	1 per cent.
Travel insurance	35 per cent–40 per cent.
Coach holidays	10 per cent.
British Rail ticket	7 per cent.
Cruises	9 per cent.

These figures should only be taken as a guide, since commission levels can fluctuate in response to competitor activity. Some principals offer incentive commission, where the amount paid increases as the sales volume rises. Override commission is another type of extra payment, often paid when an office has 'sole agency' status with a particular principal; for example, British Rail often appoints only one ticket agency in a town and will advise other agencies to deal with this 'sole agent' when they want rail products. The override commission allows the sole agency to pay the standard 7 per cent commission to the agent and retain a small 'override' to cover its own costs.

Most people associate high street travel agencies with the sale of one particular product; overseas package holidays (also known as inclusive tours). An analysis of the work of a typical agency, however, shows that it actually offers a wide range of products and services, including:

- Overseas package tours.
- UK short breaks.
- 'Flight-only' sales.
- Theatre bookings.
- Car hire.
- Cruising holidays.
- Rail tickets.
- Coach holidays and tickets.
- Travel insurance.
- Foreign exchange.
- Visa and passport applications.

As the market for overseas travel becomes even more competitive, travel agencies will be looking for ways of increasing their income from the sale of products other than the traditional inclusive tours.

Components of package holidays

The majority of overseas inclusive tours have three separate elements:

1 Accommodation.
2 Transportation.
3 Other services.

Accommodation
The accommodation component of the package can be either serviced or self-catering. There has been a steady growth in the demand for self-catering holidays over the last 10 to 15 years. Serviced accommodation is usually in a hotel that can offer a range of meal arrangements, including:

- Full board (sometimes called American plan), which means that three meals are provided.
- Half board (or modified American plan), which on overseas package holidays usually refers to breakfast plus either a midday or evening meal.
- Bed and breakfast (sometimes called Continental plan).

Hotels in some parts of the world do not include any meals in their standard room rates, an arrangement sometimes known as European plan. This is common in the USA and the Far East.

Customers can usually request a room with extra facilities or a particular aspect for the payment of a supplementary charge, e.g. a room with a sea view or a ground floor room.

Fig 11.3 A typical high street travel agency *(courtesy of Airtours PLC)*

Self-catering can be in a wide range of accommodation:

- Studios.
- Villas.
- Apartments.
- Tents.
- Caravans/mobile homes.
- Boats.

Self-catering accommodation will usually provide cooking facilities and utensils, although many people often choose to eat out and avoid household chores. Some self-catering accommodation will include a daily maid service.

Transportation

The transport element of a package holiday can be travel by:

- Air.
- Coach.
- Rail.
- Ship.

Whichever type of transport is used, the tour operator will be offered preferential, discounted rates, known as inclusive tour (IT) rates. Depending on the volume of business generated, a ferry company, for example, can offer a tour operator prices which may be discounted by as much as 50 per cent of their standard tariff. It is increasingly common for tour operators to offer their clients free or discounted travel within the UK to their destination point.

Three-quarters of all package holidays sold in the UK use air travel to transport clients to their chosen destinations. Inclusive tours use either chartered or scheduled services; package holidays that use seats on chartered aircraft are known as Inclusive Tours by Charter (ITC), while those based on scheduled services are referred to as Inclusive Tours by Excursion (ITX). Aircraft may be chartered for specific flights or for blocks of time, usually a whole year or for the duration of a season. This is known as time series charter and is financially more attractive than 'ad hoc' arrangements. Many tour operators will charter their aircraft on a flight series basis, contracting for the same time and destination each week, for example. By using flight series charters and setting very high load factors for each flight (the percentage of seats that needs to be filled before the operator starts to make a profit), tour operators have been able to keep prices down and stimulate demand. It is not uncommon for an operator to set a break-even load factor as high as 85–90 per cent.

One disadvantage of flight series charters is that there will inevitably be an empty flight home at the beginning of the season and an empty flight out at the end of the season. These flights are referred to as empty legs. In order to maximise capacity, some travel companies will operate a 'bus stop' arrangement, whereby an aircraft will take off from one UK airport, say Manchester, but stop at another, perhaps East Midlands, to pick up passengers, before flying on to its final destination airport. If bookings from one particular regional airport are low, the tour operator may decide to consolidate, i.e. cancel the flight altogether and transfer the passengers by coach to another departure airport.

Other services

Apart from accommodation and transport, package holidays will usually include other services, which may include:

- Transfers.
- The services of a representative.
- Car hire.
- Excursions.
- Equipment hire, e.g. skis.

Depending on the number of passengers, transfers will be by taxi, minibus or, most commonly nowadays, coach. Operators will schedule flight arrivals so that maximum use can be made of coaches, without undue delay being caused to clients.

Resort representatives ('reps') will provide information and support for their clients, deal with any emergencies, arrange excursions and generally ensure the smooth running of the holiday while the clients are in the resort. Many reps will only be employed for the duration of the season, either summer or winter, with some returning to work at head office out of season.

Travel agency organisation

Arranging travel for leisure purposes accounts for the bulk of the work in most high street travel agencies. Some agencies, however, may have a business travel specialist or even a business travel department, catering solely for the particular needs of this sector of the travelling public. There are also agencies, sometimes known as business house agencies, which deal exclusively with business travel. Figure 11.4 gives an example of the organisational structure of a typical retail travel agency serving the leisure and business market.

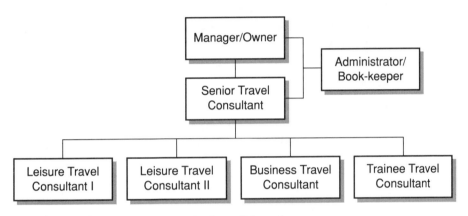

Fig 11.4 The organisation of a typical retail travel agency

The manager or owner of the travel agency will have ultimate responsibility for its management and profitability. The manager of an agency that is part of a chain is likely to be responsible to an area manager for achieving sales and revenue targets. Policy on details such as commission and 'racking' (which brochures are to be displayed in the agency) will normally be dictated by head office. Day-to-day operations management and control of staff may well be delegated to a senior travel consultant or supervisor, who will have had considerable experience in the travel industry. He or she will oversee the work of sales clerks or consultants, one or more of whom may specialise in business travel. In the absence of a dedicated foreign exchange clerk, the senior travel consultant is likely to handle this function.

It is a condition of ABTA membership that an agency must have at least one qualified person working in the office full time; 'qualified' means at least two years' relevant practical experience or a lesser amount of experience plus COTAC (Certificate of Travel Agency Competence) qualifications.

ABTA – The Association of British Travel Agents

Introduction

ABTA is the trade body that represents over 90 per cent of travel agents and tour operators in the UK. It was formed in 1950 at a time that coincided with the dawn of a new era for British travellers, when new aircraft technology and greater personal freedom were giving people the means to travel further afield. Foreign travel came to be seen as a temporary escape from the drabness of post-war Britain and the mass market holiday boom was beginning to take shape. Today, holidays are the high point in the year for many millions of UK travellers, with travel for business purposes remaining an important element of the UK travel scene. In our fast-moving society, we have come to take ease of travel for granted, to the extent that some 11 million Britons book an overseas package holiday every year. Many millions will also take short breaks, holidays in the UK, trips by rail or ferry, or travel on business.

ABTA's aims

The principal objects of the Association of British Travel Agents are:
1 To establish an organisation that is fully representative of travel agents and tour operators in the UK.
2 To promote and develop the general interests of all members of ABTA.
3 To establish and maintain Codes of Conduct between members and the general public, with the object that membership of the Association will be recognised as a guarantee of integrity, competence and high standards of service.
4 To discourage unfair competition without in any way interfering with initiative and enterprise based on fair trading.
5 To promote friendly relations with others in the travel industry.
6 To provide means for negotiations and liaison with other bodies concerned with the development of travel both in the UK and abroad.

How ABTA works

The Association is a self-regulatory body run by its membership. A network of Councils and Committees, appointed by member travel agents and tour operators, make up the policy-making and enforcing machinery of the Association and help to ensure that ABTA remains in close contact with the whole of its membership. The Association has an education and training function that is carried out by the ABTA National Training Board, which liaises with validating bodies such as BTEC and City & Guilds to ensure that the industry has programmes of education and training which are appropriate to its needs.

Up until the end of 1993, ABTA legally operated a type of 'closed shop' arrangement known as the 'stabiliser', which stated that ABTA travel agents could only sell package holidays from tour operators that were themselves members of

ABTA, and vice versa. The stabiliser was introduced 20 years ago to safeguard the public against unscrupulous agents and operators. The arrangement was dismantled in 1993, since it was considered to be a restrictive practice and also because, in theory at least, the introduction of the EC Package Travel Directive rendered the stabiliser obsolete.

Membership of ABTA

Those granted membership of ABTA are required to adhere to strict rules, which govern their business practice. These are contained in ABTA's Codes of Conduct, which regulate all aspects of tour operators' and travel agents' relationships with their customers and which have been drawn up in conjunction with the Office of Fair Trading (OFT).

The Tour Operators' Code of Conduct lays down the minimum standards of brochures, requiring that they contain clear, comprehensive and accurate descriptions of facilities and services offered. It details rules that govern booking conditions in brochures as they relate, for example, to the cancellation or alteration of tours, holidays or other travel arrangements by the tour operator. The Code also contains strict rules concerning the prompt handling of complaints and regulations relating to the conduct between tour operators and travel agents. Similar, stringent rules apply also to travel agents that are bound by their own Code of Conduct. The Travel Agents' Code of Conduct regulates all aspects of travel agents' relationships with their customers, covering their responsibility with regard to the standard of service they provide and the information they give to clients. It also lays down rules concerning travel agents' trading relationships with tour operators.

In addition, members of ABTA are required to adhere to precise financial specifications, overseen by ABTA's Financial Services Department, which checks all members' accounts at least once a year.

Protection and redress for the travelling public

In addition to its Codes of Conduct, ABTA seeks to protect the interests of travellers through its Conciliation and Arbitration schemes.

The ABTA Conciliation Scheme is a free service for clients who have booked with an ABTA-registered travel agent or tour operator and who have reason to complain about some aspect of the service they have received. ABTA will look into the complaint and seek to redress the situation without recourse to law. If the dispute cannot be resolved through conciliation, the client may pursue the claim through ABTA's Arbitration scheme, for which a fee is charged depending on the amount of the claim; at present the scheme is restricted to claims of less than £1,500 per person or £7,500 per booking form, with fees ranging from £23.50 to £29.38 for the first claimant, with lesser amounts for additional claimants. The ABTA Arbitration Scheme, administered by the Chartered Institute of Arbitrators, gives the client the opportunity for redress without incurring high legal costs.

Tour operators and travel agent members of ABTA are required to provide bonds to protect their customers in the event of financial failure. The bond can take a number of forms, but is often an insurance policy for the amount required by ABTA, or a bank guarantee. The financial protection offered by the bonding system enables ABTA, in the event of a member's financial failure, to:

- Arrange for clients whose holidays are in progress at the time of the failure to continue their holidays, as far as possible as originally planned, and in any event to make certain that customers abroad are returned to the UK.
- Reimburse customers whose holidays have not started, the money they paid for their holidays or to make alternative arrangements for the holidays to proceed.

(Information courtesy of ABTA)

The role of tour operators

If we consider that travel agents are the retail arm of the travel business, then tour operators can be likened to wholesalers, since they buy in 'bulk' from the providers of travel services, such as the hoteliers and airlines, break the bulk into manageable 'packages' and offer the finished product, the inclusive tour (IT), for sale via a travel agent or direct to the consumer. Figure 11.5 shows the relationship between travel agents, tour operators and the suppliers of travel products and services.

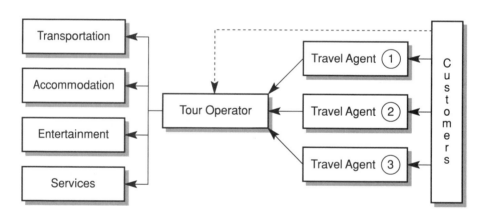

Fig 11.5 The relationship between travel agents and tour operators

In the case of foreign package holidays booked by British people, most customers approach a travel agent rather than booking direct with the operator (the dotted line in Figure 11.5). There are, however, a number of 'direct sell' operators, such as Portland, Tjaereborg and Martin Rooks, who advertise their holidays through newspapers and other media. They stress that, since they do not have to pay a commission to a travel agent, they are able to pass this saving on to the client who should benefit with a cheaper holiday. The more specialist the product on offer, the more likely the customer will deal direct with the operator, for example skiing holidays and mountain exploration tours.

Types of tour operators

There are approximately 600 UK tour operators, most of which are small companies specialising in a particular destination of type of product. Most operators fall into one of the following four categories:

- Mass market operators.
- Specialist operators.
- Domestic operators.
- Incoming tour operators.

Mass market operators

These tour operators include some of the best-known names in the industry, such as Thomsons, Airtours and Cosmos. They organise inclusive tours, often referred to as package holidays, for around 11 million British people each year, thereby dominating the UK outbound tourism market.

At present, three companies together share well over 50 per cent of the total package holiday market:

1 Thomsons: 29 per cent.
2 Airtours: 15 per cent.
3 Owner's Abroad: 14 per cent.

As the figures show, Thomson is the market leader in the UK tour operating market, followed by Airtours and the Owner's Abroad Group, which owns such companies as Sunmed, Falcon, Enterprise and Martyn Holidays. There has been a great deal of uncertainty in the outbound tour operating industry over the last 12 months, ever since Airtours announced a takeover bid for Owner's Abroad in January 1993. Had the bid not failed, due mainly to an injection of capital by Thomas Cook, the industry would have been left with two major companies controlling over 50 per cent of all package holiday sales. The collapse in 1991 of Intasun (together with the rest of the International Leisure Group, ILG), had already strengthened Airtours' position in the market, since it gained the majority of Intasun's previous clients.

The three top tour operators all have their own airlines:

- Thomson own Britannia.
- Airtours operate their airline under the same name.
- Owner's Abroad own Air 2000.

This is a further example of vertical integration in the travel industry, which we saw earlier in this unit with the major tour operators owning travel agency chains, e.g. Thomson owns Lunn Poly.

Specialist operators

Although less well-known than the mass market operators, there are literally hundreds of specialist operators in the travel industry, including:

- Those that offer holidays and other travel arrangements to a particular geographical region or destination, e.g. Paris Travel Service and Magic of Italy.
- Those that cater for a particular segment of the market, e.g. PGL Adventure Holidays for young children and Saga Holidays who specialise in the 'senior' market.
- Those that specialise in a particular type of activity, e.g. walking holidays offered by the Ramblers' Association and Susie Madron's 'Cycling for Softies', which offers all-inclusive packages to France.
- Those that cater for the special interests of their clients, e.g. wine tasting holidays in the Loire and art history tours to Italy.
- Those that specialise in sporting holidays and breaks, e.g. Roger Taylor's tennis holidays in the Algarve and tours to see the motor racing Grand Prix around the world.
- Those that use a specific type of accommodation or form of transport, e.g.. EuroSites, part of the Airtours Group, which organises self-drive camping holidays on the Continent and operators who offer nostalgic tours using steam railways.

A glance at the *Travel Trade Directory* will show that the range of specialist operators is vast, indicating that the travel industry is not afraid to rise to the challenge of meeting the needs of many different types of customers.

Domestic operators

Although, in general, the British tourism product has not been extensively 'packaged', there are a number of UK operators who put together inclusive tours for the home market. Probably the best-known are coach operators, such as Shearings and National Holidays, who offer value-for-money products geared mainly to the older age groups.

The packaging and marketing of UK short breaks has been something of a success story in recent years. Companies such as Superbreak and Rainbow Holidays have led the development of city and country breaks offered for sale through travel agencies. Some local authorities, keen to boost their visitor numbers, have worked with tour operators to feature their particular destinations in brochures and tour programmes.

Special interest groups are well catered for by domestic operators. Activity holidays are growing in popularity and operators, large and small, are emerging to cater for the demand, e.g. YHA Holidays and HF Holidays. Companies offering specialist services and facilities, ranging from sketching holidays to ballooning breaks are being increasingly sought by a public looking for something unusual to do in its leisure time.

Hotel groups and marketing consortia (for example Best Western Hotels) have created and marketed domestic tours for some time, often in conjunction with coach companies. The competitive situation that has arisen in the hotels sector in recent years, however, has forced some hotel groups to widen their customer base, by developing themed breaks and activity and special interest tours.

Incoming tour operators

Information in Units 1 and 13 show that incoming, or inbound, UK tourism is concerned with meeting the needs of the increasing numbers of overseas visitors who choose to visit Britain; outbound tourism, on the other hand, deals with UK people taking holidays abroad. Just as we would visit a travel agency to book our annual overseas holiday or business trip abroad, so many overseas visitors do the same in their own country when they want to come to Britain. A travel agent in the USA, for example, who has a client wanting to spend a week in Scotland, has to contact a tour operator to make all the arrangements; this operator, who may be based in the USA or in Scotland, is known as an incoming tour operator, since it is providing a service for overseas visitors to Britain.

There are around 300 incoming tour operators in this country who specialise in dealing with the incoming market. Some are little more than handling agents offering a transfer or 'meet and greet' service on behalf of an agent or operator. Others, such as British Heritage Tours, Frames Rickards and Evans Evans Tours, offer complete package tours of the UK, which are sold through overseas agents. The packages are often themed, including tours based on British heritage, gardens or castles. Approximately 100 incoming tour operators in the UK are members of BITOA (the British Incoming Tour Operators' Association). Founded in 1977, BITOA is an independent organisation that aims to provide a forum for the exchange of information and ideas, to follow an accepted code of conduct and to act as a pressure group in dealing with other bodies in the UK with a common interest in tourism matters.

Tour operator organisation

A typical mass market outbound tour operator will have a main UK head office, regional offices and overseas offices. The UK head office will be organised on a departmental basis in order to carry out the following functions:

- *Marketing* – staff employed in the marketing department will be responsible for planning and developing products, which will be aimed at particular segments of the market. They will focus on the selection of resorts, choice of accommodation and selection of regional UK departure airports. Typical segments of the market include:
  - Singles.
  - Families.
  - Couples without children.

- Disabled travellers.
- Groups.
- Business travellers.
- Youth market.
- Elderly travellers.

- *Research* – a great deal of background research is undertaken to ensure that the products have the best chance of meeting their sales potential. Sources of research data include:
  - Internal sales data.
  - External sales data (available from commercial sources).
  - Analysis of competitors' programmes.
  - Analysis of customer comment questionnaires.
  - Financial analysis.

- *Contracting* – once the structure of the programme is finalised, staff in the contracts department will negotiate with accommodation providers over the number of beds and names of accommodations required.

- *Flights* – teams working on different programmes and products liaise with the flight or aviation department over how many seats they will need, which regional airports are to be used and whether day or night flights are required. The flight department must make optimum use of its resources.

- *Brochure production* – the brochure is the most visible part of the marketing process. Teams working in the marketing department will work with brochure production staff to finalise design, copy and photographs. A lot of brochure printing takes place outside the UK to save on costs.

- *Brochure distribution* – sales staff will make decisions about how many brochures are required and to which travel agents they will be distributed.

- *Promotion* – marketing staff will plan and co-ordinate a range of activities including advertising, direct mail, sales promotion and PR.

- *Reservations* – systems are developed by computer operations personnel and sales staff are fully briefed on the features of products included in the brochure.

- *Agency sales support* – sales representatives will regularly visit agencies and offer product training and POS (point-of-sale) materials, such as posters and window displays.

- *Administration* – the administration department is responsible for producing invoices, receiving payments and issuing tickets and other documentation.

- *Customer services* – this department will be responsible for handling complaints and queries from agents and members of the public. It will try to ensure that all matters are dealt with quickly and efficiently in order to retain goodwill.

The overseas office of a major tour operator will be responsible for:

- Feeding back to head office any formal or informal research findings.
- Organising transfers to and from the accommodation and airport.
- Selling and arranging excursions and other 'extras' such as car hire.
- Finalising contracts with hoteliers and transport operators.
- The well-being, training and deployment of representatives.
- The handling of complaints and emergencies.

Britain's number one tour operator – Thomson

Introduction

Thomson Travel is part of the International Thomson Organisation, which has interests not only in travel, but also in publishing and oil. Thomson Travel consists of:

- Thomson Tour Operations (tour operator).
- Portland Holidays (direct sell operator).
- Britannia Airways (charter airline).
- Lunn Poly (retail travel agency chain).

History

In 1965 Lord Thomson, a Canadian businessman, took the first step towards the creation of the Thomson Travel Group when he acquired Universal Sky Tours, Britannia Airways and Riviera Holidays. In 1974 when the then number one operator, Clarksons, failed at the height of the holiday season, Thomson Holidays inherited the enviable number one position that it still retains today. The Lunn Poly travel agency chain with 60 retail outlets was acquired in 1972 and Thomson Travel Group was made even stronger with the founding of Portland Holidays in 1979, now the UK's leading direct-sell operator. In 1988 the Horizon Travel Group was acquired; this brought Orion Airways and Horizon Holidays into the Thomson Group, plus the Horizon brands of HCI, Wings, OSL and Blue Sky, as well as Horizon Travel Centres. In 1989, Thomson Tour Operations was set up as the new company operating all programmes run by Thomson and Horizon. By summer 1991, all brands and products had been realigned to operate separately but under the Thomson banner. Only Portland continues to operate as a separate company.

Company aims

Thomson's mission is:

> To be the leader in terms of quality, profit and volume of the ex-UK tour operating industry.

Its aims are:

- To have the best team of people in the industry working for the company.
- To provide all its employees with a challenging, rewarding and secure working environment.
- To ensure that the quality of product and service is better, and is perceived to be better by holiday-makers, suppliers and travel agents, than all major competitors.
- To operate within a lower cost base, quality for quality, than all major competitors.
- To be the clear market leader in terms of size of the ex-UK inclusive tour business.
- To achieve a superior level of profitability compared to all major competitors to ensure the long-term viability of the business.
- To carry out all tasks with due responsibility towards the communities in which they operate and towards the environment.

Company structure

The job of Thomson's Marketing Department is to identify and plan to meet holiday-makers' needs; in other words providing the right holiday at the right price to the right person. The department has staff concerned with creating products, providing a customer service function, producing brochures, undertaking market research and liaising with the press and media.

The Overseas Department is mainly concerned with operations outside the UK and co-ordinates the overseas operation of all holidays. Its responsibilities include the contracting of all types of accommodation, providing a high standard of service to clients while in the resort and maintaining and improving the standards of accommodation and service on offer. The aviation team draws up the initial flight plans from the capacity requirements, i.e. the number of holidays planned to be sold and the number of aircraft needed.

Personnel services are divided into two departments, one serving UK staff and the other dealing with staff overseas. The main activities of the overseas personnel department include planning staffing levels, recruitment, job evaluation, salary and benefits administration and staff relations. UK Personnel has the task of assisting managers to recruit the right calibre of staff in the most effective way. This may be by internal progression, transfer or external recruitment. Staff training and development is also handled by the personnel department.

One of the main objectives of Thomson's sales department is to maintain excellent relationships with travel agents in order to create sales opportunities. This is done through the agency sales force, which provides agents with sales and market information and trains agency personnel in products and procedures. Another responsibility of this department is co-ordinating a merchandising team that visits the top agents at regular intervals to check on brochure stocks and visibility on shelves.

The systems division provides computing services for all areas of the company.

The viewdata-based reservation system for travel agents (TOP) is recognised as the standard for the UK travel industry. There is also an automated funds transfer system for payments from agents. Thomson's computer systems provide the means to hold, change and update all business and holiday related information. They handle all reservations on about 28,000 travel agent terminals around the country.

The responsibilities of the finance and legal department include working with Marketing on the pricing of each programme, preparing budgets, reporting actual results against the budgets and analysing any variances. It handles all financial transactions including credit control and payments to accommodation providers and airlines. Company secretarial and legal matters are also dealt with in this department.

The future

At the start of 1991, Thomson's Managing Director set out the agenda for Thomson Tour Operations for the 1990s. He stressed the following points as the way to ensure that Thomson remained at number one:

- Diversity.
- Reliability.
- Quality.
- Value for money.
- Efficiency.
- People.
- Environment.

Whether Thomson can hold on to its number one position throughout the 1990s remains to be seen, in the light of the ambitious expansion plans of some of its major rivals.

(Information courtesy of Thomson Tour Operations)

The impact of technology on travel organisers

New technology equipment and systems have had a profound effect on travel organisers over the last 15 years or so. With the right equipment, even the smallest specialist tour operator or independent travel agent can now:

- Access databases to check availability of products and services.
- Make reservations on behalf of clients.
- Print and issue tickets and other travel documents.
- Confirm fares for transportation.
- Provide management information.
- Access information on countries and their health and visa requirements.

- Fax or telex a manifest (list of passengers) anywhere in the world.
- Accept payment by EFT (electronic funds transfer).
- Target selected customers for promotional purposes.

Section three of Unit 6 on management information systems in leisure and tourism looked in detail at the role of new technology in travel agents, tour operators and airlines. Reference should be made to this section in order to give a fuller picture of information technology in travel organisation.

In summary, travel agents cannot hope to remain competitive if they do not invest in the latest equipment. There is a gradual move towards tour operators accepting only reservations made via their computerised reservations systems (CRSs). Changes in the nature of work and leisure mean that people are demanding instant information and immediate confirmation of their travel arrangements. New technology systems can offer this immediate service. Tour operators have seen their margins fall drastically in recent years and must have the ability to offer mass market or specialist products to a market still looking for value for money. New technology equipment is vital to future success of the tour operating industry.

Section 2 Profitability in travel organisation

What determines profitability?

Any travel organiser, whether a small independent travel agent employing just a few people or a multi-million pound tour operator with hundreds of staff, will hope to trade successfully and profitably. For the small independent agent, his or her profit will be the return for devoting time and energy to the business, as well as a reward for management expertise and risk-taking. The large tour operator will have shareholders, who will expect the company to trade sufficiently well to give them a return on their investment. In either case, profits can also be 'ploughed back' into the business to update equipment or introduce new systems.

Profitability is a function of two principal internal factors:

- Income (also known as revenue, sales volume or turnover).
- Costs (also known as expenditure).

A third important and related factor is management expertise. Good management will motivate staff to actively seek out new business rather than waiting for it to arrive, thereby increasing revenue. Good management will also ensure that costs are kept under control. Taken together, these three factors can be considered to be within the control of the organisation, hence the term internal. External influences, generally outside the control of the travel organiser, will also have an important part to play in determining profitability. Factors such as the state of the economy, exchange rates, political unrest and changes in tastes and fashions will all contribute to an organisation's profitability.

Income by itself is no indication of profitability; a tour operator may have a turnover running into many millions of pounds, but still be running at a loss. In contrast, a small travel agency's turnover may only be £1 million, but its profits may be very healthy. This is because in any business, regardless of its size or volume of sales, the income must exceed the costs of generating that income, in order for it to be profitable. A company that has either not costed its products correctly or cannot maintain control over its expenditure may never make a profit, however large its income.

Income

Travel agents

We saw in Section 1 of this unit that travel agents' main source of income is the commission they receive from principals, i.e. tour operators, hotels, car hire companies, etc. Commission varies between as little as 1 per cent on foreign currency transactions up to as much as 40 per cent on sales of travel insurance. Most tour operators pay 10 per cent commission on package holidays, so that an agent would receive £150 for booking a holiday with a brochure price of £1,500. This figure of £150 is not clear profit for the agent, since it does not take account of overheads such as staff costs, heating, postage and telephone charges. Once these costs have been accounted for, most travel agents will make on average only 1 per cent net profit over the course of a year's trading. Put another way, an independent travel agent who has recently set up in business and is hoping to make a net profit equivalent to the salary of £18,000 per year she earned in her last job, would need to achieve sales of £1,800,000.

Although commission is by far the biggest source of income, travel agents can also earn revenue from arranging their own tours. This practice is becoming an increasingly common way of injecting extra income into the business, while at the same time giving clients a more personal service than they might receive on a standard package tour.

Another important source of funds is the interest gained on any money held on behalf of the principal. Deposits and balances paid by clients may stay in the agent's account for some time, thus accruing interest. It is generally in the agent's interest to negotiate a credit rather than cash arrangement with principals. This gives the agent the benefit of simpler administrative procedures and, more importantly, credit agents can hold on to clients' payments longer.

Some agents supplement their income in other ways, by, for example, selling luggage and other travel goods, running training courses or teaching on evening classes, writing a regular column in a local paper or appearing on local radio, or selling maps and guide books.

Tour operators

A tour operator's main source of income are the payments it receives from clients for its products. This revenue may come direct from the customer if it is a 'direct sell' company, or, more usually, through a travel agent that will sell the holiday on behalf of the operator. A large tour operator such as Airtours may have a number of separate operating divisions, each of which will contribute to overall group profits; Airtours owns its own airline, runs camping holidays under the EuroSites brand and operates a chain of travel agencies under the 'Going Places' banner. Mass market tour operators will usually offer a range of holiday products catering for different sectors of the market. Although this range will vary from time to time in response to fluctuating demand, there are likely to be a series of brochures that include:

- A main summer programme.
- A winter programme.
- City breaks.
- Flight only.
- Programmes featuring particular countries or regions, e.g. the Caribbean.
- Holidays geared to the youth market.
- Programmes for 'seniors'.
- Budget holidays.
- Specialist programmes, e.g. golf or sailing.

Other sources of income to tour operators include:

- *Interest on money held in account* – deposits for holidays are sometimes paid up to 12 months before departure and balances settled six to eight weeks before the start of the holiday. This money accumulates for the tour operator who receives interest on it.
- *Commission on 'extras'* – commission for items such as car hire, insurance, flight only and excursions is generally paid direct to the tour operator. Most operators will offer their own insurance and car hire in their brochures, hoping to benefit from the high commission levels that these two products attract.
- *Currency dealing* – large operators may buy foreign currency in advance if rates are favourable to use later for payments to suppliers. Surplus funds can be invested to provide a return.
- *Vertical integration* – tour operators that have financial interests at more than one level of the distribution chain, can generate income from a greater number of sources, e.g. duty-free sales on aircraft and hotel bar sales.

- *Charges* – tour operators levy charges for cancellations and amendments to holiday arrangements, which are another source of income.

Costs

Having considered the sources of income available to travel agents and tour operators, we now have to look at the costs which they must bear in order to generate revenue. Travel organisers' costs can be categorised as either fixed or variable.

Fixed costs

These are the costs of running a business which do not alter with changes in the level of activity. For example, the rent or rates for a travel agency will be fixed over a period of time, regardless of the number of holidays sold. Similarly, the insurance and cleaning costs for the headquarters of a tour operator will be the same whether it has a successful or poor season. Fixed costs for travel organisers include:

- Rates.
- Rent or mortgage.
- Interest on loans.
- Essential maintenance.
- Cleaning.
- Insurance.
- Permanent staff.
- Lighting and heating.

Variable costs

Variable costs alter in direct proportion to the volume of business generated by travel organisers and include:

- Postage.
- Telephone, fax and telex charges.
- Computer time and equipment hire.
- Printing and stationery.
- Advertising and publicity.
- Part-time staff.
- Professional fees and charges.
- Bank charges.
- Transaction charges, e.g. credit cards.

A good manager or supervisor in a travel agency will be constantly looking for ways of reducing the costs of the business, by, for example, instructing staff to:

- Make telephone calls at off-peak times whenever possible.

- Make use of freecall, freephone and freepost facilities offered by principals.
- Avoid wastage of stationery and materials.
- Only use lighting and heating when necessary.

Pricing policy

In the same way that it is important for travel organisers to control their costs, pricing their products is crucial to overall profitability. Pricing is a very risky business; a tour operator that sets the prices of its main summer programme holidays too high in relation to the competition will not achieve optimum levels of sales. Too low, on the other hand, and it will find it difficult to produce an adequate profit.

Determining tour prices

There are two basic methods that can be adopted to arrive at the cost of an inclusive tour:

- Cost-based pricing.
- Market-based pricing.

Cost-based pricing involves calculating all the fixed and variable costs of a tour, including any commission payments to agents, and setting the price at a level that covers all these costs and allows a profit margin. This is the method adopted by small, specialist operators that are unlikely to be operating in such a competitive environment as the mass market holiday companies and whose product will have a degree of uniqueness. In large tour companies, apportioning all costs to particular cost centres may be a very difficult task; while it will be relatively easy to determine the variable costs of a tour programme, calculating the proportion of fixed operating costs to be allocated to that programme is much more difficult.

Sometimes referred to as 'what the market will bear', market-based pricing sets pricing in a wider context by taking account of what competitors are charging when determining prices. Re-issuing brochures with revised prices is now commonplace among tour operators that are constantly checking competitor activity and making adjustments to maintain their market share. Following the market leader's pricing is a risky business, if a company has not fully taken into account its own costs of operation; the collapse of Intasun in 1991 is a good example of this type of 'overtrading'. The hope is that the economies of scale involved in tour operating will enable the larger operators to reduce their costs but still allow a profit margin at the end of the day.

To show that pricing is often a combination of market- and cost-based approaches, we will look at a simplified example of how the pricing policy for a typical overseas package holiday is worked out.

EXAMPLE: COSTING AN INCLUSIVE TOUR TO MAJORCA – 14 NIGHTS HALF-BOARD

	£	£
Flight costs		
Twenty-six return flights during the season @ £12,000 per flight	312,000	
Empty leg at beginning and end of the season	12,000	
Total flight costs	324,000	
Cost per occupied flight (£324,000 divided by 26)	12,461	
Cost per seat based on 90% load factor using Boeing 737 with a capacity of 130 passengers		106.50
Hotel costs per person for 14 days		90.00
Transfers and handling fees		7.50
Total costs of tour per person		204.00

Having calculated that £204 is needed to cover the direct costs of the holiday, the tour operator will now determine a price that covers these costs plus a mark-up to cover a proportion of fixed costs, the commission payment to travel agents and leaves a profit margin for the operator. The exact amount of the mark-up, and hence the final price of the holiday, will be determined by:

- Prices of similar holidays offered by competitors.
- The cost of the holiday last year.
- The season in which the holiday is being taken.

Assuming a mark-up of 25%, the final brochure price of this holiday to Majorca will be:

£204 × 25% = £255

This figure is known as the break-even point. The operator will sell the holiday at above break-even when demand is high and below £255 when demand is low out of season.

Discounting

We have seen that tour operators rely on obtaining the elements of their inclusive tours at discounted rates, from suppliers such as hoteliers and airlines, which are happy to negotiate a discount in return for releasing an agreed amount of stock.

Discounting is also prevalent at the other end of the distribution chain, namely discounted holidays offered for sale in travel agencies. In the past, tour operators have frowned on travel agents that have offered cut price holidays, but in today's very competitive holiday industry, discounts are a common way for a travel agent to attract custom. At the time of writing, high street travel agents offer up to 11 per cent off the brochure prices of most tour operators, in return for the clients taking out the agents' holiday insurance.

Section 3 The future for travel organisers

Introduction

Over the last five years, the trading situation for travel agents and tour operators has been very difficult. The inclusive tour market grew rapidly during the first half of the 1980s, when the economy as a whole was buoyant and bookings were growing at about eight per cent annually. The package holiday market in the UK relies heavily on volume sales to offset small profit margins and the recession of the late 1980s and early 1990s has put pressure on the tour operators, which in turn has been reflected in the low profitability of many travel agents. In recent years, tour operators have tended to cut back on the supply of holidays made available to the public, rather than trim their already perilous margins even further.

Key factors influencing the UK travel market

The challenge for operators for the remainder of the 1990s is to retain or improve their market share by, among other things, forecasting the likely changes in consumer demand for travel services. There are a number of important factors that they will need to take into account in order to remain competitive:

- The rise of the 'new tourist'.
- The state of the economy.
- Statutory intervention.
- New technology.
- Wider changes in society.

The rise of the 'new tourist'

The 1980s brought rapid changes in UK society, some good and some bad, which have filtered through into the travel industry and have influenced, in particular, the way that people now use their leisure time and choose their holidays. We have seen the emergence of the 'new tourists', who exhibit some, or all, of the following characteristics:

1 *A wish to be more independent in their holiday habits* – there are clear signs that a certain section of the market is moving away from the traditional package

holiday to a holiday that is 'tailor made' to its own specifications. Figure 11.6 shows the recent growth in the independent holiday sector at the expense of inclusive tours.

Figure 11.6 shows that while there was a small decrease in the number of package holidays taken by British tourists between 1986 and 1991, the number of independent visits grew by 38 per cent over the same period to nearly 10 million. There are many reasons for this change in emphasis; a disillusionment with the 'mass production' nature of the package holiday, poor image, variable quality and a move away from 'sun' destinations, have all contributed to this change.

YEAR	INDEPENDENT HOLIDAYS		INCLUSIVE TOURS	
	'000 Visits	% Change on previous date	'000 Visits	% Change on previous date
1976	3,153	–	3,871	–
1981	6,297	+ 100	6,835	+ 77
1986	7,235	+ 15	10,661	+ 56
1991	9,984	+ 38	10,646	– 0.1

Fig 11.6 UK travellers abroad 1976–91 (source: IPS)

2 *Greater travel experience* – the first generation to have been 'brought up on travel' are now the holiday purchasers of today and tomorrow. They are looking for excitement, variety, entertainment and fun, when choosing their travel products. They may well have experienced the traditional British seaside holiday or have been on 'sun, sand and sea' packages to Spain and are now looking to expand their horizons.

3 *More environmental awareness* – the 'green consumer' of the 1980s is now the 'green tourist' of the 1990s. Travellers will continue to demand greater environmental appreciation and respect from their tour operators and travel agents, both in terms of the travel products they sell and their organisational policies and practices.

4 *Greater flexibility* – people whose working lives may well have taken on greater flexibility in recent years will demand the same from their travel organisers. Changes in working practices, such as short-term contract working and working from home with the help of new technology, will alter the patterns of holiday-taking and accelerate a trend towards late booking and short holidays.

5 *More health conscious* – a section of society that 'works hard and plays hard' will seek to combine active pursuits with their holiday and leisure experiences. More generally, a move towards healthier lifestyles in the population will need to be reflected in holiday products.

6 *More conscious of quality* – most tour operators and travel agents have reduced their profit margins to the bare minimum, leaving little scope for further competition on the basis of price. They will increasingly seek to compete on quality, both of the travel products they are selling and their own level of service. Customers are increasingly demanding higher standards of service and better quality from their travel organisers.

The state of the UK economy

In many respects, the uptake of holidays by British people in recent years has been surprisingly recession-proof. Many regard an annual holiday as essential, not optional. Having a holiday, however, may seem a very remote possibility to a family whose main income earner has just been forced to join the ranks of the unemployed, along with three million others. Some commentators believe that the current economic recession, which began in the late 1980s, may not end until the mid-1990s. If this is the case, it is likely that the package tour sector will continue to be squeezed by supply outstripping demand, with reduced profit margins for tour operators and travel agents. A continuing recession may well influence the type of holiday taken, if not the decision of whether or not to have a holiday at all. Holiday-makers may choose to stay with friends and relatives or swap an overseas holiday for a break closer to home.

Statutory intervention

Central government and the European Union (formerly EC) control over the activities of travel organisers is likely to have important repercussions for the UK travelling public in the 1990s and beyond. The EC Package Travel Directive (see Section 3 of Unit 2 for more on this) came into effect on 1 January 1993, with the aim of making travel organisers in the 12 Member States legally liable for the proper operation of the 'packages' they offer for sale to the general public, even when third parties are involved. A tour operator, for example, can no longer deny responsibility for poor standards of accommodation or transportation used on any of its package holidays simply by saying that the matter is outside of its control. A 'package' is defined as a pre-arranged combination of at least two of the following:

- Transport.
- Accommodation.
- Other tourist services.

The Directive will not only affect the outbound travel market; it applies equally to domestic operators that arrange packages, such as coach companies, hotels, tourist information centres, resorts and conference organisers. While it is taking the industry some time to come to terms with the full effects of the EC Package Travel Directive, most commentators agree that one of its major effects will be to increase the cost of most package holidays, perhaps by as much as 10 per cent, in order to allow tour operators to take out extra insurance to cover themselves in the event of claims under the terms of the Directive.

In 1993, the UK government unveiled a package of EC measures designed to liberalise the airways of Europe. If it follows the pattern of developments in the USA, this deregulation of European air services should result in greater competition between the carriers, leading to reduced prices for travellers.

The abolition of the 'stabiliser', the arrangement whereby ABTA travel agents could only sell holidays from operators that were also members of ABTA, and vice versa, could lead to other institutions deciding to enter the holiday and travel marketplace. Building societies, banks and retail outlets are understood to be investigating this new opportunity.

New technology

Rapid growth in new technology equipment will lead to new developments in both travel products and reservations systems. Further improvements to aircraft technology will make travel to long-haul destinations even more affordable, as well as accelerating the trend towards greater domestic air travel. High-speed rail networks within Britain and to the Continent through the Channel Tunnel will tempt business and leisure travellers to leave their cars at home. The development of high-speed links will stimulate greater demand for short breaks in the UK and in near-European countries. New technology will help travel organisers manage their businesses more efficiently, through the constant development of management information systems (MIS).

Changes in technology will alter the way in which travel products and services are offered to the public. Travel agencies will continue to use even more sophisticated software packages to access principals' databases, offering clients a more immediate and responsive service. There are likely to be further developments in ticket technology, particularly at airports where self-service ticketing using a credit card will evolve.

Wider changes in society

Changes to the demographic profile of UK society, with an ageing population and fewer young people between now and the year 2000, will alter the demand for particular travel products (see Figure 11.7).

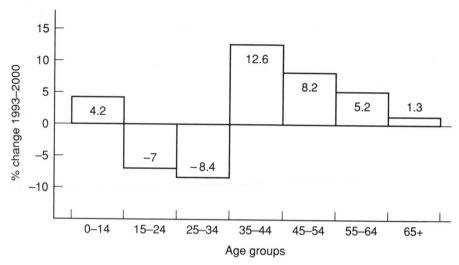

Fig 11.7 Britain's ageing population *(source: Leisure Futures, 1993 Henley Centre for Forecasting)*

The chart in Figure 11.7 shows the expected changes in the age structure of the UK population between now and the end of the century. It shows that the numbers of young adults in the 15–34 age group will decline by around 8 per cent in the next six years. In contrast, there will be an increase of about 8 per cent in the number of middle aged (45 to 64 year olds). The largest increase will be in the 35–44 age group at 12.6 per cent.

Similarly, increases in the number of single-parent families, more couples choosing not to have children and the trend towards early retirement, will all offer opportunities which travel organisers will be able to exploit.

Future developments in the travel organising sector

The continuing recession in the UK economy will mean that the market for outbound and domestic leisure and business travel products and services is likely to show little growth over the next 2–4 years. Profit margins of tour operators and travel agents will be further squeezed and all companies will be constantly monitoring their costs of operation, making cuts in staffing and premises whenever the need arises. Within this rather gloomy overall picture, however, there will be successes and opportunities for expansion; some of the most likely future developments include:

1 *Continued growth in the long-haul market* – helped by new aircraft technology and the consequent availability of charter flights, destinations such as the USA, Australia, the Caribbean and the Far East will continue to be popular with both package and independent tourists.

Fig 11.8 Older travellers are a growing sector of the market *(courtesy of Magic of Italy)*

2 *Growth in independent holidays* – the trend away from inclusive tours towards more independent travel is likely to continue. In order to retain market share, tour operators will need to offer more flexibility in the design of their holidays, while some travel agents will seize the opportunity and offer a more customised service to their clients.

3 *Growth in short holidays and breaks* – both domestic and outbound operators will continue to provide short breaks to meet growing demand. Developments in transportation, such as the Channel Tunnel and the deregulation of European air fares, will stimulate increases in this sector.

4 *Increase in demand for activity and health-related holidays* – growing interest in health and fitness will offer an opportunity for travel organisers to develop greater variety in their activity programmes.

5 *Continuation of the trend towards late bookings* – changes in life-style and work patterns will mean a shorter lead time for travel purchases.

6 *Increasing outlets for travel purchases* – the loss of the 'stabiliser' arrangement will encourage other retail and banking concerns to consider competing with established travel agents in the sale of travel products, especially when the UK economy begins to come out of recession.

7 *Greater concern for quality* – concern over indifferent standards of package holidays have dogged tour operators in recent years, making it crucial for tour operators to put quality at the top of their agenda when planning new products.

8 *Heightened concern for the environment* – customers will expect their travel organisers to operate in a manner which is respectful of the long-term well-being of the environment when choosing the elements of their packages.

Assignment 11

Situation

The Chairman of the ABTA National Training Board has accepted an invitation from your college principal to open a new combined Travel Office and Tourist Information Centre at the college, which will handle enquiries from staff, students and the general public. The new facility will give students valuable experience in dealing with face-to-face and telephone enquiries and will offer them the chance to use the latest in viewdata technology.

Tasks

Part of the programme to welcome the ABTA NTB Chairman will be a 15-minute presentation by your group, entitled: 'Travel organisers – past, present and future'.

Your task for this assignment is to research and prepare the script for the presentation and to make a presentation to the rest of your group by way of a 'dress rehearsal'. Your script should include information on:

- The recent historical developments in travel organising.
- The present structure and scale of the travel organising business.
- The role of ABTA.
- Future developments in travel organising.

You should supplement the script with relevant visual aids and statistical data. You will be assessed both on the content of the script and the effectiveness of your presentation.

Unit 12
PRODUCT AND SERVICE DIVERSIFICATION

Section 1 The scope for diversification

What is diversification?

To diversify is to introduce variety into an organisation by experimenting with the introduction of products, facilities and services that are outside its current sphere of activity. It is possible to identify three levels of diversification within the leisure and tourism industry:

- Diversification into and out of the industry.
- Diversification into different sectors of leisure and tourism.
- Diversification within an individual organisation.

Diversification into and out of the industry

At the industry level, it is relatively rare for enterprises wholly within leisure and tourism to diversify into other activities that are not related to the industry. This is partly because few leisure and tourism organisations have sufficient assets to be able to consider acquiring outside enterprises and, if they were looking to expand, they would most probably look first to opportunities within their own industry. By contrast, we frequently find examples of diversification into the leisure and tourism industry from all manner of industries and public sector agencies. The Thomson Travel Group is a good example of this; its founder, Lord Thomson, initially built his empire on publishing, choosing to diversify into tour operating in 1965.

There are many reasons why leisure and tourism is often given serious consideration by organisations wishing to diversify their activities. These include:

- *As an industry, it has few barriers to entry* – anybody can open a travel agency, set up a restaurant, become a tour operator or open a health and fitness club.
- *It often has a low capital requirement* – being a service industry, enterprises in many sectors within leisure and tourism can be set up with small amounts of capital, e.g. a travel agency, incoming tour operator, a local guiding service or a sports coaching business.
- *It is perceived as a growth industry* – we have looked at statistics in Unit 1 which point to overall growth in leisure and tourism up to and beyond the year 2000. Within this general picture, there are sectors with above and below average growth potential.
- *Perceptions that it is a glamorous industry* – organisations outside the leisure and tourism industry are attracted by its apparent glamour, which, with one or two notable exceptions, is not always quite so obvious to those actually working in the industry!
- *It is considered easy to operate a leisure and tourism enterprise* – some entrepreneurs consider that the skills they have put to good use in other industries, can be easily applied to leisure and tourism.
- *It offers opportunities for investment in multi-use ventures* – a large company in the entertainments sector, for example, could develop a mix of activities on one site. With flexibility of design and management, these activities could be re-organised in response to changing market needs.

Diversification into different sectors of leisure and tourism

There are a number of examples of leisure and tourism organisations that have diversified their interests into different sectors of the industry. The Rank Organisation, for example, has interests in:

- *Film and television* – it operates over 300 screens in 70 Odeon cinemas in the UK and runs Europe's premier film studio at Pinewood.
- *Holidays and hotels* – Butlin's, HavenWarner and Shearings are all part of the group.
- *Entertainments* – Rank is the leading operator of amusement centres in Britain trading under the Top Rank, Grosvenor and Mecca brand names.
- *Leisure* – 50 UK nightclubs are operated by Rank, including Ritzy, Fifth Avenue and Central Park. It also owns and operates ten Hard Rock Cafés in Europe and the USA, with another 12 franchised in other parts of the world.

Diversification into different sectors of the same industry is sometimes referred to as either horizontal or vertical integration. Thomson Holidays is a very good example of an organisation that is vertically integrated, owning companies at different levels in the distribution chain, as shown in Figure 12.1.

Richard Branson's Virgin Group is also vertically integrated, with interests in air transport with Virgin Atlantic Airways, tour operating with Virgin Holidays

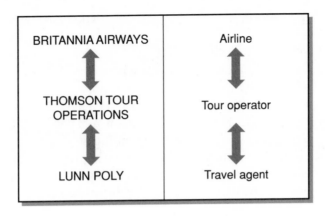

Fig 12.1 Vertical integration in the leisure and tourism industry

and leisure retailing with Virgin Megastore and Virgin Games. Virgin is reported to be considering further product diversification and is showing a keen interest in both the new National Lottery and British Rail franchising.

Horizontal integration is the term given to organisations at the same level in the industry working together for mutual benefit. In the airline sector, for example, British Airways is seeking to achieve its ambition of becoming the world's biggest airline by developing alliances with other companies such as US Air, QANTAS and TAT, a French domestic carrier. It has also recently taken over Dan Air in the UK and has interests in Germany with Deutsche BA. Horizontal integration is also common in the hotels sector, where hotel chains such as Forte and Inter-Continental achieve economies of scale by controlling the marketing and operation of large numbers of individual hotels.

Diversification within an individual organisation

In the fast-moving world of leisure and tourism, there are few organisations that can afford the luxury of not having to think of new ideas and ways to earn extra revenue. Diversification into new markets or with new products is essential for the majority of commercial leisure and tourism enterprises. In the public sector also, organisations are constantly experimenting with new or adapted products in order to achieve their social and community objectives.

Diversification into new markets and leisure and tourism products is not without its risks. In deciding how to diversify, an organisation has a number of alternative courses of action open to it:

1 Least risky is modifying an existing product to make it more attractive to its present market. A leisure centre, for example, may replace old training weights with new state-of-the-art fitness equipment.
2 It could choose to introduce a totally new product to its existing market, with

the expectation that the present satisfied customers will give the new product a try.

3 When it comes to exploiting a new market, an existing product could be re-fashioned in order to have a wider appeal. For example, swimming lessons in a local pool which are at present only run at weekends could be extended to evenings as well, in order to attract a new market.

4 Perhaps the most risky situation is to try to introduce a totally new product to a new market. In the tour operating sector, Airtours did this in 1990 with the launch of EuroSites, when its market research indicated there was scope for expansion into the self-drive camping market. Within two years, EuroSites had become the number two in this sector behind Eurocamp.

Why diversify?

There are many reasons why leisure and tourism organisations decide to diversify into new product and market areas. Some of the most important are:

- *To maintain profitability* – an organisation may have a product that has reached the 'maturity' or 'saturation' stage in its life cycle (see Unit 4 for more on the product life cycle concept). Diversification may be a way of recouping the losses from its existing products.
- *To defend market share* – in response to competitor activity, a company may diversify into new areas so as to maintain its overall share of the market.
- *To stimulate profit growth* – by increasing its range of products and services through diversification, an organisation may be able to generate new sources of profits.
- *To maintain its status as a product innovator* – an organisation that has built its reputation on responding quickly to changes in the marketplace, may diversify to maintain its favourable image.
- *To exploit technology* – installing new technology equipment and systems for one particular reason may open up possibilities for diversification into new markets and products. A conference organising business, for example, may develop a direct mail service for hoteliers using new database software.
- *To make best use of staff* – staff with specialist knowledge and expertise in a specific field may be able to carry through diversification into new areas. The seasonal nature of some leisure and tourism enterprises makes them particularly suitable for diversification.
- *To use excess capacity* – a facility that has spare capacity, whether it be a theatre, sports hall, aircraft, hotel, restaurant or museum, may look to diversify into new market areas in order to fully utilise its resources.
- *To widen customer appeal* – an expanded range of products and services is likely to make facilities more attractive to the paying public.

- *To increase visitor spend and length of stay* – attractions may wish to experiment with new and modified products and services as a way of lengthening visitors' stay and increasing the amount they spend on-site.

In deciding whether or not to diversify, leisure and tourism organisations must fully consider all the implications that the process might entail. There is no guarantee that diversification will work; there are countless examples of companies that have diversified into product areas of which they have little knowledge, only to get their fingers burnt in the process. Diversification that is well planned can be a positive benefit to an organisation in helping to maintain profitability and make fullest use of all available resources.

Diversification in leisure and tourism sectors

There is scope for diversification in all areas of the leisure and tourism industry, whether in the private, public or voluntary sectors and in all sizes of enterprises. We shall investigate some of the avenues open to organisations looking to diversify into new markets and products.

Visitor attractions

Unit 13 shows that the UK attractions sector is constantly evolving in response to the changing fads, tastes and fashions of the visiting public. Attractions have to be sure they are providing the services and facilities demanded by increasingly discerning visitors. Given the very broad nature of the UK attractions sector, there is considerable scope for diversification within individual attractions. If we take as an example a farmer in a popular holiday region who decides he will move some of his bygone farm machinery into some disused barns and create a farm museum, this in itself is an example of diversification from farming into tourism. Having developed the machinery and barns as his 'core' attraction, he could then consider diversifying into:

- Retail.
- Catering.
- Themed events.
- Working demonstrations.
- Tours of the farm.
- An animal sanctuary.
- An educational centre.
- Worksheets and materials for school visits.
- Visits for parties of leisure and tourism students to see how the enterprise is managed.

Diversification into any of these areas will provide an additional source of income and create employment for local people.

Larger visitor attractions, such as theme parks, stately homes and other historic buildings, are all competing for visitors in their own particular catchment areas and will be looking to offer the visitor a 'unique' experience, while at the same time looking for ways to increase visitors' secondary spend. The owners of many stately homes and historic buildings, including Chatsworth House, Beaulieu and Warwick Castle, have all diversified into the leisure and tourism business in order to generate income that can be used to help cover the rising costs of maintaining the buildings. Recognising that the family market is a prime source of visitors, most large attractions offer a children's adventure play area, each competing with the other for the most daring structures and rides! Retail and catering are again vital when it comes to earning revenue, with the most popular attractions offering a range of eating places and retail opportunities. Strict health and safety requirements, especially concerning food handling and storage, are an important consideration when diversifying into food and drink. Some historic buildings have also diversified into hosting conferences, corporate hospitality events and hiring out their facilities for shooting films and TV programmes.

CASE STUDY — Diversification – increasing customers' secondary spend

Secondary spend is the term used to denote the money spent by customers over and above the cost of the primary reason for their visit to a leisure and tourism facility. Many organisations devote a great deal of attention to providing secondary spend opportunities, which often yield a higher profit margin than their primary activities. Examples of secondary spend include:

- Money spent in the café at a visitor attraction.
- Drinks bought from a vending machine at a sports centre.
- Money spent on duty-free goods on a cross-Channel ferry.
- A payphone in a restaurant or hotel.
- A bookshop in a museum.
- Charging for car parking.

As well as providing a welcome source of extra revenue in what is a highly competitive industry, the inclusion of services and facilities that generate a secondary spend also adds to the quality of the visitor experience. Many of these services are now taken for granted by visitors; we would think it strange when visiting a tourist attraction if we could not buy a drink or a souvenir of the visit. Moreover, the provision of retail outlets and catering services can give a leisure and tourism enterprise a competitive advantage. Research has shown that it is often the quality of the shop or cafeteria at a museum which persuades a visitor to make a return trip or to recommend the attraction to friends and relatives.

Tourist attractions, including museums, theme parks and stately homes, have developed a number of ways of increasing the secondary spend of their visitors. Chatsworth House in Derbyshire has recently opened a restaurant in a converted coach house while Alton Towers boasts 76 catering outlets generating in excess of £6.5 million during a 32-week season. Shops are another prime source of secondary spend in tourist attractions. Most of the larger National Trust properties now have retail outlets selling anything from a postcard to a cardigan. To increase revenue further, the National Trust also operates a chain of shops in high street locations, through National Trust Enterprises. Eureka! the Museum for Children, 1993 Museum of the Year in the England for Excellence Awards, has a shop that caters for the needs of families and school parties. Some UK theme parks, including Alton Towers and the American Adventure, have installed instant camera facilities giving visitors the chance to buy a photograph of themselves immediately after they step off a ride. Charging for car parking is another way of increasing revenue, although if the charge is too high the number of repeat visits may fall.

Tour operators and travel agents will try to increase their clients' secondary spend in a number of ways, including:

- Offering a programme of excursions at the resort, usually organised by the tour operator's representative.
- Hiring out items such as cars, bicycles, mopeds, sailboards and ski equipment.
- Selling travel insurance as an addition to the main holiday.
- Offering a 'shuttle' service to the airport or seaport in the UK.
- Providing duty-free sales in conjunction with the carriers.

Leisure centres are constantly trying to offer the widest possible range of events, facilities and services, in order to encourage customers to visit more often and to stay longer when they do. Staying longer means they are more likely to make use of the various secondary spend sources, which include:

- Vending machines for drinks and snacks.
- Cafeteria.
- Sports shops.
- Payphones.
- Amusements and computer games.
- Juke boxes and videos.
- Fitness testing equipment.

While initially a little slow to recognise the full potential of secondary spend sources, most leisure and tourism organisations are now providing a range of opportunities to meet the increasingly sophisticated demands of their customers, while at the same time generating the extra revenue that is so vital to their continued success.

Transport operators

Operators of all forms of transport are keen to make maximum use of their vehicles and reap the benefits of economies of scale. Airlines have very complex fare structures for different types of travellers and categories of travel, with charter flights offering considerable savings when compared with scheduled services. One way in which the airlines diversify is by offering seats to tour operators at reduced rates in return for guaranteed take-up; this is on the basis that any revenue for an empty seat is better than no revenue at all (Unit 11 has more detail on the costing of tour operations). Capitalising on new developments in aircraft technology, some airlines have exploited the demand for trips to 'long haul' destinations, such as Gambia, Goa and the Caribbean. Diversification into the European city breaks market has also been a feature of UK airlines in recent years, in response to the growth in short breaks.

The majority of UK coach operators are small operations, offering a service to local people in their immediate area. Diversification in this sector has led to many coach companies offering a range of inclusive tours both in the UK and on the Continent. Major rock concerts and sports events are other areas that coach operators have targeted for increased business. The growth of incoming tourism to the UK is an opportunity that has been seized by coach operators, by contracting with incoming tour operators to run parts of their UK tours. Coach operators in Britain's main tourist cities have also diversified into offering guided tours for overseas visitors; Roman City Tours based in Bath is a good example of a coach operator that serves the tourists in the summer season and offers a local service in the winter, thereby offering year-round employment for its drivers.

British Rail and some privately-owned railway companies have been successful in diversifying into the 'nostalgia' market, aimed at both UK and overseas visitors. Tourist 'specials' operate from London to the most popular tourist cities, including Stratford-upon-Avon and Oxford. Steam-hauled locomotives, offering hospitality and catering facilities, are to be found in Wales, the Highlands of Scotland and many regions of England.

Accommodation providers

Hoteliers and other providers of accommodation are constantly looking for ways of increasing their revenue by diversifying into new markets and product opportunities. In recent years, some of the more enterprising ideas have included:

- *The addition of leisure complexes and fitness suites to hotels, to offer a facility both to hotel guests and local people on a membership basis* – the idea has been attractive to business travellers, who tend to use the hotels on a Monday to Thursday basis, as well as guests on weekend breaks. Queens Moat Houses have been active in this field with their Metropolitan Leisure Clubs.
- *The development of themed breaks, especially at weekends, to utilise spare bed capacity*

– working independently, or in conjunction with a tour operator or coach company, hotels have created a range of breaks and short holidays, covering subjects as diverse as murder mystery weekends, fine art appreciation and wine tasting. Family breaks, with activities provided for children, have also proved popular.

- *Diversifying into the conference market* – hotels in the city and the countryside have geared themselves up to cater for small business meetings, breakfast seminars, business lunches and large conferences.
- *Diversification by some large leisure organisations into the 'lodge' concept* – offering basic overnight facilities for both leisure and business travellers, lodges, such as those operated by Forte and Granada, have been developed along the UK's motorway and trunk road network.
- *Targeting the overseas market* – some enterprising hoteliers, often in country areas, have made a point of working with the BTA to attract high-spending overseas visitors from the USA, the Far East and Europe.

Public leisure facilities

Although local authorities are not obliged by law to provide leisure facilities for the people living in their areas, they all allocate a proportion of their budgets for this purpose. The more imaginative district and county councils have gone beyond the basic provision of public open spaces for recreation and have diversified into providing:

- Tourist attractions.
- Golf courses and practice driving ranges.
- Sports stadia.
- Tourist information services.
- Local guides for visitors.
- Seminars and conferences.
- Health and fitness suites at leisure centres.

Public sector leisure centres, swimming pools and sports centres are charged with offering a wide range of facilities and services to their local community. Under CCT, the facility may well have targets to meet in terms of offering services for minority groups currently under-represented. This has offered managers the opportunity of diversifying into new products and services in order to cater for the very different needs of all sections of the local community. Some forward thinking local authorities have experimented with the following ideas:

- Offering a range of fitness sessions and courses – for example, aerobics, callanetics, step aerobics and circuit training.
- Staging events such as a Mexican evening or roller disco.
- Expanding vending outlets selling drinks and snacks.

- Providing a health screening service for local people, sometimes in conjunction with local GPs.
- Running specialist courses in, for example, sub-aqua techniques, life-saving and first aid.
- Offering management consultancy services to other local authorities, covering such matters as CCT and health and safety requirements.

Travel organisers

We saw in Unit 11 that a few of the UK's largest tour operators have diversified into owning their own airlines and travel agency chains in order to increase their profitability in this highly competitive sector. Individual operators have seen their profits being squeezed and have diversified into different market sectors by offering:

- City breaks.
- Holidays for senior citizens.
- 'Up market' hotel packages.
- Budget holidays.
- Family holidays.
- Activity breaks.

Some travel agencies have sought to widen the range of products they offer to travellers by diversifying into:

- Selling UK holidays and short breaks.
- Offering foreign exchange facilities.
- Selling luggage and other products such as maps and travel books.
- Promoting their own travel insurance products.
- Offering 'shuttle' services to airports and seaports.
- Taking bookings for theatres and events.

Entertainment and sporting venues

Venues such as nightclubs, indoor arenas and cinemas are constantly looking for ways of increasing their profitability by altering their facilities in response to changing customer tastes and fashions. There has been a revival in cinema-going and ten-pin bowling with the development of multi-screen complexes and 'super-bowl' facilities. The popularity of 'virtual reality' has persuaded some entertainment complexes to offer this activity in addition to their standard facilities. Catering and retail outlets, either staffed in-house or contracted out on a concession basis, are important generators of cash. A number of large indoor arenas have exploited the demand from local and national organisations for exhibition and conference facilities.

Some sporting venues are keen to diversify into new product and market areas to make maximum use of facilities that may only be used for short periods of time during a normal year or season. Football clubs have added sports and leisure facilities that are made available to the local community at specific times during the week. Aston Villa Football Club has diversified into conferences, exhibitions and banqueting, with the addition of specialist facilities. Wembley Stadium runs tours of the venue to see 'behind the scenes'. Many golf courses have been successful in offering corporate events, where companies are given full use of all facilities to entertain business clients or reward their own staff.

Pubs and catering outlets

Many pubs have looked to entertainment and catering as their principal ways of generating extra revenue through diversification. Entertainment has taken many forms, from karaoke evenings and themed fancy-dress events to the leasing of slot machines and computer games equipment. Catering has involved revamping menus to offer a wider range of a higher quality. Offering outside catering for special events and providing facilities for weddings and other special occasions are other ways in which pub landlords and landladies have diversified into new areas. Restaurants and other serviced food outlets have tried to exploit the business market by creating menus specifically aimed at this sector of the market and by renting out rooms for meetings and seminars.

Operational implications of diversification

If planned in advance and managed effectively, any type of diversification within a leisure and tourism organisation will have the potential to achieve its aims, whether they be social or financial. There will, however, be implications for the management to consider, including:

- Legal restraints.
- Staffing implications.
- Effects on physical resources.

Legal restraints

We looked in detail in Unit 2 at the specific legal requirements relating to health, safety and security in leisure and tourism organisations. Under the Health and Safety at Work, etc. Act 1974, all leisure and tourism enterprises owe a general duty of care to visitors and staff when on their premises. When it comes to diversifying into new products or new market areas, some of the most important legal considerations are likely to include:

- *Food safety* – any leisure and tourism organisation considering diversifying into any operation involving the sale of food to customers or visitors must work within the Food Hygiene Regulations introduced under the Food Safety Act 1990.
- *Public order* – an enterprise looking to diversify into areas that are likely to increase the number of visitors or their vehicles is well advised to consider whether, under the Public Order Act of 1986, nuisance will be caused to neighbours in the immediate vicinity of the facility.
- *Fire precautions* – diversification of an existing enterprise may mean that it falls within the scope of the Fire Precautions Act 1971, requiring the owner or manager to apply for a Fire Certificate and meet certain minimum safety requirements.
- *Planning regulations* – diversification into any areas that involve a change of use, constructing new buildings or making significant alterations to the structure of existing buildings is likely to fall within the scope of local authority planning and building regulations.
- *Licensing* – a leisure and tourism enterprise considering selling wines, beers and spirits, will have to apply, through local magistrates, for the appropriate liquor licence. Types of licence vary from a full on-licence, which allows the sale of alcohol for consumption on the premises during permitted licensing hours, to an occasional licence, which allows the holder to sell beers, wines and spirits for a particular occasion, such as a sports event or entertainment function. If a facility is to be used for social and entertainment events involving music and dancing, it may be necessary for the management to apply for a special licence known as a Public Entertainment Licence (PEL).

Staffing implications

The managers of leisure and tourism organisations will have two important questions to answer when it comes to providing staff for any diversified activities:

1 Does our present staffing level and structure give us the flexibility to be able to provide the quantity of employees needed for the new activity?
2 Can we provide the quality of staff needed from our current resources?

Quantity of staff

Depending on the precise nature of the diversified activity, it is possible that the leisure and tourism enterprise may be able to supply the right number of staff from within its existing workforce. From a financial point of view, this is obviously preferable to having to go through the sometimes lengthy process of recruiting new staff, even if the present employees have to be paid overtime if there is insufficient scope for job transfer. It may be possible to recruit volunteers to help, for example at an event or sports match.

If the extra staff for the diversified activity cannot be found from within the existing workforce, the organisation will need to implement a recruitment campaign in order to find the best people for the job (see Unit 9 for more details of the recruitment process in leisure and tourism).

Quality of staff

Even if an organisation can find sufficient existing staff to take on the new roles, they may not have the right qualifications or experience to be able to cope with the demands of the diversified activity. For example:

- An outdoor activity centre, which is considering branching out into offering courses in hang gliding, may not have staff with the correct qualifications to be able to run the courses.
- A tour operator hoping to diversify into selling package tours to the Far East for the first time may not have existing staff with the necessary language skills.
- A restaurant owner who wants to change from providing 'middle of the road' fare to an 'à la carte' menu may not find the necessary skills within his existing staff.
- A hotel that is opening a health and fitness suite is unlikely to have existing staff with the necessary qualifications and experience to be able to manage the new facility.

The problem of not having staff with the necessary skills and qualifications can be tackled in one of two ways; either by sending existing staff on a programme of training to give them the opportunity of gaining the extra qualifications needed, or by taking on new staff who already possess the necessary skills, qualifications and experience. Such staff may be employed on a short-term contract basis, in order to give the organisation flexibility with its human resources.

Effects on physical resources

As well as having impacts on staffing resources, diversification within an existing leisure and tourism organisation will also have an effect on its physical resources. An enterprise will need to consider whether the proposed diversified activities can be accommodated in existing buildings or whether new structures will be needed. It may be that existing resources are simply being 'repackaged' in order to appeal to a different market sector; a hotel, for example, may be offering themed weekend breaks using only existing accommodation and catering facilities and resources. In cases such as this, the need for new buildings or equipment will not arise, making only minimal demands on physical resources.

When a leisure and tourism organisation is embarking on a diversification that will take it into a completely new product area, for example a tourist attraction deciding to add accommodation units to its facility or a tour operator considering the purchase of a chain of hotels, there will need to be a very careful feasibility study undertaken in order to determine the likely costs and benefits of such a development. The feasibility study should be designed so as to answer a number of important questions, including:

- Will the new enterprise produce a satisfactory return on investment?
- Will it be compatible with the overall aims and objectives of the existing operation?
- Is there a market of sufficient size to warrant the proposed diversification?
- What will be the projected revenue and capital costs of the development?
- What impact will the new enterprise have on existing physical resources?
- Can the project be accommodated on existing land or will the purchase of new areas be required?

Having considered these questions, the organisation will be in a better position to make a judgement on the merits or otherwise of the proposed diversification.

Section 2 Planning and managing additional products and services

The planning process

Leisure and tourism organisations that adopt a methodical approach to planning and managing additional products and services are more likely to reap the full benefits that diversification can offer. Indeed it may be that a feasibility study into the possible introduction of a new development will indicate that it is unlikely to provide a worthwhile return and that the project should not go ahead.

Assuming that a feasibility study has been undertaken and has concluded that a particular product or service should be introduced, Figure 12.2 shows the stages that need to be considered in the planning process.

Organisational aims

It is important that the diversified activity should in no way conflict with the overall aims of the leisure and tourism organisation. These aims are frequently

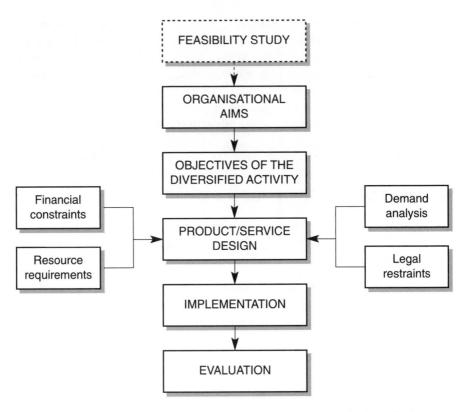

Fig 12.2 The planning process for diversification in leisure and tourism

expressed in the form of a mission statement or statement of policy. When considering diversifying into new products or new market areas, it is likely that an organisation will consider a range of possible alternatives, rejecting some at an early stage because they do not conform to the spirit or the letter of its overall aims.

A local authority leisure services department may decide, for example, not to diversify into large-scale entertainment events in its leisure centres, since the increased noise and disturbance caused may not conform with its aim of being a 'good neighbour' to those people who live close to its facilities. Similarly, a tourism company may not wish to expand its package holiday programmes into new countries or areas with particularly 'fragile' habitats, as to do so would be contrary to its environmental policy. Diversification by local authorities into products and services that could be considered 'exclusive' may also lead to accusations that they are not complying with the aim of providing services that are accessible to all sectors of the local community, irrespective of their social status or ability to pay.

Some leisure and tourism organisations will be very conscious of the effect that any new developments will have on their image. In service industries, the customers' perception of an organisation is a very important element in the purchasing process. Thomson Holidays, for example, has a reputation for high standards of service and good quality products; indeed their current TV advertising campaign reinforces these images by using phrases such as 'we don't go there' and 'we don't do that'. Thomson, along with many other private and public sector leisure and tourism organisations, would certainly reject diversification into any product or market areas that adversely affected its positive image in the marketplace.

Objectives of the diversified activity

We looked in Section 1 of this unit at why leisure and tourism organisations consider diversification (see page 12.4). Specific objectives of additional or amended products and services could include:

- To increase the use of a facility, such as a leisure centre, hotel or tourist attraction.
- To generate extra revenue to re-invest into new equipment and services.
- To use up spare capacity, perhaps in an aircraft or a self-catering complex.
- To increase customer satisfaction by offering a wider product range.
- To change the image of an organisation, by perhaps offering a more 'up market' product or service.
- To increase the amount spent by customers.

In order to be of use, the chosen objectives must be:

- Specific.
- Realistic.
- Achievable.
- Measurable.
- Set within a timescale.

Objectives that are vague and imprecise are of little use to managers and staff in leisure and tourism organisations which are keen to achieve success with their diversification and, more importantly, to be able to measure their success against their aims.

Product/service design

The final design of the diversified product or service will depend on a number of factors, including:

- *An analysis of demand* – feedback from customers, surveys of users, customer comment forms and knowledge of what competitors are offering will all help to ensure that the final product or service offered to customers will meet their requirements.

- *Legal restraints* – we saw in Section 1 of this unit that there may be legal restrictions on what can be developed (see page 12.11).
- *Financial constraints* – the budget of expected revenue and expenditure for the new or modified activity will indicate the maximum investment that can be made and a break-even point for the project. Determining the appropriate price for the new enterprise will be critical to its popularity.
- *Resource requirements* – the organisation will need to consider the effects on existing staff and physical resources of the diversification (see pages 12.12 and 12.13).

Implementation

When all the financial, legal and operational aspects of the proposed diversification have been agreed, the time has arrived for the plan to be put into practice. Some organisations may choose to 'test market' the new concept for a particular length of time or to a specific sector of the market, in order to monitor results. If the decision has been made to implement the plan fully from day one, a promotional campaign will have been developed in advance, using, depending on the nature and scale of the new product or service, a mixture of advertising, public relations activity, sales promotion techniques and direct marketing. Staff will have been fully trained and briefed on their particular roles and responsibilities.

Evaluation

Evaluation of the diversified product or service is essential in order to measure whether or not it is meeting its objectives. As well as an evaluation at the end of the activity or after an agreed period of time, there should also be monitoring while it is taking place. Evaluation should be both quantitative and qualitative; quantitative data concerning the number of customers buying or using the new or modified facility and actual financial costs and revenue will provide useful feedback to management. As important as this quantitative information will be the qualitative data, such as customers' views on the new venture and their suggestions for improvement. Such information can be obtained from formal and informal survey techniques. The views of staff should also be included in any evaluation, so that their opinions can be included should it be felt necessary to alter any elements of the programme.

Diversification in practice

In order to analyse how diversification in leisure and tourism works in practice, we shall look in detail at two examples, one from the leisure sector and one in tourism.

Diversification in leisure – running courses in a leisure centre

Running courses of different types is a good way for a local authority leisure centre to broaden the range of facilities it offers to its local people, while at the same time generating additional revenue to help reduce any operating deficit that may exist.

Types of courses

A course is any activity run over a pre-determined number of sessions, involving instruction on the part of the provider of the course, for which the course participants normally pay a charge. The types of courses offered in a local authority leisure centre could include:

- *Courses in specific sports and activities* – for example badminton, squash, trampolining, volleyball and swimming.
- *Courses aimed at those with different skill levels* – courses are sometimes graded beginners, intermediate and advanced to cater for the needs of people with different levels of experience, who can be given the chance to progress when appropriate.
- *Courses for trainers* – specialist courses, often leading to awards of the governing bodies of individual sports, can be offered to 'train the trainers'.
- *Courses for particular segments of the market* – women, the over 50s, disabled people, school children and ethnic minorities are sometimes attracted to leisure centres with the help of courses that are designed for their specific needs.
- *'Taster' courses* – as a promotional exercise, a leisure centre may hold a special event at which the general public are able to try out new sports and activities they would not otherwise have attempted.
- *Courses that complement a promotional campaign* – courses with specific themes are sometimes run to coincide with a particular sport or health campaign, which may focus on 'looking after your heart' or 'fitness for the over 40s'.

Why diversify into running courses?

In addition to general reasons for introducing courses, such as to make maximum use of available resources and to provide additional revenue, leisure centres will have specific objectives when they decide to diversify into this area, including:

- To offer existing customers a new experience, in the expectation that they will want to use the facility again and hopefully recommend it to their friends and relatives.
- To increase the use of a specific facility, such as an indoor bowling hall or table tennis room, which is currently under-used.
- To increase the use of particular time-slots in the programme which are presently

not fully utilised, e.g. courses for the over 50s during a 10.30 a.m.–11.30 a.m. morning period that is under used.

- To maximise the use of a new facility that has just been opened.
- To provide a marketing opportunity by attracting new customers to the centre and keeping them up to date with what is happening through a regular newsletter mailed to their homes.
- To increase the use of the leisure centre by specific minority groups in order to meet targets specified in a CCT contract, e.g. ethnic minorities and disabled people.
- To make use of staff experience and expertise in particular areas.
- To make full use of equipment that may otherwise be under utilised.

Forecasting demand

The leisure centre will need to carry out market research in order to discover what the demand is likely to be for particular courses and what specific needs customers may have. For example, mothers with young children may prefer the courses at a certain time of the day and with crèche facilities. Market research will also give an indication of how much customers would be willing to pay for courses. Such information can be collected by using formal questionnaire surveys and interviews, or informally by staff talking to existing customers and asking their views. The centre may well already have information from past surveys which could be of use, as well as data from non-user surveys which may highlight possible areas for course developments.

Pricing the courses

In determining its pricing policy for the courses, the leisure centre will take into account a number of factors:

- Any feedback from customers on what they would be prepared to pay.
- The prices of any similar courses being run locally.
- The time of day that the courses are being run.
- The characteristics of the target group, including their ability to pay.
- The potential for sponsorship.
- Any grant-aid that may be available.

Having considered these points, the leisure centre can take a number of alternative courses of action:

- It can choose to run the courses on a commercial basis by adopting a cost-based pricing policy. This involves calculating all the variable costs of running the courses, plus a proportion of the total fixed costs of the centre and adding a profit margin.
- It can set the prices for the courses in order to break-even, making no surplus profit margin.

- It can subsidise the costs of running the courses from other sources and offer them at a price that is less than their running costs. This is sometimes known as a loss leader situation.

Demands on resources

Running a programme of courses in a leisure centre will have repercussions on the resources of staff, buildings, equipment and finance.

Staffing

The courses will need to be run by a coach who has sufficient experience and the right qualifications for the task. Such a person may already be employed in the centre and may need to be released from other duties in order to prepare for and run the courses. If it is necessary to employ somebody from outside the organisation, references should be taken up before the appointment is confirmed. The coach should be consulted as to whether any additional help will be needed and if there are any special requirements.

Buildings and equipment

The management of the centre will have to ensure that suitable premises are made available for the courses and that they are accessible to all participants. Liaison with the coach will determine whether any audio-visual aids are needed or if specialist equipment is required.

Finance

A budget should be devised, detailing all the variable and fixed costs associated with running the courses, the projected revenue and a final surplus or deficit figure. As we discussed when the pricing policy was being considered, the budget will reflect whether the courses are being run to maximise returns, break-even or as a subsidised loss leader.

Publicising the courses

Depending on the time and financial resources being made available for publicising the courses, the leisure centre has a number of possible promotional tools it can use, including:

- Distributing leaflets and posters locally.
- Mounting a display in the centre itself or in nearby premises, for example the local library, building societies, council offices, etc.
- Advertising the courses in the local press and on local radio.
- Public relations work with local journalists.

- Direct mail to leisure centre users.
- Personal selling by leisure centre staff.

Any publicity material should carry simple yet imaginative messages and basic information about price, timing, location and facilities.

Monitoring and evaluation

Once the courses are underway, management and staff should monitor their effectiveness by checking attendances and asking participants for their reactions. At the end of the series of courses, there should be a formal debrief at which an evaluation should be carried out to determine if the courses met their aims, both financial and social, and to decide if there are any improvements that could be made for the future. The evaluation should include feedback from:

- The coach.
- Course participants.
- Leisure centre management.
- Staff at the leisure centre.

Only if the courses are methodically evaluated can future developments be proposed with any degree of certainty.

Diversification in tourism – farmhouse bed and breakfast

Bed and breakfast accommodation is one of the most popular types of enterprises offered by farmers and their families who have decided to diversify into tourism. It is one of the many forms of farm tourism, which also includes:

- Self-catering cottages and annexes.
- Camping sites.
- Caravan sites.
- Farm open days.
- Farm museums and other attractions.
- Farm restaurants.
- Farm shops.
- Activity holidays on farms.
- Off-road driving centres.

Diversification into farm tourism enterprises became popular in the early 1970s in Britain, when many farms were looking to supplement the income they earned from purely agricultural sources. Farmers were beginning to see their incomes drop to levels that threatened the very existence of some agricultural holdings, particularly those that supported one or more families. This situation has been exacerbated by reductions in farm subsidies from the EC, in an attempt to reduce the stockpiles of food and grain. Farm tourism was seen as a way of helping

Fig 12.3 Many farmers diversify into tourism
(courtesy of Michael D. Smith, Festival of the Countryside)

farmers in marginal areas to continue their businesses, although in the early days of farm tourism development, it was often the more profitable farms that seized the opportunity that diversification into tourism offered. Enterprises were developed all over rural Britain, with Welsh farmers leading the way in many new initiatives, with the support of the Wales Tourist Board.

Farmhouse bed and breakfast

Providing bed and breakfast on a farm is a relatively cost-effective way of supplementing the income from agricultural sources, since it requires little start-up capital and often relies on members of the family supplying the labour. From the visitor's point of view, farmhouse B&B offers good value accommodation, home-cooked food and a chance to experience the farming way of life. In the remoter regions of Britain, or in areas where the supply of restaurants and other eating places is limited, the B&B proprietor may need to offer evening meals in order to attract custom, although they rarely prove profitable when all costs are taken into account. In line with other types of tourist accommodation, guests are not only looking for good value but also high standards, not just in the quality of the accommodation and food, but also in the warmth of the welcome and attention to detail. The number of farms diversifying into bed and breakfast makes it a very competitive sector of the market, especially in the more popular holiday regions of Britain. Many farms have applied for classification of their accommodation under the Crown Classification Scheme (see Unit 13), while those in Wales can apply for the WTB Farmhouse Award after completing a period of training and meeting certain standards. Although guests often choose to stay in farmhouse accommodation rather than in a hotel, they still expect good facilities, with many now prepared to pay extra for such items as *en suite* accommodation, colour television in their rooms and even four-poster beds!

The market for farmhouse bed and breakfast

The particular nature of farmhouse B&B makes it especially popular with city dwellers and families with children. Guests are keen to escape the hustle and bustle of urban life and enjoy the fresh air of the countryside. The main season for bookings is during the school holidays in July and August, with peaks also at Easter, Whitsun and half-term breaks. With imaginative marketing and promotion, there is scope for offering off-season holidays and weekend breaks to sectors of the market that are free at these times, such as couples without children and those whose families have grown up and left home; the so-called 'empty nesters'. Short breaks that 'package' the farmhouse accommodation with local events, attractions or activities are particularly popular. Farmhouse B&B is increasingly popular with overseas visitors to Britain, especially those on their second and subsequent trips who want to explore the more remote regions and make contact with genuine country people.

Financing farmhouse bed and breakfast

All new ventures require a certain amount of capital to get started. With farmhouse B&B, there may be certain alterations that will be needed to the house, for example, extra washbasins, another shower or *en suite* bathrooms. Other capital costs are likely to include:

- Extra bed linen.
- More kitchen equipment.
- Extra furniture.

Sources of funding from public agencies to establish the venture are no longer easy to find. Grants from the English Tourist Board were withdrawn in 1989, although the Wales and Scottish Tourist Boards do still have limited funds for the development of farm tourism. The Ministry of Agriculture will be able to offer advice on diversification into tourism and leisure, but is severely restricted when it comes to grants and loans for development. The Rural Development Commission, Highlands and Islands Enterprise and the Development Board for Rural Wales can sometimes offer financial help for potential developers.

Profitability

Before starting a farmhouse bed and breakfast enterprise, it is essential to calculate the costs of running the venture and the expected income, drawn up in the form of a budget. The fixed costs, which will remain fairly constant whatever the level of occupancy, will include:

- Insurance.
- Marketing and promotion.
- Tax.
- Capital and interest repayments.
- Telephone rental.
- Water rates.
- Equipment hire.

Variable costs, which will alter depending on the level of business activity, include:

- Food and drink.
- Laundry charges.
- Casual labour.
- Cleaning materials.
- Energy costs.
- Postage.
- Telephone charges.

It is also wise to take account of depreciation to fixtures and fittings and any redecoration that may have to be carried out.

The venture will reach a 'break-even' point when total income is equal to total expenditure. Profitability is difficult to assess, since it relies on so many different factors, such as:

- Location and accessibility.
- Length of the season.
- Occupancy rates.
- Number of letting bedrooms.

In the height of the season, most farmhouse bed and breakfast establishments would hope to achieve a 75 per cent occupancy of their accommodation, dropping to 30 per cent–40 per cent for the 'shoulder' months. Imaginative marketing can help to boost these figures.

Staffing

Most farmhouse bed and breakfast enterprises are run using only family labour. At peak times, there may be the need for extra help, particularly for those establishments which offer evening meals or packed lunches. The enterprise may provide a living for a young son or daughter who might otherwise have to leave the area to find work.

Legal aspects

Most farmhouse bed and breakfast establishments restrict their number of guests to six, in order not to have to comply with the Fire Precautions Act. Under the terms of the Act, any establishment that takes more than six guests must apply for a Fire Certificate, a process that may involve carrying out costly alterations to the property, which would make the venture financially unprofitable. The proprietor of the bed and breakfast will need to comply with the requirements of the Food Hygiene Regulations introduced under the Food Safety Act 1990. The local planning authority will need to be informed of the venture if it results in a significant change of use of the premises.

Marketing

Good marketing is often the key to success with farmhouse bed and breakfast enterprises. Farms that are 'off the beaten track' sometimes find it difficult to attract custom. Since the early 1970s, there has been rapid growth in the number of farms that have formed joint marketing groups, often with the help of ADAS (the Agricultural Development and Advisory Service). Typically, 12–15 farms in a local area have joined forces and pooled resources in order to have a greater impact in the market-place, by producing and distributing a joint brochure. One of the farms acts as a central booking point, acting on behalf of all farms in the group. A further development of this idea came with the establishment of the Farm Holiday Bureau, based at the National Agricultural Centre at Kenilworth, which produces a comprehensive guide to farmhouse bed and breakfast and self-catering accommodation in England and Wales. Many farms register with their regional tourist board and use the services of their local tourist information centre, which usually offers a bed booking service for a small fee or commission. Some farms attract custom from 'where to stay' guides and published guides to farm holidays. Most find that advertising in national newspapers is not cost-effective. Bed and breakfast proprietors who are skilled in handling the media often benefit from good publicity.

Assignment 12

Situation

You have been the Assistant Manager of a small, city centre museum for the last three years, during which time visitor numbers have remained static at around 58,000 per year and margins have steadily declined. Of the current visitors, 18,000 are school children on organised trips. The museum is funded by the local city council, which has indicated that if the fortunes of the museum do not change for the better, it will have no alternative but to shut it down, making you and the four other permanent members of staff redundant. The manager, Paul Scott, has decided that the museum must generate more revenue, thus reducing the burden on the local council tax payers and, hopefully, keeping it open. At present the facilities in the museum include:

- Local exhibits, traditionally displayed, of the history of the city.
- A small cafeteria with seating for 65 people.
- A kiosk selling souvenirs of the museum.
- Toilets.
- A small office for the staff.

The museum is attached to the city library which has more extensive facilities, including, as well as the book stock, two large meeting rooms and a rather overgrown walled garden, at present closed to the general public.

Tasks

You have been asked by Paul to prepare a report for the Leisure Services Committee of the city council, outlining three ways in which the museum could diversify and achieve its aim of reducing the financial burden on the council. The Committee will want to see in your report:

- The objectives of each venture.
- Financial feasibilities.
- Other resource implications.
- The market for the proposed ventures.

Your report should include relevant facts and figures and be no longer than 1,500 words.

Unit 13
INVESTIGATING THE UK HOLIDAY INDUSTRY

Section 1 Overview of the UK holiday industry

Introduction

Mention the word 'holiday' to a British person and their thoughts may turn towards a 'package' holiday to a sunny Mediterranean beach resort or a winter ski trip to the Alps. What may come as quite a shock to most British people is that far more of them take holidays in the UK every year than venture abroad on holiday. Latest figures from the 1992 United Kingdom Tourism Survey (UKTS) show that 80 per cent of all tourism trips made by UK residents were taken in England, Scotland, Wales or Northern Ireland, with only 20 per cent taken abroad. What these figures do not show is that the UK domestic tourism market has remained static over the last 30 years, while trips to overseas destinations by British people have grown from around 10 million per year in the mid-1970s to just below 25 million per year at the beginning of the 1990s.

The UK has a tremendous variety of cultures, traditions, architecture, history, countryside, heritage and leisure facilities to cater for the needs of all types of tourists, both from within Britain as well as overseas visitors. Even though Britain must now compete for visitors on a global scale with countries such as France, Italy, the Far East, USA and Australia, it still has great appeal to visitors from all over the world. With a few notable exceptions, however, the British holiday 'product' has failed to keep pace with the demands of an increasingly sophisticated and discerning public that has come to expect high standards of customer service. While the steadily growing number of overseas visitors to Britain over the last 30 years is evidence of effective marketing and product development in this category, the British tourist looking for quality products and high standards of service has had little to choose from. It is ironic that the outbound package holiday market is inflicting a double blow on UK domestic tourism; first in terms of attracting holidaymakers away from UK resorts and second by exposing the tourists to the very standards of product and service they find lacking when they take holidays in Britain.

In spite of this gloomy picture of the domestic scene, tourism is still viewed by private and public sector organisations throughout the length and breadth of Britain as having major growth potential. Many local authorities see tourism as a way of creating jobs and providing income, while at the same time reviving areas of dereliction and improving the image of both town and country.

The rise of UK tourism

Throughout history, people have travelled across Britain for purposes of trade, education, religion and to fight in battles. It was not until the eighteenth century, however, that the foundations of what we now regard as the British tourist industry began to be laid. Spa towns such as Leamington Spa and Buxton were frequented by the wealthy classes who came to sample the health-giving properties of the saline waters. Seaside resorts grew in popularity, helped by the introduction of the railways from 1830 onwards. The Industrial Revolution, which had been the catalyst for the development of the railways, also led to improvements in the road and canal networks in the UK. What the Industrial Revolution also began was the desire for workers to escape from their normal harsh routine and dirty environment, in favour of the relative purity of the countryside and coast.

The 1938 Holidays with Pay Act gave a stimulus to mass tourism in the UK, with 80 per cent of workers being entitled to paid holidays by 1945. Holiday camps flourished immediately before the outbreak of the Second World War, the first having been opened by Billy Butlin in 1937 at Skegness. Two years later, there were around 200 camps offering self-contained 'package' holidays to 30,000 people per week.

In the early 1950s, two-thirds of all domestic holidays were taken at the seaside and the majority of holidaymakers travelled to their destinations by coach or train. The late 1950s saw the establishment of the British Travel Association, forerunner to the British Tourist Authority, which was given the role of encouraging the development of hotels and resorts.

The 1960s can be chronicled as the time when tourism came of age. Increasing car ownership, the development of jet aircraft and the growth of the overseas 'package tour' were to have far-reaching implications on the UK domestic scene. British resorts were faced with stiff competition from overseas destinations in the Mediterranean. Today the competition is even fiercer with the introduction of long-haul destinations such as Goa, the Gambia and the Dominican Republic, and European resorts which are investing heavily to 'reposition' themselves in the market-place and regain their popularity.

The facts about UK tourism

BTA figures published in November 1993 show that the total value of tourism to the UK in 1992 was £29,659 million, of which:

£10,665 million (36 per cent) was spent by UK residents staying overnight.
£9,003 million (30 per cent) was spent by UK residents on day trips.
£7,891 million (27 per cent) was spent by overseas visitors in the UK.
£2,100 million (7 per cent) was paid to UK carriers by overseas visitors to the UK.

As these figures clearly demonstrate, UK tourism can be divided into two main categories:

- Overseas visitors to Britain.
- UK residents taking holidays in Britain.

As these two elements of the domestic market have distinct characteristics, we will look at each separately in greater detail.

Overseas visitors to Britain

Despite the world-wide recession and increased competition from other countries around the world, British Tourist Authority statistics show that a record 18.5 million visitors came to Britain in 1992, keeping it among the world's top five destinations (BTA Annual Report 1993). Earnings from these visitors amounted to nearly £7.9 billion, meaning that incoming tourism accounted for one-third of Britain's total income from 'invisible' items on the Balance of Payments (see Section 3 of Unit 1 for more detail on tourism and the Balance of Payments).

The importance of incoming tourism to Britain

As well as contributing vital income to Britain's Balance of Payments, overseas visitors also bring a variety of other benefits:

- An influx of tourists to an area helps create or sustain jobs, thus increasing the wage-earners' spending in the locality and leading to an improved local economy.
- The money spent on accommodation, food, transport, entertainment, attractions and leisure facilities creates profits that are used to generate more business for companies.

- The government benefits from incoming tourism since overseas visitors pay VAT and other taxes on a range of products and services including liquor, tobacco, petrol, accommodation and souvenirs.
- Overseas visitors' spending on facilities such as leisure facilities and public transport can help to keep costs down for local people, who may also benefit from a greater range of facilities provided for both tourists and residents alike.
- Income from overseas visitors can be channelled into improvements to the local environment, thus improving the quality of life for everyone.
- British theatres and the arts in general benefit from spending by tourists from overseas.
- Income from overseas visitors may help to preserve historic buildings and conserve areas of special environmental significance.
- An international reputation for cultural and sporting events can be maintained if large numbers of visitors are attracted from overseas.

The BTA, through its headquarters in London and network of offices around the world, works hard to ensure that information on the requirements of potential visitors to Britain is used to create products and services they will want. This 'market intelligence' is vital for the continued success of incoming tourism to the UK (Unit 1 has a case study giving more information about the work of the BTA).

The trend in overseas visitors to Britain

Table 13.1 shows that, despite the world recession of the early 1980s and the downturn in the economy in the late 1980s, together with the lingering effects of the Gulf War, the numbers of overseas visitors to Britain showed healthy growth between 1981 and 1992, the last year for which figures are currently available.

Statistics on spending by overseas visitors to Britain are equally impressive and are shown in Table 13.1.

Table 13.1 Expenditure of overseas visitors to Britain 1981–92

Year	Total spending (£m)
1981	2,970
1982	3,188
1983	4,003
1984	4,614
1985	5,442
1986	5,553
1987	6,260
1988	6,184
1989	6,945
1990	7,785
1991	7,386
1992	7,896

Source: BTA Annual Reports 1991/92 and 1993

The two charts show that 1992 was not only a record year in terms of number of overseas visitors to Britain, but that the expenditure was the highest ever recorded.

Table 13.2 gives a broad indication of where the majority of overseas visitors to Britain originated in 1991 and 1992.

Table 13.2 Regional origin of overseas visitors to the UK 1991/92

Region	Number of visits		
	1991 ('000)	1992 ('000)	Change 1991/91 %
European Community	9,381	9,977	+6
Other W. Europe	1,747	1,768	+1
North America	2,867	3,377	+18
Rest of the world	3,131	3,413	+9

Source: BTA Annual Report 1993

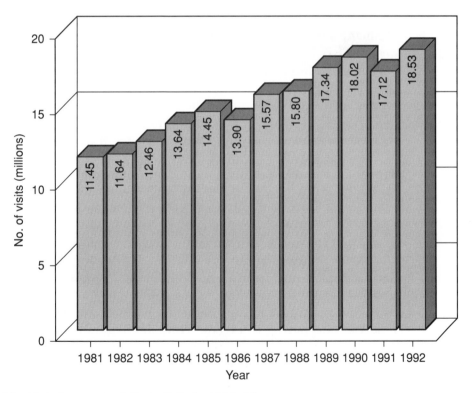

Fig 13.1 Overseas visits to Britain 1981–92 *(source: BTA Annual Reports 1991/92 and 1993)*

As Table 13.2 shows, the majority of overseas visitors come from within the 12 European Community (now EU) countries, which showed a 6 per cent overall increase in visitor numbers between 1991 and 1992. In this group, Belgium and Luxembourg (+16 per cent), Denmark (+15 per cent) and Spain (+10 per cent) were the top three countries to show an increase in visitor numbers. Notably, visitors from Holland fell by 11 per cent over the same time period.

Of the other Western Europe countries, Austria (+14 per cent) and Norway (+5 per cent) exhibited the largest increases in numbers between 1991 and 1992.

North American visitors increased by 18 per cent overall, with the USA and Canada showing an 18 per cent and 15 per cent increase respectively.

Visitors to Britain from the rest of the world showed an overall increase of 9 per cent between 1991 and 1992. The top three countries in this region in terms of the percentage growth in number of visitors to Britain were Hong Kong, Malaysia and Singapore (+22 per cent), Japan (+21 per cent) and Latin America (+17 per cent). North Africa showed a decrease of 17 per cent over the same time period.

Visitors from the USA, the Middle East and the Far East are particularly beneficial to the UK tourism balance since they have a higher than average spend per head when compared to visitors from Europe.

Why do visitors come to Britain?

The many images of Britain, from the pageantry associated with the great cities of London, Edinburgh and Cardiff, to the quaint towns and villages of Wales, England, Scotland and Northern Ireland, all paint a picture of a wealth of experiences and adventures for the overseas visitor. Many tourists from overseas put Britain's heritage as the number one reason for their visit; famous buildings such as St. Paul's Cathedral, the castles of Stirling and Caernarvon, the Elizabethan architecture in Shakespeare's birthplace, Stratford-upon-Avon, rural and industrial heritage are all focal points for overseas visitors. The aristocracy, too, in the form of the Royal Family, their palaces and ancestral homes such as Kensington Palace and Hampton Court, is an important reason for visiting the UK.

Museums, art galleries, theatres, the ballet, and events such as the Chichester Festival and Cardiff Singer of the World, are all part of Britain's rich and varied culture and customs which attract the overseas visitor. Sporting events, such as Wimbledon, international rugby matches, Henley Royal Regatta and the Open Golf Championship, are popular with tourists from abroad. Some visitors are attracted by the excellent shopping facilities, not only in London's West End, but also in historic cities such as Chester, Cambridge, Oxford, Edinburgh, Bath and York. Many overseas visitors come to Britain to study, perhaps learning English in one of the many language schools that can be found throughout Britain. Business tourism, too, is important to Britain's tourism balance; more than 20 per cent of all trips by overseas visitors to Britain in 1992 were for business purposes.

Most first-time visitors to Britain will visit London as part of their stay, or may choose to remain in the capital for the whole of their trip. They may visit the cities and regions most frequented by overseas visitors and become part of what is known as 'the milk run'; this is a round trip that includes London – Oxford – Bath – Cardiff – Chester – the Lake District – Edinburgh – York – Cambridge – London. Increasingly, however, overseas visitors are beginning to explore the parts of Britain located far from London, in search of the 'real Britain', as it is sometimes promoted. In recent years, BTA marketing campaigns have highlighted the attractions of the whole of Britain, rather than just concentrating on the well-known images of London; the Beefeaters, Tower of London, the British 'bobby', Big Ben, etc. Such campaigns have been particularly targeted at visitors on their second and subsequent trips to Britain.

UK residents taking holidays in Britain

According to figures from the 1992 United Kingdom Tourism Survey (reported in an article in *Insights*, September 1993), people in the UK took more than 118 million trips of one night or more away from home during 1992, spending more than £25 billion in the process. Eight out of ten of these trips were taken within the UK (65 per cent in England, 7 per cent in Wales, 7 per cent in Scotland and 1 per cent in Northern Ireland) and 20 per cent were taken abroad.

Where do the British go for their UK holidays?

UKTS statistics show that in 1992, the West Country, with its relatively mild climate and pleasant scenery, continued to be the most popular holiday destination with the British, accounting for 21 per cent of all holiday tourist trips. The Southern Tourist Board region was next in popularity, with 12 per cent of total holiday trips, closely followed by East Anglia accounting for 11 per cent and Yorkshire and Humberside 10 per cent.

When we look in detail at holidays rather than trips (a holiday generally refers to a stay away of four nights or more), the British National Travel Survey (BNTS) figures for 1992 show that British people took an estimated 53.75 million long holidays (4+ nights) away from home in 1992, a small increase on the 1991 statistics. The number of holidays taken in Britain was down by two million when compared with the previous year, while holidays taken abroad increased by 1.5 million (*Insights*, July 1993). In 1992, just over three-quarters of long British holidays were spent in England. Within Britain, the most popular destination for holidays was again the West Country, which accounted for nearly a quarter of all long holidays.

The 1992 Seaside Campaign – English Tourist Board

English seaside resorts have been losing market share over the past ten years to both overseas and other UK destinations. Many of the resorts were developed to cater for the needs of a type of tourist who has all but disappeared; one who travelled by train, stayed in a boarding house and was content to walk along the promenade, play in the sand or spend money on the amusements.

Despite the excellent efforts of some individual seaside resorts, most notably the 'English Riviera' campaign, which has helped to attract extra visitors to the Torbay area of Devon, there was a need for resorts to join together and aggressively promote the overall concept of seaside resorts as holiday destinations. This happened in 1992 when 35 resort areas throughout England and the Isle of Man joined together with the ETB to fight for customers. The London-based advertising agency Travis Dale & Partners won the contract to design and implement the campaign.

Objectives of the campaign

The 1992 Seaside Campaign had three principal aims:

- To improve the public image of domestic seaside resorts.
- To arrest the long-term decline in the share of tourism taken by the resorts.
- To pioneer new, cost-effective brochure response generating mechanisms.

Target market

Research had suggested that children were a prime target through which to attract more families to the seaside resorts. After discussion by the members of the resorts consortium, the target market evolved into parents with children, and specifically parents in the C1, C2 social groups. Britain's coastal resorts appeal most to this group, accounting for 57 per cent of all holidaymakers at the British seaside.

Campaign strategy

TV advertising led the campaign, with two commercials, one of 30 seconds and one of ten seconds, screened in the Central, Granada, HTV and TVS regions between 26 December 1991 and 26 January 1992, and again in the Central region from 6–29 March 1992. As well as the TV advertising, other above and below the line techniques used included:

- Black and white press advertising with a direct response coupon, which appeared in various titles during the campaign period to support the TV advertisements.
- Press and PR support, which included a launch media briefing and distribution of syndicated radio tapes and press features by ETB's Travel Press Office.

Many of the partner resorts made considerable efforts in terms of press and PR, contributing to an estimated overall media value of some £1–£1.5 million.

- A travel agency promotion was staged throughout March with the support of 13 major operators. This involved a merchandising team calling on 2,200 agencies distributing point-of-sale material and highlighting the ready availability of the easily-booked commissionable resort products.

Outcome of the Campaign

The ETB is convinced that the campaign has been highly successful in re-awakening interest in the English seaside holiday. According to their Assistant Marketing Director, quoted in an article in *Tourism Marketplace*, the seaside campaign generated 'as much as £22 million additional business for resorts last season' (1993). The third year of the campaign has been launched with a national television advertising campaign. New brochure response initiatives tested as part of the campaign have also proved very cost effective. In the longer term, it remains to be seen if the campaign, and any related promotional activities that build on its innovative work, will help stem the drift of UK visitors away from seaside resorts.

(Adapted from an article by Peter Travis in Insights, September 1992)

This particular example of the ETB Seaside Campaign, together with Torbay's 'English Riviera' strategy, highlight the fact that professional and targeted marketing activity has an important role to play in generating extra business for resorts. Marketing alone, however, is unlikely to achieve the desired effect. Coupled with promotional work must be investment in the 'product' that the visitors will buy, namely the hotels, attractions, entertainment venues and the improvements to the environment and infrastructure. Partnerships between the private and public sectors must secure funding to invest in 'bricks and mortar' projects and in training the managers and staff to offer the high standards of service that today's customers expect.

A number of coastal and inland resorts in Britain have made the decision to stop gambling with the most unpredictable element of the domestic holiday scene, the weather, and have developed all-weather leisure attractions. The Rhyl Suncentre and the Sandcastle development at Blackpool were two of the first such attractions to be built in the UK. Companies such as Pontin's and Butlin's have invested millions of pounds in the last decade to upgrade their former holiday camps, now called 'holiday centres', to cater for the increased expectations of the British holiday-maker. The well-known Center Parcs developments at Sherwood Forest and Elvedon near Cambridge are based on the concept of a high quality short break or holiday centred on a covered leisure pool in a wooded location. A third UK Center Parcs is due to open at Longleat in the summer of 1994.

Another response to the downturn in the UK holiday industry has been the development of more 'user friendly' visitor attractions, particularly museums, which have combined sophisticated electronics and immense imagination to produce such places as the Jorvik Centre in York, the Oxford Experience and Eureka! in Halifax. New types of tourist destinations have also emerged, many of which have used their former industrial heritage as the springboard for a new kind of economic activity – tourism. Bradford was one of the first to enter the market promoting its links with the Brontë sisters, but now there is scarcely a town or city in Britain that isn't working hard to gain its share of the tourist pound.

Section 2 The structure of the UK holiday industry

Tourism in the UK is a highly fragmented industry, employing some 1.5 million people who help provide a vast range of products, services and facilities to cater for the needs of British residents and visitors from overseas. Tourism in Britain is sustained by thousands of small businesses, a smaller number of large well-known companies and a number of public sector agencies that assist the industry at European, national, regional and local levels. The diagram shown in Figure 13.2 shows how the major sectors of Britain's tourist industry interact.

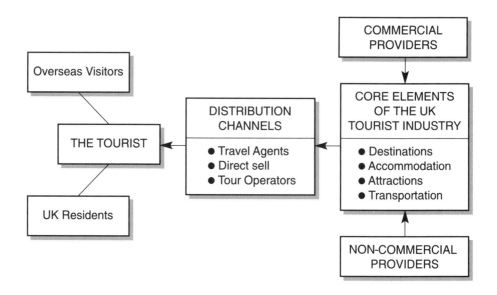

Fig 13.2 The structure of the UK tourist industry

The diagram rightly places the tourist as the focus of tourist activity in the UK, since without tourists there would be no need for an industry, a fact that private and public sector operators ignore at their peril! The core elements of the industry – destinations, accommodation, attractions and transportation – are provided by a mixture of commercial and non-commercial organisations, ranging from multi-million pound companies such as Forte Hotels and British Midland Airways, to local councils that provide leisure facilities and tourist information services for visitors. Private sector companies are responsible for providing the bulk of tourist facilities and services in the UK, with the public sector usually acting in a regulatory or co-ordinating role. Increasingly, however, local authorities are becoming more commercially orientated in their tourism marketing activities, with many now acting as tour operators in their own right and aggressively promoting their destinations. Figure 13.2 shows that UK tourism 'products' are made available to people in the UK and overseas tourists via a number of distribution channels, including 'direct sell', where operators offer their facilities direct to the paying public, through travel agencies and from tour operators.

The accommodation sector

Accommodation is one of the most important sectors of UK tourism. Department of Employment figures indicate that it employs around 20 per cent of the total tourism workforce, a figure which excludes the self-employed, many of whom are attracted to the idea of running their own country guesthouse or small seaside hotel. The accommodation sector is also a significant revenue earner; BTA estimates that more than one-third of all expenditure by overseas visitors to Britain and UK residents is for accommodation.

Visitors to Britain and UK residents can choose to stay in a wide range of establishments, all of which can be classified as 'accommodation'. There are city centre hotels, motels, farm guesthouses, country house hotels and self-catering cottages, to name but a few. For those looking for something a little different, the Landmark Trust specialises in self-catering accommodation in unusual settings, including a lighthouse and a disused railway station!

UK accommodation can be classified in a number of ways:

- Either serviced or self-catering.
- Commercial or non-commercial.
- Urban or rural.
- Static or mobile.

Perhaps the most usual classification is to categorise a type of accommodation as either serviced or self-catering. As its name implies, the term 'serviced accommodation' is used when a service is provided along with the overnight stay, for example meals and housekeeping. In this category, therefore, we find:

- Hotels.
- Motels.
- Guesthouses.
- Bed and breakfast establishments.
- Youth Hostels.
- Farm guesthouses.

Self-catering, or self-serviced accommodation, includes:

- Cottages.
- Villas and apartments.
- Chalets and log cabins.
- Camping and caravan sites.
- Hired motorhomes.
- Second homes.
- Timeshare.
- Educational institutions.
- Camping barns.
- Home 'swaps'.

The distinction between serviced and self-catering accommodation is not quite as clear as these lists suggest; for example, it is quite common now for self-catering establishments, particularly if they form part of a complex, to offer visitors the option of buying food and ready-to-eat meals. Some even have on-site restaurants, cafés and snack bars.

The accommodation sector in the UK is dominated by the commercial sector. The only significant non-commercial suppliers of accommodation are the YHA, universities and colleges, and premises operated by religious groups.

An analysis of the accommodation used by British people on long (4+ nights) holidays in the UK in 1992 shows that, in general, self-catering was more popular than serviced accommodation, although the single most popular type of accommodation was hotels accounting for 25 per cent of all accommodation used. Staying in a friend's or relative's home is a significant category of tourist accommodation, used for 20 per cent of all holidays in Britain in 1992. This category, often referred to as VFR (visiting friends and relatives), is often overlooked as a contributor to tourism revenue; how can it be that somebody who stays for free with a friend or relative in their home, is helping tourism in an area? The answer to this question is that the visitor, although enjoying free accommodation, is likely to spend money on other goods and services in the locality, such as food, entertainment and transport, so contributing to the local economy. Indeed, the very fact that he or she is not paying for accommodation may well be an incentive to spend more on such things as eating out and entertainment. VFR is a very important part of the UK accommodation scene; the United Kingdom Tourism Survey shows that 46 per cent of all trips by British people in the UK in 1992 were to friends and relatives.

Hotels and serviced accommodation

The annual English Hotel Occupancy Survey (EHOS), carried out on behalf of the regional tourist boards by consultants Howarth and Howarth, defines a hotel as:

An establishment having five or more bedrooms, not calling itself a guest-house or a boarding house, and not being listed as providing bed and breakfast accommodation only.

Using this definition, BTA statistics show that there are in the region of 27,000 hotels in England, Wales, Scotland and Northern Ireland. Although gathering data on accommodation stock is always difficult, since different regions use different classification criteria, it can be estimated that, in addition to this figure of 27,000, there are around 20,000 guesthouses, farm guesthouses, boarding houses and bed and breakfast establishments. The majority of this total of 47,000 establishments are operated by owner-proprietors who usually live on the premises. Many large hotels in the UK are run by hotel groups, such as Forte and Queens Moat Houses, which benefit from 'economies of scale' in terms of purchasing, recruitment and marketing. The top ten hotel groups in the UK, ranked by number of rooms, is shown in Table 13.3.

Table 13.3 Top ten hotel groups in the UK 1993

Rank	Group	Hotels in the UK	Rooms in the UK
1	Forte	344	30,343
2	Mount Charlotte		
	Thistle Hotels	109	14,071
3	Queens Moat Houses	102	10,407
4	Hilton UK	40	8,501
5	Whitbread Group	94	4,438
6	Swallow Hotels	35	4,397
7	Accor UK	28	4,120
8	Holiday Inn Worldwide	23	4,052
9	Stakis Hotels	30	3,688
10	Jarvis Hotels	43	3,522

Source: Caterer and Hotelkeeper, 1993

Self-catering accommodation

Self-catering accommodation was used on just over half of all long British holidays in 1992 (53 per cent), compared with 30 per cent for serviced accommodation. Holiday-makers like the freedom and value-for-money that all forms of self-catering can offer; families with young children find it particularly convenient and flexible.

Self-catering can take many forms:

- The former holiday camps, now **holiday centres**, quickly converted much of their accommodation to self-catering in the 1970s and 1980s in response to customer demand. Today, the leaders in this market are Warner's, Butlin's, Haven and Pontin's, which together account for approximately 20 per cent of all UK domestic holidays. Since the mid-1980s, Butlin's has invested £100 million in upgrading its five holiday centres, which between them now welcome over 1.5 million tourists every year. Aiming at a more 'up market' clientele, Center Parcs offer self-catering accommodation in their villages in Sherwood Forest and Elvedon, near Cambridge.
- **Self-catering cottages** are popular with the more affluent AB social groups, who appreciate the rural location of many of the properties and the convenience of booking through one of the many agencies now operating in Britain, such as English Country Cottages, Blakes, Wales Holidays, Hoseasons and Country Cottages in Scotland. The National Trust and Forestry Commission offer self-catering accommodation throughout Britain to supplement their income.
- Self-catering is an increasingly popular form of **farm tourism**. The Ministry of Agriculture and tourist boards have given grants to farmers to convert redundant buildings into accommodation units. The owners, in general, prefer self-catering to serviced farmhouse accommodation as it involves less day-to-day work.
- **Timeshare** is a particular type of self-catering involving the purchase of a period of time (usually in blocks of weeks) in a property, allowing the purchaser to use that property for the same time each year. Although most commonly associated with overseas developments, there are many timeshare properties in the UK, the first having been built at Loch Rannoch in Scotland in 1974. Most UK timeshare resorts are in the rural parts of Britain such as the Lake District, North Yorkshire, Scottish Highlands and Cornwall. As well as self-catering villas or log cabins, apartments in seaside resorts and city centres are also available.
- **Camping and caravanning** are excellent choices for those wanting good value self-catering accommodation. Camping accounted for 4 per cent of all long holidays in Britain in 1992, with caravanning at 23 per cent. Camping and caravanning parks in Britain have developed considerably in recent years, offering a range of entertainment and eating facilities aimed principally at the family and youth market, although touring caravans are particularly popular with older age groups, many of whom are members of the Caravan Club or Caravan and Camping Club of Great Britain.

Accommodation grading schemes

The 1969 Development of Tourism Act allowed for the compulsory classification and grading of British hotels, but it was not until 1987 that the English, Scottish and Wales Tourist Boards introduced a workable scheme that had the support of the majority of accommodation providers. This classification system, based on 'crowns' was, however, entirely voluntary, unlike many European countries, which had implemented compulsory schemes to maintain and improve standards. The scheme categorised accommodation of an acceptable standard within one of six bands:

- Listed.
- One crown.
- Two crown.
- Three crown.
- Four crown.
- Five crown.

Establishments were classified solely according to the range of facilities and services they provided. During 1990, by which time the Crown Classification Scheme had more than 16,000 participating establishments throughout England, Scotland and Wales, it was refined to include a subjective assessment of quality, for which establishments could be categorised as:

- Approved.
- Commended.
- Highly Commended.

This was based on the premise that a luxury five crown city centre hotel may have excellent facilities but poor staff, with little respect for the customer. A small farm guesthouse, on the other hand, may have minimal facilities but a welcome that would put any top-flight hotel to shame. The quality gradings, which were introduced first by the Scottish Tourist Board, could be applied to accommodation with any number of crowns or was 'listed'.

The English Tourist Board adopted a similar scheme for self-catering accommodation based on 'keys' rather than 'crowns'. By 1990, over 10,000 self-catering holiday homes had applied for a key rating (see Figure 13.3).

Fig 13.3 The Crown and Key classification schemes adopted by the ETB

Issues and trends in the UK accommodation market

We have seen earlier in this unit that the domestic tourism industry has faced many challenges in recent years, not least the fierce competition from overseas destinations and an infrastructure that was designed and built for a market that has all but disappeared. Accommodation in the UK, as one of the key sectors of tourism, has also gone through a difficult period and has evolved in response to changing market needs. Some of the most important issues and trends in UK accommodation include:

1 The growth of self-catering accommodation at the expense of the serviced sector. The flexibility and value-for-money offered by self-catering is popular with UK tourists.
2 The relative decline in the use of unlicensed accommodation. Accommodation that does not have a liquor licence is often at a distinct disadvantage.
3 The development of 'budget' hotels and 'lodges', such as Forte's Travelodge chain and Campanile.
4 The addition of leisure complexes to hotels to cater for business and leisure travellers.
5 The introduction of weekend breaks and short holidays to make maximum use of accommodation, which, in the case of hotels, tends to be used by business clientele mainly on a Monday–Thursday night basis. Themed breaks, such as 'murder mystery' weekends and industrial heritage packages, have helped fill unused bedspaces in country and town hotels. According to the Henley Centre for Forecasting, the UK short breaks market is set to grow by 20 per cent in the next five years.
6 The growth of 'chain' hotels, such as Forte, Mount Charlotte Thistle Hotels and Swallow Hotels, which have consolidated their position by taking over many independent hotels.
7 The development of marketing consortia, including Best Western Hotels and the many farm holiday groups in the UK, which have benefited from a joint approach to marketing and promotion.
8 The increased use of new technology for functions such as reservations, marketing and finance.
9 A general upgrading of facilities and focus on quality in both serviced and self-catering establishments, e.g. the addition of *en suite* bathrooms, direct-dial telephone systems and improved customer care training for staff.
10 The changing nature of holiday centres, providing improved facilities for an increasingly discerning public.

The tourist attractions sector

Attractions are a vital component of the UK tourism scene; indeed, they are often the very reason why visitors decide to venture out. BTA estimates that there were in the region of 350 million visits to tourist attractions in the UK in 1992. We saw in Unit 1 that attractions can be either natural or man-made. While this section is concerned principally with man-made attractions, the British countryside (and in particular its 'protected' areas including National Parks, Areas of Outstanding Natural Beauty and Heritage Coasts) is a major resource for leisure and tourism. ETB figures estimate that there are in the region of 550 million day visits to the countryside each year, a quarter of which take place in July and August. The Countryside Commission, charged with protecting the countryside and providing facilities for its enjoyment, suggests that some 18 million people visit the countryside on a fine summer Sunday. In certain parts of Britain, the pressure on the countryside is such that the visitors are in danger of damaging the environment permanently, and are certainly guilty of spoiling the very thing that attracted them in the first place.

Man-made attractions

The term 'tourist attraction' usually brings to mind a purpose-built facility, designed to provide fun and entertainment. If asked to give the name of the first major tourist attraction in Britain that comes to mind, an overseas visitor may well mention the Tower of London, while a UK resident is likely to name Alton Towers, the well-known theme park in Staffordshire. The official National Tourist Board's definition of a visitor attraction is:

> *A permanently established excursion destination, a primary purpose of which is to allow public access for entertainment, interest or education.*

In collecting data on the popularity of tourist attractions, statistics are sometimes sub-divided into attractions that charge admission and those that are free. Table 13.4 gives details of the 1992 top ten UK tourist attractions charging for admission and Table 13.5 lists those that offered free entry.

A comparison between the two tables shows, not surprisingly, that attractions which have no entry charge are visited more frequently than those that charge an entry fee. Blackpool Pleasure Beach remained the UK's most popular free attraction of 1992 and, for the first time ever, Alton Towers attracted the highest number of visitors of all attractions that charged for admission, overtaking Madame Tussaud's in London which held the top spot in 1991. Alton Towers recorded a very impressive 27 per cent increase in visitors between 1991 and 1992, due to two major new rides, increased promotional activities and the media publicity surrounding EuroDisney.

Table 13.4 Top ten UK attractions charging admission 1992

	Attraction	Number of visits 1992
1	Alton Towers, Staffordshire	2,501,379
2	Madame Tussaud's, London	2,263,994
3	Tower of London	2,235,199
4	Natural History Museum, London	1,700,000
5	St. Paul's Cathedral, London	1,400,000*
6	Tower World, Blackpool	1,300,000
7	Science Museum, London	1,212,504
8	Chessington World of Adventures	1,170,000
9	Thorpe Park, Surrey	1,026,000
10	Royal Academy, London	1,018,114

Source: Insights, July 1993
* Estimated

Table 13.5 Top ten free attractions 1992

	Attraction	Number of visits 1992
1	Blackpool Pleasure Beach	6,500,000*
2	British Museum, London	6,309,349
3	National Gallery, London	4,313,988
4	Strathclyde Country Park, Motherwell	4,220,000*
5	Palace Pier, Brighton	3,500,000*
6	Pleasure Beach, Great Yarmouth	2,250,000*
7	Pleasureland, Southport	2,000,000*
8	Tate Gallery, London**	1,575,637
9	Bradgate Park, Leicestershire	1,300,000*
10	Frontierland, Morecambe	1,300,000*

Source: Insights, July 1993
*Estimated
**Free entry most or all of the time

The two tables show that the list of visitor attractions that charge for entry is dominated by three main categories of attraction:

- Theme parks.
- Museums.
- Historic monuments.

Theme parks have been a major growth sector of UK tourism over the last 15 years. They have developed from the idea of amusement parks, offering visitors a range of activities spread over a large area. All parks differ in terms of what they offer, but typical facilities include:

- 'White knuckle' rides.
- Live entertainment.
- Catering outlets.
- Historic houses and gardens.
- Events.
- Extensive parking.
- Shops.

The introduction of the National Curriculum in schools has also given theme parks, as well as other attractions, an opportunity to exploit the school trip market, by offering group visits tailored to the teachers' requirements. Most large UK theme parks have experienced growth in their attendances in recent years, but only by updating their facilities in order to sustain their market share. There is evidence that the theme park market is becoming saturated in some parts of Britain, resulting in a very competitive situation. UK theme parks have yet to develop into the 'resort' complexes seen in the USA and Europe, where the attraction is supplemented by on-site accommodation in hotels and apartments.

Museums have always been popular places to visit both for entertainment and educational purposes. Museums of national significance in Britain are not only located in London, but are also to be found in places as diverse as Bradford (the National Museum of Photography), Liverpool (Tate Gallery), Cardiff (National Museum of Wales), Birmingham (National Motorcycle Museum) and Beaulieu (National Motor Museum). Local museums and galleries also play an important role in meeting the needs of visitors to both town and country areas. Museums have changed a great deal in recent years and we have seen the introduction of living museums and heritage centres, which have attempted to change the sometimes 'stuffy' image of museums and widen their appeal. The Jorvik Viking Centre in York, the Tales of Robin Hood in Nottingham and 'The Oxford Story' are three examples of the new wave of heritage centres, while Beamish Museum, Wigan Pier and Ironbridge Gorge Museum are examples of sites that have 'brought the past to life' by faithfully recreating the past using actors and authentic memorabilia.

Historic monuments, such as the Tower of London and Edinburgh Castle, have great appeal to overseas visitors to Britain. Most are in public ownership, with many London monuments under the management of the Historic Royal Palaces Agency, a division of the Department of National Heritage. Castles and stately homes play an important role in attracting tourists to an area. Castles are a particular feature of the attractions scene in Wales, where Caernarvon Castle receives approximately 300,000 visitors per year.

Museum of the Year 1993 – Eureka! The Museum for Children

Introduction

Eureka! is the first museum of its kind in Britain. It is wholly designed to teach children between the ages of five and 12 about the world in which they live using a 'hands-on' educational approach. Visitors to the museum in Halifax are encouraged to touch, listen and even smell, as well as look; Eureka! is truly at the forefront of the new breed of 'interactive' museum attractions. It draws on the traditions of the international community of children's museums which are to be found all over the United States and throughout the world.

Since its official opening in July 1992 by HRH The Prince of Wales, the museum has been a runaway success. So successful that it has recently been voted Museum of the Year 1993 in the ETB 'England for Excellence Awards'. Within six months of opening, Eureka! had attracted 250,000 visitors and the figure at nine months had risen to over 375,000. The museum is well on course to reach its target of 500,000 visitors per year within its first three years of operation.

Aims

The aims of Eureka! The Museum for Children are as follows:

- To promote, maintain, improve and advance public education by the creation of an informal learning centre, designed primarily for children up to the age of 12.
- To pay particular attention to children with special needs and the adults who care for them.
- To offer an educational resource for use both in the context of schools and the National Curriculum, and as a leisure facility.
- To encourage dialogue between adults, children and all sections of the community that have an interest in children's development and welfare, such as the family, the school and industry.
- To enable children to become aware of their future importance as citizens, examining the issues and problems of today.
- To help visitors, both child and adult, to discover their unexpected abilities, and to give them a desire to learn new skills.

Museum facilities

Eureka! is housed in a new 4,500 sq. metre building designed by Building Design Partnership (BDP). The steel, stone and glass structure has been designed to be the biggest exhibit of all. Development costs totalled £9 million, a third coming from private sponsors and the remaining two-thirds from the Clore and Duffield Foundations. Eureka!, a registered charity, was conceived and built without any local or central government funding.

The focus of the museum is the exhibition, which has three main parts, entitled:

- *Me and My Body* – where children are encouraged to explore how the body and senses work.
- *Living and Working Together* – investigates how the individual fits into an extended family and into society.
- *Inventing and Creating* – provides opportunities for children to use their imagination, shared skills and knowledge to solve the problems of today and to open up new perspectives for tomorrow.

The market

The prime target market for Eureka! are the 8.5 million people who live within a 90-minute travelling distance of Halifax, of whom 2.7 million are in family groups with children under the age of 14. The museum is situated at the centre of a densely populated area, with major conurbations including:

Greater Manchester   population 2,500,000.
West Yorkshire   population 2,053,000.
Merseyside   population 1,468,000.
South Yorkshire   population 1,298,000.

School groups account for 25 per cent of all visitors and tend to be from within a 50-mile catchment area. Weekends outside the main holiday periods tend to attract family groups from a 50–60 mile radius. Most visitors during peak holiday times tend to be on holiday in the region.

The future

There is talk of Eureka! Mk 2, which may be housed in the Great Northern Railway shed adjacent to the existing building and would be aimed at the 12–14 year age group. Continuing the phenomenal achievements of the present museum will be no easy task.

(Information courtesy of Eureka! The Museum for Children)

Issues and trends in the UK attractions sector

In the same way that the UK accommodation sector has had to change its image and facilities in response to changing customer needs, so too have UK tourist attractions. Some of the most important issues and trends facing the attractions sector include:

1 The changing nature of the visitor experience. Rapidly changing lifestyles and changes in fashions mean that attractions must constantly adapt to customer demand. The continuing success of some of the UK's leading theme parks and heritage attractions is testimony to this need to adapt.

2 Changes in technology mean that attractions today can use a bewildering range of sophisticated electronic and computer-generated equipment to produce exciting and life-like exhibits, rides and 'hands-on' features; good examples are

Eureka! and the Jorvik Centre in York. At the same time, increased exposure to new technology in everyday life, particularly among the young, has created a demand for attractions based on 'virtual reality'.

3 Increased environmental awareness means that attractions which incorporate a 'green' theme or subscribe to sustainable principles in their management and operation are likely to appeal to the growing sector of the population that is environmentally aware. The gradual replacement of zoos by safari parks and wildlife parks since the mid-1960s was one of the first steps in this trend.

4 The provision of 'all weather' facilities has paid dividends for attractions such as Center Parcs, Butlin's Holiday Worlds and Rhyl Sun Centre, by providing an experience that the British weather can't spoil.

5 The power of the media, particularly television, has been demonstrated over the last ten years with the rise of attractions based on TV programmes or personalities. The 'Howard's Way' television series prompted the commercially-minded Southampton City Council Tourism Department to offer weekend breaks modelled on the programme, while the set for 'Coronation Street' at Granada Studio Tours in Manchester is a magnet for tourists.

6 The funding of tourist attractions, particularly in the public sector, will continue to be problematical. Local authorities faced with static or reduced budgets will look hard at the viability of their local museums and galleries. Investment in major new attractions is likely to be minimal during the present recession.

Transportation in UK tourism

Transportation for UK tourists and overseas visitors to Britain can be divided into surface, sea and air travel. Unit 1 gave information on the UK transport networks, including seaports and motorways. BTA estimates that in 1992, £2,564 million was spent on travel within the UK, accounting for 14 per cent of all spending by domestic and overseas tourists.

Surface transport

Surface transport, or land transport, includes travel by road and rail. The private car is the main mode of transport used by UK tourists and overseas visitors to Britain (see Table 13.6).

Increasing car ownership and access to private transport has meant that the use of cars for tourist trips has grown dramatically since 1951, at the expense of rail and coach/bus travel, both of which have experienced dramatic losses in market share.

Although the growth in the use of the private car for tourism has given people the freedom to explore the lesser-known parts of Britain that are not well served

Table 13.6 Modes of transport used for holiday travel in the UK 1951–90

Year	Car %	Train %	Coach/bus %
1951	28	48	28
1961	49	28	23
1971	63	10	17
1981	72	12	12
1985	70	10	14
1990	78	8	9

Source: Insights, January 1993

by public transport, there is increasing concern about the environmental problems they cause. Congestion and pollution in historic cities, coupled with erosion and congestion in popular countryside areas, has increasingly led to calls for cars to be banned from some areas, or their use strictly controlled. The city of Cambridge, for example, is undertaking a pilot scheme of 'road pricing' in an effort to improve traffic management, while the 'honey pot' areas of popular National Parks are experimenting with 'park and ride' schemes and restrictions on car access.

Rail travel is an altogether more environmentally friendly mode of transport, but one that has lost popularity with UK tourists in recent years. Tourist trips by train are now at only 16 per cent of their 1951 level. There are, however, one or two growth areas in tourist travel by rail, notably short breaks and the popularity of narrow-gauge scenic railways, particularly in Wales. The number of short breaks by rail increased from 28,000 in 1980 to 135,000 in 1985 (*Insights*, January 1993). Some operators have successfully exploited the market for 'nostalgia' travel by introducing rail holidays using steam locomotives, e.g. the Venice-Simplon Orient Express, which is sometimes chartered for special excursions in the UK.

Travel by coach consists of holidays, offered by companies such as Shearings and Frames Rickards, and networked, timetabled services between major cities and towns operated by National Express, a former state-run enterprise that was bought by its management in 1988 (see Figure 13.4).

Many smaller coach companies also run extensive programmes of tours and excursions for their local markets and visitors on holiday in their area. Flexibility and good value for money make coach travel particularly popular with the youth market and senior citizens. The ageing of the UK population will be an opportunity for coach operators to increase their business to the 'senior' market (see Figure 13.5).

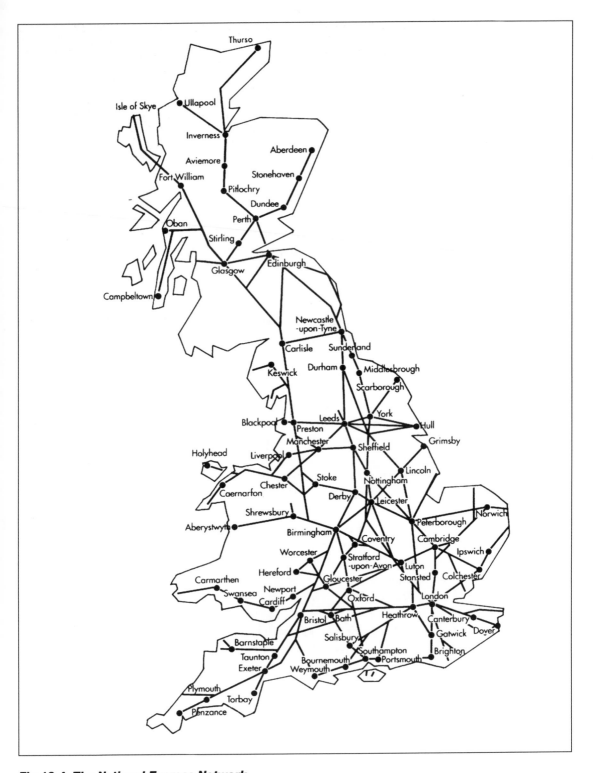

Fig 13.4 The National Express Network

Fig 13.5 Coach operators are an important sector of UK tourism
(courtesy of Frames Rickards)

Sea transport

Approximately 9 per cent of all overseas visitors to the UK arrive by car using the many seaports around the coast (see map on page 1.50 in Unit 1). If, however, we concentrate on European visitors to Britain, the figure rises to 19 per cent (*Insights*, January 1993). Faster, more frequent and more comfortable cross-Channel services, using new generation 'super ferries', hovercraft and hydrofoils, have given the incoming tourist, who wishes to come by car, a range of opportunities for travel to the UK. Ferry companies are gearing themselves up for the fierce competition that is likely to follow the opening of the Channel Tunnel, planned for May 1994, which is likely to mean lower prices for the travelling public.

Air travel

The majority of overseas visitors, approximately two-thirds, travel to Britain by air, particularly those from long-haul destinations such as Australia, the Far East and the USA. With the introduction of off-peak and stand-by fare arrangements and new types of aircraft, e.g. STOL (short take-off and landing), domestic air travel for holiday purposes is being given serious consideration by growing numbers of British travellers. Heathrow and Gatwick Airport alone handled 100,000 domestic flights in 1993.

London is the principal gateway for overseas visitors to Britain arriving by air. The capital is currently served by five airports:

- Heathrow.
- Gatwick.
- Luton.
- Stansted.
- London City.

Outside the South-East of England, Manchester Airport ranked third to Heathrow and Gatwick in 1989 in terms of passenger traffic (see Table 13.7).

Table 13.7 Volume of passenger traffic at principal UK airports 1989

Airport	No. of terminal passengers
Heathrow	39,610,600
Gatwick	21,182,700
Manchester	10,072,585
Glasgow	3,861,900
Birmingham	3,333,285
Luton	2,850,000
Edinburgh	2,368,500
Stansted	1,322,100

Source: Civil Aviation Authority

The number of passengers flying by air is predicted to double in the next 20 years, making the issue of airport expansion versus conservation of the environment very important. At present, some of the expansion plans being considered include:

- A new runway for Manchester Airport to cope with an expected throughput of 30 million passengers by the year 2005.
- A fifth terminal for Heathrow.
- Expansion of the runway at East Midlands Airport.
- A new terminal for Liverpool Airport.
- A multi-million pound development at Southampton Airport.

- A new terminal for Bristol Airport.
- Expansion at Gatwick.

There are likely to be heated debates concerning the economic benefits that airport expansion can bring to an area and the environmental damage such expansion can cause.

Issues and trends in the UK transportation sector

The rapid rise in transport networks and demand for new services and facilities, has led to severe pressures on many aspects of the UK transportation scene since the rise in 'mass tourism' more than 30 years ago. The following issues and trends are some of the most important that have been noted:

1 Congestion resulting from the growth in car ownership and the expansion of air services is having a serious impact on the movements of UK and overseas tourists. Unrestricted use of the private car is causing traffic congestion and pollution in both town and countryside. London is considered by overseas tourists to have a very poor transportation system when compared with other European cities.
2 The privatisation of the railways may well reduce even further some train services in the UK, hitting rural areas, many of which rely on income from tourism to help their economies, particularly badly.
3 The impact of the Channel Tunnel, and the associated high-speed rail link to London, remains uncertain. What is clear is that Britain will not have the fast link to London in place until well into the next century, putting UK incoming tourism at something of a disadvantage compared to other European countries.
4 Competition in all sectors of transportation is likely to benefit the travelling public by forcing prices down, e.g. competition between airlines, and the fight for cross-Channel passengers.
5 New technology will lead to new methods of payment, route selection and booking, as well as more efficient and faster modes of transport.
6 Airport expansion and the development of new roads will continue to bring conservationists and developers into conflict over the loss of land and buildings. The current problems concerning the development of Manchester Airport and the extension of the M3 motorway at Twyford Down come readily to mind.

Public sector tourism in the UK

Public sector involvement in UK tourism can be traced back to before Victorian times when many 'resorts', both inland and on the coast, benefited from investment in tourist facilities by their local councils. Central government recognition of the economic significance of tourism was not forthcoming until as late as 1969, with the passing of the Development of Tourism Act. This first piece of tourism legislation, now 25 years old, still applies today, although the nature and scale of the industry has changed dramatically. The principal outcomes of the Act were:

1 The establishment of the British Tourist Authority (BTA), English Tourist Board (ETB), Wales Tourist Board (WTB) and Scottish Tourist Board (STB).
2 The introduction of 'section 4' grants for tourist developments.
3 The establishment of a hotel development grants scheme.
4 Legislation to introduce a compulsory registration scheme for accommodation.

The Northern Ireland Tourist Board was not included in the Act since it had already been set up in 1948.

The structure of public sector tourism

Figure 13.6 shows the relationships between the various public sector organisations with an interest in tourism in the UK.

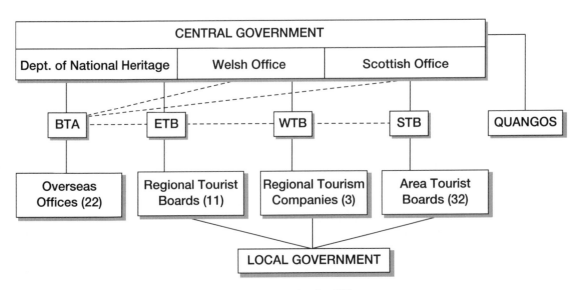

Fig 13.6 The structure of public sector tourism in the UK

While the Department of National Heritage (DNH) can be regarded as the 'lead' government department when it comes to tourism matters, other departments, including the Department of the Environment and the Ministry of Agriculture, all undertake activities that can impinge on tourism. Quangos (quasi-autonomous non-governmental organisations) include bodies such as the

Highlands and Islands Enterprise and the Welsh Development Agency, which have interests in tourism in their respective regions.

The British Tourist Authority, which is responsible for promoting the whole of Britain to overseas visitors, is the subject of a case study in Unit 1 (page 1.26), where its aims and structure are considered in detail.

The role of the tourist boards

Tourist boards in Britain exist at two distinct levels:

1 National tourist boards.
2 Regional tourist boards (RTBs).

National tourist boards

The national tourist boards aim to set the framework and policy for their particular country, within which the private and public sector can operate. The English Tourist Board, for example, has the following objectives:

- To stimulate the development of English tourism by encouraging the British to take holidays in England and by the provision and improvement of facilities for tourists to England.
- To develop and market tourism in close co-operation with regional and national tourist boards, the BTA, local authorities and public sector organisations, and the private sector.
- To advise government and public bodies on all matters concerning tourism in England.
- To maximise tourism's contribution to the economy through the creation of wealth and jobs.
- To enhance the image of England as a tourism destination by all appropriate means, including undertaking and encouraging innovative marketing.
- To encourage and stimulate the successful development of tourism products of a high standard, which offer good value for money.
- To bring greater recognition of tourism as an industry for investment, employment and economic development, by providing information and, where appropriate, advice and financial support.
- To produce and disseminate information on tourism to the trade and the consumer.
- To research trends in tourism and consumer requirements to show marketing and development needs and opportunities and evaluate past performance, future prospects and the impact of tourism.
- To improve the industry's status and performance by encouraging and stimulating the adoption of up-to-date business methods and appropriate technology and the provision of education and training programmes.
- To ensure that England's unique character and heritage is recognised and protected through the sensitive management of tourism.

In order to achieve these objectives, the ETB is engaged in a wide-ranging programme of work with public bodies and commercial companies, including:

- *Marketing* – direct to the consumer and via the travel trade, through the production of publicity materials and development of new products.
- *Information services* – the co-ordination of the network of Tourist Information Centres and a research function.
- *Tourism development* – co-ordinating national and regional development policies on tourism and advising on local tourism initiatives.

Unlike the Wales and Scottish Tourist Boards, ETB no longer has powers to fund tourism projects under 'section 4' of the 1969 Development of Tourism Act, meaning that its ability to stimulate new investment and development is severely limited. ETB suffered another funding blow in 1992, when the 1993/94 allocation of funds to the Tourist Boards was announced by the government; ETB's grant had been cut from £15.6m in 1992/93 to £14.2m in 1993/94, with further planned reductions to £10.8m in 1994/95 and £9.1m in 1995/96.

Regional tourist boards

The work of tourist boards at regional level is altogether more commercial, with close liaison between public and private sector concerns. In order to manage its three designated regions, the Wales Tourist Board has recently established associated companies, namely 'North Wales Tourism', 'Mid Wales Tourism' and 'Tourism South Wales'. The number of English regional tourist boards is now 11, following the recent demise of the Thames and Chilterns Tourist Board, which ran into financial difficulties (see Figure 13.7).

The commercial nature of regional tourist organisations is shown by the ways in which they have to generate revenue, which include:

- Grants from central government sources via the DNH, Welsh Office or Scottish Office.
- Subscriptions from local authorities.
- Subscriptions from commercial members.
- Revenue from sales, e.g. selling advertising space in regional publications and letting space on exhibition stands.

A typical English Regional Tourist Board will have a diverse range of members, including:

- Hoteliers and other providers of accommodation.
- Operators of tourist attractions.
- Local district councils.
- County councils.
- Restaurateurs and owners of pubs.
- Coach companies.
- Local tourist guides.
- Providers of tourism training.

Fig 13.7 The regional tourist boards in England *(courtesy of ETB)*

The main responsibilities of the English Regional Tourist Boards are to:

1 Have a thorough knowledge of tourism within the region: the facilities and organisations involved in the tourism industry.
2 Advise the National Board on the regional aspects of major policy issues and to supply management information.
3 Service enquiries attributable to nationally developed promotions and to provide literature.
4 Co-ordinate regional tourist information services as part of the national TIC network.
5 Maintain close liaison with planning authorities on policies affecting tourism.
6 Carry out a continuing domestic public relations campaign with the local authorities, the travel trade and the public within the region, with a view to ensuring that issues are understood and the regional and national objectives are known; to create awareness of the need for tourism to be managed for the benefits of residents as well as tourists.
7 To promote tourism to the region both from other parts of the country and from overseas.

Local authorities and tourism

At the local level, District and County Councils in the UK are keen to develop tourism in their areas as a way of injecting income into the local economy and creating much needed employment. Many will support the establishment of local tourism groups and associations that will bring together the private and public sector. The Local Government Act of 1948 gave local authorities the powers to set up information and publicity services for tourists. This was reinforced by the Local Government Act 1972, which empowered them to publicise their areas for tourism and provide facilities for visitors.

Today, there are few local authorities in the UK which are not actively involved in some way with promoting their areas to tourists; places as diverse as Brighton and Barnsley, Newcastle and Nottingham, Scarborough and Shrewsbury are all competing for a slice of the 'tourism pound'. The scale of involvement is very variable, ranging from authorities with a single person given the responsibility for tourism promotion, to councils with separate tourism departments under a Director of Tourism. Some local authorities see tourism as a natural extension of their planning function and house their tourism officer and staff in this department. The more pro-active authorities consider that tourism is an integral part of economic development and so assign individuals into this section. Still others view tourism, and particularly the marketing and promotion of tourism, as a PR activity that lends itself very well to their press and PR department.

Local authorities play a significant role in providing facilities and services for tourists. Depending on the location, size and priorities of the council, it may provide some of the following:

- Tourist Information Centre.
- Publicity and promotion.
- Caravan site.
- Parks and gardens.
- Leisure centre.
- Country parks.
- Pleasure beach.
- Promenades.
- Nature reserve.
- Outdoor activity centre.
- Golf course.
- Festivals and special events.

Regardless of how tourism is organised within a particular local council, it is clear that it will remain a vital and increasing part of the work of local authorities in the future.

The future of the UK tourist industry

We have seen that Britain has been very successful in attracting overseas visitors, with a record year in 1992. The recent history of tourism by the British in the UK, however, is far from encouraging. English Tourist Board and BTA figures indicate that the number of UK holidays taken by British people has remained static over the last 30 years. Some industry experts have pointed to the recent drop by two million in the number of long holidays taken by the British in the UK as a sign that the UK holiday industry, far from being static, is now in decline. This situation has been brought about by a number of factors:

1 Competition from overseas destinations.
2 Lack of responsiveness on the part of the industry to the changing nature of the market for UK holidays.
3 Lack of investment in infrastructure.
4 Inadequate management and staff training.

There is no doubt that the most significant impact on UK domestic tourism has come from the 'package' tour operators that have competed aggressively on both price and quality with their UK rivals. While it is often not the case, there is a general feeling among the UK population that it is cheaper to buy a two-week package holiday to a Mediterranean destination than to stay for the same length of time in a British seaside resort. So concerned were the English Tourist Board about the prospects for English seaside resorts, that they developed and co-ordinated the Seaside Campaign featured on page 13.8.

Opportunities do exist in what is overall a growing market; the Henley Centre for Forecasting estimates growth rates of between 1 per cent and 3 per cent per year for the number of British holidays taken by UK residents and overseas visitors between 1994 and 1997. Potential for the fastest growth is likely to be in:

- Short breaks.
- Activity holidays.
- Holiday products geared to single person households.
- Holidays for 'early retirers'.
- Environmentally friendly holidays.

While there is scope for optimism, UK tourism providers must not be complacent and must remember that quality and value for money are likely to be the bywords of the 1990s.

Section 3 The development potential of UK tourism

Introduction

Sections 1 and 2 of this unit looked in detail at the very varied nature of the UK tourist industry. What is evident from any analysis of data and information on UK tourism is that, if planned and managed effectively, it does have proven development potential, offering:

- Financial returns for the commercial sector.
- The provision of facilities for communities.
- Injections of income into urban and rural areas.
- The creation of jobs and new businesses.
- The ability to help promote a positive image of an area.
- A contribution towards the regeneration of derelict industrial areas.
- The ability to stimulate environmental improvements in an area.

In order to understand the many development benefits tourism can offer, the next part of this unit will look in detail at three pioneering projects that have set their sights on harnessing the full tourism potential of their particular areas. The three projects are:

1 *The Dartmoor Area Tourism Initiative* – a project that combines visitor management with sustainable tourism development.

2 *Castlefield Urban Heritage Park* – an initiative that aims to revitalise an area to the south and east of Manchester city centre.
3 *Islington Tourism Development Action Programme* – a north London partnership project with the aim of enhancing local facilities and creating job opportunities through a series of tourism initiatives.

Tourism development in rural areas – Dartmoor Area Tourism Initiative

Introduction

The Dartmoor Area Tourism Initiative (DATI) is a public and private sector partnership co-operating to develop 'green tourism' in the Dartmoor National Park and its surrounding areas. It is one of a number of Local Area Initiatives, some formerly known as Tourism Development Action Programmes (TDAPs), whose primary aim is to strengthen local economies through tourism. Funded principally by the English Tourist Board, DATI began its work in 1990 from a base at Princetown, in the heart of the Dartmoor National Park. The Initiative is directed by a Project Manager, who leads a small team that includes a Project Officer and a Project Secretary. Although the team is small, there are many sponsors and supporters of the Dartmoor Area Tourism Initiative which are all involved, to a greater or lesser degree, in helping to 'steer' the Project and ensure that it is successful in meeting its aims. These partners include:

- The English Tourist Board.
- West Country Tourist Board.
- Dartmoor National Park Authority.
- Countryside Commission.
- Devon County Council.
- West Devon Borough Council.
- South Hams District Council.
- Teignbridge District Council.
- Dartmoor Tourist Association.
- The Duchy of Cornwall.

Objectives of the Dartmoor Area Tourism Initiative

DATI has eight main aims:

1 To protect and enhance the natural resources upon which the tourism industry depends – the landscape, heritage and culture of the area.
2 To increase tourism's contribution to the local economy.
3 To minimise existing and potential negative effects of tourism on local communities.

4 To enhance the visitor's experience of the area, thereby encouraging greater understanding and respect for it.
5 To ensure tourism activities support the conservation and enjoyment of the intrinsic attractions of the area.
6 To raise the profile of the areas surrounding the National Park in such a way as to reduce pressures within.

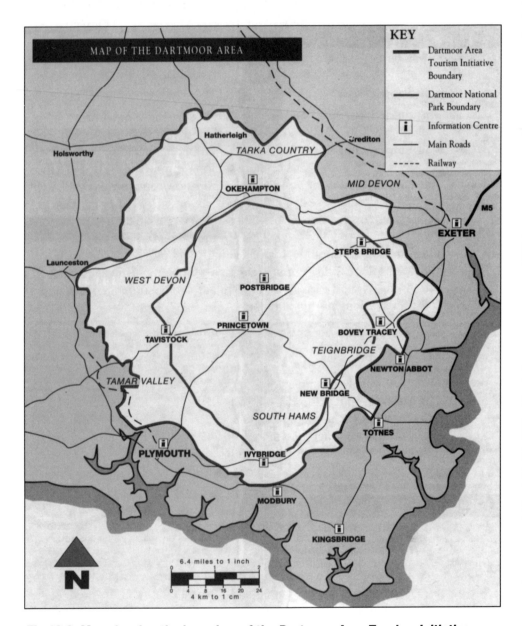

Fig 13.8 Map showing the boundary of the Dartmoor Area Tourism Initiative
(courtesy of D.A.T.I.)

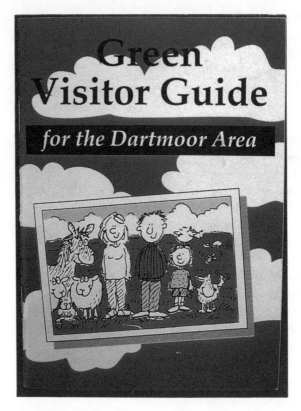

Fig 13.9 Dartmoor 'Green Visitor Guide' produced by D.A.T.I.

7 To spread the benefits of tourism to the areas surrounding the National Park.
8 To demonstrate that 'green' tourism is the way forward for the industry, and gain local and national support for progress.

The work programme

The overall responsibility for the co-ordination of the work programme rests with the Project Manager, working closely with the agencies listed above. DATI's innovative programme of work focuses on:

- *Marketing* – including familiarisation tours for journalists, participation in road-shows and events, a campaign for longer stay holidays, specific campaigns to promote 'theme' breaks, organisation of training seminars and the publication of leaflets including the 'Green Visitor Guide for the Dartmoor Area' (see Figure 13.9) and the 'Green Business Guide', both of which encourage, among other things, the use of local products and services, respect for the natural environment and developing close supportive links with local conservation groups.
- *Development of public transport* – including the publication of 'suggested tour' routes and 'briefing packs' for coach operators, to advise on the best routes to follow.

- *Farm diversification* – farmhouse bed and breakfast, farm activity days, guide-lines for farm tourism enterprises, co-operative marketing schemes and the development of 'bunk barn' accommodation, are some of the projects the team are involved with.
- *Sustainable tourism* – DATI aims to promote the principles of 'green tourism' to all involved and to cultivate and disseminate best practice in sustainable tourism. Specific projects involve assessing how the local tourist industry might best contribute to the sustainable management of the area and the develop-ment of a 'Green Charter' for the Dartmoor Area.
- *Public relations* – the Project aims to use local and national media to stimulate interest in its work and to encourage a favourable image for both the Project itself and the tourism industry within the area.
- *Advisory and information role* – an important part of DATI's work is to develop co-operation with possible sponsors and the tourism industry by the provision of clear, precise and up to date information. Without this information network, much of the work of the Project may go unnoticed and work may be duplicated by other agencies.
- *Interpretation strategy* – specific projects include the production of interpretive leaflets, guided walks, farm interpretation, improving access to countryside viewpoints and forest interpretation.
- *Managing the pressure* – the Project Team hope to implement demonstration sites to show how practical measures to combat the negative effects of visitor pressure can be carried out.

The future

DATI has been recognised as a pioneering project in the field of visitor manage-ment in rural areas; it was 'Highly Commended' in the 1991 ETB 'England for Excellence Awards'. The Dartmoor Area Tourism Initiative formally comes to an end in March 1994, but the principles and priorities it set will continue through a number of subgroups of sponsors.

(Information courtesy of the Dartmoor Area Tourism Initiative)

CASE STUDY

Tourism and economic regeneration – Castlefield Urban Heritage Park

Introduction

The Castlefield area of Manchester markets itself as 'Britain's first Urban Heritage Park' and has been the focus for substantial investment over the last few years by both the public and the private sector. The area has been recognised by the English Tourist Board as having significant tourism potential, currently attracting around one million visitors per year to its two main attractions:

- The Museum of Science and Industry.
- Granada Studios Tour.

Other attractions within the Castlefield area include:

- G-Mex Exhibition Centre.
- Castlefield Gallery.
- Roman fort.
- The canals.
- Castlefield Hotel.
- Salford Quays.

The job of controlling the regeneration of the area rests with the Castlefield Management Company Limited, a separate arm of Central Manchester Development Corporation (CMDC), which was established by the government in

Fig 13.10 Castlefield Urban Heritage Park, Manchester

1988 for a period of five years and given the remit of revitalising the Castlefield area.

The area is characterised by a railway and canal network that has played an important role in its history. The whole area is currently undergoing rapid transformation with old warehouses being renovated, new hotels and attractions being built, and significant environmental improvements taking place.

Aims of the scheme

Castlefield Management Company has two principal aims:

1 To improve standards of management and maintenance in the area.
2 To improve visitor facilities and services.

It is hoped that the presence and work of the Management Company will result in:

- Increased cleanliness of the waterways.
- Improved litter control.
- Better maintenance of public areas and private land.
- Improved visitor services.
- Increased activities and events in the area.
- Increased numbers of visitors.
- Increased security.
- Improved co-ordination of the management of the area.

Objectives

In seeking to achieve its overall aims, the Castlefield Management Company has identified the following specific objectives:

- To set up and manage an Urban Ranger service for the Castlefield area.
- To establish measurable maintenance standards for the area, identify maintenance problems and encourage those responsible to take remedial action.
- To establish and gain commitment to measurable cleanliness standards for the area, identify problems and find solutions.
- To establish good working relationships with local owners and operators.
- To play an active role in establishing a programme of events and ways of marketing the area to draw in additional visitors and maximise their enjoyment of Castlefield.

The ranger service

The unique Castlefield Urban Rangers, complete with distinctive uniforms, radios and mountain bikes, patrol daily around the Heritage Park ensuring the canals and tow-paths are kept free of debris and take on environmental issues with tenants and businesses. They also provide a link to local authority services, inform Castlefield residents of events happening in the area through an in-house newsletter 'Castlefield Today', give guided tours around the site and enhance visitor interpretation through the provision of interpretation boards and trail leaflets.

Funding and the future

During the first three years, funding for the Castlefield Management Company will come from a mix of private and public sector agencies:

- Central Manchester Development Corporation.
- English Tourist Board via its Area Initiative Fund.
- Local authorities of Manchester and Salford.
- Local landowners and businesses.

Future funding will be dependent on the Manager's ability to convince the sponsoring bodies of the effectiveness of this form of area management. CMDC's financial support will continue in an appropriate form if the project proves viable beyond the life of the Corporation.

(Information courtesy of Castlefield Management Company Limited)

CASE STUDY — *Tourism development in a north London borough – Islington TDAP*

Introduction

The Islington Tourism Development Action Programme (TDAP), with the working name Discover Islington and promotional slogan 'Discover Islington – the real London', was set up in 1991 as a partnership of public and private sector organisations to promote and develop tourism in this part of London. Established for an initial three-year period, it is supported and sponsored by:

- English Tourist Board.
- Department of the Environment.
- Islington Borough Council.
- London Tourist Board.
- Arsenal Football Club Ltd.
- Barclays Bank PLC.
- British Waterways.
- Business Design Centre.
- Grand Metropolitan Estates Ltd.
- The Heritage Consulting Consortium.
- Holden Matthews.
- Ian Lerner and Co.
- Islington Chamber of Commerce.
- Thames Water PLC.

The Discover Islington TDAP is unusual, if not unique, in that it deals with only one local authority (Islington Borough Council), which no longer has a Tourism Officer and, in essence, has 'contracted out' its tourism promotion function to the TDAP.

The aims

The underlying purpose of Discover Islington is to improve perceptions of the area, enhance local facilities and infrastructure, and help create job opportunities for local people through increased revenue from visitors. It aims to balance the benefit to visitors with those living and working in the area.

At the outset, the following key objectives were established:

- *To reach new markets* – by, among other things, developing a marketing and PR strategy based on the targeting of selected specialist markets likely to be interested in visiting Islington. Promotional materials and activities include a tour leaflet for groups, a tourist guide, guided walks, an arts package and a speciality shopping guide.
- *Building up the resource* – an audit of tourist attractions and facilities in Islington was produced in August 1992 to provide a base from which to develop accommodation and visitor services, including bed and breakfast in private homes, accommodation in pubs and the upgrading of the accommodation stock through registration with the London Tourist Board.
- *Improving the visitor experience* – the programme seeks to improve access both to and between attractions and encourages the improvement in the local infrastructure, including a clean environment, toilet facilities, appropriate signs, interpretation and information provision. A new tourist information centre was opened in August 1993 offering a range of services and publications for visitors. In partnership with other agencies, Discover Islington aims to identify gaps in training provision and encourage professionalism and quality throughout its area.
- *Promoting investment* – the first priority in this category was the encouragement of investment in accommodation facilities to cater for a broad range of visitors to the area. The identification of development opportunities for new attractions and facilities, involving both the private and public sector, remains an important aspect of Discover Islington's work.

The opportunities

Islington is still a largely undiscovered tourism resource. It has a rich architectural heritage and boasts the biggest concentration of theatres and performing arts venues of international standing outside the West End of London. It has a first class antiques market at Camden Passage and a range of speciality shopping. There is an unbeaten choice of pubs, bars and cafés with character and a range of restaurants with fine foods from all over the world.

The future

The three-year TDAP officially comes to an end in November 1994. Given the undoubted tourism potential within the area, it is the hope of the small and dedicated team at Discover Islington that the innovative work they have begun can be continued beyond this date, so that the area has a sound base from which to develop to the full.

(Information courtesy of Discover Islington TDAP)

The negative effects of tourism development in the UK

While tourism development can bring significant benefits, as the three case studies above have shown, unrestricted or unplanned development does have its negative impacts on local communities. These adverse effects can be categorised as:

- Economic impacts.
- Effects on the local environment.
- Social and cultural effects.

Negative economic effects of tourism

Most public sector bodies develop tourism principally because of the economic benefits it can bring, especially income and jobs. There are, however, some negative effects of tourism development, including:

- Extra charges levied on the local community to finance facilities and services for visitors. Through their Council Tax, local people may have to pay for such facilities as tourist information centres and promotional literature, which are purely for the benefit of tourists.
- The price of land and houses may rise as a result of tourist development, making it difficult for local people to buy their own property. In rural areas of Wales, England and Scotland, the purchasing of second homes, which may only be used for a small proportion of the year, can inflate house prices and put them beyond the reach of the local population, particularly young couples looking for their first property.
- Areas of the country that become particularly popular with tourists may lose their local shops in favour of retail outlets geared specifically to the needs of the tourists, such as gift shops and cafés. This means that local people have to travel further to buy their staple foods, thus incurring extra travel expense. Rural areas are again particularly at risk; the village of Holmfirth, which has become famous as the location where the TV programme 'The Last of the Summer Wine' is recorded, has seen many of its village shops being replaced by facilities for visitors.

Negative environmental effects of tourism

In the UK, negative environmental impacts of tourism are not confined to countryside areas, but are to be found in cities and on the coast.

Negative impacts in the countryside are most acute in the National Parks, which together accommodate over 100 million visits per year (see page 1.46 for a map of the National Parks in England and Wales). Parks close to urban centres come under particular pressure; at summer weekends, some parts of the Peak District and Lake District National Parks reach saturation point, with traffic jams for many miles. The large numbers of people visiting the countryside, most travelling by car, put pressure on the physical environment, resulting in erosion by walkers, cars, cycles, horse-riders and motorcyclists. Litter and the pollution of fields and waterways are a constant problem, resulting in harm to the natural flora and fauna.

Tourism's harmful effects on the city environment affect many historic destinations popular with tourists, such as York, Bath, Chester, Cambridge, Stratford-upon-Avon and Oxford, to name but a few, as well as our capital cities, Cardiff, London and Edinburgh. Congestion, pollution and litter are three of the most common problems concerning tourism in the urban environment.

On the coast, sensitive areas such as sand dunes and estuaries can be harmed by tourist pressure, while the popular seaside resorts, including Scarborough, Brighton and Newquay in Cornwall, have to deal with the huge influx of visitors for a relatively short period of time and all they bring with them. In areas of the country prone to drought, water supply can be a problem in the peak tourist season, while sewage disposal is a constant challenge.

Negative social and cultural effects of tourism

While it is possible, in most cases, to put measures in place to rectify the adverse environmental and economic effects of tourism development, its negative social and cultural impacts are somehow more deep-rooted and, therefore, not easy to manage. We are thinking here, for example, about the loss of a language through lack of use, traditional activities (e.g. farming, forestry and fishing) losing labour to tourism and tourists' own social values and behaviour distorting local customs. Traditional crafts may be lost in favour of imported, mass-produced items and the religious codes of the 'host' population may be altered. Many commentators consider that the need to consider ways of alleviating the negative social and cultural impacts of tourism is the biggest challenge the industry faces in the 1990s.

 Assignment 13

Situation

You are the first Tourism Officer for your local area, employed initially on a three-year contract with funding from the tourist board and local tourism businesses. Your job is to promote the local area for leisure and business tourism and act as a catalyst for private and public sector tourism developments.

Tasks

Your first priority is to develop a tourism strategy for the area, highlighting both marketing and development opportunities. Your strategy should include:

- An overview of the UK tourism industry, with indications of market trends.
- An audit of the present tourist businesses and facilities in your area.
- An analysis of the development potential of current tourism facilities and services.
- Specific market and development opportunities that may arise in the area.
- The views of local people and local traders on the development of tourism.
- Potential economic, environmental and social impacts of your recommendations.

Your strategy should include national, regional and local data on visitor numbers and should consider the wider business environment within which the tourism industry operates. The strategy should be no longer than 1,500 words in total.

Unit 14
FINANCIAL PLANNING AND MONITORING IN LEISURE AND TOURISM

Section 1 The importance of financial management

Introduction

The information and examples examined in the different units of this book have highlighted the fact that leisure and tourism is an extremely fragmented industry, covering sectors as diverse as visits to stately homes, home-based leisure and ten-pin bowling. It is a young and dynamic industry, providing products and services for an increasingly discerning public. Despite the broad range of the industry, there is one element common to all its constituent parts, namely finance. Indeed, without finance there would be no leisure and tourism industry. Most managers would agree that controlling the financial aspects of their organisation is the most important task they undertake.

What is financial management?

Financial management is the general term used to denote the planning and control of an organisation's financial resources and their appropriate deployment. All leisure and tourism organisations approach the management of their finances in different ways, but they will all, at some stage in their development, need to:

1 Find appropriate sources of capital to fund their operations.
2 Record all the financial transactions associated with the operation and present the information in an appropriate form to outside agencies.

3 Use financial information to measure current and past performance, for decision-making purposes and to plan for the future.

We will now look at each of these areas of financial management in a little more detail.

1 Sources of capital

Most leisure and tourism organisations, whether in the private, public or voluntary sector, will operate with a mix of funding from internal and external sources. Funds from internal sources include retained profits, which are re-invested ('ploughed back') into the business, and the owners' capital. Many small businesses in the leisure and tourism industry rely heavily on internal sources of capital, fearing a loss of control over their operation when investors from outside are involved. However, in all but the smallest of ventures, internal sources of capital are unlikely to provide sufficient scope for further expansion, given the capital-intensive nature of many leisure and tourism enterprises. At some stage in their development, most organisations will need to raise funds from external sources. These include funding from non-commercial sources, such as central and local government agencies involved with leisure and tourism. Section 4 of Unit 1 has more details of potential providers of public funds, including the Arts Council and Sports Council. Commercial sources of finance available to leisure and tourism organisations include:

- Bank loans and overdrafts.
- Commercial mortgages.
- Share issues.
- Leasing and hire purchase.

As recent press coverage of the financial losses at EuroDisney have highlighted, raising finance from external sources is not without its risks. Organisations that are seeking funds from commercial sources will need to consider a number of factors before entering into any short- or long-term commitments. These include:

- Their ability to meet the costs of the borrowing.
- The current interest rates.
- The state of the economy.
- The state of the leisure and tourism market.
- The length of the borrowing term.
- The security required by the lender.

2 Recording financial transactions

Financial accounting is the process by which an organisation records all its financial inputs and outputs and produces its accounts. In the private sector, the statutory accounts the organisation is required to produce are:

- The profit and loss account.
- The balance sheet.
- The cash-flow statement.

These are the items that will appear in its annual report and accounts, which is made available to shareholders and other interested parties (Unit 8 shows extracts from the annual report and accounts for the Centre for Alternative Technology in Mid Wales). Financial accountants are bound by legislation contained in the various Companies' Acts concerning the method of presentation of financial data and the disclosure of certain information. As well as meeting the needs of shareholders, the financial accounts will include information required by the Inland Revenue and the Registrar of Companies. The accounts of all leisure and tourism companies are subject to auditing, a technique that attempts to ensure that the financial information disclosed to shareholders and other interested parties is objective and fair.

Leisure and tourism organisations in the public sector are also required by law to produce annual accounts. Under the Local Government Finance Act 1982, local authorities are required to produce Statements of Accounts that include income and expenditure, summaries of capital expenditure, the consolidated balance sheet and the statement of sources of funds. With the development of 'contracted out' services through CCT, individual business units within local authorities, including leisure and tourism facilities, are required to produce a separate annual report, prepared along the lines of accounts in the commercial sector.

3 Using financial information for evaluation and decision-making purposes

Leisure and tourism organisations will use the financial information collected as part of the financial accounting process, as a basis on which managers can make decisions about the most effective use of their resources . We saw in Unit 6 concerning management information systems (MIS) in leisure and tourism, that a flow of accurate, relevant and up-to-date financial data is essential for successful management. The process by which the financial data is presented and used for management purposes is known as management accounting. The emphasis of management accounting is to adopt a wide approach to planning and control, not only providing information on actual expenditure and income, but also on expected costs and revenues.

In particular, information made available from management accounts will be used to:

- Measure actual performance against plans and budgets.
- Analyse the viability of various courses of action.
- Plan future strategies.

We looked in detail in Unit 8 at how performance indicators, such as financial ratios and targets, are used in both private and public sector leisure and tourism organisations to measure performance within facilities and between industry sectors. Measuring actual against planned income and expenditure data is essential if management is to be able to fully control their financial resources. Analysing the viability of various courses of action may involve the manager in sensitivity analysis, a technique which looks at the likely impact of different scenarios on the overall financial outcome of a project. Sometimes referred to as 'what if' calculations, sensitivity analyses look at what would happen if, for example, attendance at a theme park turned out to be 20 per cent less than predicted over a 30-week season. Investors are often keen to see the likely effects of 'worst case' scenarios. Planning future strategies involves devising budgets, the action plans of financial management, which we consider in detail in Section 2 of this unit.

Finance and the planning process

The very diverse nature of the leisure and tourism industry, when coupled with the constant changes in both the internal and external environment, mean that managers must develop their services and facilities within an objective planning framework. Leaving things to chance or relying on intuition is unlikely to lead to business success in the very competitive leisure and tourism industry. There needs to be both short- and long-term planning, the latter often referred to as strategic planning.

Strategic planning

A strategic plan will indicate the broad direction that an individual company or local authority leisure and tourism department is intending to follow over a three to five-year time-scale. The strategic planning process will seek to answer the following questions:

- What do we want to achieve?
- Where are we now?
- Where do we want to be in x years time?
- What do we have to do to get there?
- How do we know when we've arrived?

In trying to answer these questions, the strategic plan will recommend a process that will include the following stages:

1 Clarification of the organisation's aims and objectives.
2 Analysis of current financial and market position.
3 Development of action plans to achieve desired aims.
4 Implementation of the action plans.
5 Monitoring and evaluation of the plans.

Financial planning will have a fundamental role to play at every stage in the strategic planning process. The clarification of aims and objectives will almost certainly refer to financial objectives, which will differ depending on which sector the organisation operates in. Wealden District Council, for example, in its Leisure Strategy 1993–6 document states that:

> *The initial objective for the department was to operate the leisure centres at break even level on operational costs, thereby minimising the burden on the community chargepayer. A commercial approach was adopted, involving the use of marketing and business plans and a staffing structure evolved which was customer orientated, to ensure the centres were synonymous with quality and choice.*

Stage 2 of the strategic planning process, the analysis of the current financial and market position, will rely heavily on financial information, such as spend per head, revenue per member of staff, total number of visitors and other relevant financial ratios.

The development of action plans (stage 3), will involve developing budgets that will forecast likely revenue and expenditure, plus the application of sensitivity analyses to predict a range of outcomes if circumstances change.

Stages 4 and 5, the implementation and monitoring of the plans, will involve management in measuring actual against planned performance and making any necessary adjustments or alterations to the plans.

Business plans

Whereas the strategic plan of a leisure and tourism organisation or department will consider its broad objectives and future policies over a three to five-year time period, managers will need short-term operational plans as a way of meeting specific targets. A business plan, reviewed on an annual basis and including an annual budget, is the most appropriate tool for this job. Such a plan will give the manager a focus for his or her activities and the freedom to organise, co-ordinate, motivate and control resources to achieve optimum efficiency and effectiveness. The concept of using business plans applies equally to the private, public and voluntary sectors of leisure and tourism.

When to develop a business plan

Business plans have a number of applications in the leisure and tourism industry. Historically, they have been prepared by organisations when they are:

- Considering the expansion of an existing product, service or facility.
- Diversifying into a new product or sector of the market.
- Seeking extra finance from external sources.
- Establishing a new enterprise.

Given the fast-moving nature of leisure and tourism, the preparation of business plans is now common management practice in the industry, since managers are constantly evaluating the services they offer to their customers and redefining their actions. Typical examples of when a business plan would be prepared include:

- A hotel planning to add a leisure facility to its existing building.
- An airline considering the purchase of another aircraft.
- A local authority leisure centre aiming to break-even within a given time period.
- A museum considering an expansion of its retail outlet.
- A young entrepreneur setting up a chauffeur-drive service for overseas visitors to Britain.

The structure of a business plan

The layout and contents of a business plan will depend upon a number of inter-related factors:

- The purpose for which the plan has been prepared.
- Whether the organisation is within the private, public or voluntary sector.
- Who the business plan has been prepared for.

The purpose for which the plan has been prepared may be to examine the feasibility of expansion or to help management make the best use of their existing resources. Business plans drawn up with the aim of securing extra funding for expansion, will need to include sections on:

- The proposed product or facility expansion.
- The market in which the organisation operates.
- Details of the management team who will be implementing the plan.
- Legal aspects of the expansion.
- Financial considerations including projections and funding requirements.

Business plans whose purpose is principally to help management make the best use of its existing resources often focus more on financial aspects than those that are principally concerned with expansion of facilities or services.

Which sector a leisure and tourism organisation operates in, and who it is prepared for, will influence what is included in the business plan. A local authority leisure services business plan, for example, will seek to ensure councillors that the authority is making the best use of its finances. They may not be as interested in seeing complex financial data as, perhaps, the directors of a private sector company may be. The business plan of a voluntary sector organisation may well be most concerned with raising funds for future developments and will be aimed at encouraging potential sponsors.

Financial aspects of the business plan

The section covering finance is often the most important part of a business plan, particularly when the prime purpose of the plan is to raise finance for a specific project. Potential investors will want to be assured that the organisation seeking the extra funding has been objective and realistic in its assessments of future financial performance. Since a business plan is essentially concerned with looking to the future, the financial information must include projections of anticipated

	ESTIMATE	PROJECTED	
	1991/92	1992/93	1993/94
EXPENDITURE			
Employees	253,310	265,000	285,000
Premises and transport	166,030	160,000	165,000
Supplies and services	84,280	55,000	60,000
Agency and contracted services	59,040	55,000	60,000
Total expenditure	£562,660	£535,000	£570,000
INCOME			
Grants	46,140	50,000	55,000
Fees and charges	290,000	360,000	475,000
Catering	5,000	30,000	40,000
Total income	£341,140	£440,000	£570,000
Net cost	£221,520	£95,000	£ Nil

Fig 14.1 Financial projections from a leisure centre's business plan
(courtesy of Wealden District Council)

costs and revenue, based on current performance and the best available data. It is likely that the business plan will give details of the following:

- Cash flow projections.
- Anticipated profit and loss figures.
- Balance sheet projections.

An extract from a local authority leisure centre business plan is shown in Figure 14.1.

Written in the early 1990s, the financial information presented in Figure 14.1, shows that the leisure centre is aiming to break-even at the end of the trading year 1993/94 by reducing costs and increasing income. The projections are based on certain assumptions that the management considers to be reliable, including current data on the performance of the facility.

Depending on the purpose of the business plan, the financial information it contains will relate to a three to five-year time period, with projections relating to the first two years presented on a monthly basis.

Section 2 Budgets in leisure and tourism

Introduction

Good management in leisure and tourism involves not only reviewing past performance and the progress of current work, but also looking ahead to the future development of the organisation and the products and services it offers to its customers. The leisure and tourism market is constantly evolving, new technology is being introduced, customers are demanding better quality and tastes and fashions are changing. To be successful in such a diverse and dynamic industry, private, public and voluntary sector organisations must identify and anticipate market changes and plan accordingly. We saw in the first section of this unit that to be able to achieve this needs both long- and short-term planning. Long-term planning sets out the strategic objectives of the organisation, while short-term planning details the tactical objectives for the coming financial period, usually the next 12 months.

Strategic plans are expressed in general terms and cover periods of at least three to five years. They illustrate the expected growth in the market, the organisation's target market share and its anticipated profitability. Short-term plans relating to the next 12 months, sometimes called business plans, will include much greater detail and take account of recent forecasts concerning economic activity, inflation, costs and revenues for the coming period. The financial element of this detailed plan of action is usually referred to as the budget.

What is a budget?

In simple terms, a budget is a forecast of likely income and outgoings over a given period of time. We all have to budget in our everyday lives, trying to balance our income, in the form of wages, salary or government benefits, against our living expenses, including rent, energy costs, taxation and costs for food and clothing. Another type of budget is that presented by the Chancellor of the Exchequer every year to Parliament, setting out the income and expenditure plans of the government for the next 12-month period. The present Chancellor is having to grapple with a budget that is £50 billion pounds out of balance, the so-called budget deficit. This is leading to increased direct and indirect taxation for the general public and falling expenditure on local and national services, including local authority leisure and tourism facilities.

At organisation level, a budget can be defined as a plan, quantified in financial terms, prepared and agreed in advance, showing the anticipated revenue and expenditure over a given time period. The budget is the action plan for the coming financial period, which can be used to delegate responsibility to departmental managers or supervisors, leaving senior management to concentrate on investigating any major deviations from the plan. This delegation will mean that, in practice, a leisure and tourism organisation will have many different budget heads, i.e. a range of budgets that sets out the financial responsibilities of each manager or supervisor. These detailed budgets will be consolidated into one master budget for the organisation, which will detail its overall short-term financial plan. The budget is the principal tool for allowing managers to co-ordinate and control the activities of their organisation. Performance is constantly monitored against the budget plans and feedback is an important part of the budgetary process.

The budgetary planning process

This process of agreeing budgets and managing their implementation has three principal elements:

1 Setting objectives.
2 Planning.
3 Monitoring and control.

1 Setting objectives

It is the function of senior management within a leisure and tourism organisation to outline its short-term financial objectives for the coming period and to communicate them to all other management areas. As we saw in Unit 8, objectives will not always be only concerned with profit maximisation. Public and voluntary organisations will have wider social and community objectives, in addition to managing their financial resources efficiently.

The budgets that are set must reflect the overall objectives of the organisation, whether financial or social. When setting budgets, it is important to involve all levels of management in an organisation, in order to engender a degree of ownership of, and commitment to, the budgets, on the part of those managers who will be responsible for their achievement. Agreeing the fine detail of the budgets can be a lengthy process, involving elements of co-operation and teamwork from all involved. In the public sector, the setting of budgets for leisure and tourism services will be the responsibility of a leisure services committee working in conjunction with the finance committee, often a sub-committee of the authority's policy and resources committee. In larger private sector leisure and tourism organisations, there will be negotiation on budgets by individual section heads, with a single manager, often a management accountant, responsible for collating the individual budgets into the master budget.

2 Planning

Constructing a budget

Budgets are based on a set of assumptions about an organisation's future performance and the general awareness of the economic and market conditions that are likely to prevail in the future. In many respects, setting budgets relies on informed guesswork and is never an exact science. In setting its overall budgetary requirements, a commercial leisure and tourism organisation will follow a number of steps, including:

- Preparation of the sales budgets.
- Preparation of the expenditure budgets.
- Preparation of the capital budgets.
- Amalgamation of departmental budgets into the master budget.
- Agreement of the budget.
- Translation of the master budget into a cash budget, profit and loss budget and a forecast balance sheet.

Types of budget

The sales budget

This is normally the starting point for all budgets, since market demand is often the overriding factor in determining success or failure. In attempting to forecast its future sales pattern and volume, a leisure and tourism organisation will need to take a number of important matters into account, including:

- Past levels of sales, unless it is a new business just starting.
- Market research.
- The state of the economy.
- Trend analysis.
- Existing and potential competition.
- The state of the market in which it is operating.

A high street travel agency, for example, will be concerned with a number of factors when producing its sales budget, for example:

- Last year's sales figures.
- Local competition from other agents.
- Inflationary effects on its principals' product prices (i.e. the cost of package holidays, airline flights, etc.).
- Results of marketing and promotional activity.
- The resources of its own agency staff, including training.
- National trends in holiday bookings and destination choices.
- The state of the local economy.

Figure 14.2 gives an example of a monthly sales budget used in an independent travel agency.

The sales budget in Figure 14.2 uses the sales figures for 1993 as a base for forecasting likely sales in the same month in 1994. To the January 1993 figures is added an allowance for inflation in each of the product categories plus any forecast growth in volume of sales, perhaps as a direct result of increased marketing and promotion or the closing of a competitor agency in the same locality. Monthly sales targets would be consolidated into a complete sales budget for the 12-month period.

The expenditure budget

The expenditure budget shows the spending limits that must be adhered to so that the department or organisation as a whole achieves its financial targets. It will include all the fixed and variable costs attributable over a given period of time, which could be annual or monthly. The example given in Figure 14.3 shows an expenditure budget for an independent travel agency that chooses to budget on a monthly basis.

MONTHLY SALES BUDGET				
Product Type	Value of sales January 1993 (actual)	Inflation allowance	Forecast share of market growth	Sales target January 1994 (budget)
Inclusive tours – Europe				
– Long haul				
– Domestic				
Scheduled air				
Flight only (charter)				
Cruising				
Car hire				
Hotel reservations				
Car ferries				
Miscellaneous				

Fig 14.2 Sales budget used in a typical independent travel agency

Showing monthly expenditure will allow management to rectify any variances in the budgeted and actual expenditure by taking the appropriate action.

The performance of the expenditure budget cannot be divorced from the figures contained in the sales budget and it is a matter or preference whether the two budgets are kept separate. Many organisations choose to operate a combined sales and expenditure budget, as shown in the simplified example given in Figure 14.4, again modelled on an independent travel agency.

The combined budget allows for monthly figures and a cumulative total combining data from previous months. Any variations from the budgeted figures are included in the variance columns, which may contain actual figures or a percentage difference.

3 Monitoring and control

Once budgets have been agreed and the mechanisms for recording the financial data are in place, it is necessary to introduce a monitoring and control process. Control is based on the concept of management by exception, i.e. the investigation of any items which deviate from the agreed budget. This is done by comparing

ITEM	1st Quarter		2nd Quarter		3rd Quarter		4th Quarter	
	Budget	Actual	Budget	Actual	Budget	Actual	Budget	Actual
Rent								
Rates – general								
– water								
Salaries and NI								
Casual labour								
Lighting								
Heating								
Telephone/fax								
Telex								
Prestel/Istel								
Postage								
Stationery								
Cleaning								
Insurance								
Travel – motoring								
– subsistence								
Maintenance								
Promotions								
Advertising								
Reference books								
Accounts charges								
Legal fees								
Bad debts								
Training								
Petty cash								
Miscellaneous								
Total								

Fig 14.3 Expenditure budget used in an independent travel agency

Item	Current month			Cumulative totals		
	Budget	Actual	Variance	Budget	Actual	Variance
Sales						
– product 1						
– product 2						
– product 3						
Total sales						
Expenditure						
– item 1						
– item 2						
– item 3						
– item 4						
Total expenditure						
Gross profit (loss)						

Fig 14.4 The structure of a combined sales and expenditure budget

the actual costs with the budgeted costs to identify any over or under expenditure. The differences are known as variances and their investigation is known as variance analysis. Variances may arise in any items of revenue or expenditure, including labour costs, sales figures and energy costs. Where actual costs are greater than budgeted costs, the term unfavourable or adverse is applied and where actual costs are below budget, the variance is favourable. The opposite is true of revenue variances, where favourable variances occur when the actual sales are above budget.

The aim of variance analysis is to highlight areas needing immediate attention. Minor variances from budget are common and unlikely to require detailed analysis, but when the variance is large either in percentage or monetary terms, the situation will need reviewing. Once a variance has been investigated and a cause identified, remedial action can be taken. For example, a visitor attraction that experiences a 10 per cent adverse variance in its admission income for a particular month will need to investigate the cause and put matters right immediately if it is to achieve its annual budget targets. However, not all causes of variances from budget are capable of immediate solution. A permanent change in market demand, perhaps away from an existing type of home entertainment product that loses its appeal with the buying public, will force an organisation to feed the information back into its planning stage for alteration to projected sales figures.

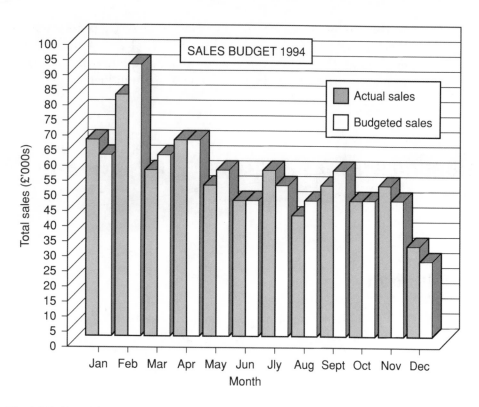

Fig 14.5 Graphical representation of budget data

There must be a degree of flexibility in any budgetary planning system, which takes account of the fact that leisure and tourism is a very dynamic industry.

A budget is generally broken down into shorter periods for control purposes. These are normally monthly but can be shorter or longer as the case demands. As well as a comparison of actual with budgeted figures, budgetary control often involves a comparison with data from the same period in the previous year. Whatever time period is agreed, managers will need a constant flow of financial information that they can use for control purposes. The combined sales and expenditure budget shown in Figure 14.4 includes columns for variances, which could be expressed in either percentage or monetary terms. Information presented in this tabular form may be supplemented by graphical presentation of the results, now made easier with the use of readily available graphics computer software. Figure 14.5 gives an example of the data contained in a monthly sales budget for a typical independent travel agency.

The presentation of information in this form provides a quick and easy way of identifying problem areas and is often an easier means of identifying budget variances. Graphical presentation should also be considered for comparing current year data with that from past years.

As well as comparing actual with budgeted results, the budget information can be used to measure performance of individual cost centres within the organisation. This is done by developing financial ratios that allow performance evaluation. Unit 8 looks in greater detail at the use of financial and other performance indicators in the leisure and tourism industry.

Section 3 Cost controls in leisure and tourism

Introduction

It is essential for managers in leisure and tourism to have accurate, relevant and up-to-date information on the costs of running their organisation. Without this detailed information, they will not be in a position to be able to appraise past performance and control future developments. The organisation's management information system (MIS) should be designed in such a way as to provide data on costs at regular intervals and in an appropriate format (see Unit 6 for more detail on MIS in leisure and tourism).

Classification of costs

As well as having detailed cost data on which to base their management decisions, organisations and their personnel need to understand the different types of costs they will encounter and their likely impact on organisational performance. Costs may be classified according to:

- Function.
- Type.
- Nature.

Classification by function

This method groups costs on the basis of the functional department that incurs them, such as administration, sales, marketing and personnel. Each of these departments would have several cost centres, which are readily identifiable locations or functions against which costs can be charged. If we take the example of a large mass-market tour operator, for example, the expenditure incurred by its marketing department may be divided into the following cost centres:

- Product development.
- Customer services.
- Brochure production.
- Brochure distribution.
- Photographic costs.
- Market research.
- Above-the-line activity (e.g. consumer and trade advertising).
- Below-the-line activity (e.g. sales promotions, PR, direct marketing).
- Agency sales support.
- Agency marketing and merchandising.

Each cost centre will be allocated a cost code to ensure that all the costs it incurs are easily identifiable. In a local authority leisure centre, each of the main facilities and services, including the leisure pool, sports hall, outside pitches, health and fitness suite, restaurant/café, squash courts, vending and courses, will be independent cost centres, each with its own cost code.

Classification by type

Costs can be classified into two types, direct and indirect. Direct costs are those that can be directly identified with the service or facility, for example the costs of hiring equipment and employing an extra instructor to run a series of health and fitness courses at a leisure centre. Indirect costs, also known as overheads, are those costs within an organisation which cannot be readily allocated to a specific function. Taking the case of the leisure centre organising the health and fitness courses, indirect costs would include the rent and rates for the centre, insurance and energy costs. It is not easy to calculate an exact proportion of the overhead costs that should be allocated to the running of the courses.

Classification by nature

The nature of costs varies between those that remain constant despite changes in the level of activity (fixed costs) and those that alter in direct proportion to the volume of business generated (variable costs). Fixed costs for a museum, for example, would include rent, rates, interest charges and permanent staff costs, all of which stay the same regardless of how many people visit. The same museum's variable costs could include casual labour, telephone charges, postage, advertising and stationery, all of which will vary, depending on the level of use. Figure 14.6 shows the relationship of fixed, variable and total costs to output.

A third category of costs is semi-variable costs, which are made up of both a fixed and variable element. Energy costs, telephone, telex and fax costs fall within this category, since there is a fixed charge for rental with added usage charged thereafter.

The costs incurred by the majority of leisure and tourism organisations tend to be fixed rather than variable, given the high staffing, buildings and equipment costs associated with the industry.

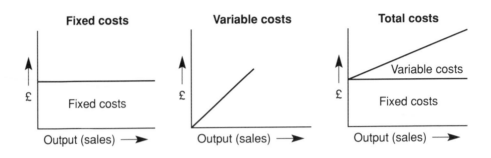

Fig 14.6 The relationship of fixed, variable and total costs to output

Costing systems

The different ways of classifying costs described above enables managers in leisure and tourism to apply different approaches to solving problems. This is illustrated by looking at two different methods of costing products and services, one concerned with the treatment of overheads and the other with marginal costs.

Absorption costing

Under an absorption or full cost system, the variable costs and a proportion of the fixed costs are allocated to cost centres in an effort to ascertain the full cost of running a facility or service. The method of sub-dividing all the fixed costs and charging them to a particular cost centre is known as apportionment. The way in which apportionment is carried out varies from one organisation to another, making the process a rather inexact science and sometimes a little too subjective. As an example, the rent and rates of a leisure centre could be apportioned to individual activities on the basis of the floor area that each occupies as a percentage of the whole building. Similarly, total energy costs could be divided according to the cubic capacity of each facility. An example of absorption costing in a leisure centre is shown in Table 14.1.

Table 14.1 Absorption costing in a leisure centre

	Leisure pool £	Squash £	Badminton £	Catering £	Total £
Income	350,000	80,000	120,000	90,000	640,000
Variable costs	120,000	20,000	30,000	40,000	210,000
Fixed costs	170,000	40,000	60,000	20,000	290,000
Profit	60,000	20,000	30,000	30,000	140,000

Table 14.1 shows that out of a total sum for fixed costs of £290,000, different amounts are apportioned to the four principal cost centres in the facility.

Some leisure and tourism organisations consider that absorption costing is not only a very complicated procedure, but one that does not always deliver realistic results. There are, however, occasions when apportioning fixed costs is helpful, such as when adopting a cost-based pricing policy and costing leisure service contracts.

Marginal costing

Marginal costing, sometimes referred to as contribution costing, is another technique that finds favour with leisure and tourism professionals. Marginal costing adopts the view that in the short run, fixed costs cannot alter and will have to be borne anyway, whatever the level of sales or revenue. The variable costs, which are relatively easily allocated to particular cost centres, are termed the marginal costs. The difference between the marginal costs and the selling price is known as the contribution towards the fixed costs. No attempt is made to apportion fixed costs with the marginal costing method; the total contribution is set against the fixed costs. If the contribution is greater than the fixed costs, a profit is made; if the contribution is less, then a loss is incurred. Using the same data shown in Table 14.1 but working on a marginal cost basis, allows the manager to ascertain the contribution each activity makes to the leisure centre as a whole, as shown in Table 14.2.

Table 14.2 Marginal costing in a leisure centre

	Leisure pool £	Squash £	Badminton £	Catering £	Total £
Income	350,000	80,000	120,000	90,000	640,000
Variable costs	120,000	20,000	30,000	40,000	210,000
Contribution	230,000	60,000	90,000	50,000	430,000
		Less fixed overheads			290,000
Profit					140,000

Table 14.2 shows that presenting the figures for the leisure centre on a marginal costing basis gives a more realistic picture than by adopting the absorption costing method of Table 14.1. For example, a comparison of the two tables shows that although the badminton and catering cost centres show an equal profit of £30,000 each under absorption costing, when we look at the results under the marginal costing method, catering contributes significantly less (£50,000) towards the fixed costs than badminton (£90,000). Making management decisions on the basis of absorption costing alone is clearly very risky.

Break-even

Break-even analysis makes use of the division of costs into fixed and variable in order to determine the minimum output where all costs are just covered by income. In other words, the break-even point is reached when an organisation's total revenue exactly equals its total costs (see Figure 14.7).

Figure 14.7 shows the break-even chart for a hypothetical national conference on sport and the community. The chart shows that, with a delegate fee of £80 per head, 250 delegates will need to attend in order for the event to break-even. At this point, costs and revenue will be in balance at £20,000. Delegate numbers in excess of 250 will result in a profit for the organisers, while less than 250 will mean that they will incur a loss.

Break-even analysis has many applications in leisure and tourism and is frequently used in hotels, leisure centres, restaurants, visitor attractions and by transport operators. We saw in Unit 11 that airlines use a form of break-even analysis known as load factor to calculate the minimum number of seats they must fill before they begin to make a profit. Although it is widespread through-

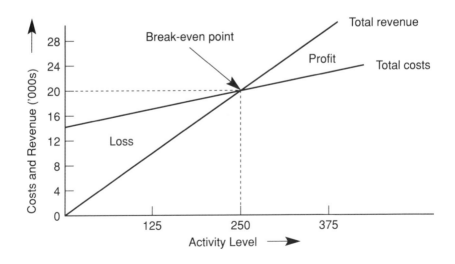

Fig 14.7 Break-even analysis

14.20   Financial planning and monitoring in leisure and tourism out the industry, break-even does have its limitations; it assumes that costs will remain constant over a given time period and that costs and revenue are only affected by changes in volume and no other external factors.

Pricing policy

Price is a key influence on the purchasing habits of consumers, whether they are buying a loaf of bread, a package holiday or a round of golf. In times of economic recession, when peoples' disposable income is limited, price becomes a very important factor in the purchasing patterns for leisure and tourism products and services. A family may be forced to postpone an overseas holiday in favour of a cheaper break closer to home. A weekend break in the country may be for just the Saturday night rather than two nights. Price will have a critical role to play in determining the volume and type of sales of leisure and tourism products.

In any organisation, pricing has two major roles:

- Price must be pitched at a level that enables the organisation to cover all its costs and provide a profit.
- Price is a key element of the marketing mix, which must be balanced against the type of product, how it is promoted and where it is made available (see Unit 4 for more on the marketing mix in leisure and tourism).

In the language of the economist, price is all about supply and demand. There exists a price where the wishes of suppliers and buyers are brought into equilibrium at a market price. If the price of the product or service is too high, demand falls and a surplus of supply develops and drives the price down. Too low a price, on the other hand, will lead to a situation where demand exceeds supply and the price will rise.

In the real world, pricing policy has to be set within the overall objectives of an organisation. As we have discussed, public and voluntary sector leisure and tourism organisations will have social and community aims alongside their financial goals, making pricing a very difficult task. Pricing is a little more straightforward in the commercial world since the principal objective of most private sector leisure and tourism organisations is to maximise their profits.

In determining price levels, organisations can choose between two basic approaches:

- Cost-based pricing.
- Market-based pricing.

Cost-based pricing

This involves calculating the total costs of providing a product or service and adding a given percentage as a profit margin. Unit 11 showed that cost-based pricing is used by many specialist tour operators. It is considered to be a rather crude technique since it takes no account of the fact that the total costs are made up of variable costs, which vary in proportion to changes in volume, and a proportion of fixed costs, which will not vary with output. The problem is compounded by the fact that the organisation may achieve economies of scale through expanding output, as is the case with mass market tour operators. Nevertheless, accurate information on costs is vital to an organisation for a number of reasons:

- The profit contribution of individual transactions can be measured.
- The most profitable products, services, customers or market segments can be identified.
- The effect of changes in output on profits can be measured.
- The organisation can determine whether a product or service can be developed and sold at any price.

In practice, an organisation can adopt a number of approaches to determining its prices under a cost-based system. Absorption pricing involves determining the total revenue needed to cover all costs and dividing this figure by the number of customers, to arrive at an average selling price per customer. Rate of return pricing works the other way round, by setting a predetermined rate of return on capital employed and setting prices which will achieve this required rate of return. Marginal cost pricing involves identifying the variable costs associated with a service, product or facility and adding a gross profit margin to determine the price. The price is fixed so as to maximise a contribution towards fixed costs and profit.

Market-based pricing

While cost-based pricing techniques are preferred by accountants and economists, they take no account of the demand for leisure and tourism services and facilities. Marketing personnel would argue that of equal importance to costs in determining pricing levels are factors such as:

- The quality of the service provided.
- Competition from other providers.
- The amount of marketing and promotion.
- The 'uniqueness' of the product or service.
- The location of facilities.

The users of leisure and tourism facilities and products are becoming increasingly more sophisticated, with many looking beyond the narrow concept of price when making their purchasing decisions.

In following a market-based pricing strategy, an organisation may decide to set its prices in line with those of competitors offering a similar product or service; this is sometimes referred to as going rate pricing. This is a common policy in the public sector, with leisure facilities pricing at similar levels to their neighbouring authorities. Demand-led pricing involves setting prices at levels that the market will bear, taking into account the nature and characteristics of the customer and the existence of similar facilities operated by competitors. Perhaps the most extreme example of a demand-led pricing strategy is that operated by Concorde, a truly unique experience! Demand-led pricing presupposes a high degree of knowledge of the market in which the services are being offered, including both detailed customer profiles and extensive awareness of competitors' products and services.

Section 4 Investment in leisure and tourism projects

Introduction

The growth and development of Britain's leisure and tourism industry depends on its ability to generate a return on investment. Returns are generally measured through the financial rewards that the investor receives, in the form of interest or a dividend. Capital growth, for example the rise in value of a resort complex or a restaurant, is another way of measuring returns on investment in leisure and tourism.

Financial information has a crucial role to play in helping a potential investor decide whether or not to support a leisure and tourism project. It is often the most important part of a feasibility study that considers all the relevant factors to determine whether or not a project should be given the 'green light'. In general, a feasibility study will include information on:

- Initial project ideas and concepts.
- An analysis of the market within which it will operate.
- Likely social and environmental impacts of the proposed development.
- Financial and economic feasibility.
- Site analysis.

The potential developer will be looking to the feasibility study to answer a range of questions, including:

- Is the specific project site suitable?
- Is there a market of sufficient size available to support the development?
- What style of operation and quality levels should be provided?
- What will the capital costs of the project be?
- What are the projected revenues and costs that the project will generate?
- Will the project produce a satisfactory return on investment?
- Should the investors and developers proceed with further analysis of the project?

Why invest in leisure and tourism?

Throughout this book we have seen that the UK leisure and tourism industry is constantly developing and reacting to changes in customer fashions, tastes and expectations. When the economy is in recession, future developments are difficult to forecast with any degree of certainty in an industry that provides products and services that people buy with their discretionary income.

If leisure and tourism is such a risky business, why do people bother to invest in it? While there is no single answer to this question, it is interesting to note that the amount of investment in the UK leisure and tourism has fallen sharply since the late 1980s. The depressed state of the economy, leaving people with low levels of disposable income to spend on leisure, has halted the growth in major development projects. There is, however, still investment in the industry, for a number of reasons:

- The most obvious reason for investing in a leisure and tourism project or organisation is that the investor expects to receive a healthy return on his or her investment, in the same way as if the investment was in any other commercial sector of the economy.
- Some governments undertake investment in leisure and tourism for non-commercial reasons, such as social and community benefit. Investment in leisure centres, parks, tourist information centres, transport infrastructure and visitor attractions may be justifiable on social if not always commercial grounds.
- A lot of investment in leisure and tourism is property-driven, meaning that entrepreneurs who are essentially property developers will invest in capital projects such as hotels, resort complexes and theme parks, as alternatives to shops, factories and offices.
- Some investments in leisure and tourism are made for 'life-style' reasons such as an extension of a hobby or as a tax loss. Investment in tourism may also be needed to subsidise an existing enterprise, such as a stately home or family farm. Leisure and tourism has an appeal to investors outside the industry who consider that it is an easy sector in which to operate and brings with it significant life-style benefits.

- Many investments in leisure and tourism can be justified on the grounds that they are joint-use. Leisure centres are often joint enterprises between a local authority leisure services department and a school or college. Major out of town retail developments often include leisure facilities such as multi-screen cinemas and ten-pin bowling facilities.

Investment appraisal

Before any potential developer invests in leisure and tourism, he or she will need to consider the future profitability of the proposed project. This can be estimated using a number of techniques concerned with the evaluation of investment proposals, known as investment appraisal. Since investment decisions are often irreversible and can tie up substantial amounts of capital for long periods of time, it is important to approach the decision in the rational and precise manner offered by the investment appraisal techniques.

The four most common methods of investment appraisal are:

1 The payback method.
2 Accounting rate of return (ARR).
3 Net present value (NPV).
4 Internal rate of return (IRR).

All four techniques take account of the future stream of benefits or savings expressed in cash terms and the cost outlay required to effect the investment.

The payback method is the quickest method that can be used to calculate how long it will take to recoup the original investment in a project. The payback period is measured from the time of initial outlay to the time it is recovered. If a potential investor is considering one or more projects, the one with the shortest payback period may well be chosen.

The accounting rate of return method expresses the average annual profit of a project as a percentage of the initial capital outlay. In comparing alternative projects, which are mutually exclusive, the project with the highest ARR will be chosen. The disadvantage of the ARR method is that it takes no account of the cash flow of a project and the timing of receipts.

The net present value (NPV) and internal rate of return (IRR) methods both use the discounted cash-flow technique. NPV takes account of the timing of cash flows. It recognises that a given sum of money received now is worth more than the same sum received in the future, since the sum could be invested today to yield a return. For example, £100 invested now at an interest rate of 10 per cent would be worth £110 in one year's time and £121 in two years' time. In other words, £121 received in two years has a net present value of £100. Cash flows received at different times need to be adjusted to take account of the time value of money and it is this adjustment of future flows into present values that is known as discounted cash flow (DCF). The internal rate of return method also uses DCF, with the aim of determining which project will produce the highest rate of return over its life.

DCF methods of estimating the profitability of capital projects are considered to be superior to payback and average rate of return. ARR ignores the timing of the returns while payback ignores the cash flows after payback. Despite these problems, many organisations choose to use more than one method. Whichever method is used, they all depend on the accuracy of the cash flow forecasts, which themselves may be subject to wide margins of error. It must also be remembered that investment appraisal is only one facet of the total picture when a potential investor is considering going ahead with a project. Other non-commercial factors, such as how will the workforce react to the project and how the project fits into the organisation's overall objectives, are also important considerations.

Assignment 14

Situation

Your best friend has been working as a Senior Consultant in a local branch of Lunn Poly for the past eight years, but has always fancied the idea of being her own boss. The opportunity arises when a distant relative leaves her £30,000 in his will. She decides to look into the possibility of setting up her own travel agency, but she has little idea of how to go about the financial side of the business. As you have some knowledge of the travel industry and finance, she has asked you to help her prepare a financial plan for the bank manager.

Tasks

The financial plan that you prepare must include:

- A sales budget.
- An expenditure budget.
- A cashflow statement.

The plan should be as realistic as possible and should include a 'worst case' scenario. The capital requirements of the business should be stated in the financial plan together with the level of borrowing required.

Unit 15
INVESTIGATING LEISURE FACILITY OPERATIONS

Section 1 Leisure facility products and services

Introduction

In order to remain competitive, leisure facility operators, whether in the private, public or voluntary sectors of the industry, must constantly review the products and services they offer their customers. Successful leisure and tourism organisations need to be 'customer driven'; in other words, they must put the customer at the centre of their operation by researching their needs and offering facilities, products and services that satisfy these needs. Moreover, the products on offer must meet the high standards of quality demanded by an increasingly sophisticated public, which also expects high levels of customer service from leisure and tourism providers.

For the purposes of this unit, 'leisure facility operators' include:

- Establishments offering accommodation – for example, hotels, guesthouses and self-catering.
- Catering and hospitality facilities – such as cafés, restaurants, fast-food outlets, bars and pubs.
- Arts and entertainment venues – for example, art galleries, theatres, arenas and casinos.
- Sport and recreation facilities – such as leisure centres, recreation areas, parks, golf courses and outdoor stadia.
- Heritage and cultural facilities – including museums, historic houses and ornamental gardens.

- Outdoor centres – offering activities such as canoeing, orienteering, mountain biking and countryside events.

In deciding which products and services to offer, as well as individual characteristics such as price and quality, each type of leisure facility operator needs to take a number of factors into account, including:

- Product range.
- Market trends.
- Pricing policy.

Product range

It may seem strange that we are using the term 'product range' when considering leisure, which is essentially a service industry. It is easy to think of a range of soap powders or a range of cars, but not so easy to think of 'intangible' leisure products in the same way; a 30-minute session on a sun bed or a round of golf are 'experiences' rather than tangible products. None the less, these and many other leisure experiences are purchased by the general public and, as such, the leisure industry has adopted the same terminology as manufacturing industry, including FMCGs (fast moving consumer goods, such as food and toiletries).

When considering its product range, a leisure facility operator will use the same basic principles as any other organisation in the service or manufacturing sector of the economy. Depending on its overall objectives, an operator may be aiming to capture as big a share of the market as possible in order to maximise its profit, or it may be seeking to achieve more social objectives by providing community facilities for certain sectors of the local population.

In order to maximise their returns, or the use of their facilities, most leisure facility operators will offer a range of products that is geared to different sectors of the market. Taking the example of a country house hotel, for example, the range of products it offers its guests could include:

- Accommodation in standard *en suite* rooms.
- Executive rooms with special facilities, e.g. a four-poster bed.
- A suite of rooms.
- Weekend breaks.
- Gourmet events.
- Sunday family lunches.
- Business lunches.
- Afternoon teas.
- Weddings and other special events.
- Activity breaks, e.g. fishing, walking or bird watching.
- Outside catering for functions.

- Small seminars and conferences.

The proprietor of the hotel will adjust the range of products in response to demand and any commercial opportunities that arise.

Local authority leisure centres, while not operating in the same commercial world as the proprietor of a country house hotel, are nowadays expected to work with a high degree of financial efficiency, while at the same time offering the widest possible range of facilities and services for their local community. The following extracts from a leisure centre's promotional leaflet demonstrate that in order to fulfil these often competing functions, leisure centres have to offer an imaginative programme of high quality products covering a wide range of interests.

> *Utopia Leisure Centre offers a superb range of activities and prides itself on its friendly welcome and family facilities. The tropical atmosphere of the free-form leisure pool with its shallow lagoon, bubble tub, health suite, 55-metre water slide and splash pool is ideal for all the family. The centre operates a variety of sessions, including 'Sunrisers', 'The Family Fun Plunge', adults, ladies and a popular lessons programme. The pool is available for hire for parties, shows, product launches and other events and is perfectly complemented by the poolside terrace and bar/cafeteria.*
>
> *The four badminton court sports hall is used for a vast range of sporting activities: aerobics, step aerobics, five-a-side football, trampolining, basketball, etc. A balance of clubs, courses and casual use is maintained and the hall is a sought after venue for a variety of events, competitions and tournaments.*
>
> *The impending refurbishment at Utopia promises exciting new developments for the Centre; the existing Fitness Suite with its quality exercise machines, regular induction programmes and various conditioning and fitness courses will be extended and will boast the latest hi-tech fitness equipment. The creation of a Dance Studio provides Utopia with the perfect opportunity to initiate a whole new dimension to the Centre's facilities with the future possibility of a programme including ballet, tap, jazz, Tai-Chi, etc.*
>
> *An attractive lounge bar and social area offers a relaxing atmosphere for that after-activity refreshment, with the imminent development of a restaurant area completing the service.*
>
> *With its wide range of facilities for all ages and abilities, Utopia is the perfect place to either learn new skills or improve existing ones, get fit, meet new people or just simply have fun!*
>
> (Courtesy of Wealden District Council)

The success and continued support for theatres and other entertainment venues, whether in the public or commercial sector, depends on them offering a wide range of products aimed at a broad cross-section of their local or regional audience. Sheffield City Hall, for example, in its autumn programme for 1993, offered a range of activities that included:

- The rock band Jethro Tull.
- A Storehouse fashion show.
- The BBC Philharmonic Orchestra.
- The Siberian National Folk Dance Ensemble.
- The comedians Jack Dee and Lenny Henry.
- Pinocchio.

The City Hall's near neighbour, the Crucible Theatre, is known internationally as the host of the World Snooker Championships every year. What is not quite so well known, is that the Snooker Championships is but one event in a range of activities aimed at a wide section of the general public.

The popularity of visiting the countryside for holidays, short breaks and day visits, means that outdoor centres must provide a full range of products and services to meet the needs of all sections of the community. Rother Valley Country Park, for example, situated between the urban centres of Sheffield and Chesterfield, offers its visitors:

- A model yacht regatta.
- Grass skiing.
- Nature photograph workshops.
- Cycling events.
- Road races and fun runs.
- Watersports facilities.
- Wildlife walks and events.

Market trends

In helping to secure their range of products, services and facilities, leisure facility operators need to keep abreast of trends and developments in their particular market sector. There are constant changes in tastes and fashions throughout UK society, which are reflected in the demand for leisure facilities, both home-based and outside of the home. Leisure facility managers will become aware of changes and demand from running their own organisations and by having an effective feedback mechanism, whereby ideas from both staff and customers are collected and considered when developing new products and services or altering the existing provision.

As well as information on changes in the market collected from within their own organisations, leisure facility managers will also look to external sources of data in order to keep up to date with events in their sector. There are many sources of information that are publicly available to leisure facility operators, including:

- Statistics on local and national population trends available from central and local government.

- Reports from consultants such as the Henley Centre for Forecasting and Leisure Consultants, which analyse past demand and future prospects.
- Journals and magazines, including *Leisure Manager, Caterer and Hotelkeeper, Leisure Management* and various arts and countryside sources.
- Information from professional bodies such as ILAM (the Institute of Leisure and Amenity Management), HCIMA (the Hotel, Catering and Institutional Management Association), ISRM (the Institute of Sport and Recreation Management) and the Tourism Society.

Awareness of competitor activity is also important when it comes to deciding which products, services and facilities to offer. It is often said in the leisure sector that there are very few products and services that are totally unique. Most are the adaptation of existing ideas to meet local circumstances. It is important to remember that there is not only competition between operators offering the same facility, for example local authority leisure centres in neighbouring boroughs, but that all facility operators are competing for a share of peoples' discretionary income which they choose to spend on leisure activities. In this respect, the local authority leisure centre in borough A is not only in competition with the centre in borough B, but also with local cinemas, restaurants, casinos, bingo halls, tennis clubs, golf courses, and so on. Having knowledge of what is happening in all sectors of the industry is important when aiming to offer a good quality experience geared to the customers' needs.

Major changes in tastes and fashions which have influenced the demand for leisure products and services in the recent past include:

- An increasing awareness of health and fitness – for leisure facility operators, this trend has opened up a whole range of issues and new opportunities. The number of hotels with leisure facilities has increased dramatically in recent years, while restaurants have responded by offering 'healthy eating' and vegetarian menus. Leisure centres have devised courses and activities in response to customer demand (see Figure 15.1).
- Increased environmental awareness – this has resulted in customers actively seeking out organisations and facilities that demonstrate a respect for their environment and offer facilities for its enjoyment. For example, indoor entertainment venues, pubs and clubs have responded to customers' demands to operate 'no smoking' policies. Hotels and other accommodation providers have increased the range of activity holidays and short breaks they offer, while countryside centres are increasingly updating the courses and facilities they offer to the visiting public.
- Developments in technology – new developments in this area have influenced leisure products and services both in the home and in public leisure facilities. Museums have responded to the demand for a more 'hands on' approach by installing computer-controlled animations and facilities. The growth in the market for home computers and electronic games is also evident in entertainment complexes, which offer virtual reality and other electronic simulations.

Fig 15.1 Fitness suite in a local authority leisure centre
(courtesy of Wealden District Council)

Pricing policy

In view of the current economic recession, with the subsequent decrease in disposable income, leisure facility operators must be aware that pricing policy is a crucial element of the marketing mix. Pricing levels must be set within a framework that allows flexibility to meet changing demand, yet allows management to plan for the future profitability of the leisure facility.

Pricing tactics

Within an overall pricing policy that will reflect the operator's financial objectives, management will need to develop short-term tactics on prices in order to make maximum use of the facility. The particular pricing tactics undertaken by an operator could include:

1 *Variable pricing* – this is one of the most common price tactics in both private and public sector leisure operations. It involves charging different customers

JUBILEE HALL PRICELIST

GOLD MEMBERSHIP
MONTHLY & YEARLY GOLD CARDS (inclusive)

Monthly Weights	£40.00
Monthly Weights & Classes	£55.00
Yearly Weights	£375.00
Yearly Classes	£375.00
Yearly Weights & Classes	£500.00

TARIFF MEMBERSHIP
Annual Tariff   £45

Activity	Member	Non-member
Classes	£3.00	£4.00
Weights	£3.50	£5.00
Badminton ($^1/_2$ hr.)	£2.50	£2.50
Football ($^1/_2$ hr.)	£8.00	£8.00
Entrance		£1.00

Residents and students who live or study in the Covent Garden area are entitled to a discount of £15.00 off the tariff membership

SUNBEDS

	Members	Non-members
Normal Pressure	£4.00	£4.50
Course of 10	£35.00	£40.00
High Pressure	£7.00	£8.00
Course of 5	£35.00	£40.00
Jomi Seabreeze	£5.00	£6.00
Course of 10	£45.00	£55.00

NB Jomi Seabreeze has high powered facial unit.
Towell hire 50p plus £10.00 Deposit

Prices as at January 1994

Fig 15.2 Variable pricing in a leisure centre (courtesy of Jubilee Hall Sports Centre)

varying prices for the same service or product. Local authority leisure centres often charge different rates for users who are members or non-members and for those who live inside and outside the borough (see Figure 15.2).

In addition, leisure centres, along with most other leisure facilities, will offer concessionary rates to children, students and senior citizens. It is also common for many leisure facilities, including theatres, sports stadia, museums and art galleries, to offer concessions to unemployed people.

2 *Time-price differentials* – charging different prices at different times can help to level out peaks and troughs in demand for facilities. Many restaurants and bars offer a 'happy hour', often in the early evening, when drinks are reduced in price to attract custom and 'two for the price of one' may be on offer.

3 *Loss leader pricing* – this involves setting a price below break-even, in the hope of attracting extra business overall for the facility. Discos, clubs and casinos often operate a policy of a low initial admission price to get customers interested, knowing that they are more than likely to make up any shortfall by increased spend at the bar and on slot machines. Pubs sometimes offer meals at loss leader prices, earning revenue from the sale of drinks.

4 *Diversionary pricing* – this is similar to the loss leader tactic, but does not involve selling products at a loss. Rather, prices of a few items are kept deliberately low in order to give an impression of a low overall pricing structure. Restaurants and pubs will offer a 'dish of the day' on their menu, knowing that customers may be tempted to other, higher-priced alternatives once in the establishment.

5 *High price maintenance* – this is the opposite of any form of discount pricing, since it involves setting high prices that reflect quality and exclusivity. An example of this would be the top end of the hotel market, where customers will pay a premium for excellence in service and product quality.

6 *Competitive pricing* – this is when a leisure facility sets its prices at a similar level to competitors offering comparable products and services. Restaurants and fast-food outlets sometimes operate this system of pricing, along with leisure centres in the same locality.

Whatever pricing system a leisure facility operates, it must have the flexibility to be able to respond quickly to competitor activity and be able to seize any market opportunities which arise. As the 1991–4 Business Plan of Wealden Leisure Services Department comments in its section on pricing in leisure centres:

> *There is no captive market in leisure services and, although charges have been increased significantly over the past two years (within the level of inflation), pricing cannot be a 'bottomless pit', but must be service-related with inbuilt flexibility to respond to market forces.*

The Business Plan goes on to say:

> *The annual review of charges should continue to take into account a variety of factors, including demand and the results of market research, and not slavishly follow increases in line with inflation. Public perception of 'value for money' can be enhanced considerably by improving the quality of the leisure experience. Pricing experiences, rather than activities, should feature strongly in the marketing approach in order to encourage favourable comparisons with similar activities. Flexibility in pricing must extend to minority and disadvantaged groups, including disabled, the young, the elderly and socially deprived, in order that the social objective of non-exclusion is satisfied.*

Section 2 **Programme evaluation**

What is a programme?

In the context of a leisure facility, a programme is a series of activities or events that is planned to:

1 Make the maximum use of the resources of the facility.
2 Meet the needs of many different types of customers.
3 Achieve the aims of the organisation which is running the facility.

Making maximum use of the resources of the facility means the best use of staff, buildings, equipment and the financial resources of the organisation. An individual programme will be developed using the skills and expertise of employees and management, who will exploit the facility's physical and financial resources to the full. Types of customers will vary enormously, from individuals to groups, able-bodied to disabled and specialists to non-specialists. A well developed programme should cater for the needs of many different sectors of the population. The organisation's aims will have an important part to play in the design of a programme for a facility. Public sector leisure facility operators will have social and community objectives to achieve, over and above any financial aims. A local authority leisure centre, for example, will be aiming to make its facilities and services available to as wide a cross-section of the local community as possible. In contrast, leisure facilities operated in the private sector will have profit maximisation as their main objective. Odeon cinemas, for example, will put on a range of programmes that they hope will attract a wide range of customers, thus maximising the revenue to the organisation.

Programming takes place in a wide range of leisure facilities, in the private, public and voluntary sectors, including:

● Leisure centres.
● Theatres.
● Community centres.
● Sports halls.
● Cinemas.
● Outdoor and indoor arenas.

Figure 15.3 shows an imaginative pool programme for a local authority leisure centre.

The key features of the programme shown in Figure 15.3, are:

● Opening for 15 hours per day, 7 days per week (excluding a four-hour period on Sunday evenings for cleaning and maintenance).

Utopia — UCKFIELD'S LEISURE CENTRE — POOL PROGRAMME

	7am	8	9	10	11	12	1pm	2	3	4	5	6	7	8	9	10pm
MONDAY			SCHOOLS				HAPPY HOUR	SCHOOLS		LESSONS		OPEN SWIM			X-RATED END-TO-END STUFF	
TUESDAY	SUN RISERS		OPEN SWIM (AQUAFIT ... YOUNG AT HEART)							LESSONS		OPEN	ZOOM ZONE	SWIM	ADULT LESSONS	
WEDNESDAY			SCHOOLS				HAPPY HOUR	SCHOOLS		LESSONS		OPEN	ZOOM ZONE	SWIM	MERMAIDS / AQUAFIT	
THURSDAY			SCHOOLS				HAPPY HOUR	SCHOOLS		LESSONS		OPEN	ZOOM ZONE	SWIM	LIFE SAVING	
FRIDAY	SUN RISERS		OPEN SWIM (AQUAFIT)							LESSONS		H₂O			LESSONS	CLUB USE
SATURDAY		SCHOOLS	LESSONS	FAMILY FUN PLUNGE (PLUS FLOATS)				ZOOM ZONE			OPEN SWIM	CLUB USE	POOL PARTY HIRE TIME			
SUNDAY		END-TO-END STUFF X RATED		FAMILY FUN PLUNGE (PLUS FLOATS)				ZOOM ZONE			OPEN SWIM	CLEANING AND MAINTENANCE				

Fig 15.3 Pool programme in a local authority leisure centre
(courtesy of Wealden District Council)

- Targeted at different user groups; for example, 'Sun Risers' is early morning swimming for adults only, 'Family Fun Plunge' is aimed at the family market, 'Mermaids' is exclusive use by female swimmers and 'Young at Heart' are sessions for the over 50s.
- Differentiates between club, schools and casual use.
- Includes specialist uses, such as life saving and 'Aquafit'.
- Includes lessons at selected times of the week.
- Encourages use by offering discounts during the 'happy hour'.
- The programme shows variety and is 'customer led', offering a wide range of activities, carefully timed to appeal to different sectors of the market.

Difficulties in leisure facility programming

All leisure facilities will, to a greater or lesser extent, experience difficulties when developing their programmes. Depending on the overall objectives of the organisation and whether it operates in the private, public or voluntary sector, these problems could include:

- *Fluctuating demand* – demand from customers for leisure facilities will fluctuate dramatically during each day, week, month and year. Facilities such as ice rinks, cinemas and leisure centres will experience heavy use at weekends, in the evenings and during school holidays. Outside of these peak times, venues such as these are likely to be underused. Effective market research can help to identify potential markets for use during off-peak periods and allow the organisation to actively encourage participation from selected target groups. People who are sometimes targeted for use outside of the peak periods include the unemployed, retired and mothers with pre-school age children. Promotion and marketing will have an important role to play in making the leisure facilities widely known to potential customers. In the public sector, leisure centres sometimes employ staff to go out into their local area and encourage more community involvement in the design of the facility programme. The use of the price mechanism can also boost usage during off-peak times; reduced rates for afternoon matinees in cinemas and theatres, discounted rates for certain customers and leisure centres charging less at certain times of the day, are all examples of the way in which price can influence demand.
- *Conflict between users* – by their very nature, programmes are aiming to maximise the use of facilities. This will inevitably lead to conflicts between different groups of customers from time to time. It is sometimes possible to predict when conflict may arise and implement measures to minimise its impact. The opening night of a heavily-publicised programme of taster courses in a leisure centre, for example, may well lead to problems with car parking and handling the volume of enquiries and bookings. Management can have contingency plans drawn up, such as overflow car parking spaces and additional staff available, should the need arise. It is quite often the ancillary facilities, such as changing rooms, toilets, refreshment areas and information points, which give rise to conflict. There are also the obvious conflicts that can arise when individuals or groups are sharing the same or adjacent space in a leisure facility. Noise and congestion are frequent problems in this respect. The net effect of the conflict, from whatever source, is to detract from the customers' total leisure experience and may make them consider going elsewhere in the future, making the management of any conflict which does arise very important.
- *Clubs versus casual usage* – managers working in public sector leisure facilities are constantly faced with the problem of clubs demanding more booking time for their members to enjoy the facilities on offer. While accepting that club bookings are more financially secure than casual use of facilities, managers have to be aware of their social and community aims by making sufficient time available in their programmes for the needs of individual customers. The trend in local authority leisure services departments in the recent past has been to discourage expanding club sessions in their leisure centres in favour of open centre sessions. This has been partly due to the desire to leave time available in the programmes to encourage specific targeted groups to participate in activities, and partly out of a feeling that membership of clubs that are based on

sporting excellence and high standards of achievement will exclude many potential participants. Open membership schemes and temporary membership arrangements can be introduced to overcome conventional objections to extensive use of facilities by clubs. Given all the activity that goes into developing programmes that target specific sections of the community, there is sometimes a tendency to forget the needs of the casual users, even though they may generate a far greater revenue than clubs. Publicity materials and events should not overlook the casual user and catering for their needs while in the facility should not be forgotten; some leisure centres will rope off part of a pool for casual use during school or other group sessions, for example.

- *Staffing implications* – leisure facility managers do not always fully appreciate the demands that a varied and targeted programme can have on their staffing resources. In a local authority leisure centre, a programming policy that favours community groups currently under represented in the facility may mean that staff with specialist skills will be needed to fully implement the programme. For example, targeting mothers with pre-school age children is likely to mean providing a crèche staffed by a qualified helper. Devising programmes that include activities appealing to specialist groups, such as karate and sub-aqua training are likely to need staff with the appropriate skills and qualifications from outside the organisation. Some targeted groups may demand exclusive use of a facility, thereby adding to staff supervision costs, e.g. an Asian women's swimming session cannot be held with men in the pool. A varied and innovative programme may also lead to an increased workload for administrative and clerical staff, who may have to establish and carry out new systems for particular groups in the programme.

- *Poor take-up rates* – there may be many reasons why a programme fails to achieve its aims, perhaps even the fact that its aims were not clearly worked out before the programme was developed. Without a specific objective in mind, management will find it hard to put together a programme that is attractive to the public. Staff, too, will be unsure of their role in achieving success with the programme. Another reason for failure of the programme may be that insufficient research was carried out to show that there was a sufficient demand. Programmes are sometimes designed with little flexibility, so that an unexpected occurrence, such as the non-arrival of a coach or the failure of equipment, can render the whole programme useless. Last of all, it may simply be that the activities included in the programme are just not attractive to the paying public, since they lack variety, imagination and novelty value.

Programme evaluation

Evaluation is an essential part of programme planning. Without a critical review of the successes and weaknesses of a programme, management will be uncertain as to whether it has actually achieved what it set out to do. In carrying out an evaluation, the manager will be looking for the answers to a number of interrelated questions, including:

- Did the programme meet its financial targets?
- Did it reach the intended sector or sectors of the market?
- Were all the elements of the programme fully in line with the organisation's policy and objectives?
- Did the programme make maximum use of available physical resources?
- Were staff resources fully utilised?
- Did the programme meet customers' needs and expectations?
- Were there any major weaknesses or problems?
- What were the measurable successes of the programme?

Torkildsen advocates a three-stage approach to programme evaluation, namely:

- The inputs.
- The process.
- The outcomes.

The inputs to the programme focus on what went into planning, design and organisation. Inputs need to be quantified whenever possible, so that an organisation has statistics on which to base its judgements and conclusions during the evaluation of the programme. Data on how much staff time went into planning the programme, the cost of any promotional work and any charges for hiring extra staff and equipment will all be useful when looking at overall inputs to the programme. Evaluation of the process is concerned with considering the running of the programme and aims to quantify what actually happened. It can give clues as to why a programme was successful or not, as the case may be. All those who were involved in planning and carrying out the programme should be given the chance to comment on such matters as management style, leadership effectiveness and administrative support. In seeking to identify elements of good and bad practice, the management should not be seen as embarking on a 'witch hunt', but rather reflecting constructively on events and learning lessons for the future. The outcome stage of the evaluation involves comparing programme objectives and targets with actual performance. Financial information will be used to compare budgeted with actual costs and revenue. More subjective conclusions, such as whether customers' expectations were fulfilled, can be answered with the aid of surveys and analysis of informal feedback.

While evaluation takes place at the end of a programme, it does not mean that all feedback on performance is left until after the programme has finished. Staff and management will need to monitor frequently during the life of the programme and make any necessary adjustments. All those with a stake in the programme should be included in the evaluation process, in order to make it as representative and effective as possible; the staff running the programme (internal and external), the customers, senior management and policy makers will all have constructive comments to make about the elements of the programme and their views as to improvements for the future. The evaluation exercise should be co-ordinated by one member of staff, chosen for his or her sensitivity, in what can sometimes be difficult circumstances.

Section 3 **Administrative systems**

Introduction

It is not always easy to distinguish exactly between purely administrative and distinct management tasks; indeed it is very easy to find many managers who complain that their management tasks have been taken over by an ever increasing administrative workload (and administrators who, likewise, are sometimes left to make important management decisions). The widespread use of personal computers (PCs) has served to blur the distinction between the two functions even more. It is not uncommon nowadays for leisure facility managers to have a PC permanently on their office desk and to process their own management information, with the help of sophisticated word processing, database, spreadsheet and DTP (desk top publishing) packages. Another reason for lack of clarity between administrative and management functions, is the greater involvement of administrators in the day-to-day management of leisure facilities. This trend, while welcomed by administrators who have for a long time felt divorced from the teamwork approach of running a facility, has nevertheless made role clarification more difficult.

Administrative functions in leisure facilities

Irrespective of who actually carries out the tasks, there are a number of important areas within leisure facilities which need administrative support. Some of the most important concern:

- Booking systems.
- Handling and recording of cash.
- Stock control.
- Cleaning and maintenance.

Booking systems

Booking systems in leisure facilities can be either manual or computerised. Many organisations that formerly used manual systems have transferred their data on to computers, because of the greater speed and storage capacity they offer. A computerised booking system in a leisure centre will need to be able to handle a range of different types of bookings, including bookings from individuals and club bookings, which may be in advance or on a casual admission basis. Hire of equipment and bookings for particular facilities, e.g. badminton courts and fitness equipment, will also be logged into the computer. A membership system may also be handled by a computerised booking system. Unit 6 on MIS in leisure and tourism gives examples of computerised booking systems.

Smaller leisure facilities may choose to adopt a manual system that meets their particular needs. An example of an advance booking sheet for a small hotel that uses a manual booking system is shown in Figure 15.4.

In Figure 15.4, the room numbers are entered in the left-hand column, while the days of the month run along the top of the chart. When a customer makes a booking in advance, it is a simple matter to complete the appropriate square or squares on the chart.

Handling and recording of cash

Cash is the lifeblood of any leisure facility. As such, it requires very strict control to record its movement through the organisation and to provide a check against negligence and fraud. It is essential that everybody working in the leisure facility is aware of the importance of cash and that money, in its various forms, is credited to the organisation's bank account with safety and without any undue delay. A daily receipts summary, similar to that shown in Figure 15.5, will help keep track of cash takings.

Most leisure facilities will receive payment by one or more of the following means:

- Bank notes and coins.
- Cheques and postal orders.
- Credit cards, debit cards and charge cards.
- Banker's drafts and certified cheques.
- Travellers' cheques.

Although it is becoming a little unfashionable to carry coins and notes, there are still a lot of people who wouldn't think of using anything else. Cash is the main payment method in many leisure facilities, such as leisure centres, museums, catering outlets and sports venues. It is usual practice to issue a receipt immediately for cash transactions, which acts as proof of purchase. Cash paid into a bank account does not need 'clearing' and is immediately credited to the organisation's account.

Advance Booking Chart

Room No.	1	2	3	4	5	6	7	8	9	10	11	12	13	14	15	16	17	18	19	20	21	22	23	24	25	26	27	28	29	30	31

Fig 15.4 An advance booking chart

Maesmawr Hall Hotel
Daily Receipts Summary

W/E	Monday	Tuesday	Wednesday	Thursday	Friday	Saturday	Sunday	Total
Accom/Room hire								
Restaurant								
Lounge bar								
Wines								
Bar Meals								
Functions Food								
Functions Wines								
Functions Bar								
Telephone								
Miscellaneous								
Deposits								
Total								

Fig 15.5 Daily receipts summary as used in a hotel (courtesy Maesmawr Hall Hotel)

Accepting cheques is a very common means of payment in many leisure facilities. Once paid into a bank account, it will take a minimum of three working days for the cheque to be processed, during which time it remains 'uncleared'; clearing is the process of passing the cheque to the customer's bank, debiting their account and crediting your own. Staff should always ask for a cheque guarantee card to be presented; most will honour cheques up to the value of £50, although it is becoming increasingly common to see £100 cheque guarantee cards in use. Cheques for values in excess of that quoted on the card should not normally be accepted; it is safer to ask the customer to provide another form of payment.

Credit cards are widespread in hotels, restaurants and other catering outlets. The two most common cards in use in Britain are Access and Visa, used on a whole range of credit cards offered by banks, building societies and even car manufacturers (Vauxhall and Ford have recently introduced credit cards). For the customer, credit cards are a very convenient way of making payment, since they can be used for postal and telephone bookings, as well as payment in person. They offer an interest-free period subject to certain conditions. Debit cards, such as Switch and Delta, should not be confused with credit cards since they have a completely different function. A debit card is used in place of a cheque, with the holder's bank account being debited within three working days. Charge cards, such as American Express and Diners Club, offer no extended credit facility, as with credit cards. Their use in leisure facilities is mainly for business and corporate customers.

A banker's draft or certified cheque will be used when payment is required immediately and there is no time to go through the normal clearing process. Some people will pay a large amount by a certified cheque issued by their building society. Banker's drafts are an easy way of accepting payment in a foreign currency.

While not common in leisure facilities, travellers' cheques may be used for payment in hotels and restaurants by overseas visitors. Care should be taken to ensure that the cheques are not already countersigned before they are presented for payment.

Whichever method of payment is accepted, and depending on the policy of the individual organisation, the stages that the payment will go through are as follows:

1 Payment received by the leisure facility.
2 Receipt issued to customer.
3 Entry made on daily cash summary entry (see Figure 15.5).
4 Receipts and summary sheets reconciled.
5 Bank paying in slips completed.
6 Monies paid into the bank account.
7 Paying in slips stamped by bank.

Stock control

Although leisure is essentially a service industry, providing 'experiences' rather than 'products', there are a number of areas where it is necessary to undertake some form of stock control. These include:

- Catering outlets.
- Bars.
- Retail units.

Leisure facilities often generate healthy extra revenue, sometimes known as 'secondary spend', from the sale of food, drinks, souvenirs, equipment and clothing, all of which will need careful control of stock. Stock control is a broad term that covers:

- Storage.
- Recording of stock levels.
- Stocktaking.
- Withdrawing stock.

Careful attention to stock control is particularly important in the case of food, which will deteriorate in quality if not stored in the right conditions. Holding too much stock of any sort is wasteful, since it ties up money unnecessarily and takes up valuable space. Records will be needed for all receipts of stock and stock issues.

Cleaning and maintenance

The importance of maintaining the fabric of a leisure facility goes well beyond the routine tasks associated with keeping the weather out. With visitors now demanding high quality in their leisure provision, a facility that is poorly maintained and not cleaned on a regular basis will not be able to compete effectively with those organisations that give cleaning and maintenance a high priority. The image of a facility and its management is closely linked to its physical appearance. Add to this the fact that legislation demands a healthy and safe environment for both staff and visitors, plus the fact that a poorly maintained building will decrease in value, it is not surprising that the cleaning and maintenance of leisure facilities has taken on greater importance of late.

Types of maintenance

Maintenance of leisure facilities can be either routine or exceptional. Work carried out as a matter of routine is often referred to as planned maintenance, while corrective maintenance involves tasks carried out in response to an emergency or failure of equipment or services. It is expected that by adopting a policy of planned maintenance, carried out at pre-determined intervals and according to prescribed criteria, the probability of the failure of systems or equipment and hence the need for corrective maintenance will be reduced.

The normal cleaning routine of the facility should be part of the programme of planned preventative maintenance. Any minor defects should be reported to the appropriate authority and remedial action carried out. However, as well as this day-to-day activity, there also needs to be a systematic inspection of essential equipment and systems on a regular basis. Managers or supervisors should also implement frequent inspections of all parts of the facility, recording the findings on a report form (see Figure 15.6).

It makes good sense to carry out a programme of planned inspection and maintenance of equipment and facilities for a number of reasons, including:

- It is a cost-effective exercise, since preventative measures can save on costly major works in the future.
- It will provide a healthy and safe environment for staff and customers.
- It will ensure all areas are cleaned on a regular basis.
- It will reduce the incidence of failure of equipment and systems.

CLEANING AND MAINTENANCE INSPECTION REPORT				
Name of Facility				
Area inspected	Date	Time	Comments/action required	Inspection carried out by

Fig 15.6 Inspection report form

Section 4 Legal requirements

Introduction

No leisure facility operator, whether in the private, public or voluntary sector, can afford to disregard the impact of UK and European legislation on his or her organisation. Although the present government is committed to reducing bureaucracy by cutting out a lot of 'red tape', most leisure managers and policy makers would agree that there is still plenty of legislation that has to be taken into account when operating a facility.

Principal legal requirements in leisure facility operation

Health and safety

We looked in detail in Unit 3 at the main legislation concerning health and safety in the workplace including:

- The Health and Safety at Work, etc. Act 1974.
- The new EC Directives on health and safety.
- The Fire Precautions Act 1971.
- The Food Hygiene Regulations.
- COSHH (the Control of Substances Hazardous to Health) Regulations 1988.

Employment legislation

Unit 9 on human resource management in leisure and tourism featured information on the main employment legislation affecting leisure facility operators, including:

- Employment contracts.
- Redundancy and dismissal.
- Equal opportunities.
- Discrimination.

Licensing legislation

Many of the activities that leisure facility operators consider when designing their programmes and facilities will need a licence before they can go ahead. Licensing exists to regulate those providing public facilities and to ensure that they are providing a safe and secure environment for their customers. It is important to remember that it is not sufficient to meet the standards only when applying for a particular licence, but that the standards applying to the licence must be maintained throughout its duration.

Types of licence

The main types of licence that a leisure facility operator may need to consider are:

- A Public Entertainments' Licence (PEL) – this will be needed by any facility that provides public dancing, music or other public entertainment of a like kind in any building and may even extend to entertainment in the open air in certain areas.
- An Indoor Sports' Licence – this may be required if the facility operator is promoting sporting events to which the public is invited as spectators.
- A Theatre Licence – this is required for any public performance by one or more persons of any play.
- A Cinema Licence – this covers the showing of films, videos, video juke boxes and the broadcasting of boxing matches or similar live events to an audience.
- A Liquor Licence – all premises where alcohol is sold or consumed must hold a suitable licence. Licences range from a full on-licence, where the licence holder can sell alcohol for consumption on the premises, to a seasonal licence, which allows the leisure facility to sell alcohol only at certain times of the year.

Licensing authorities

In the case of the liquor licence, application must be made to the Magistrates' Court. For most other licences, application is via the local District Council. Some licences require that the application is copied to the police and fire authorities.

Assignment 15

Situation

The range of leisure facility operations in an area is very broad and will differ from one region to another. What is available will be in part a reflection of historical trends and will be partly due to commercial and political priorities. Leisure facility operations can include:

- Hotels and other types of accommodation.
- Restaurants and other catering outlets.
- Arts and entertainment venues.
- Sport and recreation facilities.
- Heritage and cultural attractions.
- Outdoor pursuits and countryside centres.

Tasks

While on work experience, or carrying out a part-time or seasonal job, you should gather information on the detailed management of the facility where you are based. This information, which must be gathered with the full consent of the facility managers, should include details on:

- The facility's administrative systems.
- The management structure and objectives of the organisation.
- Relevant legal requirements related to the operation of the facility.
- Any programming that takes place at the facility.
- The products and customers of the facility.

This information should be converted into a report that should evaluate the effectiveness of the facility in relation to its objectives and within any budgetary or other constraints. The report should look objectively at the resources and systems used in the facility and make recommendations for its future management. The report should be in the region of 1,500 words in length.

Index

C

Capital, sources of 14.2
Car ownership 1.12
Careers in leisure and tourism 1.36
Cash handling 15.15
Cashflow statement 8.13, 8.17
Castlefield Urban Heritage Park 13.38
Center Parcs 3.26
Centre for Alternative Technology 8.16
Cleaning and maintenance 15.19
Climate 1.40
Commission 11.5
Complaints, handling 3.11
Compulsory competitive tendering (CCT) 1.32
Computers 6.9
Control of Substances Hazardous to Health (COSHH) Regulations 2.13
Costs, in leisure and tourism 14.16
Courses in leisure centres 12.18
Customer, definition of 3.2
Customer care 3.16
   care programme 3.21
   care, training 3.24
   comment form 8.25, 8.26
   existing 3.15
   needs, identifying 4.7
   satisfaction 8.22
   service, factors influencing 3.4
   service, importance of 3.1
   service, obstacles to 3.8

D

Dartmoor Area Tourism Initiative 13.35
Data analysis 10.11
Data Protection Act 6.11
Department of National Heritage (DNH) 1.25, 1.56
Direct mail 10.26
Direct marketing 10.25, 4.26
Disciplinary procedures 9.21
Discrimination 9.24
Dismissal 9.20
Display Screen Equipment Regulations 2.10
Diversification 12.1

Diversification, implications of 12.11
Domestic tourism 1.7

E

Economic impacts 1.52, 13.43
Employment, contracts of 9.18
Employment in leisure and tourism 1.35
Entertainment facilities 1.43
Environmental impacts 1.53, 13.43
EPOS 6.18
Equal opportunities 9.23
Equal pay 9.25
Eureka! Museum for Children 13.20
European tourism 1.17
Events 5.1
    evaluation 5.23
    planning 5.13
    resource implications 5.5
    sources of advice 5.8
    staffing 5.26

F

Farmhouse bed and breakfast 12.21
Financial accounting 8.13
    performance 8.12
    planning 14.1
    ratios 8.18
Fire precautions 2.11
Fire Precautions Act 1971 2.11
First aid 2.11
Fixed costs 14.18
Food Hygiene Regulations 2.15
Front office 6.8, 6.9, 6.28
Funding, leisure and tourism 1.55

H

HavenWarner 3.13
Health and Safety EC directives 2.6
    hazards 2.1
    sources of advice 2.17
Health and Safety at Work, etc. Act 2.3
Heritage Coasts 1.47

History of leisure and tourism 1.8
Holidays 1.41
Holiday camps 1.12
Hotels 6.32
Human resource management (HRM) 9.1

I

Impacts of leisure and tourism 1.51, 13.43
Incoming tour operators 11.15
Independent travel 11.27
Induction 9.13
Industrial relations 9.33
Industrial Revolution 1.10
Infrastructure 1.49
Investment, in leisure and tourism 14.23
Investment appraisal 14.25
Investors in People 9.15
Islington TDAP 13.41

J

Job description 9.8

L

Legal requirements 15.21
Leisure, complexes 6.21
    definition of 1.2
    factors affecting participation 1.3
    future of 1.39
    scale of the industry 1.14
Leisure and recreation, in the 20th century 1.11
Leisure and tourism, future of 1.38
    local government involvement in 1.30
    national government involvement in 1.24
Licensing 15.22
Life cycle classification 4.10
Lifestyle classification 4.11
London Marathon 5.9
London Tourist Board 10.22

M

Management accounting 8.15

U

UK tourism, facts of 13.3, 13.7
    future of 13.33
    rise of 13.2
    structure of 13.10
Utopia Leisure Centre 10.38

V

Variable costs 14.18
Vertical integration 12.3
Voluntary sector in leisure and tourism 1.32

W

Wales Tourist Board (WTB) 3.20, 3.21